Lacrosse

Chris Watson puts pressure on Navy star freshman Nick Mirabito in the Blue Jays' 9–8 overtime win against the Mids in 2005. *Jay Van Rensselaer*

Lacrosse

Technique and Tradition

David G. Pietramala and
Neil A. Grauer

The Second Edition of the
Bob Scott Classic

The Johns Hopkins University Press
Baltimore

© 2006 The Johns Hopkins University Press
All rights reserved. Published 2006
Printed in the United States of America on acid-free paper
9 8 7 6 5 4 3 2

The Johns Hopkins University Press
2715 North Charles Street
Baltimore, Maryland 21218-4363
www.press.jhu.edu

Library of Congress Cataloging-in-Publication Data

Pietramala, David, 1967–
   Lacrosse : technique and tradition / David G. Pietramala and Neil A. Grauer.—2nd ed.
     p. cm.
   Rev. ed. of: Lacrosse / Bob Scott, c1976.
   Includes index.
   ISBN 0-8018-8371-7 (hardcover : alk. paper) — ISBN 0-8018-8410-1 (pbk. : alk. paper)
   1. Lacrosse. I. Grauer, Neil A. II. Scott, Bob, 1930– Lacrosse. III. Title.
   GV989.S36 2006
   796.347—dc22   2005027696

A catalog record for this book is available from the British Library.

Contents

Preface

As has been said by others whose efforts follow and build upon the work of prominent predecessors, we stood on the shoulders of a giant when writing this book.

Bob Scott was and remains a giant in the world of lacrosse. His two decades as head coach at the Johns Hopkins University earned him the respect, admiration, and affection of countless players, fans, and fellow coaches. Writing the first edition of *Lacrosse: Technique and Tradition* made his name — and coaching principles — synonymous with the game wherever it is taught and played around the world.

To update such a landmark book—considered by many the "bible" of lacrosse—has been a daunting task and has taken more than two years. We are indebted to Bob Scott for his encouragement and counsel throughout this process and are humbled by his approval of what we have done. At Mr. Scott's urging, much of this book was rewritten. In some sections, however, we saw no reason to change what Mr. Scott wrote and have retained his original wording, with his approval.

We were extremely pleased and honored to be asked by the Johns Hopkins University Press to undertake this project. After the press approached Coach Pietramala to revise the book in 2003, he asked Neil A. Grauer, a longtime Hopkins lacrosse fan, a friend since Pietramala's days as a player, and a professional writer, to help. During lengthy meetings, Coach Pietramala and Mr. Grauer reviewed each chapter in the first edition. Coach Pietramala detailed the revisions he wished to make to the text, and Mr. Grauer subsequently put his words on paper. The "I" in the text now is Coach Pietramala, not Coach Scott. Mr. Grauer did the research to add thirty years of season recaps and other developments in the sport to the chapters on national and Hopkins lacrosse history, including in them Coach Pietramala's recollections of events in which he participated.

Special thanks are due to Robert J. Brugger, senior acquisitions editor at the Johns Hopkins University Press, for his faith in our ability to do this work and his patience while we tackled the job. We also are grateful to Jay Van Rensselaer and Will Kirk for their exceptional photos and to Jade Myers of Matrix Art Services for the play diagrams. In addition, we appreciate the insights on goaltending and face-offs, two highly specialized positions, provided by Hopkins All-American, Hall-of-Fame goalies Dr. Les Matthews, Mike Federico, and Larry Quinn and by former Hopkins face-off men and coaches Howard Offit and Patrick Miller. Their combined expertise would be hard to match.

Mr. Grauer thanks Coach Pietramala and all of his predecessors going back to Bob Scott for the generous and kind welcome into their exciting world; he also expresses his appreciation for the enduring friendship of all the players and their families whom he has been privileged to know. He is grateful that his grandfather, the late Albert L. Grauer (JHU 1907), and father, Dr. William S. Grauer (JHU 1936), established his family's century-long love of Hopkins lacrosse.

Having the honor of revising this book simply reflects again the enormous debt Coach Pietramala owes to his parents and the great coaches, players, teammates, opponents, and administrators at the universities he has been privileged to work for and with throughout his career. It is said that you are only as good as those with whom you are surrounded, and he has been blessed to be around some of lacrosse's finest. Without these people, he would not have been able to accomplish either what he did as a player or what he now tries to do as a coach.

Ernie Larossa, associate director of athletics at Hopkins, heads a superb sports information department. We are grateful for his assistance in compiling statistics and photos and for proofreading portions of the text. Tremendously important additional assistance was also provided by the Special Collections Department of the Milton S. Eisenhower Library of the Johns Hopkins University and by university archivist James Stimpert; Josh Christian, managing director of programs and services at US Lacrosse; Joe Finn, US Lacrosse's archivist; and Leighton Beamsley, executive director of the International Lacrosse Federation.

Coach Pietramala has had the good fortune to be associated with some wonderful young men. All of his current and former players have helped fulfill his life. The time they have spent together has taught him many lessons and given him the opportunity to watch these great, talented young athletes grow as people, develop as players, and graduate as men. He will continue to cherish every day he is able to share with these exceptional individuals.

Seth Tierney, Bill Dwan, and Jeff Tambroni have been at his side during his eight years as a head coach at Cornell and Johns Hopkins. (Jeff now heads Cornell's program.) These outstanding men have had a profound influence on him, not only as a coach but also as a person.

Last, and most important, Coach Pietramala thanks his wife, Colleen, and their twin boys, Dominic and Nicholas. Their unwavering love and support mean everything to him. His life would not be complete without them.

I

The Game and Its History

Hopkins attackman Kevin Huntley ('08) surrounded by Duke defensemen in the 2005 NCAA national championship game. *Jay Van Rensselaer*

1

The Game of Lacrosse

Lacrosse, first played by Native Americans before recorded time, now is one of the fastest growing games on the local, national, and international sports scenes. From the United States to Japan, from Great Britain to the Czech Republic, players of all ages are propelling lacrosse to new heights in participation and popularity. It is booming particularly at the youth level, not only captivating novice players and casual observers but also strengthening its ties with those who get to know it well.

A game of constant action and exceptional grace, lacrosse combines the individual skill of baseball, the physical demands of football, the team strategies of basketball, and the conditioning required in soccer. It has made its way from youth league tournaments in local parks to collegiate championships in the National Football League's Baltimore Ravens' 69,084-seat M&T Bank Stadium and the Philadelphia Eagles' 68,532-seat Lincoln Financial Field and into countless homes through television coverage.

Spectators cannot help but be caught up in the thrills—and beauty—of lacrosse. Whether a pass from a midfielder to an attackman, creating a fast break that leads to a goal and clinches a 17–16 win; a smoothly executed slide by a defenseman who, with one swift poke check, knocks the ball to the ground, scoops it up, and sprints past the opponents; a bone-crunching hit that up-ends an opposing player in the middle of the field; or a spectacular save by a goalie that secures a 9–8 victory—lacrosse offers participants and fans alike tremendous, nonstop excitement.

Today's youngsters take part in more organized sports than their parents or grandparents did, and more opportunities exist now than ever before for young men and women to become involved in lacrosse. In addition, because of lacrosse's increased presence on television, the efforts of US Lacrosse (the sport's national governing body), and sports clinics held by high school and college coaches, the number of adults who have knowledge of the game and a greater ability to teach it has grown.

Because of all this, lacrosse has experienced a growth rivaled by few other sports in the past three decades. When Bob Scott's *Lacrosse: Technique and Tradition* first appeared in 1976, lacrosse was being played by an estimated eleven thousand high school and college athletes. Today, some 120,000 young men and women enjoy playing the game in high schools and colleges. Recreation leagues offering lacrosse have sprouted across the country for players as young as five years of age. With more high schools sponsoring lacrosse teams, the sport—once confined mostly to America's mid-Atlantic region—now has expanded to Ohio, Texas, Colorado, and California. At different times of the year, the number of lacrosse tournaments around the country, from Lake Placid, New York, to Vail, Colorado (perhaps the largest, most popular of these tournaments), also has energized the lacrosse boom, spotlighting the talents of many college players. Even youth league teams travel across the country and overseas to compete in tournaments.

Television has played an especially large role in the explosive growth of lacrosse. Fans no longer have to pack the family up in the van and take them to see a game. Now you can sit in your own home and watch classic matchups between Johns Hopkins and the University of Maryland, or Syracuse, or Princeton. "Game of the Week" broadcasts, initiated in Baltimore during the late 1990s, now are syndicated on a tape-delayed basis all over the country. The college championships have become a fixture on national television over the past twenty years and now are covered on ESPN and ESPN2. New cable networks devoted to collegiate sports, such as College Sports Television (CST) and ESPNU, are airing more and more lacrosse. In addition, the creation of professional lacrosse leagues during the past two decades has given the game a previously unimagined year-round exposure, with the National Lacrosse League's wintertime season and Major League Lacrosse's summertime games also appearing on television frequently.

The parity of our sport at the Division I level has promoted growth as well. More college teams, in more areas, now are having success, which in turn is sparking interest in local high schools. For example, the long-running success of the Princeton lacrosse program has prompted a surge of new youth and high school programs in New Jersey, which previously had not been a hotbed of lacrosse talent. Having a six-time national champion in that state surely has helped expand the sport there. New programs, such as the one at the University of Denver, also have helped spawn the growth of lacrosse in Colorado and elsewhere.

The growth of the game actually has become a year-round phenomenon at all levels. In addition to its traditional season in the spring, the Division I collegiate level now has a nontraditional season and tournaments in the fall, plus strength and conditioning and individual workouts throughout the winter. The youth level also has fall tournaments, Thanksgiving tournaments, Christmas tournaments, and winter leagues.

Taking a cue from our Canadian friends, we now find that playing indoors in the winter has become part of our lacrosse culture, with indoor facilities popping up around the country, allowing young boys and girls to participate in lacrosse regardless of the weather. Years ago, lacrosse was seen as a second choice to baseball as a spring sport for youngsters. Now it has become a first choice for many kids. In addition, for many years lacrosse was considered a spring conditioner for football players, but that no longer is true. Many potential college-level football players now are playing lacrosse instead during the fall, preparing themselves to enjoy playing the game in the spring. The dramatic rise in the number of summer lacrosse camps—now estimated at more than three hundred—also has fueled the sport's growth and taken it to new heights of participation.

What all these new players are delighted to discover is that lacrosse practices often are more enjoyable than those in many other sports. Jim Brown, thought by many to be among the greatest all-round athletes of the past half century—and best known for his Hall of Fame–winning accomplishments in football both at Syracuse University and with the Cleveland Browns—also was an All-American lacrosse player at Syracuse. He has been quoted as saying that football was his favorite sport on game day, but overall, when considering both practices and games, his favorite sport was lacrosse because it was more fun.

Lacrosse practices are more enjoyable because they are not monotonous. They are not a struggle to endure because the participants do so much playing—and in practicing the sport of lacrosse, nothing takes the place of playing. Even when drilling, which sometimes can take up more than 60 percent of a practice, you're still playing. For example, when you're drilling the one-on-one techniques of the game, you're still actively involved in competition, and there is a certain level of excitement to those mano a mano matchups.

Drilling in lacrosse is unlike drilling in other sports. It's unique because as you work on the fundamentals of the game and on specific techniques, you're still playing, competing against your teammates. In basketball, for example, you practice dribbling—and you don't do that against anyone else. In football, you work on your technique of rushing a passer, maybe without someone else. In lacrosse, everyone is playing.

As the next chapter, on lacrosse history, will explain in more detail, Native Americans were playing the sport long before European settlers established colonies in North America. The descendants of those settlers began playing lacrosse in the nineteenth century and introduced rules of their own. Today's lacrosse rules are based on variations of those nineteenth-century regulations. They are similar to the rules that govern all team sports, such as football, soccer, basketball, and ice hockey, and are used wherever the sport now is played—whether the athletes are Native Americans or some of the game's latest enthusiasts in China or Chile.

In Canada, both the field game and box lacrosse—an indoor version—are played, but box is considerably more popular there. It is played in ice hockey arenas with six players on a team, compared with ten in the field game. Physical contact highlights the box game, and its general makeup is more similar to ice hockey than to field lacrosse.

A neophyte can learn the important rules of lacrosse easily by watching a game or two with a veteran player, a spectator, or a radio or television commentator to provide a running explanation of the action. Spectators become as devoted to lacrosse as players. In Baltimore and at the Johns Hopkins University, the sport has had strong support for more than a century. With many other cities and college campuses now developing strong roots in the game, as large a number of expert spectators can be found in these locations as has long been routine at Hopkins's Homewood Field.

Over the years, Hopkins students, even freshmen who never saw the game before, have been quick to learn the rules of lacrosse. During Orientation Week, I now even give a lecture on lacrosse in a noncredit "Hopkins 101" course, during which various aspects of life on the Homewood campus and at Hopkins are discussed. Students who are not from this area or who don't know about Hopkins lacrosse learn of the traditions of our sport and of the big part it plays in our community during the spring.

After watching their first game or two, Hopkins spectators start to get a feel for the sport. By mid-season they are knowledgeable fans—ready to voice their negative reactions to the officials' calls against Hopkins (which in their opinion are always wrong) and their positive reactions to clever maneuvers by our players. I know. Having been on the cheering side of these avid spectators as a player, an assistant coach, and now head coach at Hopkins, I've also been on the jeering side of the passionate fans at Homewood as an assistant coach and head coach for visiting teams. I can attest to the level of excitement and understanding that the fans bring to the game. By the end of their freshman year, Hopkins students can be considered veteran spectators, and by graduation, they are "All-American" spectators.

In the United States today, lacrosse is played at more than four hundred colleges and universities at all levels—Divisions I, II, and III—and at junior colleges. Spectator attendance at major games is soaring. The 2002 Hopkins-Navy game packed 17,000 fans into the Naval Academy's Navy–Marine Corps Memorial Stadium, the Hopkins-Syracuse game in 2003 brought 15,000 fans to Syracuse's Carrier Dome, and the Hopkins-Syracuse semifinal championship game was played before more than 37,000 rain-soaked spectators in the Baltimore Ravens' stadium. A year later, more than 46,900 fans saw Syracuse and Hopkins battle again in the semifinal. The 2005 semifinal game between Hopkins and the University of Virginia was played before 45,275 sun-baked fans at the Philadelphia Eagles' stadium; overall, more than 90,000 spectators were on hand to see the 2005 Final Four, featuring Hopkins, the University of Virginia, Duke, and the University of Maryland. On average, when a major opponent comes to Homewood Field, anywhere from 8,000 to 12,000 people will be there to watch—despite the fact that most of these games now are on television.

Sports are an integral part of American life, and the playing and practice fields are critical venues for the development of young men and women. A certain level of discipline is required to balance athletics and academics at the high school and college levels. Lessons of time management are taught, one's ability to handle adversity is challenged, a work ethic is instilled, a sense of leadership is fostered, and one's sense of loyalty and the ability to work within the framework of a team is built. In my opinion, there is no better place to learn the qualities that are necessary to be successful in life than on the athletic field.

An athlete learns to live with victory and with defeat, and these experiences are basic to daily living. The opportunity for growth in personal character traits is as great in athletics as in any other activity—possibly even greater. Athletic competition demands complete commitment. Learning to say "no" to cutting corners, to cheating, and to telling "white lies" and learning to put the good of the team above personal ambitions are perhaps the most important factors in the development of a person's character. Respect for others (teammates, coaches, opponents, and referees) helps the individual to appreciate the necessity of getting along with people. The athlete who respects other people gains self-respect as well.

As a student, lacrosse was an important part of my life—and now it has become my job. I have the opportunity to work at a world-renowned academic institution and the distinct privilege of interacting with forty outstanding young men on a daily basis each year. Lacrosse also can provide players with many wonderful opportunities. I have been able to travel to Australia, Great Britain, and China—places I might never have visited if I had not been involved in lacrosse.

Lacrosse has touched thousands of lives, and in chapters 19 and 20 I will give a few examples of its influence on others from my own experience as a player and a coach at Hopkins.

Flanked by assistants Seth Tierney (left) and Bill Dwan, Hopkins Head
Coach Dave Pietramala (center) displays the 2005 NCAA Men's Lacrosse
Championship Trophy. *Jay Van Rensselaer*

Native Americans of the Choctaw tribe playing lacrosse
in 1834, by George Catlin (1798–1872). *Courtesy of US
Lacrosse, Inc.*

2

A Brief History

Lacrosse is so ancient a game that its Native American originators say it was a gift to them from the Creator, in whose honor they play it.

When Europeans first settled in North America during the 1600s, they found the native peoples playing many varieties of ball games. The Indians played these games for recreation, for settling diplomatic disputes, for making spiritual tributes, and as physical training for hunting or war.

As historian Donald M. Fisher notes in his book *Lacrosse: A History of the Game* (Johns Hopkins University Press, 2002), all of the sports involving a ball were played on rough fields, sometimes more than a mile long. The players used sticks topped with a loop or pocket to carry and pass the ball toward a goal. The tribes living in the Northeast who spoke the Iroquoian language used one stick that was four or five feet long and had a string-laced pocket. In the Great Lakes region and upper Mississippi River area, the Algonquian and Siouian tribes used a stick that was two to three feet long and had a wooden pocket. In the Southeast, the Chicakasaw, Choctaw, Cherokee, and Creek Indians played with two small sticks, one in each hand.

The Native Americans had different names for these ball games. The Sauk and Ojibwa Indians of the upper Midwest called their game "baggataway." The Mohawk tribe in the Northeast called it "tewaarathon." The name that the Creeks of the Southeast used was translated as the "younger brother of war."

The French settlers on what now is the New York–Canadian border gave the game its present name because the sticks the Indians used looked like the crosier (*la crosse*), which is the staff that bishops carry in religious ceremonies as a symbol of their church office.

The first use of the word *crosse* in reference to the game was made in 1636 by a Jesuit missionary, Jean de Brébeuf, who saw the Hurons play it near Thunder Bay, Ontario, and mentioned it in a report to his superiors back in France. He said nothing of how the game was played, and it was not until eighty-five years later that another Jesuit, Pierre de Charlevoix, described the action of the sport as it was played by the Algonquins in 1721.

According to these early reports, the ball rarely touched the ground, even in daylong contests. The ball was about the size of a modern tennis ball and was a stone or was made of baked clay, wood, or deerskin stuffed with deer hair. Indian lacrosse was a mass game. Most teams were made up of about a hundred players and sometimes of more than a thousand. Distance between goals usually was between five hundred yards and a half mile, but on occasion the goals were several miles apart. Some tribes used a single pole or tree or rock for a goal, and scores were made by a hit with the ball. Other tribes used two goalposts, six to nine feet apart, and the ball had to pass between them. There were no sidelines, and play ranged over the countryside in all directions.

Games lasted as long as two or three days, starting at sunup and ending at sundown. If a player seemed to be lagging behind the game's top pace, the women of his tribe would rush onto the field and beat him with switches. Players wore only breechcloths and some decorative paint; they usually played barefoot.

The roughness of the game served to prepare players for the conditions of close combat, and its length developed endurance for hunting parties and war. The historian Francis Parkman wrote in 1870 of how a century earlier, in 1763, during a rebellion against the British colonists led by the Indian chief Pontiac, an intertribal game of baggataway was used to lure soldiers out of an English garrison at Fort Michilimackinac, near today's Detroit. As the unsuspecting soldiers watched the game with fascination, the Indians suddenly dropped their sticks, picked up weapons, and killed the English troops.

In early colonial days, the Jesuits sought to convert Indians who were part of the Six Nations of the Iroquois Confederacy and the Huron tribe, living in w   . Members of these tribes who converted to Christianity moved to Canada because they feared reprisal from the other tribes. They settled at Caughnawaga, near Montreal, or at St. Regis, near Cornwall. It was among these people that the prototype of the modern lacrosse stick was developed.

After the Revolutionary War, the Canadian Indians lived peacefully as wards of the British Crown. Lacrosse, as played around Montreal in the 1790s, underwent a number of changes. Teams were limited to sixty men, playing fields took on a specific size, and the goals were set about five hundred yards apart. The pure sport of the game replaced the warrior-training aspects of play. By 1825, Indians were playing with seven-man teams on fields fifty yards long. To make the tribal team was a great honor.

Some histories say that a group of French pioneers were the first Europeans to play the Indians at their own game, as far back as 1740. If this is true, the occasion must have been a monumental fiasco for the settlers, since another hundred years went by before white men tried to play lacrosse again. Even then it was the general opinion that no group of whites could match a good Indian team.

In 1834 a group of Montreal gentlemen arranged for the Caughnawaga Indians to play an exhibition game in Montreal. The game was well reported in the newspapers, and it is probable that settlers began experimenting again with the game as a result of these reports. In 1844, as part of an athletic program conducted in Montreal, a team of five Indians easily defeated seven white men. In 1851, more than two hundred years after Europeans first saw lacrosse, a group of seven white players finally succeeded in defeating an Indian team of the same size.

Canadian enthusiasts formed the Montreal Lacrosse Club in 1856, and its members introduced changes that improved their style of play. They used a longer stick with wide, triangular netting that was tightly strung with gut. This stick encouraged passing and teamwork, as compared with the bagged net that the Indians used to mass-attack the goal. The white man was successful with this style of attack, and the Indians eventually adopted it, too. Montreal thus became the cradle of modern lacrosse.

In 1867, Dr. William George Beers, a Montreal dentist often called "the father of modern lacrosse," formed the Canadian National Lacrosse Association. He later claimed that on the same day that the Dominion of Canada was created, July 1, 1867, lacrosse was declared its national sport—although historical research a century later proved that was not so. Nevertheless, Beers's enthusiastic promotion of lacrosse as a Canadian pastime was successful. Early in 1867, there were only six clubs in Canada; at the end of the year, there were eighty. Among the clubs formed in 1867 was one representing Upper Canada College of Toronto, which thus became the first college to play lacrosse.

Beers drew up the first written rules for lacrosse, which included the following regulations:

The crosse could be of any length, with netting that had to be flat when the ball was not in it.
The ball should be made of India rubber sponge not less than eight inches and not more than nine inches in circumference.
The length of the field was to be decided by the team captains. (Dr. Beers recommended that it be two hundred yards.)
The goalposts were six feet high, with a flag on top of each, and were six feet apart.
The goal crease was a line six feet in front of the goalposts. No opponent could cross the line until the ball had passed it.
Teams consisted of twelve men. Their positions were goalkeeper, point, cover point, center, home, and fielders. No substitution was permitted after a match was started, not even if a player was disabled.
Matches were decided by three goals (or "games") out of five, unless otherwise agreed upon by the captains. If, because of darkness or other reasons, neither side won three games, the match was considered unfinished and was called a draw, unless the captains had agreed that should one side score two goals and the other none, the former would be declared the match winner. Teams changed goals after each game and rested at least five minutes, but not more than ten, between games.

Players could not touch the ball with their hands (although goalkeepers might block a shot with their hands). Players also were forbidden to wear spiked shoes, throw a crosse at a player or at the ball, hold another player with the crosse or hands, or strike, trip, or threaten opposing players.

In 1867 an Indian team went to England, Ireland, France, and Scotland. As a result of the interest aroused in England, clubs were formed at Blackheath and Richmond, near London, and at Liverpool. In 1868 the English Lacrosse Association was formed. It adopted a code of laws that differed from the Canadian regulations in several respects. One change prescribed a time limit for a game. That was well in advance of the game's eventual development; a time limit was not used in championship club play in the United States until 1883 or in Canada until 1888. Another important new rule provided for a tape across the tops of the goalposts, which were seven feet apart. That definite target was the forerunner of the goal net.

A troupe of Indians from Canada demonstrated lacrosse at New York's Saratoga Springs fairgrounds during racing season in 1867. This event brought the first mention of lacrosse in the United States by American newspapers. Soon afterward, an exhibition was played in Troy, New York, between eight Canadian Indians and eight Americans. The Indians won, but an offshoot of the game was the formation of the first lacrosse club in the United States, the Mohawk Club of Troy. In 1868 the Mohawk Club played and lost four games to good Canadian clubs. Soon there were clubs in the Midwest, North, and East.

When the game was first played in New York City in 1868, the *New York Tribune* said, "Lacrosse may be called a madman's game, so wild it is." The *New York World* called it the "most exciting and at the same time the most laughter provoking among the whole range of outdoor sports." The *Times* rated it as "a noisy game and one of much excitement."[*]

In 1874 the sport was introduced in Australia, and in 1878 it spread to New Zealand. Dr. Beers

---

[*] As quoted in Bob Scott, *Lacrosse: Technique and Tradition* (Baltimore: Johns Hopkins University Press, 1976), 9.

took a club team and an Indian group to the British Isles in 1876. On June 26 the teams played before Queen Victoria at Windsor Castle. The queen was reported to be quite pleased with the game.

On their return to North America, the teams that had appeared before the queen were invited by the Westchester Polo Club to visit its grounds at Newport, Rhode Island, and demonstrate lacrosse for the vacationers at that exclusive resort. The game was played before a crowd of eight thousand. The *New York Herald* reported that "the immense popular success of the game caused lacrosse to be the talk of Newport. The universal verdict is that lacrosse is the most remarkable, versatile, and exciting of all games of ball."[*]

Intercollegiate lacrosse had its beginning in New York City, in the fall of 1877, when New York University played Manhattan College. By the time the game was called for darkness, NYU was ahead 2–0.

John R. Flannery was so active in promoting lacrosse in Boston and New York that sometimes he is called "the father of American lacrosse." He initiated the movement that resulted in the formation of the United States National Amateur Lacrosse Association in 1879. Harvard and New York University joined the association along with nine club teams: Ravenswood, New York, Brooklyn, Westchester, and Bay Ridge from the metropolitan area of New York; Elmira and Osceola from Elmira, New York; Union from Boston; and Bradford from Bradford, Pennsylvania. Modern-day counterparts to these club teams, featuring former collegiate stars, would remain major competitors of leading college teams well into the twentieth century.

The Baltimore Athletic Club did not join the association until 1880 but had gotten its start in lacrosse more than a year earlier after a trip by a Baltimore track and field team to Newport to compete at a sports carnival of the Westchester Polo Club. They saw the exhibition lacrosse game played there, liked it, brought sticks back to Baltimore, and resolved to master the sport. The first formal lacrosse exhibition conducted by the Baltimore Club was at old Newing-

ton Park in Baltimore on November 23, 1878. About four thousand turned out to get what was, for many, their first view of lacrosse. The first interclub game to be played in Baltimore took place on May 29, 1879, when the Ravenswood Club beat the Baltimore Athletic Club 3–1. By the spring of the following year the Monumentals and the Ivanhoes were also playing lacrosse in Baltimore. Many of the players on these club teams, especially the Monumentals, who later became the famous Druids, were high school students.

During the spring of 1881 Princeton and Columbia fielded lacrosse teams. Lawrason Riggs, a Baltimorean and a football star for Princeton, started the sport there and was the Tigers' first captain. Princeton, Columbia, Harvard, and New York University competed in the first intercollegiate tournament sponsored by the National Association. In the final game of the tournament, Harvard beat Princeton for the first intercollegiate championship.

The Intercollegiate Lacrosse Association was formed in March 1882. Yale fielded its first varsity team in the fall of 1882 and formally joined the association in 1883. The Johns Hopkins Club was organized in the fall of 1882 and played its first game, against the Druid Club, the following spring. However, the team disbanded and was not officially reorganized until 1888.

Lacrosse gradually spread to other colleges and universities before 1900. Stevens Institute and Lehigh began playing in 1885 and joined the association in 1886 and 1888. Rutgers formed a team in 1887, as did Union. City College of New York began playing in 1888, the University of Pennsylvania and Lafayette in 1890, Cornell in 1892, and Hobart in 1898. None of these schools was a member of the association.

The association championship was dominated by Harvard and Princeton in the 1880s and by Lehigh, Stevens, and Hopkins from 1890 to 1903. Swarthmore began the sport in 1891 and won championships in 1904 and 1905.

Just before the beginning of the twentieth century, several innovations greatly improved the game. During the 1897 season, Rossiter Scott, Stevens's captain, had the idea of fastening a tennis net to the goalposts. He passed this idea on to his friend Ronald

---

[*] Bob Scott, *Lacrosse: Technique and Tradition* (Baltimore: Johns Hopkins University Press, 1976), 9.

Abercrombie, the Hopkins center. Hopkins adopted that primitive form of goal net in 1898. Other colleges soon followed suit. That same season, Abercrombie, a short man, cut a piece from the handle of his stick, which was long, in the custom of the day. Other Hopkins players liked the modification, and the team, after some experimenting, ordered special sticks. The following year Hopkins used shorter, lighter sticks with smaller nets for attackmen in order to present smaller targets to opposing defensemen. The goalies' sticks were shorter, and while defensemen continued to use long sticks, these were made lighter. These sticks, which increased maneuverability, gave rise to the short passing game that was installed by Hopkins coach and captain William H. Maddren. This change was considered by many to have been Hopkins's most important contribution to the tactics of lacrosse.

In 1900, William C. Schmeisser began a distinguished career as a player, outstanding coach, and pioneer in the development of the game. Not only was he a great player and coach at Hopkins, he was instrumental in the early organization of Baltimore's Mount Washington Club, a top power for decades, and in 1904 he published *Lacrosse: From Candidate to Team*, a 113-page textbook on the coaching of lacrosse that was the standard instructional book for many years.

In 1905, the United States Intercollegiate Lacrosse League (USILL) was founded, with Northern and Southern Divisions. A champion was selected for each division based on the difficulty of the schedule each team played and the number of its wins, but in some years it was difficult to determine the national champion because the division champions did not play each other.

Under the USILL's new rules, the dimensions of the crease were fixed at eighteen by twelve feet. Substitutes could be used at any time, but once a player was removed he could not return. Games were divided into halves of thirty-five minutes each. The penalty for a foul was suspension for three minutes or until a goal was scored. For a second offense, the offending player was suspended for the remainder of the game.

During the first four years of the new league arrangement, Johns Hopkins, under the tutelage of Bill Schmeisser, not only won the Southern Division championship but probably had the best college team in the country. Johns Hopkins did not lose to another college team during that period and beat the Northern Division champions three times: Cornell in 1906 and Harvard in 1908 and 1909. Hopkins did not play the Northern Division champion, Cornell, in 1907 or the cochampion, Columbia, in 1909.

The service academies began playing lacrosse within a year of each other. In 1907, the U.S. Military Academy played its first game and continued to field a team for four years but dropped the sport after the 1910 season. It was revived in 1921. Navy's beginning was more auspicious. In 1908 Navy accepted a challenge from Harvard to play a game. James M. Irish, who had learned the game at Hobart, was appointed captain and coach. With some assistance from Hopkins's Frank Breyer and other Blue Jay players, Irish assembled and trained a team. Navy's first game was with its instructors on April 4, and the instructors won 6–1. In the challenge game, Navy lost to Harvard, but in 1909, its first season under an official coach, L. Alan Dill from Hopkins, it beat the Crimson 6–3.

In 1910, Navy turned on its mentors and defeated Hopkins 7–6. Swarthmore gained the Southern Division title by soundly trouncing Hopkins 13–3. Harvard lost to Hopkins but won the Northern Division title for the third straight year. Maryland Agricultural College (now the University of Maryland at College Park) organized a team with Edwin E. Powell, a former Mount Washington Club player, as captain and coach. At the Carlisle Indian School in Carlisle, Pennsylvania, athletic director Glenn "Pop" Warner substituted lacrosse for baseball and built an impressive program. During Carlisle's first year in the game, it rose to great heights by defeating both Navy and Mount Washington, but the school lost to Swarthmore, Lehigh, and Stevens.

The next ten years of the game's development were eventful, although World War I curtailed lacrosse activity from 1917 to 1919. Hopkins and Harvard repeated as sectional champions in 1911, but Hopkins had beaten the Crimson 3–2 early in the season. The story was repeated in 1913 and 1915, with Hopkins beating Harvard. A formal postseason play-off between the regional champions was held in 1912, with Harvard beating Swarthmore 7–3, but Navy pulled the biggest upset of that year when it defeated the previously unbeaten Crescents Club team. In 1914, Navy, coached since 1911 by Canadian George Finlayson, was tied by Carlisle but won all other games and compiled the best collegiate record. However, Navy was not a member of the USILL and therefore could not be considered for the league championship. Lehigh and Cornell were division champions and played to a 1–1 tie during the season. These same schools again won their division championships in 1916, but Lehigh edged Cornell 5–4 in the regular season.

In the shortened wartime schedules of 1917, Stevens and Lehigh were division champions, and Navy was undefeated in its two-game schedule. This began a unique period in college lacrosse annals, as the Midshipmen went on to win every game they played for the next seven seasons, with Finlayson coaching them during this period of glory. Because Navy was not in the USILL, however, it unfortunately could not be identified as champion. In 1918, Hopkins and Stevens were the regional champions. Hopkins was Southern Division champion again in 1919, but a Northern Division champion was not named. After World War I, schedules returned to normal.

Each era in lacrosse, and every championship team, has had its legendary players, led by accomplished coaches. All of them were as famous in their time as the top stars and coaches of today are now, and they merit mention in any brief history of the game. For example, in 1920, Syracuse and Lehigh were division champions and Lehigh won the postseason title 3–1, but Navy, still not a member of the league, defeated both of them and was the best of the nation's college teams. Navy's defense, built around two football All-Americans, Eddie Ewen and Emery "Swede" Larson, was superb in allowing only six goals in nine games. Navy's next-door neighbor in Annapolis, St. John's College, ventured into lacrosse competition for the first time and was defeated by Maryland—but soon would become a significant power itself.

In 1921 a major technical change occurred in lacrosse: An offside rule was instituted for the first time, dividing the field in half by a center line. Each team was required to keep at least three men, exclusive of the goalies, in each half of the field. This relieved the problem of defense players massing in front of the goal and preventing a wide-open offense. The penalty for violation of that rule was suspension for three to seven minutes.

Navy continued its unbeaten ways in 1921, 1922, and 1923. Lehigh, the Southern Division champion, once again beat Syracuse, the Northern Division champion, 3–1 in a play-off game in 1921. Irving B. Lydecker captained the 1922 Syracuse team to an undefeated seventeen-game season, which included victories over the Crescents Club and the University of Pennsylvania, the Southern Division champion. Victor Ross of Syracuse led the nation in scoring for the second year in a row. In 1922 an All-American lacrosse team was first selected. Hopkins won the Southern Division championship in 1923, but Army, Navy, and Syracuse shared the limelight as the top teams in the country.

Coach Laurie Cox's 1924 Syracuse team was undefeated in fourteen games, with impressive wins over Navy and the Crescents. Navy's first loss after forty-six consecutive victories came at the hands of the University of Maryland, which made an impressive debut in the association under the leadership of Dr. Reginald V. Truitt. Maryland also knocked Hopkins, the Southern Division champ, from the unbeaten ranks with a 4–2 victory. The first Army-Navy game was played in 1924 at West Point, and Navy won 5–0.

In 1925 Navy bounced back with another undefeated season. In Navy's 3–2 victory over Army, Fred Billing, Navy's captain, scored two goals against the Cadets and gave them their only loss for the season. Harold "Soft" Wood and Walt Townsend guided Syracuse to a Northern Division championship, and Maryland won in the Southern Division by virtue of a 3–1 victory over Hopkins. Doug Turnbull captained the Blue Jays and became the first player ever selected for the first All-American team for four straight years. The University of Virginia fielded a team for the first time in twenty years, and Brown University took up the sport.

Most of the colleges that had adopted lacrosse wanted to be members of the USILL, which was not able to accommodate them. In 1926, the league was replaced by the United States Intercollegiate Lacrosse Association (USILA), with unlimited membership. The Northern and Southern Divisions of the old league were merged. Rutgers, Navy, Union College, New York University, Colgate University, and St. Stephen's were admitted to full membership. Playing for the first time or resuming play that year were Dartmouth, Lafayette, City College of New York, the University of Georgia, St. John's of Annapolis, and Randolph-Macon College.

Amazingly, for the next fifty years—well into the 1970s—collegiate lacrosse was dominated by teams from Maryland: Johns Hopkins, Navy, Maryland, and St. John's. There were several reasons for this. Lacrosse was the major spring sport at the two largest public high schools in Baltimore, the Polytechnic Institute and Baltimore City College, and at almost all of Baltimore's private high schools. Players from these schools stocked the teams of the four collegiate lacrosse powers in the state. During the early years of the USILA, if you drew a wide circle around the neighborhoods near the Johns Hopkins campus and Baltimore's Mount Washington area, you would find most of the children with lacrosse sticks in their hands in the springtime, while elsewhere in Baltimore youngsters were seen with baseballs and gloves. In the 1950s, this circle began to widen, and today most of the high schools in Baltimore's outlying areas are playing lacrosse.

In addition to its superb high school players, Baltimore and the Maryland area may have dominated lacrosse during this period because, as former Hopkins assistant athletic director Andy Bilello once observed, lacrosse was the one sport in which the region excelled. Baltimore then had no Major League sports teams. The Colts weren't founded until 1947. They left in 1984 and were not replaced by the Ravens until 1996. The original Major League Orioles left town in 1904 and went to New York to become the Yankees; the modern Orioles arrived in 1954. Baltimoreans consequently focused on the quintessential amateur sport, lacrosse, and continue to support it with great fervor. Baltimore media still give

lacrosse greater coverage than it receives anywhere else. Princeton coach Bill Tierney told a reporter in 1998, "I grew up on Long Island, went to college in upstate New York and first coached there. But it meant a lot to be in Baltimore [as an assistant coach at Hopkins] and see lacrosse be that important in an area. Nowhere else will lacrosse ever have that history or that importance or carry the weight it does in Baltimore."

Besides the Maryland teams, Army and Princeton won a number of championships during this fifty-year period, but their teams were coached by men who had strong Baltimore lacrosse backgrounds: William Logan and Ferris Thomsen at Princeton, and F. Morris Touchstone and Jim Adams at Army. Most of their key players were also Baltimoreans. When Coach Howard "Howdy" Myers Jr. moved from Hopkins to Hofstra University in 1950, he joined forces with William Ritch of Sewanhaka High School, Jason Stranahan of Manhasset High School, and Joseph "Frenchy" Julien, the president of the Lacrosse Officials Association, to spread the game among Long Island high schools. Today these schools often surpass Baltimore and Maryland high schools in developing the largest number of outstanding collegiate lacrosse players.

In 1926 the USILA decided to rate the teams officially and award gold medals to the leaders. Although Navy was undefeated (8–0) and Syracuse lost only to the Crescents, Johns Hopkins, coached by Ray Van Orman to a 9–0 record, won the gold medal. In 1927 the Blue Jays were again victorious over all opponents, and their only close game was a thrilling come-from-behind 6–5 win over Navy. But in 1928 it was a different story. Gold medals were given to four teams—Johns Hopkins, Maryland, Navy, and Rutgers—as each finished its regular season with only one loss to an association rival. Army was not a member of the association, but the Cadets had an excellent record, which included a 5–3 victory over Hopkins and a 4–4 tie with Navy. Rutgers gave Army its only loss (8–3). Army's "Light Horse Harry" Wilson achieved the distinction of being selected to the All-American team in football, basketball, and lacrosse. At the conclusion of the 1928 season, Hopkins won a play-off series to determine the U.S. representative to the Olympic

Games in Amsterdam, where lacrosse was featured as an exhibition sport. The Blue Jays won all three play-off games (Mount Washington, 6–4; Army, 4–2; and Maryland, 6–3). In the Olympic Games, the Blue Jays beat Canada 6–3 but lost to Great Britain 7–6. Canada downed the Englishmen 9–5.

St. John's of Annapolis moved into the limelight for the next three years under the leadership of Coach William H. "Dinty" Moore. Although the team was not a member of the association in 1929, it was undefeated in thirteen games. The offense was led by Ferris Thomsen and Clem Spring; the defense was led by "Long John" Boucher. The Johnnies gave Maryland its first defeat on its home field in thirteen years. Navy and Union, both undefeated, were awarded goal medals that year by the association. In 1930, St. John's joined the association and was given the gold medal with a 10–1 record. Its only loss was to Hopkins after twenty-one consecutive victories. The next year the Johnnies won all ten of their games, scoring 108 goals and giving up just 7. Goalie Bill Armacost and defensemen Ed and Phil Lotz spearheaded the defense, which registered six shutouts, five in a row. Bobby Pool was outstanding on the attack, as were Bill Ziegler and Ernest Cornbrooks Jr. in the midfield. In an international competition between the United States and Canada, St. John's beat the Canadian team made up of amateur club players in two of three games. This was the last time such a U.S.-Canadian competition was held for the next three decades, because the amateur clubs of Canada chose to abandon field lacrosse in favor of indoor box lacrosse.

During 1932, Hopkins was undefeated in the regular season as well as in the Olympic play-offs and won the right to represent the United States in the Olympics again. Jack Turnbull and Don Kelly were the offensive leaders of the team. In the Olympic Games in Los Angeles, Hopkins beat the Canadians in two of three games for the world championship.

Although no champion was selected by the USILA from 1932 to 1935, Hopkins was considered by many as the leading team in 1932, 1933, and 1934, as the Blue Jays did not lose to a college team during that period. In 1935, St. John's, Maryland, and Navy each won all of its games except one, but

Princeton was undefeated for the third straight year under the expert coaching of Albert B. Nies and had an important 4–3 victory over Navy to boost its claim for the championship.

Some of the most drastic rule changes in modern lacrosse history were enacted in 1933, aimed at speeding up the game and giving it more wide-open play. The number of players on a side was reduced from twelve to ten. The distance between goals, which had been 110 yards since 1922, was reduced to 80 yards, and the playing area in the rear of each goal was fixed at 20 yards. It had been as much as 35 yards in 1930. Playing time still was sixty minutes, but it was divided into four quarters, with teams changing goals after each quarter.

In 1936, lacrosse lost a devoted friend and an influential supporter when W. Wilson Wingate, a Baltimore sportswriter, died. He was credited with being the first to call lacrosse "the fastest game on two feet" (hockey, of course, is played on skates). Wingate was an editor of the *Official Lacrosse Guide* and was appointed an official to accompany the Johns Hopkins teams to the Olympic Games in both 1928 and 1932. Wishing to honor his memory, a group of Wingate's friends bought a silver trophy to be awarded each year to the team voted the intercollegiate champion by the executive board of the USILA. The Wingate Trophy was the top award for lacrosse until the National Collegiate Athletic Association assumed control over the championship competition in 1971.

The University of Maryland, coached by Dr. John E. Faber, won the first Wingate Trophy in 1936. In 1937 the Terps shared the trophy with Princeton, coached by William F. Logan and captained by C. M. Dering. Both were undefeated in collegiate play. Jack Kelly (goal) and Charles Ellinger (attack) starred for the Terps as first-team All-Americans in both years. John Christhilf and Bobby Neilson were the leading Terp scorers in 1936 and 1937, respectively.

Dinty Moore, who had coached St. John's College to national championships, moved to the Naval Academy in 1936. His 1938 Navy team, captained by Frank Case, was undefeated in collegiate play and the unchallenged winner of the

Wingate Trophy. The University of Maryland won the championship in 1939, with Jim Meade and Rip Hewitt leading the way, and again in 1940, when Milton Mulitz (defense) and Oscar Nevares (attack) were the top Terp players. After the 1939 season, St. John's College discontinued participation in all forms of intercollegiate athletics.

In 1940, the first annual North-South all-star game, highlighting the best players from each area in the association, was played in the old Baltimore Stadium. It was introduced partly to take the place of the U.S. games with Canada, which had been discontinued after the Canadians' adoption of box lacrosse. The North won the game 6–5.

In 1941 Kelso Morrill and Gardner Mallonee coached Hopkins to an undefeated season that was climaxed with a 7–6 victory over the Mount Washington Club team. Hopkins's first-team All-Americans were John Tolson and Nelson Shawn on defense and Charlie Thomas on attack.

Although World War II reduced lacrosse activity, with many college players entering the military, Princeton's team of 1942 went undefeated in college ranks and was the first northern team to defeat the "big three" of the South (Maryland, Navy, and Hopkins) in the same year. Captain Elmer Weisheit had a hand in ten of the goals scored in a 12–10 victory over Maryland, and Ty Campbell's play in the goal was outstanding throughout the season. Navy won the Wingate Trophy in 1943, and Army won it in 1944. This was the Cadets' first national championship and came under the fine coaching leadership of F. Morris Touchstone, who had transferred to West Point in 1928 after having met with considerable success at Yale. In 1945 Army and Navy shared the championship after they had battled through two extra periods in a driving rainstorm to a 7–7 tie.

After the war ended in 1945, lacrosse returned to full-scale competition. Navy, although beaten by Hopkins, compiled the best record and won the Wingate Trophy in 1946. In the Army-Navy game, Navy, behind by six goals at one point, rallied to beat the Cadets 12–10.

The years 1947 through 1950 were dominated by Hopkins. The Blue Jays did not lose a collegiate game during those four years. The 1949 Navy team, led by All-Americans Richard Seth (goal), Philip Ryan (defense), and Lee Chambers (attack), also went undefeated and shared the championship that year with Hopkins. Howdy Myers coached the first three of those undefeated Blue Jay teams, but when Howdy left Hopkins and went to Hofstra University, Dr. W. Kelso Morrill directed the 1950 Hopkins team. Quite a few players were outstanding during that period. Two of the best were Brooke Tunstall, a two-year captain and first-team All-American attackman, and Lloyd Bunting, a three-time first-team All-American defenseman.

Princeton, coached for the first time by Ferris Thomsen and led by Captain Don Hahn (attack) and Reddy Finney (midfield), shared the championship with Army in 1951. Finney was an All-American in both football and lacrosse, as was West Point's Dan Foldberg. Bruno Giordano combined with Foldberg to give Army an excellent defense. Ray Wood of Washington College established a new national record by scoring 187 goals in four years of varsity play.

Cochampions again were named in 1952. Robert "Pic" Fuller coached Virginia to a 7–1 collegiate season, and Ned Harkness directed Rensselaer Polytechnic Institute to a 10–0 record, although its opposition did not include any of the traditional collegiate powers. The offensive leaders were Gordon Jones and Dick Godine for the Cavaliers and Lester Eustace and Ken Martin for Rensselaer.

A significant new rule went into effect in the 1953 season. It allowed free movement of players when play was stopped. Since the adoption of the initial rules in 1867, a player was required to freeze in position at the sound of a whistle or had to leave his stick to mark his place if he moved.

Princeton, led by All-American attackman Ralph Willis, won the Wingate Trophy in 1953 but gave way to an undefeated Navy team in 1954. The Navy defense, headed by goalie John Jones and defenseman Stanley Swanson, limited their opponents to an average of 3.1 goals per game. The University of Maryland, coached by Dr. Jack Faber and Albert Heagy, dominated the game for the next two years with identical 11–0 seasons. Its only close games were with Navy in 1955 and Mount Washington (12–11) in 1956. The Terps had a powerful team with one exceptional player at each position: Charles Wicker (attack), James Keating (midfield), John Simmons (defense), and James Kappler (goal).

Bill Morrill Jr. and Mickey Webster led Hopkins to two unbeaten collegiate seasons the next two years. The Blue Jays won the Wingate Trophy in 1957 but were denied a share of it in 1958, when Army, under the fine leadership of Jim Adams, was also undefeated and selected as the champion. Another major star of the game during this period was Jim Brown of Syracuse, who compiled an incredible record even though Syracuse's teams did not win any championships under rules that emphasized the quality of the opponents a team played.

In 1959 Army, Maryland, and Hopkins shared the championship, since each had one collegiate loss on its record. Don Tillar (defense) and Robert Miser (attack) were Army's top players for both championship teams, and Robert Schwartzberg and Roger Goss led the 1959 Maryland team at defense and attack, respectively.

In June 1959, the Lacrosse Hall of Fame Foundation was founded as a nonprofit organization dedicated to the support and development of the game throughout the country. Later known as the Lacrosse Foundation and now as US Lacrosse, its offices and museum are located beside the Johns Hopkins University's Homewood Field. US Lacrosse not only serves as a clearinghouse of information for the entire sport but also has been instrumental in promoting lacrosse's growing popularity in the United States and overseas.

In 1959 Willis P. "Bildy" Bilderback succeeded Dinty Moore as the Navy coach when Dinty retired. In his first season, Bildy guided Navy to a modest 6–3–1 record, but from 1960 through 1967 Navy seemed to own collegiate lacrosse. The Middies lost only three college games during this eight-year period, and two were upsets to Army in games played at Annapolis in 1961 and 1963. The 10–8 loss to the Cadets in 1961 caused the national championship to be shared by the two service academies. A 9–6 loss to Hopkins in 1967 gave Navy a three-way share of the crown with Maryland and Hopkins. During this golden era in Navy lacrosse,

there were a number of outstanding players. The most acclaimed attackmen were Karl Rippelmeyer, 1960; Tom Mitchell, 1961; George Tracy, 1962 and 1963; and one of the greatest of all time, Jimmy Lewis, 1964–1966. The top defensemen were Neal Reich, 1961; Michael Coughlin, 1963 and 1964; James Campbell, 1964; Pat Donnelly, 1965; and Carl Tamulevich, 1967. Leaders in the midfield were Roger Kisiel, 1962, and John Taylor III, 1964, and face-off specialists Neil Henderson, 1965, and John McIntosh, 1967. Dennis Wedekind, 1965, was considered by many as the best of the Navy goalies during this period.

Hopkins was involved in championship play from 1967 through 1970. After sharing the Wingate Trophy in 1967 with Navy and Maryland (led by its high-scoring attackmen, Jack Heim and Alan Lowe), the Blue Jays won sole possession of it in 1968 with a 10–0 collegiate record. In 1969 Hopkins shared the championship with Army. Pete Cramblet and Tom Cafaro were the Cadet's one-two scoring punch. Joe Cowan was the offensive leader of the Blue Jays from 1967 through 1969. During that period, Hank Kaestner (1967) and Mike Clark (1968 and 1969) were the number one defensemen. Virginia, Navy, and Hopkins shared the championship in 1970, when each had only one loss on its record.

Club lacrosse was at its peak in the 1970s. Although it seems surprising now, fans could often attend exciting games for free and see many former collegiate stars compete fiercely. The Long Island Athletic Club organized a lacrosse team in 1966 through the efforts of Al Levine and soon became the reigning power. Richie Moran coached the Islanders to their first of four consecutive championships in 1968 and was followed by Cliff Murray in 1969 and Bill Ritch in 1970 and 1971. Among the top players during this period were attackmen Jim Martone, Bruce Cohen, Jack Heim, and Alan Lowe; midfielders Ron Fraser, Dick Finley, and Tom Postel; defenseman Jack Salerno; and goalie Bob Ricci. Arlyn Marshall's Carling Club of Baltimore edged the Islanders 9–8 for the 1972 championship as Gene Fusting scored the winning goal on a pass from Charles "Chooch" Turner with twenty-eight seconds remaining in the game. Long Island won the title again in 1973 and 1974 under Jack Kaley's leadership. After a seven-year lapse, Mount Washington regained the championship in 1975 by beating Long Island 18–9. Coach Joe Seivold's key players were Dennis Townsend, Skip Lichtfuss, and Don Krohn.

The first NCAA lacrosse championship tournament occurred in 1971, and Cornell University was the first champion. After losing the season opener to Virginia 10–9, Richie Moran's Big Red team won thirteen straight games, including a 17–16 thriller with Army in the NCAA semifinals and a 12–6 victory over Maryland for the championship. Outstanding players for Cornell were Robert Rule (goal), John Burnap (defense), Robert Shaw (midfield), and Al Rimmer (attack).

Glenn F. Thiel directed Virginia to an undefeated regular season in 1971, but a loss to Navy in the opening round of the NCAA tournament knocked the team out of championship contention. In 1972, however, the Cavaliers, despite suffering three regular-season collegiate losses, were primed for the NCAA play-offs and beat Army 10–3, Cortland State 14–7, and then Hopkins 13–12 in the action-filled finals at College Park, Maryland. Pete Eldredge scored the winning goal, his fourth, with four minutes remaining in the game. Jay Connor and Tom Duquette were the offensive guns for the Cavaliers, and Bruce Mangels led the defense.

The University of Maryland, coached by Buddy Beardmore, won the 1973 NCAA championship by beating Hopkins 10–9 in overtime at the University of Pennsylvania's Franklin Field. Freshman Frank Urso scored the winning goal in the second overtime period after Doug Schreiber had tied the score with three minutes remaining in regulation time. Pat O'Meally (attack) and Mike Thearle (defense) joined midfielders Schreiber and Urso on the first All-American team. Five Terps were also selected to the second All-American team. This gives an indication of the overall depth and strength of their team.

After losing in the NCAA final by one goal two years in a row, Johns Hopkins won the gold championship plaque in 1974 with the 17–12 defeat of Maryland. This game climaxed outstanding college careers by Jack Thomas, Rick Kowalchuk, and nine other Hopkins seniors as well as the superb twenty-year coaching career of Bob Scott.

In 1975, Maryland became the first school to repeat as NCAA Division I champions. The Terps beat Navy 20–13 in the final, with Frank Urso, Doug Radebaugh, and Mike Farrell leading the way.

The 1975 championship outcome was the last one mentioned in the first edition of this book. In the thirty years since, the ranks of the major lacrosse powers have expanded and the rules and equipment have changed dramatically, and yet lacrosse still is a game that can be decided by mere inches or seconds. The names of Division I championship programs may often remain the same, but their margins of victory frequently have been razor thin. Fourteen of the championships since 1976—nearly half of them—have been one-goal wins in regulation time or overtime.

Syracuse has been the predominant team—barely. It has won eight national championships (a ninth championship game victory was vacated for off-season rules violations). More than half of the Syracuse championships—five—have been one-goal victories. Hopkins has won eight national championships, three of them by one goal in regulation time. Princeton has won six titles—four of them by a goal in sudden-death overtime. The University of North Carolina has won four championships, one by a single goal in regulation and another by one goal in overtime. Virginia has won two championships. Cornell has won two titles, one in overtime. And sometimes these teams only made their way to the championship game by winning one-goal quarterfinal or semifinal games. There has been no lack of excitement in any of the NCAA lacrosse programs, regardless of division—although I only will deal in this chapter with Division I, where Hopkins plays.

In 1976, Cornell won the Division I national championship by beating Maryland 16–13 in double overtime. There was no sudden death overtime then, as we have now. Cornell's ace attackman Mike French scored seven of the Big Red's goals. This was the first NCAA lacrosse championship to receive exposure on national television, with football Hall of Famer Frank Gifford doing the play-by-play on a shortened, tape-delayed broadcast. He called the game "without question the most exciting sporting event I've ever seen." Highlights of French's performance became part of ABC-TV's *Wide World of Sports* opening montage of victories. Joining French on the offensive for Cornell were Eamon McEneaney, Jon Levine, Bill Marino, and Bob Henrickson. Goalie Dan Mackesey, with defenseman Bob Katz in front, made twenty-eight saves. Maryland's midfielder Frank Urso also had a typically outstanding game. He became the first four-time, first-team All-American since Johns Hopkins's Doug Turnbull in the 1920s.

Richie Moran's Cornell repeated its championship win in 1977, beating Henry Ciccarone's Hopkins Blue Jays 16–8 at the University of Virginia's Scott Stadium and completing a second straight undefeated season with the NCAA's first back-to-back championships. The championship game was a showcase for Cornell's senior attackman Eamon McEneaney, who had three goals and five assists. Tom Marino, Dave Bray, and Dan Mackesey also had a great game. Hopkins was making its first appearance in the NCAA final since 1974—and also was beginning its first in a record string of nine consecutive championship game appearances. Team leaders Mike O'Neill, Dave Huntley, and Mark Greenberg would be back.

In 1978, Hopkins avenged its loss a year earlier by beating Cornell decisively, 13–8, for the championship before the then largest crowd ever, 13,527, at Rutgers University. NBC-TV broadcast tape-delayed highlights of the game later. Hopkins's freshman face-off specialist Ned Radebaugh controlled twenty out of the twenty-two face-offs in which he participated. (The next year, a USILA rules change virtually eliminated the face-off for the 1979 season. It was not a happy experiment, and the face-off was back by 1980.) Hopkins attackman Mike O'Neill was named both the game's Most Valuable Player (MVP) and Division I Player of the Year. Other Hopkins goal-scorers included Scott Baugher, Jim Bidne, Frank Cutrone, Bob DeSimone, Joe Devlin, Wayne Davis, and David Huntley. Goalie Mike Federico, fronted by defensemen Mark Greenberg, Will Hazelhurst, Mike Connor, Mike Sheedy, and Curt Ahrendsen,

was spectacular in the cage. Cornell's goalie, John Griffin, made seventeen saves; other top Cornell players were Steve Page, Keith Reitenback, and Bob Henrickson.

A World Series of Lacrosse was held in Manchester, England, that summer, with Canada beating the United States 17–16 in overtime. It was a stunning upset, especially since the U.S. team had beaten Canada 28–4 in their previous matchup in the round-robin tournament, which also featured teams from Great Britain and Australia. It was the first defeat for the United States in international competition in decades—and would be its last to date. The top player of the tournament was Mike French, playing for Canada against the U.S. team coached by his former mentor from Cornell, Richie Moran, and featuring his former Cornell teammate, Eamon McEneaney. Another top Canadian player was Stan Cockerton, who scored the winning goal. This event would begin the international lacrosse tournaments that now are held every four years, with more than sixteen nations currently represented.

Henry Ciccarone's 1979 Blue Jays went 13–0 on their way to another NCAA championship in which they beat Maryland 15–9. It was Hopkins's first undefeated, untied season since 1941; its twentieth straight win since losing to Cornell during the regular season in 1978; and its first successful defense of an NCAA title. The Blue Jay offense was led by bazooka-armed David Huntley, Jeff Cook, Scott Baugher, Jim Bidne, Wayne Davis, Joe Garavente, Steve Wey, and Ned Radebaugh; the defense of Mark Greenberg, Curt Ahrendsen, Dave Black, and goalie Mike Federico gave up fewer than seven goals a game. Maryland's top scorers Bob Boneillo, John Lamon, and Terry Kimball were repeatedly frustrated by the Jays' tough defenders.

In 1980, Hopkins became the first team to win three consecutive NCAA Division I championships. Henry Ciccarone again led the Jays to a successful defense of their title, beating Virginia 9–8 in double overtime when senior attackman Jim Bidne made a perfect feed to Jeff Harris on the crease, enabling Harris to put one past the Cavalier's goalie, Brian Gregory. Although Virginia's face-off expert Steve Kraus won nineteen out of twenty draws,

Hopkins's goalie Mike Federico continued making amazing saves, and the Hopkins offense, which included Henry Ciccarone Jr., Jim Zaffuto, and Navy transfer Brendan Schneck, brought home the win.

In 1981, North Carolina, coached by former Hopkins player and assistant coach Willie Scroggs, won its first NCAA Division I championship. Scroggs's Tar Heels beat his former coaching chief, Henry Ciccarone, and the Hopkins Blue Jays 14–13 to complete a 12–0 season and end Hopkins's twenty-two-game winning streak. Although the top offensive player of the game was Hopkins's Jeff Cook, who scored six goals, North Carolina's offensive stars Mike Burnett, Doug Hall, Kevin Griswold, and Pete Voelkel overcame an 11–8 deficit by scoring six unanswered goals, as Carolina goalie Tommy Sears made eighteen saves.

Willie Scroggs's University of North Carolina team retained the Division I championship in 1982 with a stifling defense, holding Hopkins to just five goals and winning the NCAA crown 7–5 to complete another undefeated season. Goalie Tommy Sears was MVP and Player of the Year as he and his defensive teammates, John Haus, Jamie Allen, and Gary Burns, kept the Blue Jays scoreless for the first twenty-four minutes of the game. Carolina's Dave Wingate scored all three of the team's first-quarter goals and ultimately scored five of its tallies. Mike Donnelly scored Hopkins's only goal of the second quarter—despite a Blue Jay 17–4 dominance in shots that period.

In 1982, the United States regained the international lacrosse crown in the World Games, held at Hopkins's Homewood Field in Baltimore, beating Australia 22–14 before a standing room only, sellout crowd of 11,435. A feisty Australian team had upset the reigning champion Canadians 24–18 in the round-robin tournament with exceptional offensive play by Jeff Kennedy, Paul Lynch, Peter Cann, Graeme Fox, Ken Nicholls, John Butkiewicz, and Gary Tillotson. In the championship game, the powerhouse U.S. attack of Brooks Sweet (a University of Maryland grad), former Hopkins stars Mike O'Neill and Jeff Cook, Adelphia alumnus Bob Engelke, and Bob Griebe (the 1980 club Player of the Year) scored eight unanswered goals to break open the game. Australia's Jeff Kennedy, a key to the Aussies' victory over Canada but sidelined from the championship game due to a sudden heart problem, was named the tournament's MVP. Many spectators thought the most exciting game of the tournament was the consolation match between Canada and England, which was won by Canada 20–19 in the last two minutes of the second overtime period. Great Britain's ageless goalie John Marr, then forty-three years old, made a record thirty-two saves to keep the British in the game to the last second. The ten-man All World Team included U.S. goalie Tom Sears; U.S. defensemen Mark Greenberg and Chris Kane, along with Jeff Mounkley of England; midfielders Australian John Butkiewicz, American Brooks Sweet, and Canadian Bob Teasdall; and the U.S. team's Brendan Schneck and Aussie Peter Cann joining Kennedy on the attack.

Syracuse won its first lacrosse championship since 1924 with an astounding come-from-behind victory over Hopkins in the 1983 NCAA Division I title game. After being down 12–5 going into the fourth quarter, Roy Simmons Jr.'s Orange scored six goals in seven minutes and pulled off a stunning 17–16 victory against Henry Ciccarone's Blue Jays, appearing in their seventh consecutive championship game. Syracuse's offensive leaders were Brad Kotz, Art Lux, Dave Desko, Tom Korrie, Tim Nelson, and Randy Lundblad. Hopkins's top scorers were Del Dressel, John Krumenacker, Kirk Baugher, Peter Scott, and brothers Henry Ciccarone Jr. and Brent Ciccarone.

Hoping to recapture the excitement of the 1982 World Games, the Lacrosse Foundation and Baltimore's Masonic Boumi Temple sponsored another round-robin tournament, Lacrosse International, held at Homewood Field in the summer of 1983. Organized by Baltimoreans Hugh Mallon, Bob Kearney, and Val Donley, the five-day event featured nearly four hundred players in every level playing in games before some seventeen thousand spectators. The newly crowned NCAA Division I champion Syracuse team beat Team Canada 14–13 in another come-from-behind game, and Division III champion Hobart demolished the Iroquois Nationals 22–14.

In 1984, Hopkins completed a 13–0 season for first-year coach Don Zimmerman by regaining the NCAA Division I championship, its fifth in ten years, beating Syracuse 13–10 at the University of Delaware stadium before a then-record crowd of seventeen thousand. The defense by John DeTommaso, Steve Dubin, Brad McClam, Chris Wickwire and defensive middies John Krumenacker and Steve Mitchell limited the Orange to just thirty-three shots, and goalie Larry Quinn make thirteen saves, some of them spectacular. The Blue Jays' offensive leaders Del Dressel, John Tucker, Peter Scott, and Brian Wood propelled Hopkins to a 5–0 lead in the first quarter and never flagged.

The 1985 Division I championship game saw the Hopkins defense, coached by the legendary Fred Smith, hold Syracuse scoreless for thirty-three minutes and beat the Orange 11–4 to retain the crown. The Jays' defense set a record for the least goals scored by an opponent in a championship game, as senior captains goalie Larry Quinn (who received a standing ovation from the crowd of 17,500), Guy Matricciani, and John Krumenacker led teammates John DeTommaso and Brad McLam to stifle hard-driving Syracuse. The Orangemen had quickly gone ahead 3–0 at the beginning of the game, but then the Blue Jay defense shut them down. Greg Matthews took twelve of eighteen face-offs, and the Hopkins offense of Del Dressel, Brian Wood, Craig Bubier, and Mike Morrill put Hopkins ahead 6–3 by the half. (Even defenseman McLam scored a goal.) Del Dressel later became only the third player in history to be named a first-team All-American for four straight years.

In 1986, for the first time in twenty years, none of the top-seeded Division I teams made it to the championship game. It also marked the first time in nine years that Hopkins was not appearing in the title contest, ending a consecutive streak of championship game appearances that has not been equaled since. The 1986 Final Four saw three games decided by four goals—two of them in overtime. North Carolina beat the Blue Jays 10–9 in overtime during one semifinal game, then beat Virginia, a 12–10 semifinal winner over Syracuse, 10–9 in overtime to win the championship. (Ironically, Hopkins had beaten North Carolina by a lopsided 16–4 during the regular season, handing Willie Scroggs his worst career loss.) North Carolina's

goalie Barney Aburn made thirteen saves in the championship game, while Gary Seivold scored the winning goal.

At the 1986 World Games held at the University of Toronto, the U.S. team coached by Dave Urick successfully defended its international title, beating Canada 18–9. Named to the All-World team's defense were Larry Quinn as goalie and his U.S. teammates Jim Burke and Bob Vencak, along with Jim Aitchinson of Canada; midfielders included the U.S. team's John Tucker, Canada's Kevin Alexander, England's Mark Hodkin, and Australia's Jeff Kennedy; and the attack featured Roddy Marino of the U.S. team, Jim Weller of Canada, and Peter Cann of Australia. Pete Cann also was named the best and fairest player of the tournament.

Upsets also ruled the 1987 Division I championships, as Hopkins—ranked only fourth in the tournament—beat defending champion North Carolina, then Maryland and Cornell, the two top teams, on its way to regaining the championship for the third time in four years. Freshman goalie Quint Kessenich sparkled in the cage; offensive leaders Brian Wood, Craig Bubier, Mike Morrill, Larry LeDoyen, Brendan Kelly, John Wilkens, and John Ciccarone were explosive; and I was fortunate to be joined on an all-sophomore starting defense by Greg Lilly and James DeTommaso. Long-stick midfielder Steve Mitchell became the first in that position to be selected an All-American. In the quarterfinal, Quint made twenty-two saves, and Hopkins defeated North Carolina 11–10 on Mike Morrill's sixth goal with just one minute, fifty-seven seconds left to play. In the semifinal, Hopkins faced previously unbeaten Maryland—then ranked number one—and prevailed by a 13–8 tally. In the championship game against Cornell, Greg Gunning won ten of thirteen face-offs for the Blue Jays, Kessenich continued making spectacular saves, and senior attackmen Craig Bubier scored four goals, including the game-winner, in the 11–10 victory.

The Gait twins—Gary and Paul—burst upon the national lacrosse consciousness in 1988, leading Syracuse to a 15–0 season and the Division I national championship. Although the Gaits, from British Columbia in Canada's far west, began their collegiate career in 1987, it was during their sophomore year that their remarkable stick skills and extraordinary athleticism began having a profound impact on the game that lasts to this day—and led to their induction into the Lacrosse Hall of Fame in 2005.

In a semifinal game against Tony Seaman's Penn, Gary introduced "Air Gait," a spectacular move that originated in the Canadian box lacrosse game on which he and Paul had been raised but that had never been seen before in U.S. field lacrosse. Twice Gary charged from the rear of the Penn goal, then suddenly jumped clear over the cage, appearing almost to hang suspended in midair, and fired a shot past the startled Penn goalie John Kanaras before landing in front of the crease. The first time Gary did it, Tony Seaman asked to watch a video replay of the goal, saying that in twenty-two years of lacrosse he'd never seen a shot like that—and neither had most of the eleven thousand fans in the Carrier Dome. The referees ruled it a clean, fair shot, and the Gait legend was secured as Syracuse beat Penn 11–10. (Later, the NCAA would forbid such diving shots, either in front of or from behind the goal.) In the quarterfinals, Virginia upset defending champion Hopkins 11–10 in overtime, and Cornell, ranked eleventh in the play-offs, upset North Carolina 6–4. Richie Moran's Big Red then beat Virginia 17–6 to set up an "All Upstate New York" final with Syracuse, which won the championship game 15–8. Gary Gait broke the Division I record of sixty-five goals in a season, set in 1976 by Cornell's Mike French, by tallying seventy times in 1989 and also set an NCAA tournament record of fourteen goals, exceeding the thirteen goals scored by Hopkins's Franz Wittelsberger in 1974.

Syracuse successfully defended its title in 1989, beating second-seed Hopkins 13–12. Hopkins had gotten to the championship game by beating North Carolina 10–6 on the offensive talents of Matt Panetta, Brendan Kelly, John Wilkens, and Mike Morrissey; the face-off brilliance of Joe Rzempoluch, who won seventeen of twenty draws; and defensive efforts that almost shut down all of Carolina's offense, which scored only one goal in the fourth quarter. Syracuse beat Maryland 18–8 in the other semifinal. In the championship game, Quint Kes-

senich recorded seventeen saves against the Gaits, Tom Marechek, and John Zulberti, while the Orange's goalie Matt Palumb had thirteen saves, including one against a point-blank shot by Blue Jay John Dressel with only seconds remaining on the clock. I was matched up against Gary Gait, and the Hopkins defense managed to limit him to just two goals, but Paul Gait scored four times. Hopkins's offensive leader was Matt Panetta, who had five goals and one assist, but the Blue Jays—who had beaten Syracuse 14–13 in March—ended up on the short end of a one-goal game in May. After appearing in ten championship games over thirteen years, Hopkins's 1989 title match would be its last championship contest for the next fourteen years.

The Gaits concluded their college careers in 1990 with a 13–0 season and another NCAA championship game victory, beating Loyola 21–9 before nineteen thousand fans at Rutgers University. Loyola, powered by an offense led by Brian Kroneberger, Chris Colbeck, Kevin Beach, and Joe Reese, had gotten to the championship game by beating Yale 14–13 in double overtime, while Syracuse had defeated North Carolina 21–10 in what would be Willie Scroggs's last game as the Tar Heels' coach. Although the decisive 1990 final marked Syracuse's third straight Division I victory, the NCAA later took away the championship title because of off-season rules violations by the Orange.

In the summer of 1990, I was honored to be on the U.S. team that traveled to Perth, Australia, to defend—and retain—the international championship at the World Games played in the Western Australian Cricket Association stadium. Team USA won the title by beating Canada 19–15 in a rainbow-wrapped contest that alternately was played in either driving rain or brilliant sunshine. Along with my defensive teammates Steve Mitchell and John DeTommaso (both Hopkins alumni), George McGeeney (University of Maryland, Baltimore County), and Tony Resch (Yale), we managed to shut down Canada's offensive sextet—the Gait twins, brothers Tom and Bill Marechek, Kevin Alexander, and Geordie Dean—on five extraman opportunities. Steve Mitchell succeeded in stripping the Canadians of the ball four of the five times we did so during the game. Larry Quinn once again was brilliant in the goal. On the offensive end of the field, my former Hopkins teammate, Mike Morrill, had a hat trick; Kevin Cook of Cornell scored four times, as did Roddy Marino of Virginia. Additional Team USA goals were scored by Vin Sombrotto of Hofstra and John Tucker of Hopkins. Canada actually outscored Team USA 11–8 in the second half of the game, but our earlier offensive and defensive dominance had put the game out of reach. Six members of Team USA were named to the All-World Team. On the attack were Mac Ford of North Carolina, who was named best attackman; Roddy Marino of Virginia; and Canadian Bill Marechek. John Tucker was named best midfielder and was joined on the all-star team by Brad Kotz of Syracuse and by his former teammate, Canadian Gary Gait. Murray Kean of Australia, whose team placed third in the tournament, was named top goalie. I was fortunate to be named the top defenseman and the tournament's MVP; my all-star defensive teammates were Steve Mitchell and Canadian Ben Hieltjes. The chance to play with gentlemen I had grown up idolizing, including John DeTommaso, George McGeeney, Larry Quinn, and John Tucker, was a great pleasure. I learned a lot lacrossewise—and peoplewise.

North Carolina under first-year coach Dave Klarmann went 16–0 in the 1991 season and recorded an 18–13 victory over Carl Runk's Towson University team—seeded only eleventh in the tournament—in the championship game. In the semifinal game, Carolina displayed its deep offense as twelve players, led by Ryan Wade, John Webster, and Dennis Goldstein, scored in a 19–13 victory over Syracuse at its Carrier Dome. Syracuse had such a commanding home field advantage that up until then it had won sixty-seven out of seventy-one games at home, including fifteen straight play-off matches. Towson had gotten to the title game by beating Maryland 15–11 with the offensive skills of Mike DeSimone, Doug Sharretts, Rob Shek, and John Blatchley and the defensive smarts of goalie Rich Betcher.

The rest of the 1990s Division I championships belonged either to Princeton or Syracuse, except for one victory each by North Carolina and Virginia. In 1992, Bill Tierney's Princeton Tigers won their first national championship in nearly forty years by beating Syracuse 10–9 in overtime. It was the first time since 1977 that a team other than Syracuse, Hopkins, or North Carolina had won the Division I championship. Princeton's goalie Scott Bacigalupo was magnificent in the cage, as were defensive leaders Mike Mariano and David Morrow in front of him. The Tigers' offense was led by Kevin Lowe, Justin Tortolani, Andy Moe, and Greg Waller.

Syracuse won its fourth championship in six years—and its first since the Gait twins' graduation—in 1993, beating North Carolina 13–12. Carolina had been the number one seed, having beaten Hopkins in the semifinal 16–10, while Syracuse beat Princeton 15–9 before a then record semifinal crowd of 21,529 at the University of Maryland's Byrd Stadium. The championship game was a furious battle, with six ties and four lead changes. The Orange's offensive leaders were Roy Colsey, Dom Fin, and Matt Rider, and goalie Chris Surran made twenty saves to be named the championship's MVP.

Tight competition continued in the 1994 Final Four play-off games, as Princeton won another nail-biter, beating Virginia 9–8 in overtime to regain the Division I championship. To reach the title game, Princeton had beaten Hopkins 12–11 in an overtime quarterfinal game before managing a three-goal semifinal victory over Brown, which had beaten the Tigers 7–6 during the regular season. Virginia got to the championship game with a 15–14 overtime win against Syracuse in the semifinal. The tournament belonged to Princeton's seniors, including goalie Scott Bacigalupo and offensive leaders Paul Murphy, Scott Reinhardt, and Kevin Lowe. Virginia's freshmen Michael Watson and Doug Knight made impressive championship debuts, as did Tim Whiteley, Greg Traynor, and goalie James Ireland.

The 1994 World Games returned to Manchester, England, site of the 1978 upset victory by Canada for the lone non-U.S. championship of modern international competition. The Gait twins, Tom Marechek, and others were typically acrobatic and athletic for Canada (as they had been in Perth, Australia, four years earlier), but the Australians, led by the legendary attackman Peter Cann, attackman Chris Brown, and midfielder Gordon Purdie, once again surprised Canada in the semifinals with an 18–17 victory. Once more, I was fortunate to play for Team USA, which won the championship by defeating Australia 21–7. I was honored again to be selected as a member of the All-World Team. The defense once again included my fellow Hopkins alum, Team USA's John DeTomasso; Steve Mounsey of Australia; and U.S. goalie Sal LoCascio, who also was named the tournament's best goalie. The All-World midfield included Gary and Paul Gait along with Gordon Purdie, and the attack included my former Hopkins teammate, Mike Morrill; Australian Chris Brown; and Mark Millon, who also was named the tournament's MVP.

The NCAA celebrated a quarter century of its championship tournaments in 1995 by naming a twenty-fifth anniversary team (on which I was honored to be placed) and setting incredible records for attendance at its Final Four, which featured typically surprising outcomes.

Syracuse won the 1995 championship—their third of the 1990s—by beating Maryland 13–9, but since the Orange had lost both to Virginia and Hopkins during the regular season, they were not ranked first going into the tournament. The number one team was Tony Seaman's Hopkins Blue Jays, who had gone undefeated during the regular season on the strength of the record-setting scoring of Terry Riordan and Brian Piccola, and the record-setting goaltending of Jonathan Marcus. In the tournament's semifinal game, however, it was Maryland goalie Brian Dougherty who performed miraculously in the cage, leading the Terps to a 16–8 upset victory. In the first quarter alone, Dougherty made twelve of the twenty-three saves he would register that day. So dominating was the Maryland defense that Hopkins fell behind 4–1 in the first period, even though the Jays outshot Maryland 19–8. Maryland's offensive leaders Matt Hahn and Peter Hilgartner each scored three goals in the upset victory. Syracuse avenged its regular-season loss to Virginia by beating the Cavaliers 20–13 in the other semifinal.

A then record crowd of 30,327 attended the semifinal matchups at Maryland's Byrd Stadium. With a crowd of 26,229 attending the Division I championship game and 15,768 attending the Di-

vision III title match, the championship weekend recorded 72,389 in attendance, easily surpassing the 60,600 record set during the 1994 Final Four. As *Lacrosse* magazine noted, "Of the 79 championships the NCAA conducts, only one outdrew 1995's lacrosse semifinals—the men's basketball Final Four (38,461) held in Seattle" that March.[*]

In the championship game, Syracuse's offensive stars were Nick Licameli, Mark Fietta, Jim Morrissey, Casey Powell, Paul Sullivan, Paul Carcaterra, and Rob Kavoit, who had four goals and three assists. Syracuse's defensive leaders were Chad Smith, Hans Schmid, Ric Beardsley, and goalie Alex Rosier. Maryland's top attackmen were Matt Hahn, Peter Hilgartner, and Rob Chomo. Dougherty made twenty-three saves for the Terps.

Those attending the 1995 championship game got to see some of lacrosse's greatest players of the preceding twenty-five years honored at halftime. Those assembled on the field included attackmen Tom Cafaro (Army), Mike French (Cornell), Eamon McEneaney (Cornell), Tim Nelson (Syracuse), Mike O'Neill (Hopkins), and Jack Thomas (Hopkins) and midfielders Del Dressel (Hopkins), Gary Gait (Syracuse), Paul Gait (Syracuse), Brad Kotz (Syracuse), Richard Kowalchuk (Hopkins), Jonathan Reese (Yale), Brendan Schneck (Hopkins), and Frank Urso (Maryland). I was privileged to be among the defensemen, joining my fellow Hopkins alumni John DeTommaso and Mark Greenberg along with Tom Haus (North Carolina), Chris Kane (Cornell), and David Morrow (Princeton). The goalies honored were Scott Bacigalupo (Princeton), Mike Federico (Hopkins), Dan Mackesey (Cornell), Larry Quinn (Hopkins), and Tom Sears (North Carolina).

In 1996, Princeton once more won the Division I championship—again in overtime—by beating Virginia 13–12. It was the Tigers' third championship of the 1990s, all of them in overtime. James Mitchell won thirteen of nineteen face-offs for Princeton, while Chris Massey and Jesse Hubbard (who scored the winning goal) led the offense for coach Bill Tierney. Senior goalie Pancho Gutstein, who had

[*] Keith Maynard, "Strength, Spirit Carry Syracuse to Sixth NCAA Title," *Lacrosse*, August 1995, p. 15.

entered the game in the third quarter, performed heroically in the cage, as did Virginia's Chris Sanderson. The Cavalier offense included Doug Knight, Dave Curry, Tim Whiteley, and Michael Watson, the latter of whom scored four goals.

Princeton's fourth Division I title of the 1990s was no squeaker. Bill Tierney's Tigers won the 1997 championship convincingly, beating Dick Edell's Maryland Terrapins 19–7 before a crowd of 25,317 at the Terps' Byrd Stadium—but both the Tigers' and the Terrapins' tickets to the championship game once again had been punched by one-goal victories in earlier play-off games. Before facing each other for the title, Princeton had beaten Duke 10–9 and Maryland had sidelined Syracuse 18–17. (Earlier in the quarterfinals, Duke had beaten Hopkins 12–11 in overtime, and Maryland just got past Virginia 10–9 in regulation time.) Princeton's attack of Chris Massey, Jesse Hubbard, and Jon Hess, the tournament's MVP, combined for ten goals and eight assists in the championship game; midfielder Lorne Smith also excelled, as did goalie Patrick Cairns.

Another convincing victory over Maryland, this time 15–5, secured Princeton its third straight Division I championship in 1998 and its fifth of the preceding seven titles in the 1990s. Princeton goalie Corey Popham had seventeen saves and was named MVP, while the Tigers' all-senior attack of Jesse Hubbard, Chris Massey, and John Hess were again superb, as were face-off specialist Greg Mecca and defensemen Jason Farrell and Ted Martell. In the semifinal games that year, Maryland had trounced Loyola—which had gone into the tournament ranked number one—by a score of 19–8, but Princeton once again secured a single-goal victory, 11–10 over Syracuse, to get to the championship game. Syracuse's semifinal loss was the last game coached by the legendary Roy Simmons Jr., who then retired after twenty-eight years and six national championships. By stepping down, he ended the sixty-seven-year run of a Simmons leading the Orange. His father, Roy Simmons Sr., had coached from 1931 to 1970, then handed over the head coach's whistle to Roy Jr. His long-time assistant, John Desko, succeeded him, but a third Simmons, Roy III, now is Desko's assistant.

The World Games for 1998 returned to Hopkins's Homewood Field, where the 1982 international competition had been held sixteen years earlier. In 1982, only the United States, Canada, Britain, and Australia had fielded teams, but in 1998 players from eleven nations converged on Baltimore. In addition to the Blue Division—the United States, Canada, Australia, Britain, and the Iroquois Nationals—a new Red Division made up of teams from the Czech Republic, Germany, Japan, Scotland, Sweden, and Wales participated. Nearly eleven thousand fans packed into Homewood's stands to see Bill Tierney's Team USA win another thrilling, Tierney-like special: a 15–14 overtime victory against a powerful Canadian team featuring the Gait twins, Tom Marechek, and other top players. The All-World Team named at the conclusion of the tournament featured Canada's goalie Chris Sanderson along with defenders Terry Sparks of Australia, David Morrow of the United States, and my former Hopkins teammate Brian Voelker, who also was named best defenseman. The All-World midfield included Canada's Gary Gait and John Tavares along with the U.S. team's Ryan Wade, who also was named the tournament's MVP. The attack featured Canada's Tom Marechek and the U.S. team's Darren Lowe and Mark Millon. Millon was named top attackman.

Virginia had lost overtime championship games in 1980, 1986, 1994, and 1996, but in 1999 Dom Starsia's Cavaliers finally won their first Division I championship in twenty-seven years by defeating Syracuse 12–10. In the semifinals, Virginia had beaten number two-ranked Hopkins, led by first-year coach John Haus, 16–11, avenging a regular-season 16–15 loss, and Syracuse had notched a 13–9 victory over Georgetown (a first-round winner over Princeton, 7–5). Virginia's freshman attackman Conor Gill was the tournament's MVP. The Wahoos' other offensive leaders were Tucker Radebaugh, Jason Hard, Jay Jalbert, and face-off ace David Jenkins. Defensive leaders were Ryan Curtis, Doug Davies, Court Weisleder, and long-stick middie Peter Ragosa. The quarterfinal games that season, pitting Hopkins against Hofstra and Georgetown against Duke, were played at Hofstra before a crowd of 12,292, an NCAA lacrosse quarterfinal record that also was ranked the biggest crowd for an outdoor college sports contest ever on Long Island, according to *Lacrosse* magazine.

The 2000 season began with a Division I final-four lineup—and outcome—familiar from the preceding year. Princeton won a semifinal victory over defending champion Virginia 12–11 in overtime (again!); Syracuse beat Hopkins 14–12; and the Orange then captured their first title since 1995 by beating Princeton 13–7. In the championship game, Syracuse's Ryan Powell tied his older brother Casey's record of 287 career points with an assist to Ethan Mills with just eighteen seconds remaining on the clock. (The Powells—Casey, Ryan, and Michael—were the second set of brothers to define Syracuse lacrosse in the last two decades, succeeding the Gaits.) Syracuse's Liam Banks, with six goals and an assist, was named the tournament's MVP. Mike Springer, Marshall Abrams, and goalie Rob Mulligan also had an outstanding game, while Princeton's Sean Hartoflis, Josh White, and Josh Sims played exceptionally well—as did Bill Tierney's sons, goalie Trevor Tierney and attackman Brendan Tierney.

At the conclusion of the 2000 season, coach John Haus of Hopkins received every player-turned-coach's dream offer and returned to North Carolina to lead his alma mater's lacrosse program. John's move south gave me a similar dream opportunity, when I was asked to take over as head coach of the Blue Jays. I had spent three tremendously satisfying and exciting years as the head coach of Cornell and had been honored to receive the Coach of the Year award in 2000. No place other than Hopkins could have drawn me away from there, but ultimately my heart was at Homewood, where I had learned so much as a player—and a person.

The 2001 NCAA Division I final once again matched Syracuse and Princeton—and Tierney's Tigers once again won the championship by a goal, this time 10–9 in overtime. It was Bill Tierney's sixth national championship, equaling Roy Simmons Jr.'s record of six Division I titles. And once again, Bill's extremely disciplined Tigers had gotten to the championship game with one-goal victories: an 8–7 overtime decision against Loyola in the quarterfinals, and a 12–11 victory over Towson in

the semifinal. In all, Princeton had notched eleven straight one-goal NCAA play-off victories, including four of its six championships. The most outstanding player in the tournament was Bill's son, goalie Trevor Tierney. The Tigers' offensive leaders were Ryan Boyle and B. J. Praeger, who scored Princeton's last four goals, and Princeton's top defenseman was Damien Davis. Making his NCAA championship game debut, Syracuse freshman Michael Powell sent the game into overtime by scoring the Orange's ninth and tying goal with only sixteen seconds left in regulation time.

In 2002, Syracuse and Princeton had their third straight NCAA Division I championship matchup, and it was Syracuse's turn to win the championship by one goal, as the Orange beat the Tigers 13–12. In almost Princeton-like fashion, Syracuse also had gotten to the title game by winning its first-round quarterfinal and semifinal games by a single goal. This tournament marked Syracuse's twentieth straight appearance in the NCAA Division I Final Four and its fourth straight appearance in the championship game. Michael Powell, with four goals and three assists, was the MVP of the championship game; other Syracuse leaders were John Glatzel, Solomon Bliss, Brian Solliday, Josh Coffman, and freshman goalie Jay Pfeifer, the son of former Hopkins player and assistant coach Jerry Pfeifer. Princeton's Sean Hartoflis, Ryan Boyle, Josh White, and Brad Dumont led their offense; Damien Davis continued exceptional defensive play.

The World Games of 2002 returned to Perth, Australia, where U.S. coach Jack Emmer led a star-packed team to victory over Canada 18–15 to win the sixth straight international championship for the Red, White, and Blue. Paul Gait, making his last appearance as a player on behalf of Canada, received a standing ovation, and U.S. midfielder Doug Shanahan was named the tournament's MVP. The number of participating nations jumped from eleven to fifteen. Japan won the Red Division, and Ireland won the Green Division. In addition to Doug Shanahan, the other members of the 2002 World Team were Canada's John Grant Jr., Team USA's Darren Lowe, and the Iroquois Nation's Neal Powless on attack; Canadian Gavin Prout and Australian Peter Inge on the midfield; Canada's Steven Toll and Team USA's Ryan McClay and Ryan Mollett on defense; and goaltender Trevor Tierney of Team USA.

In 2003, the NCAA lacrosse finals reached a new level of popularity when the Final Four were held in a noncollegiate location for the first time—the M&T Bank Stadium, home to the NFL Baltimore Ravens. Virginia avenged its regular-season loss to Hopkins by beating the Blue Jays for the championship 9–7 before a record crowd of 37,944, which far surpassed the previous attendance record of 26,229, set in 1995. Virginia had beaten Maryland 14–4 in the semifinals, and Hopkins was victorious over Syracuse by defeating the Orange 19–8. I was greatly pleased to coach the Blue Jays to their first appearance in the championship game since 1989—but naturally disappointed that we could not get past the Cavaliers' great goalie, Tillman Johnson, who was named the tournament's most outstanding player for his remarkable performance. He made thirteen saves, including three on point-blank shots fired at him by Kyle Barrie, Kevin Boland, and Bobby Benson in a seventeen-second span during the fourth quarter. Hopkins's goalie, Rob Scherr, also had an incredible day in the cage, recording twelve saves. Virginia's offensive leaders included A. J. Shannon, Chris Rotelli, and Jack deVilliers, who won twelve out of nineteen face-offs. Hopkins's Adam Doneger led the Blue Jays' scoring with two goals.

Hopkins again entered the 2004 play-offs ranked number one in the nation with a 13–1 record, having lost only to Virginia during the regular season. In the semifinal game against Syracuse, however, the Orange showed that it is very difficult to beat such a talented team twice in one season. Although we had trounced Syracuse 17–5 at Homewood Field in March, they got the better of us in May, winning 15–9. Syracuse then faced a magnificent Midshipmen team from Navy, making its first appearance in an NCAA championship game since 1975, having defeated Princeton 8–7 in their semifinal matchup. The Middies entered the game with a 15–2 record, the largest number of wins in Naval Academy lacrosse history. Hopkins had eked out a 10–9 overtime victory against Navy during the regular season and knew how formidable

an opponent they could be. With some former teammates now engaged in perilous action overseas—and the game being broadcast on Armed Forces Radio (as well as ESPN)—the Middies played with tremendous pride. They also had the enthusiastic support of many in the record crowd of 43,898 fans who swarmed into Baltimore's M&T Bank Stadium despite periodic downpours. The fans witnessed an incredible game that was tied ten times and had four changes in the lead—which was never by more than two goals for either Navy or Syracuse.

In the first quarter, neither team was able to take more than a one-goal lead. Navy's Ben Bailey scored an extraman goal to put the Middies on top 1–0, but Syracuse responded with two goals in just three minutes to go ahead 2–1, only to have Navy come back right away to tie the score. Navy went ahead 5–4 early in the second period, but Syracuse once again responded with three unanswered goals over a four-minute stretch to go ahead 7–5. The score was tied 8–8 in the first five minutes of the third period, but then Syracuse scored two goals in under a minute to take a 10–8 lead that lasted for the remainder of that quarter. In the fourth period, Navy fought back and had a 12–11 lead with five minutes left to play in the game, but the Orange, ever a come-back team, proceeded to outscore the Middies 3–1 in the last five minutes to win the championship 14–13. Both Syracuse's goalie Jay Pfeifer (fifteen saves) and Navy's Matt Russell (four saves) put on exceptional performances in the cage—with Russell actually playing the entire third quarter with a dislocated shoulder. (At halftime, he was named as the first-team All-American goalie for his play throughout the season.) Syracuse's senior Michael Powell, named the MVP of the game, had a game high of 6 points, with one goal and five assists, and ended his collegiate career as Syracuse's all-time leading scorer with 307 career points. He also became only the fourth player in history to be named to the All-American first team four years in a row.

The 2005 season saw significant milestones marked—and changes experienced—by a number of leading programs. Princeton, a key participant in NCAA championship play for more than a dozen years, recorded a surprising 5–7 season record, failed to win the Ivy League title for the first time in a decade, and did not make the play-off tournament for the first time since 1990. Syracuse, which had gone to the Final Four a record-setting twenty-two years in a row, instead was defeated in the opening round by a feisty University of Massachusetts. Duke, with an explosive, powerful offense and stingy defense, made its first appearance in the national championship game after manhandling Maryland 18–9 in the semifinals. And Johns Hopkins, entering the tournament ranked number one for the fourth straight year, capped its first undefeated season since 1984 by winning the national championship, its first since 1987. The Blue Jays concluded their remarkable 16–0 record with a thrilling come-from-behind 9–8 overtime victory against Virginia in the semifinals, then held Duke scoreless for twenty-seven minutes, forty-three seconds in the championship game to win it 9–8 before 44,920 fans at Philadelphia's Lincoln Financial Field.

During the past quarter century, lacrosse has undergone tremendous change, with some of the most important developments taking place only in the past ten to fifteen years. Television coverage has exploded, with all-sports channels on cable TV now offering live broadcasts of the national championship games and local game-of-the-week broadcasts being distributed nationwide. Tens of thousands of viewers who have never seen the thrills and excitement of lacrosse now are getting a good taste of it.

Professional lacrosse—something that barely had begun when I was a player—has been developing a significant following. The Major Indoor Lacrosse League (MILL), begun in 1987 with a season of games in the winter, had a television audience of some 26 million by 1992. In 1997, another indoor lacrosse group, the National Lacrosse League, merged with the MILL and assumed the National Lacrosse League name. In 2001, outdoor field lacrosse got its own organization, Major League Lacrosse (MLL), with six franchises that played a summer schedule on the East Coast. Although the rise of these professional leagues has diminished the impact of the old amateur East Coast club teams, which used to be the key place for former collegiate players to continue in the sport, club lacrosse elsewhere is growing rapidly.

Lacrosse also has benefited immensely from the creation of US Lacrosse as a national governing body for the sport. The Lacrosse Foundation, which already had done much to promote expansion of the game, merged with other lacrosse groups, in particular the United States Women's Lacrosse Association (USWLA), in 1998 to form the US Lacrosse Foundation, under the fine leadership of Steve Stenersen. He has been energetic in spreading lacrosse not only throughout the United States but also overseas.

Intercollegiate men's lacrosse has grown from 4 schools playing the game in 1881, to 32 in 1926, to 84 in 1965, to 168 in 1975, to 400 in 2004. The 42 percent growth in the number of colleges and universities participating in men's lacrosse since the mid-1970s is amazing.

The expansion of the game on the high school level is equally impressive. Thirty years ago, 416 high schools had lacrosse teams, with the greatest growth taking place on Long Island, which jumped from 5 schools in 1951 to 76 schools in 1975. Today, more than 1,600 high schools field men's lacrosse teams nationwide, either at the varsity or club level, while 600 high schools field women's teams. Altogether, they provide more than 79,500 youngsters with the opportunity to wield lacrosse sticks. High school lacrosse is flourishing not only in Maryland, New York, New Jersey, Pennsylvania, Massachusetts, and Connecticut but also in Delaware, Virginia, Georgia, Ohio, Illinois, Michigan, Colorado, California, and Washington, D.C.

Youth leagues for youngsters ages nine to fifteen got under way in Baltimore in 1959. Three teams were involved in competition that first year. Today membership in US Lacrosse-affiliated youth lacrosse teams for kids under age fifteen has reached more than sixty thousand players across the country.

Lacrosse is flourishing in the United States on all levels, and continued growth is almost inevitable for a game as old as our land and as young as the newest player to pick up a stick.

Officials conducting a stick check. *Jay Van Rensselaer*

3

The Rules

THE FIELD AND GOALS

The playing area of a lacrosse field is bigger than that of a football field. It is 110 yards long and 60 yards wide. The goals are 80 yards apart, and there is a playing area of 15 yards behind each goal, which permits considerably more behind-the-goal action than in ice hockey. The length of the field is divided in half by a center line. A circle with a 9-foot radius is drawn around each goal and is known as the crease. A rectangular box, 35 yards by 40 yards, surrounds each goal and is called the attack area. It is formed by marking a line 40 yards in length, centered on the goal, parallel to and 20 yards from the center line. A line connects the terminal points of this line with the end line. A wing area is formed on each side of the field by marking a line parallel to the sideline and 20 yards from the center of the field. The line extends 10 yards on each side of the center line. A point on the center line, equidistant from each sideline, is marked with an "X" and is designated the center of the field. There is a special substitution area on the sideline, next to the timer's table. The substitution area is marked by two lines that are two yards from the center line. See figure 3.1 for markings of the field.

The goal consists of two vertical posts joined by a top crossbar. The posts are 6 feet apart, and the top crossbar is 6 feet from the ground. A line is drawn between the goalposts to indicate the plane of the goal and is designated as the goal line. Attached to the goal is a pyramid-shaped cord netting that is fastened to the ground at a point 7 feet in back of the center of the goal. A goal is scored when a loose ball passes from the front completely through the imaginary plane formed by the rear edges of the goal line, the goalposts, and the top crossbar. If a defending

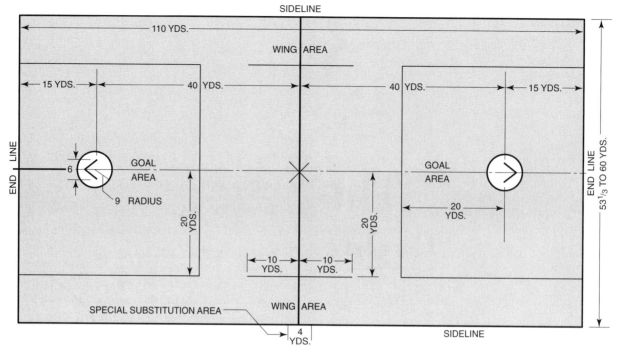

Figure 3.1 Dimensions and markings of a lacrosse field.

THE PLAYERS

There are ten players on a team, plus a number of substitutes for each of the four positions: goal, defense, midfield, and attack. The goalkeeper, or goalie, mans the goal and receives primary support from three defensemen. Since they are normally in the proximity of the goal, they are known as the close defense. The defender whose man plays primarily on the crease is called the crease defenseman. Three midfielders cover the entire field, operating as both offensive and defensive players. One of the midfielders handles the face-offs and is called the face-off man. Three attackmen spend most of their playing time around the opponent's goal and are referred to as the close attack. The one who plays on the crease is called the crease attackman. A team can have no more than four players using long sticks—fifty-two to seventy-two inches—not counting the goalie.

It is not unusual for a defenseman or attackman

player causes the ball to pass through the plane of the goal, it counts as a goal for the attacking team. A goal counts one point.

to play the entire game, because his activity is confined mainly to only one half of the field, although the fast pace at which the game is played today often requires a substitute or two, if only for a few minutes, to give the regular player a chance to catch his breath. Obviously the goalie does not need a substitute during a close game as long as he is performing capably. In today's game, the midfielders usually are more specialized in their role and are substituted with more frequency. They are divided into groups of three players each: a first offensive midfield, a second offensive midfield, and a defensive midfield unit. The defensive midfield unit has short-stick midfielders (SSMs) and long-stick midfielders (LSMs) and is comprised of two short-stick middies and one long-stick middie. Depending on the depth of a team and the skill level of the players, the first offensive midfield may play 60–65 percent and the second offensive midfield unit 35–40 percent of the game.

The lacrosse ball is solid rubber and is white, yellow, orange, or lime green in color. It is slightly smaller than a baseball and just as hard. When dropped from a height of six feet on a concrete floor, it must bounce forty-three to fifty-one inches. The

Figure 3.2 Types of lacrosse sticks: from left to right, attack, goal, midfield, defense.

ball may not be touched by the hands except by a goalie while he is in the crease. Although it is legal to kick the ball with the foot or bat it with the stick, most of the action takes place with the ball being controlled in the pockets of the players' sticks.

The lacrosse stick—or crosse—shall be of an overall fixed length of either 40 to 42 inches (a short stick) or 52 to 72 inches (a long stick), with the exception of the goalie's stick, which shall be 40 to 72 inches long. Except for the goalie's stick, the inside measurement of the head of every stick at its widest point shall be 6.5 to 10 inches. The inside measurement of the head of the goaltender's stick at its widest point shall be 10 to 12 inches. Figure 3.2 shows the various types of sticks.

Today's players have a wide variety of stick styles and materials from which to choose. Before the late 1960s, when the machine-made, plastic-headed stick

first was introduced, all sticks were handcrafted of wood. The uniformity, balance, and lightness of the plastic stick gave it a decided advantage over the wooden stick, and since the early 1970s synthetic sticks have dominated the market. One company alone has stick handles made of five different kinds of material, from titanium and aluminum to various metal alloys, and eleven types of heads featuring different designs and stringing systems. The net of today's stick usually is constructed of nylon or another synthetic material and is roughly triangular in shape. A guard stop, which is made of a rubberized material, is located at the throat of the stick and a minimum of ten inches from the outside edge of the head. The pocket of the stick may not sag to such a depth that it becomes unreasonably difficult for an opponent to dislodge the ball. This is determined by placing a ball in the pocket: if the top surface of the

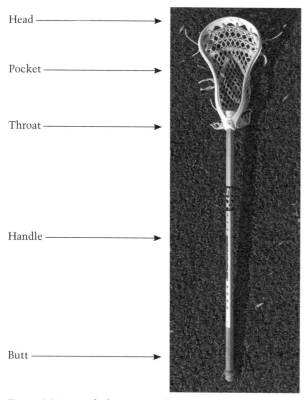

Head

Pocket

Throat

Handle

Butt

Figure 3.3 Parts of a lacrosse stick.

ball is below the bottom edge of the wall, the pocket is too deep and must be adjusted. This ruling does not apply to the goalie's stick. The end of the handle is known as the butt. Figure 3.3 identifies the parts of a lacrosse stick.

PERSONAL EQUIPMENT

The rule book requires all players to wear jerseys and shorts similar to those worn in soccer or basketball, shoes that are appropriate to the playing surface, protective gloves, and a helmet equipped with a face mask. A chin pad is secured to the mask and acts as a cushion to keep the mask from being pushed into the face. A cupped chin strap must be fastened on both sides of the helmet to keep it in the proper position. A lacrosse helmet is considerably lighter than a football helmet because the amount of physical contact in lacrosse is minimal compared with that in football. The lacrosse helmet mainly provides protection from the ball and

from blows by the opponent's stick. During play, the players must wear intraoral mouthpieces that cover all upper-jaw teeth. Gloves are worn for protection, too. They are similar to ice hockey gloves but more flexible. Although players in the past often cut out the palms and inside part of the gloves' fingers, this now is prohibited.

Arm pads and shoulder pads are required equipment for all players except the goalie, who need not wear shoulder pads or arm pads but must wear specific protective goalkeeper equipment, including a throat protector and chest protector. Elbow pads are not as cumbersome and often can be used by the goalie as a suitable replacement for arm pads. The players wear these items for protection from illegal stick checks. Midfielders and defensemen can also get by with elbow pads, although it is safer for them to wear the regular arm pads. The type of shoes worn will depend on whether the game is being played on natural grass or artificial turf. On natural grass, players wear spiked shoes with screw-in or molded cleats. Depending on the type of artificial turf, the players will wear sneakers or turf shoes.

PLAY OF THE GAME

The regulation playing time of a college varsity game is sixty minutes, divided into four periods of fifteen minutes each. High school teams play ten- to twelve-minute periods. In the event of a tie score at the end of a regulation game, sudden-death play will continue after a two-minute intermission. If no goal is scored within four minutes, another two-minute intermission is called and then sudden-death play resumes. This procedure is followed until the winning goal is scored.

The game is controlled by two officials: a referee and an umpire. The rule book recommends that a third official, who is designated the field judge, also participate. A fourth official also can be used. The referee has the final word in all decisions. The officials start the play at the beginning of each period and after each goal with a face-off. The players on each team are assigned to a specific area on the field for the face-off. Figure 3.4 shows their alignment with the goalie and three players in the defense-goal area, three play-

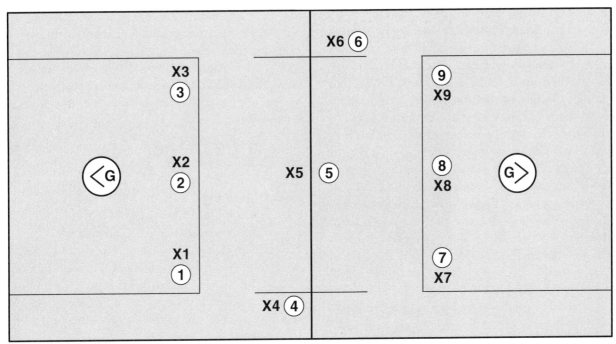

Figure 3.4 Alignment of players for a center face-off.

ers in the attack-goal area, one player in each of the wing areas, and the face-off man at the center of the field. (The particulars of face-off play are covered in detail in chapter 16; see figure 16.1 for the placement of the ball between the two opposing face-off men.) When the whistle sounds to start play, the players in the wing areas are released, but all other players are confined to their areas until a player on either team gains possession of the ball, the ball goes out-of-bounds, or the ball crosses either goal-area line. After gaining control of the ball, the team moves it toward the goal and tries to score.

The offside rule, which is peculiar to the game of lacrosse, requires each team to have three players located on its attack half of the field (between the center line and end line) and four players on its defensive half of the field (between the center line and end line). This rule prevents all ten players from jamming in front of the goal in an effort to prevent a score, as is done at times in the game of soccer, and enables lacrosse to be a more wide-open, freewheeling game with ample opportunity for scoring attempts.

When a player throws or carries the ball out-of-bounds, the opposing team gets possession. This is a basic rule for all team sports. However, in lacrosse there is one exception to this rule: when a loose ball goes out-of-bounds as a result of a shot taken at the goal, it is awarded to the team whose player is closest to it at the exact time it crosses the boundary line. This gives the offense the opportunity to maintain control of the ball after a missed shot goes out-of-bounds. An attack player is normally responsible for backing up a shot at the goal.

In recent years, substitutions have become a major aspect of the game and a critical part of coaching strategy. There are two methods of substituting players in lacrosse. The regular method follows that used in basketball, with a player entering the game whenever play has been suspended by the official blowing his whistle. The other method is similar to ice hockey's substitution of players while the game is in progress. One player at a time may enter the game when a teammate leaves the playing field. This takes place at the special substitution area at the center line.

Although the uninitiated spectator often thinks that lacrosse is a wild, stick-swinging game, it is not nearly as rough as it appears. There is physical contact in lacrosse but not nearly as much as in football, with its continuous hitting on every play. Injuries in football are more numerous and more serious. Even though body and stick checks are part of lacrosse, there are definite limitations on them that prevent injuries. In addition, the protective equipment worn by the lacrosse player minimizes injuries. Body checking of an opponent is legal as long as he either has possession of the ball or is within five yards of a loose ball and the contact is from the front or side and above the knees. A player can check his opponent's stick with his own stick when the opponent has possession of the ball or is within five yards of a loose ball. The opponent's gloved hand on the stick is considered part of the stick and can be legally checked. However, no other part of his body may be checked.

Lacrosse is similar to ice hockey in that players who violate the rules must spend time in the penalty box. This forces the violator's team to operate with one less player than its opponent, or even more if other penalties occur at the same time or while another player is already in the penalty box. The team that has been fouled is then operating with one man more than the other team and usually ends up taking a close-range shot at the goal. There are two types of fouls: personal and technical.

Personal fouls are the more serious and consist of the following:

1. *Illegal body checking.* Hitting an opponent from the rear, at or below the knees, above the shoulders, or when he is not in possession of the ball or within five yards of a loose ball.

2. *Slashing.* Striking an opponent on his arms, shoulders, head, or any other part of his body except the gloved hand holding the stick.

3. *Cross checking.* Using the portion of the handle between the player's hands to check or push the opponent.

4. *Tripping.* Obstructing an opponent below the knees with the stick, hands, arms, feet, or legs.

5. *Unsportsmanlike conduct.* Arguing with an official; using threatening, profane, or obscene language to an opposing player or official; or any act considered unsportsmanlike by the official.

6. *Illegal crosse or illegal equipment.* Using a crosse or other equipment that is not of the required specifications.

7. *Unnecessary roughness.* Excessively violent rules violations or using deliberate, excessively violent contact by a defensive player against an offensive player.

The penalty for a personal foul is suspension of the offending player from the game for one to three minutes, depending on the official's diagnosis of the severity and intention of the foul. The ball is given to the team fouled. Most personal fouls call for only a one-minute suspension. An expulsion foul can be levied against a player who deliberately strikes or attempts to strike an opponent with his stick or fist. Such a player receives a three-minute penalty and is not allowed to return to the game. His substitute may enter the game after the three minutes have elapsed.

Technical fouls are those of a less serious kind in the game and consist of the following:

1. *Interference.* Interfering in any manner with an opponent who does not have possession of the ball and thus preventing his free movement on the field. If the ball is loose, a player may interfere with an opponent only if he is within five yards of the ball.

2. *Holding.* Holding an opponent with his crosse, stepping on the crosse of an opponent, holding or pinning an opponent's crosse against the body of the opponent with his crosse, or holding an opponent with his free hand that is off the crosse. Impeding an opponent is permitted, however, under certain conditions. An opponent with possession of the ball or within five yards of a loose ball may be held from the front or side; an opponent in possession of the ball may be played with a hold check from the rear if the hold exerts no more than equal pressure (such a hold check must be done with either closed hand, shoulder, or forearm, and both hands must be on the crosse); a player may hold the crosse of an opponent with his crosse when that opponent has possession of the ball; and a player within five yards of a loose ball may hold the crosse of his opponent with his own crosse.

3. *Pushing.* Pushing an opponent with the hand, arm, or any other part of the body unless he has possession of the ball or is within five yards of a loose ball. A player may never push an opponent with his stick or push him with any part of his body from the rear.

4. *Illegal action with the stick.* Throwing his stick under any circumstances or taking part in the play of the game in any manner without his stick.

5. *Withholding the ball from play.* Lying on a loose ball on the ground or trapping it with his stick longer than is necessary for him to control the ball and pick it up with one continuous motion.

6. *Illegal procedure.* Checking the goalie's stick when he has possession of the ball in the crease; an offensive player stepping in the opponent's crease when the ball is in the attacking half of the field; a defending player with the ball in his possession running through the crease; or any player except the goalie touching the ball with his hands. The goalie may touch the ball with his hands while in the crease.

7. *Offside.* A team having fewer than three men in its attack half of the field or fewer than four men in its defensive half of the field.

8. *Warding off.* Using his free hand or arm to push or control the movement of the stick or body of an opponent applying a check.

The penalty for a technical foul is suspension from the game for thirty seconds if the offending team does not have possession of the ball at the time the foul is committed. If the offending team has possession of the ball at the time of a technical foul, it simply loses possession to the opposition. This is also the case if neither team has possession when the foul is committed.

A player who has committed a violation of the playing rules must serve time in the penalty box. He must remain there until he is substituted for or is informed by the timekeeper that he may reenter the game. The player is also released from the penalty box when the opposing team scores a goal. Expulsion fouls and unsportsmanlike conduct fouls, however, are such serious violations that they require the player to serve the full penalty time.

If a defending player commits a foul against an attacking player who has possession of the ball in the attack half of the field, a slow-whistle technique, similar to that used in ice hockey, is enacted. The official drops a signal flag and withholds his whistle until the scoring play is completed. The scoring play is considered to have been completed when the attacking team loses control of the ball, fails to move toward the goal, or takes a shot. Only one shot is allowed on the slow-whistle play.

Every player and coach should have a complete understanding of every rule in the game. The official NCAA lacrosse rule book[*] gives a detailed explanation of the lacrosse rules and should be consulted.

---

[*]Ty Halpin, ed., *2005 NCAA Men's Lacrosse Rules* (Indianapolis: National Collegiate Athletic Association, 2004).

Legendary Hopkins defensive coach Fred Smith gives pointers to future Hall of Famer John DeTommasso (JHU '86).
Courtesy of Johns Hopkins Sports Information

4

What Makes a Player

In two of the last three decades, Johns Hopkins was dominant in the sport of lacrosse at the Division I level, appearing in thirteen championship games between 1972 and 1989 and winning championships in 1974, 1978, 1979, 1980, 1984, 1985, and 1987. In the decade of the 1990s, however, teams such as Syracuse and Princeton became dominant. Even though Syracuse did not get to the Final Four in 2005 for the first time in twenty-two years and Princeton failed to make the play-offs for the first time in fifteen years, they remain powerful programs—and a greater number of programs now are vying for a place at the top.

As I described in chapter 1, the explosive growth of lacrosse and the resulting increase in young people participating in the sport have led to both a greater number of fine players and an expansion of top programs in the Division I level and throughout the game. Talented lacrosse players now have more schools to choose from than ever before, and college teams have a greater number of excellent players to recruit. The great players are not just going to Hopkins, Maryland, Syracuse, Virginia, or Cornell as they did in years past; they are also going to Princeton, North Carolina, Duke, and even Notre Dame, which has a relatively young lacrosse program but a rich athletic tradition. As in many other sports, the playing field in lacrosse has been leveled a great deal, and dominance now is more evenly shared.

What are the qualities that make talented high school players attractive to college coaches across the country?

At Hopkins, we are always looking for great athletes—the players who have speed, quickness, agility, size, and strength—but along with those tangible talents we also look for the intangible qualities of leadership, character, sportsmanship, and integrity. In my view, those attributes are critical.

With all the hoopla surrounding sports today and the poor image that some college and professional athletes have, it is important to us at Hopkins—just as I am sure it is important to many other college lacrosse coaches—to have athletes who are willing to be unselfish players and do not care who gets the credit. We want our athletes not just to be fast and strong but to be team players. We look for youngsters who are coachable, who hustle on the playing field but also hustle to the sidelines, and who understand that there are times to take over and times to involve the other players.

I would much rather coach a good player who is a great person, possessing great character, than have a great player who does not possess that quality. At Hopkins, we believe that the good player who is a great person will be willing to work hard and be coached and can become a great player. However, a very talented player who is not a good person may have difficulty fitting into our team-first concept.

Success as a lacrosse player is not just based on athleticism. As in other sports, a successful player can lack overall athletic ability but excel in specific skills. For example, a basketball player may have the talent to shoot a three-pointer, which is not a skill everyone possesses. Some of the greatest basketball players don't have it. Larry Bird, for instance, may not have been the greatest athlete in the NBA. He couldn't run fast or jump high. Yet he was a magnificent passer, could shoot the ball like no one else, and had a remarkably sophisticated understanding of the game. These skills made Larry Bird a future Hall of Famer.

While the natural athlete who is skilled in other sports has the potential to learn lacrosse quickly, an individual with less athletic ability (although he must have some) can also become an important contributor to a college varsity team in a few years—or even less. While he may not become an All-American, he still can help his team in many ways if he has an enthusiastic, competitive spirit. Having a love of the game and a willingness to work at the skills required in handling the stick are essential to the beginner's progress, but the keys to success lie in mastering the fundamentals and having the desire to be good.

There is a place on any well-rounded team for a player who has talents other than natural athletic ability: a high level of stick skills, great understanding of the game, or an ability to play without the ball—to anticipate where the action is going and to position himself to control it. All of those things don't take athletic superiority. They require exceptional smarts.

For example, in 2001, my first year as head coach at Johns Hopkins, I was fortunate to have a freshman on the team named Kyle Harrison. He was an outstanding athlete and a three-sport star in high school. He was 6'1", 175 pounds, and he had exceptional speed. He had tremendous footwork, could beat his defender at any given moment, and was able to play good, solid defense. Those are qualities that any coach would want to have in a player, and in college Kyle had the opportunity to focus just on lacrosse. By his sophomore year, he was voted an All-American—which is mighty impressive.

In his first year, however, while Kyle certainly could beat his opposing player, he was not adept at knowing what to do next. In lacrosse, once you have beaten someone, usually a defender is there to support him. Then it becomes critical to have a thorough understanding of offensive tactics and to know where to pass the ball. For that, you need to have players with strong stick skills who can locate the open man, pass the ball accurately, and shoot the ball. You can be a great athlete, but if you can't shoot the ball, you're probably not going to score a lot of goals. Ultimately, of course, you still need to score goals.

For those skills, I was fortunate also to have had Conor Ford on that 2001 team. Conor hailed from St. Paul's School, a tradition-rich lacrosse program in the Maryland Interscholastic Athletic Association (MIAA), formerly the Maryland Scholastic Association (MSA). To the naked eye, Conor wouldn't be the first guy chosen on a team if you were picking sides! He does not have the great physical gifts of speed, tremendous athleticism, or size. What Conor Ford and players like him have that allows them to be important contributing members to youth league, high school, or college lacrosse programs are tremendous stick skills and an outstanding knowledge of the game.

By combining those qualities, which have nothing to do with being a great athlete, such players can contribute significantly to their teams through their ability to play and move intelligently without the ball and through their stick skills that enable them to pass and shoot the ball effectively. Conor Ford may not run fast or appear physically imposing, but because of his high skill level and his understanding of and passion for the game, he was able to have a major impact on the success of our team.

Essentially, there is athletic ability and then there is lacrosse ability—and the two are different. One needs the other. When you have a player who combines both exceptional athletic ability and remarkable skill, such as Del Dressel, Hopkins Class of 1986, you have a four-time first-team All-American (one of only four in the history of the sport); or Syracuse University's Gary Gait, who possesses such outstanding lacrosse skills and athletic ability that he is, in the opinion of many, the greatest player in lacrosse history.

Lacrosse even is a sport in which size—so vital to such games as football and basketball—is not a necessity. The man of short stature has an equal opportunity to have an impact. Quickness, both physical and mental, can make up for lack of size. Jerry Schnydman, Hopkins Class of 1967 and a three-time All-American, was just a shade over 5'1" in height but one of the best in controlling face-offs and scooping up ground balls. Being built so close to the ground gave him a decided advantage over his taller opponents, which included every player in every game in which he competed. Not only was he able to scoop the ground balls more efficiently, he was also able to avoid the crushing body checks of his opponents. He would merely drop to his knees, which was not much of a drop, and the big guys would go sailing over him. He then would rise to his feet, scoop the ball, and be on his way, to the delight of the Hopkins fans. He was the dominant face-off specialist of his era, which earned him a place in the National Lacrosse Hall of Fame.

Even with all the changes that have occurred in lacrosse since Jerry Schnydman's day, the opportunities for shorter men still exist. Kevin Boland, Hopkins Class of 2004, became a three-time All-American on our second midfield. Bo is 5'9" and all

of 150 pounds, and while he is not gifted with size he is enormously gifted with skill and quickness. He can break down a defender and beat that player with his quickness. Speed involves distance, the ability to be fast for, say, forty yards; Kevin isn't fast for forty yards, but he's incredibly fast for five, meaning he's quick. For example, what we often did at Johns Hopkins to take advantage of Kevin's abilities would be to put him behind the goal against a much bigger and taller defender and use Kevin's quickness to beat that guy. Kevin would sprint one way and get that larger defender's momentum going that way, then stop and switch direction so quickly that he would leave that defender behind, thus drawing the slide and allowing us try to find the open offensive player best positioned to make the next pass or shoot at the goal. Kevin's outstanding vision, meaning his ability to survey the whole field in an instant and find the open man, made him even more of an offensive threat, despite his size.

To be successful in lacrosse, as in every team sport, the individual must love the game and be dedicated to self-improvement. Winning is not the only thing that counts in athletics, but certainly wanting to win is. That is another one of the intangible factors that leads to success. Along with having the strength of character that a Conor Ford or a Kevin Boland or a Jerry Schnydman possesses, having a competitive spirit and working conscientiously to develop stick-handling skills are two very important ingredients for a lacrosse player.

TALENTS FOR EACH POSITION

Each of the four positions on the field requires certain basic talents of the players. Let's take a look at each position and the talents needed for playing it.

Goal

The goalie's position is probably the most important on the field. The goalie must be the most courageous player—or some might say the craziest—because he must have no fear of being hit anywhere on his body with a solid rubber ball traveling at speeds that often reach ninety miles an hour. During the average college lacrosse game, each goalie will have between thirty and fifty shots fired at him, many coming at a distance of less than thirteen yards. He must have very quick reactions in order to stop the shot with his stick or body. Courage and quick reactions are very important credentials for the goalie.

In addition, the goalie has to be a team leader and a field general, because he must engineer and direct the position of each man on the defensive half of the field while keeping constant sight of the ball, often through a maze of sticks and bodies. He will organize and execute the clearing of the ball to the offensive half of the field. Considerable pressure is placed on him in these situations, because a failure to clear may result in a second opportunity for the opponent's offense. Even more pressure is placed on him when the opponent is on offense, because he is the last line of defense. When a goal is scored on him, however, he must keep his composure and not be hypercritical of himself or his teammates.

Although size and speed certainly are desirable for the goalie, they are not essential. Among the finest goalies who have played the game during my career—Larry Quinn, Hopkins Class of 1985; Quint Kessenich, Hopkins Class of 1990; or Sal LoCasio, of the University of Massachusetts—were some who have not looked the part of a superior athlete, being either tall and lanky or even round and pudgy, with average to below-average speed. It does help to have speed for clearing the ball, but the number one responsibility of the goalie is to stop the ball, not to clear it. So if the choice is between a slow, small goalie who is adept at stopping the ball or the tall speedster who is only average in the goal, the answer for me always has been to go with the stopper.

Defense

Considerable pressure is placed on defensemen every time the opponent brings the ball over the midline to attack the goal. It is the responsibility of the defensemen to contain the offensive players and prevent them from taking close-range shots at the goal.

With the creation of a new defensive philosophy over the past fifteen years, the defense has been moving away from one-on-one matchups to more of a team defensive game. Coaches in the past wanted an individual defenseman to be able to cover the opponent's best attackman or best midfielder and take him out of the game. Although there still is a concentration on one-on-one play, there is a much greater emphasis on the qualities it takes to be a team defender. Those qualities are different but equally as important as being a great individual defender.

Today's coaches still prefer potential defensemen to possess many of the traits that were valuable in times past, such as athleticism, size, strength, great footwork, toughness, and an ability to cover the ball and handle those one-on-one matchups.

Other traits, however, have become very valuable. To be a team defender, a player must have a strong understanding of overall defensive strategies along with the ability to anticipate the opposing team's next offensive move and react quickly to it. A defenseman must play an unselfish brand of lacrosse and be willing to support his teammates, even at the risk of having his own man score. In addition to the traditional one-on-one defenders, coaches now value the one or two guys on the defense who may not be as athletic as their teammates but make smart decisions on when to slide, know how to contain their offensive player, and dictate what areas of the field the opponent is able to enter.

Although the responsibility of a defenseman remains to neutralize the opponent's offensive players, this can be done both with that defender's specific, individual talent and with team defensive concepts. Frequently the offense will try to isolate the defender against an offensive player who knows exactly where he wants to go and what he wants to do. The key job defensively is to contain that offensive player. By properly positioning his body, a skillful defenseman can force the ball carrier into the areas of the field *he* chooses. Patience is important, because the anxious and overly aggressive defender often is susceptible to being dodged or committing a foul. If the defense takes unnecessary risks, it can get out of position and no longer contain its opponents. Containing the offense is far more important than taking the ball away from them. Ultimately, I would like my defensemen to force the opponent's offensive players to make mistakes—either to make a bad pass and throw the ball away or to take a poor shot at the goal, with a low-percentage chance of going in.

The day of the big and strong but often-slow defenseman is long gone. Although size remains a benefit, the more speed and agility a defenseman has, the easier it is for him to stay with his man. Today's defenders come in all shapes and sizes—and possess different qualities. Many are great athletes, but in today's era of team defense, a player with a thorough understanding of defensive concepts can make a great contribution to the team.

Midfield

Midfielders generally are the most athletic of lacrosse players. They have to be able to cover the entire field, swiftly running from one end to the other and playing both offense and defense. If the ball is not settled, a midfielder may find himself sprinting at full speed, up and down the field, as many as five or six times in a row without stopping. Between those sprints, he may have to battle all out for a loose ball. The action is not only strenuous and completely demanding physically but also continuous. Lacrosse players do not have that twenty-five-second break between plays that football players have, and they must cover more ground as well because a lacrosse field is bigger than a football field. Consequently, stamina and endurance are the prime essentials for the midfielder. Hustle and anticipation can make up for lack of speed.

Midfielders must also have a strong understanding of team defensive concepts, since playing defense is one of the most important jobs of a midfielder. Today, certain midfielders are used just in defensive situations because of their ability to cover the ball and play one-on-one defense. Such a midfielder must be able to react quickly and with agility when playing his man.

All midfielders do not have to be scorers, and a team can be successful with only one or two scoring threats on each midfield unit. Although every midfielder must stress his defensive play, a team actually needs players who have excellent stickwork and shooting ability as well as players who may have only limited offensive ability but are relentless in their pursuit of the ground ball and smart in playing team defense.

Specialization also has found its way into the midfield today, with four specific types of midfield-ers now participating. There are the athletes, able to get up and down the field and play both offensively and defensively. Although these players may not possess tremendous stick skills, they still can play in the offensive end. Second, there are those midfielders with great athleticism but not great stick skills. They may specialize just as defensive midfielders. Third, there are the midfielders who aren't great athletes but possess exceptional skills and a great understanding of offense as well as how to move without the ball and how to score goals. Finally, there are the guys who have it all: speed, great athleticism, defensive savvy, and scoring skills.

In 2003, the players on Johns Hopkins's first midfield combined all of these attributes and were part of the country's number one offense, averaging fourteen goals a game. We had Kyle Harrison, Class of 2005, who was a great athlete but didn't possess superior stick skills. Nevertheless, with his tremendous athletic ability, he was able to beat his man and break down the defense. In Adam Doneger, Class of 2003, we had a big, strong, physical player who could shoot the heck out of the ball. Then, in Conor Ford, Hopkins Class of 2004, we had the not-so-great athlete with exceptional skills, great savvy, and a superb understanding of the game. By combining these players, possessing all those different abilities, we were able to assemble the first midfield for the number one offense in the country, which led us to the 2003 championship game.

Attack

Attackmen normally are looked to as the team's primary scorers. The pressure is on the attack to direct the offense and to put more points on the scoreboard than the opposition does. Their stickwork should be the best on the entire team, because they must shoot and feed the ball with the accuracy of an expert marksman. They should be able to handle the stick both left- and right-handed in order to attack the goal effectively from both sides.

In today's lacrosse, teams rarely have three attackmen who go to the goal. Usually, teams have one or two guys who can handle the ball behind the goal—who can dodge and score—and often teams will have one player who is more adept at moving without the ball, scoring goals on the interior of the defense. Such a player is known as an off-ball player or a finisher; he isn't a creator of plays but specializes in finishing them. In recent years, attack squads have usually contained a variety of players. There may be a dodger, a feeder, guys who possess both of those qualities, and then a finisher.

In 1995, Hopkins had a great feeder in David Marr, Class of 1996; a great dodger in Brian Piccola, Class of 1995; and a great finisher in Terry Riordan, also Class of 1995. The combination of these outstanding players gave Hopkins one of the nation's most potent attacks. Riordan, with 184 career goals, and Piccola, with 154 career goals, became the two all-time leading scorers in Johns Hopkins history. Their success was derived in large measure from Marr's ability to find the open man and get him the ball—and Marr holds the Hopkins all-time career record for assists, with 134.

In a perfect world, a coach would like the attackmen to be athletic, but sometimes they're not. Bobby Benson, Hopkins Class of 2003, wasn't a great athlete, but he had a great understanding of offense and how to find the gray areas, so he could finish. Kyle Barrie, Hopkins Class of 2004, also is a finisher, a player who earned first-team All-American honors because he excels at shooting the ball and scoring goals, whether it's from the interior or the perimeter. Syracuse's Michael Powell, a four-time first-team All-American, combines the skills of a dodger, a feeder, and a finisher.

Being hard-nosed is as crucial for an attackman as being clever at stickwork. He should be tough enough to take the punishment of both the stick and body checks that the defense will be dishing out. If an attackman allows himself to be forced to operate closer to the end line than to the goal, his effectiveness will be minimized considerably. In addition to his stickhandling ability and physical toughness, the attackman must be sharp enough mentally to direct the offense and to make the decisions about when to shoot and when to pass. Agility, maneuverability, and speed are other qualities that make the attackman more dangerous. When the offense loses the ball, the attackman must also be a real hustler as he tries to prevent the opponent's defense from clearing the ball.

GUIDELINES FOR BEGINNERS IN DETERMINING WHAT POSITION TO PLAY

I believe that when a youngster expresses interest in lacrosse, he or she should try all the positions. This will allow the child to learn which position he or she enjoys most and is most adept at playing. Kids are not going to play if they don't get to play where they want to play. For beginners at the youth league level, the most important thing is that the game be enjoyable. Once youths move up into middle and high school, their parents or coaches—who are best equipped to judge their particular talents—probably should have a major say in where they play.

This would be especially true for the high school or college coach who is working with someone who has never played the game. In order to set the guidelines for the beginner, three categories of athletes can be identified: below average, average, and above average. The parent or coach can determine in which category the beginner belongs by evaluating the degree to which he or she possesses the following qualities: agility, maneuverability, quick reaction, speed, mental alertness, and skill. The athlete who has these qualities in abundance can be placed in the above-average category; to a moderate degree, in the average category; and to a limited degree, in the below-average category.

It is obvious that the athlete with above-average ability could have the potential to play any of the four positions in the game of lacrosse. However, the average or below-average athlete should consider playing the position that best suits his talents. Let's look at the three categories and the related guidelines.

Below-Average Athlete

The below-average athlete probably should play attack or defense and work hard at trying to improve his maneuverability. Crease attack or defense are the positions that probably require the least running, maneuvering, and stickwork and therefore are good spots for those with limited ability. He possibly can play in the midfield if he makes up for his lack of speed by being a real hustler.

The below-average athlete also can play goal—if he has exceptionally quick reactions.

Average Athlete

With some speed, the average athlete can play any of the four positions. However, it may make more sense if he starts as a defenseman or an attackman. He can become a very talented attackman if he has excellent skills and an understanding of the game; he can become a very good defenseman if he develops the ability to play team defense and makes up for his lack of athleticism with an abundance of intelligence. The average athlete without speed will need strong stick skills and a highly competitive nature to play midfield.

The average athlete who is hard-nosed and has quick reactions can be an outstanding goalie, regardless of his speed.

Above-Average Athlete

The above-average athlete who has many natural talents can play any of the four positions. Much of where he plays can be determined by his enjoyment of a specific position or by his placement by a coach because of his ability to excel in that role.

Youngsters like to score, so since scoring revolves around the attack, perhaps he will play there. If he likes continuous action, he might enjoy playing in the midfield. He can also be an outstanding defenseman or goalie if his interests are at that end of the field.

However, the above-average athlete who doesn't start playing the game until he gets to college will probably play on the midfield or defense. The skills required there probably are not as specialized or as difficult to master as the ones on the attack and in the goal.

My former teammate on the 1987 national championship team, Steve Mitchell, had been a midfielder at St. Paul's School in Baltimore. At 6'5" he had great size and also had great athleticism, but he did not possess the offensive skills that a college midfielder should have, so he was moved to long-stick midfield, where he played defense—and became the first first-team All-American long-stick midfielder ever. As my teammate again on Team USA at the 1990 World Games in Perth, Australia, he made the All World Team.

The gifted athlete who starts playing lacrosse even as late as his senior year in high school has an excellent opportunity to be successful in three of the four positions before graduating from college—midfield, attack, or defense—if he is a tough competitor and has the proper mental attitude.

II

Techniques and Tactics

Steve Mitchell (JHU '87), the first long-stick midfielder to be named a first-team All-American, checks a Cornell player decisively. *Photo by David Preece. Courtesy of Johns Hopkins Sports Information*

5

Fundamentals

Learning and mastering the fundamentals of handling the stick are the first and most important steps toward the development of a lacrosse player. It just is not possible to place too much emphasis on the proper techniques for catching, throwing, cradling, shooting, and scooping. Every player, whether a beginner or a Division I All-American, must constantly practice these basic skills. Beginners should concentrate on learning to handle the stick the right way to avoid picking up bad habits, which are difficult to break; accomplished players should concentrate on maintaining the highest level of skill they can achieve.

HOLDING THE STICK

The first step in developing the ability to handle the lacrosse stick and effectively control the ball is holding the stick properly. Figure 5.1 shows a right-handed player demonstrating the correct way to hold a lacrosse stick.

Let's start with the positioning of the hands. The left (lower) hand is used to protect the stick and guide or control its movement. The lower hand should be located just at the bottom of the stick's handle. The palm should face down, and the handle should rest on the lower part of the fingers. The thumb should be positioned so that it rests on the top of the handle, pointing in the direction of the stick head. It is important not to squeeze the handle or grip it too tightly. Gripping too tightly takes away from the player's ability to control the stick while passing, shooting, or catching. The right (or top) hand should be placed about eighteen inches from the left (lower) hand, with the palm facing up. The stick's handle again should rest on the fingers, not the palm. The thumb should

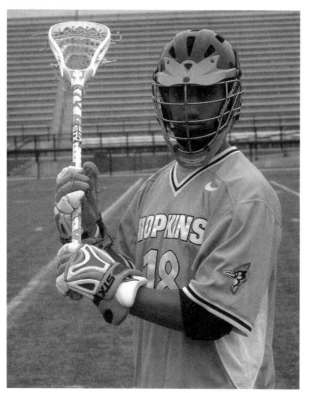

Figure 5.1 Right-hander demonstrating proper grip of lacrosse stick.

Figure 5.3 Stick positioning (triple-threat position).

Figure 5.2 Elbow positioning.

be on the top of the handle, facing the head of the stick. Often, beginners feel more comfortable holding the handle with their top hand a little closer to the head of the stick. This may allow the beginner to have more control when catching and cradling, but by moving the top hand farther up the handle, the player will lose a considerable amount of control when pass-

ing or shooting. Because of the higher location of the top hand, the player will not be able to create the kind of leverage needed to pass or shoot with power and speed.

To ensure comfort and control when holding the stick, a player must have the elbows properly positioned (figure 5.2). The left elbow should be six to ten inches away from the chest and pointing away from the body. The right elbow should be bent and pointing down, on an angle, away from the body. Placing the elbows in these positions will enable the player to catch and control the ball with greater ease.

STICK POSITIONING

Once the hands and elbows are correctly positioned, the player should hold the stick properly in reference to the body (figure 5.3).

The stick head's lower portion should be located about twelve to fifteen inches above the right shoulder (for a right-handed player) and anywhere from eighteen to twenty-four inches away from the front of the body and wide of the right ear. This places the head of the stick in what is called "the box," an imaginary area that extends about two feet above the shoulders and two feet wide. Having the stick head in this imaginary box area puts the player in what we at Hopkins call "the triple-threat position." From this position, a player can catch, throw, and cradle.

The bottom part of the handle should be placed about six to eight inches from the player's navel. Often, players at all levels make the mistake of holding the stick down by the hip. Nothing fundamental in lacrosse—passing, catching, shooting, or cradling—is done correctly with the stick on the hip. All of the fundamental movements are accomplished more effectively when the stick is held in the triple-threat position. Not even a defensive player should hold the stick by the hip. In that position, he is unable to use his stick against the offense and also loses the ability to knock down passes, since passing lanes in lacrosse are up by a player's ears, not by the hips.

Before young players reach high school, the size of the stick they use is not that important. It shouldn't be any larger than what they can handle, which is relative. A youngster who is not very tall may not be able to handle a forty-inch stick, so perhaps a thirty-five-inch stick would be better. Young defensemen may become more accustomed to handling the ball if they play with a shorter stick—one that does not go any higher than just below the chin. As players grow up, however, they must abide by the rules, which require that a stick's length be at least forty inches.

CRADLING

Cradling is one of the more difficult fundamentals for the beginner to learn. It takes patience and practice. In today's game, every player on the field, no matter what position, must be able to run at top speed and still control the ball in the pocket of his stick. This becomes even more difficult to do as a player runs up the field cradling the ball and often is pressured by the stick checks and body checks of his opponents.

The first thing to remember when cradling is to hold the stick correctly in the upright (triple-threat)

Figure 5.4 Two-handed front cradle.

position, described earlier and illustrated in figure 5.3. The key to cradling is the looseness of the top hand's wrist. The loose wrist motion of the lacrosse player's top hand is comparable to a symphony conductor's handling of his baton. When the maestro conducts, he moves his arm as well as his wrist. A lacrosse player will use a similar motion when cradling. A beginner may find it helpful to hold the stick out in front of his body with one hand and work on the cradling motion. It is critical to remember that the ball is not shaken or jiggled around in the pocket of the stick by the wrist action alone; it is rocked back and forth with a smooth, rhythmic motion of the upper arm and wrist as well as the hand. If the player's wrists are allowed to move gently with the slight, swinging motion of the arm, the ball will rest snugly in the pocket and not pop out. If you were to run with one hand on your stick, as fast as you can, the arm and wrist motion of the running would be much like that of cradling.

Although the bottom hand does not do the bulk of the work when a player is cradling, it does play a significant role. The bottom hand should be placed loosely around the bottom portion of the stick. This loose grip allows the player to turn the stick freely without having it pop loose and become a target for a defender's check. Remember to rest the handle in the lower portion of the fingers.

When practicing cradling, beginners may feel more comfortable looking at the ball. However, it is important to develop confidence in handling the ball without looking so that when a player is

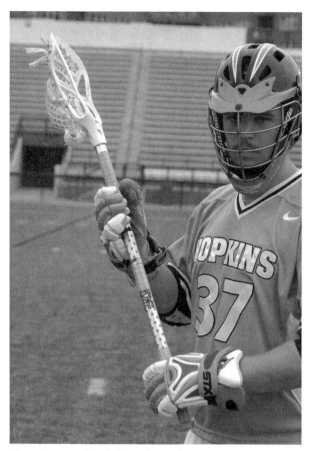

Figure 5.5 Two-handed upright cradle.

Figure 5.6 One-handed cradle.

competing in practice or a game, he will be able to survey the field as he runs with the ball.

There are different types of cradles, but each is executed in the same basic way. Figure 5.4 shows a two-handed front cradle, which can be used when carrying the ball up the field without any type of pressure from the opposing players. If the opposing players are applying pressure, I would not recommend this technique, since the stick would be more exposed for a defender to check. In figure 5.5, which shows the two-handed, upright cradle, the ball carrier's stick is in the box area and the triple-threat position. This cradle can be used when dodging or when a player is carrying the ball up the field while being pressured by an opposing defender. It allows the ball carrier to protect his stick as well as to quickly and accurately release the ball for a shot or a pass. Figure 5.6 shows the one-handed cradle, which is used more by attack-

men than any other players. It allows for additional protection of the stick. In this cradle, the ball carrier removes his bottom hand from the stick and extends it one to two feet from his body. His arm then can be used as a shield from the defender's checks. It is important to remember, however, that when doing this the ball carrier must keep his free hand stationary or else he will be called for a warding-off violation, and the other team will be given the ball.

THROWING

The techniques used in throwing a football or baseball are the same ones used in throwing a lacrosse ball with a stick. Figure 5.7 shows a right-handed player in the three phases of the throwing motion. The body is turned to the side, and the feet are staggered. The upper hand is even with the shoulders

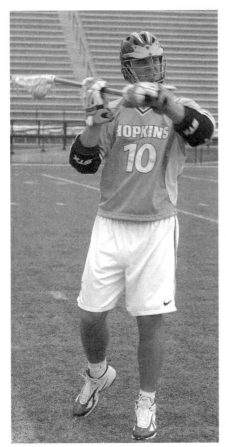

Figure 5.7 Right-hander in three phases of the throwing motion.

or slightly above and controls the stick throughout the throwing motion. When one throws a football or baseball, the upper hand is well above the shoulder. However, the lacrosse player uses his stick to place the ball in this position, and therefore his upper hand remains at about shoulder level or slightly above. The upper hand is primarily responsible for accuracy but also shares in providing the power with the lower hand, which is about six to eight inches from the body. The stick is held in the triple-threat position, with the head of the stick facing in the direction the ball is to be thrown. The ball rests in the pocket, and the thrower should have a feel for it.

In the actual throwing motion the following takes place:

1. The body weight is drawn back first to the rear leg and then transferred to the front leg.

2. The upper body is turned from a side position to one facing directly to the front. The turning of the shoulders and the waist give added power.

3. The upper hand is drawn back several inches and then follows through with a snapping motion. This wrist snap is the key to throwing with the lacrosse stick, just the same as it is in throwing the football or baseball, because it gives both accuracy and power.

4. The lower arm is bent at the elbow and places the lower hand in a position closer to the body than the upper hand.

5. The lower hand pulls down on the end of the handle, making a small arc toward the middle of the body.

6. The ball leaves the stick from the center of the pocket.

7. The ball is aimed for the head of the receiver's stick.

Figure 5.8 Positions of body and stick in catching.

8. The stick ends up pointing directly at this target and in a near-horizontal position.

To emphasize the similarity between throwing a baseball or a football and a lacrosse ball with the stick, the beginner can throw with just one hand, his upper hand, on the stick. The throw can be made with the identical motion used by the pitcher or quarterback. The accuracy and power with one hand on the stick obviously are more limited, but it is easy to feel the similarity in the throwing techniques. The wrist snap is of primary importance. At Hopkins, we compare this to swatting a fly.

The most common error the beginner makes is pushing the ball out of the pocket rather than throwing it. This can be caused by his inability to position his elbows away from his body, his failure to draw the stick back several inches just prior to his forward motion, or his failure to snap his wrist when making the throw. When a player pushes the ball out of the

stick, he has limited power and control. The beginning thrower also tends to use the pull-down move by the lower hand to release the ball—similar to the motion of a catapult—instead of using the joint action of both the upper and lower hands.

CATCHING

When a player catches the ball, the positions of both his body and his stick are important (figure 5.8). The receiving player should have his legs staggered and his upper body facing the ball in a three-quarters position as it approaches, and he should be holding his stick head in the triple-threat position, parallel to his head. The pocket of the stick is positioned so that it is completely facing the ball. In catching the ball, the player responds to its forward momentum by giving way slightly, just as he would if he were catching a raw egg to make sure it doesn't break. The stick must be withdrawn a bit,

Figure 5.9 Right-hander catching the ball on backhand side, pivoting on left foot and making the crossover with the right foot.

or the ball will rebound rather than land softly in the stick and nestle in its pocket.

In the past, it was acceptable when practicing catching and throwing for a lacrosse player to be squared off, or directly facing, the person with whom the ball was being tossed, but that is not the way the game is played on the field. The game is played moving. As players move up the field, occasionally they are throwing the ball squarely at teammates, but more often they are not. They are throwing it across their bodies, across the field, or on a diagonal, and so they rarely throw or catch it square on. Usually the player catches the ball with his feet staggered and his body turned sideways so he can catch the ball across his body.

Ideally, the player wants to start the catching motion with his stick about six inches in front of his head, and as the ball arrives he gives way and actually catches it with his stick head even with or slightly behind his head. That is not an easy thing

to do. It is a skill that takes a great deal of time to master—but it will pay off. By catching the ball even with or behind his head, a player protects his stick from being exposed to a check. In addition, as a player catches the ball, he also must be sure to keep his eye on it as it lands in his stick. Too often, as a player moves his stick to catch a ball he continues to look forward—and can miss the pass.

By positioning himself and his stick properly in the triple-threat stance when catching a ball, a player is prepared either to shoot it or pass it right away or to protect it from a check. If the player instead catches the ball with the stick in front of his head, he must pull the stick back in order to shoot, pass, or protect it—and that can leave him vulnerable.

Catching the ball on the backhand side—that is, the side opposite the receiver's stick—requires a different maneuver. For example, if the ball is thrown to the left side of a right-handed player's body, he should swing his hips around, rotate his left foot backward, and bring his stick over to his left shoulder so that the open part of the stick is facing the ball. The entire stick is moved to the backhand side, not just the head of the stick. Beginners often will move just the head of the stick and leave the butt end on the forehand side. This makes for a very awkward catch. When the player catches the ball, he should cradle the stick back to his right hand and return it to the triple-threat position. Figure 5.9 shows a right-hander who has pivoted on his left foot and made the crossover with his right foot because the ball was not near his body. The crossover step gives him extra reach.

There are several ways of playing a ball thrown directly at the receiver's head or body. The right-hander can move his body to his left by sidestepping with his left foot and then catching the ball in the forehand position, or he can pivot on his right foot and step back with his left foot, catching the ball in the backhand position. The footwork is opposite for the left-hander.

Once the receiver catches the ball, he always turns or circles into a position with his body between his stick and the nearest opponent. This gives him the best possible protection of the stick. Beginners and even some advanced players often make the mistake of turning the wrong way and bringing the stick in front of their body, where their opponent can check it.

SCOOPING

Control of the ball is a significant factor in a team's success. Since the ball is on the ground for a good portion of every game, it is vital for a team to try to gain possession of it more than 50 percent of the time. The team that wins the ground ball war usually wins the game. Scooping a ground ball that is being contested by as many as four or five players requires not only mastering the basic skills of actually scooping the ball but also determination and fierce competitiveness. A team's mental attitude usually is reflected in its ground ball play.

Maintaining the proper body and stick position is essential for the player scooping the ball. When he gets within several yards of a ground ball, a player first must determine if he or a teammate is the one who is going to scoop the ball. Once a player determines that he is going to go after the ball, he must communicate to his teammates that he is doing so by making a ball call. Two or three players from the same team should not battle each other over the ball. By making the call—"Ball!"— the player alerts his teammates that he is going for it. This also allows the player to get into position for when he scoops up the ball. Communication continues to be important while the player is fighting for the ground ball. If he hears his name being called by a teammate during the battle, he should use his stick to try to flick the ball in the direction of the teammate who is calling.

As the player approaches the ground ball, he bends his knees and upper body in a semicrouched position. If he is holding his stick right-handed, then his right foot is forward on the scoop to give a free-flowing scooping motion with his arms (figure 5.10). The left (lower) arm determines the angle of the stick to the ground during the scoop. The angle will vary according to the size of the player, but a general guideline of approximately thirty degrees can be established. Normally in the scoop the lower arm will be close to a straightened position rather than sizably bent at the elbow. A stick angle approaching sixty degrees is too steep and minimizes the effectiveness of controlling the ball in a fast-moving, pressure situation. Instead of getting their nose down near the ground to play the ball, players will often take the lazy man's approach—scooping the ball with their body in an upright position and with their stick at a sharp angle. This technique is referred to as spiking the ball and definitely should be avoided.

The end of the handle is held to the side of the body rather than in front, where the stick could dig into the ground and force the butt end of the handle into the scooper's groin or midsection. The head of the stick hits the ground one to two inches from the ball. A common mistake is for the scooper to try to place the head of his stick right next to the ball, which may cause it to hit or go over the ball. He must keep his eyes on the ball until he has

Figure 5.10 Right-hander scooping up the ball, with right foot forward.

scooped it into his stick with a shovel-like motion, and he should keep moving. He should not flip the ball into the air as he scoops it. If a player is completely ambidextrous, he may scoop the ball either left- or right-handed. However, if one hand is obviously stronger than the other, he should scoop the ball only with that hand and not try to scoop with the weaker hand in a pressure situation.

Nevertheless, stress should be placed on the importance of scooping the grounder with both hands on the stick. It may seem easier to scoop with just the lower hand gripping the stick at the butt end of the handle, but the percentages are not with the one-handed scoop. The one-handed scoop with just the upper hand should be avoided, because the end of the handle is exposed to the opponent's check. The chance for error is far less in the two-handed scoop, because the scooper gets his body closer to the ground. He can also control the stick better with two hands on it. The two-handed scoop is a must even for the most experienced varsity player.

Once the ball is in the scooping player's stick, communication between him and his teammates remains very important. The player with the ball

should shout "Release!" This alerts his teammates to the fact that he now has picked up the ball. This is essential, because at the time the scooping player yells "Ball!" and goes after the ground ball, some of his teammates naturally try to prevent opposing players from getting to it by using body checks and other tactics. If their scooping teammate then succeeds in getting the ground ball but doesn't give the "Release!" signal, they may be unaware of his possession of the ball and continue to body check and impede the opponent's efforts—which is a violation of the rules. It is a technical foul known as interference to make physical contact with the opposition when a teammate has the ball. The rules require the scooping player's teammates to disengage from any contact with the opposing players within five yards of the ball. If they do not do this and the referee calls interference on the teammates of the scooping player, he will have to give up the ball to his opponents right after having fought so hard to get it. Quick communication between teammates can prevent such a turnover.

When the scooper has the ball in his stick, his primary concern is protecting it. He has several courses of action, depending on the circumstances. As soon as he scoops the ball, he should immediately bring the stick up by his head. This is done for two reasons. First, if he needs to pass the ball immediately, he will have to do so from that position. Second, since an opponent may try to check his stick and knock the ball out, if the scooper has his stick up by his head, there is a very good chance that the opponent will make a mistake, check the scooper's helmet as well, and commit a personal foul that will cost his team a penalty.

Having scooped the ball and brought his stick up to his head, the player must determine the location of the opposition. If he is surrounded, he tucks the stick close to his head and tries to dodge out of trouble and run into an open area. If he sees an open area, regardless of whether it is toward the offensive or defensive half of the field, he bursts full-speed for daylight. If he receives pressure from his front, side, or back once he is on the run, he can hold the stick with one hand and protect it with the other. Once he is in an open area, his hands will

Figure 5.11 Right-hander, having scooped up the ball, begins to bring it up beside his head.

Figure 5.12 Right-hander, being played by an opponent on his right side, executing "snakeout" maneuver.

be free to pass the ball to a teammate in an open area (figure 5.11).

Figure 5.12 shows a right-hander being played by an opponent on his right side. If he were to keep both hands on the stick and start cradling right-handed, his stick would be an easy target for his opponent. However, by removing his right (upper) hand from the stick and holding his forearm in front of his body and parallel to the ground, he gives his stick excellent protection. The left (lower) hand remains in the same position at the butt end of the handle and cradles the ball with a minimum of motion. The stick is held to the scooper's left front and in a position close to the horizontal. Younger players have difficulty holding the stick with only one hand at the end of the handle, but as they get older and their wrists strengthen, they will have no problem. Since the scooper is able to wriggle out of trouble with this maneuver, it used to be called a "snakeout" at Hopkins. Regardless of its nickname, it is one of the most effective ways of avoiding the opponent's check.

If the pressure comes from his left, the right-

handed scooper can hold the stick with just his right hand in its normal position, about twelve inches up the handle. In this case, the left arm is held out in front of the body to protect the stick (figure 5.13).

Another technique that a player can employ when trying to scoop up a ground ball in a crowded area is to use his feet. Often players will stand over the ball and check their opponents while trying to scoop the ball up in a stationary position. It is important to remember that the ball should never be scooped up from a stationary position. The player should always "run through" or "scoop through" the ground ball, which means he scoops it, puts it up by his head, and runs away from pressure, all in one continuous sequence. However, if a player picks up the ball, it immediately gets knocked out of his stick, and a group of players continue to check each other as they battle for the ball, the player may find it difficult to regain possession of the ball. In that situation, a player might try to position himself so that he can use his feet to kick the ball into an open area where he doesn't see another

Figure 5.13 Right-hander, being played by an opponent on his left side; ball carrier holding his left arm out in front to protect the stick.

defender, then go after it and scoop it up on the run-through, just as previously described.

At Hopkins, we never start practice just with catching and throwing. We always begin with some kind of ground ball drill. Some of those drills will be discussed in chapter 17, but their importance cannot be overstated. The reason is that the name of the game in lacrosse is possession. The ball is on the ground a good percentage of the game, and we believe in dedicating a lot of time to practicing how to pick up ground balls.

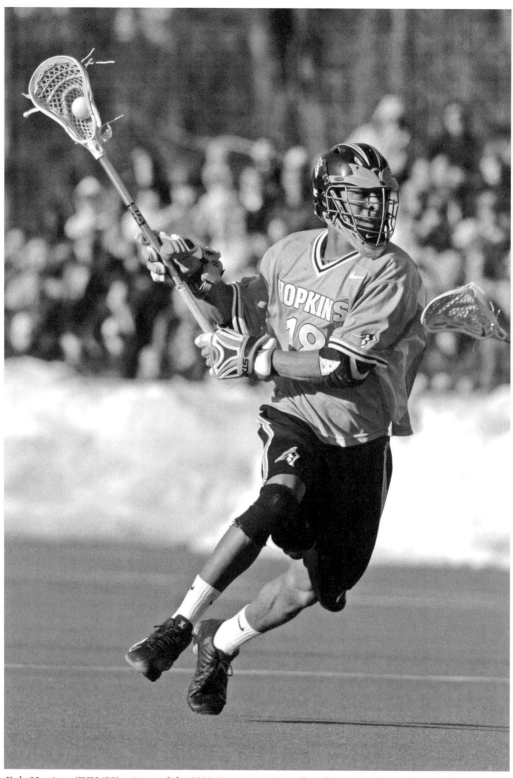

Kyle Harrison (JHU '05), winner of the 2005 Tewaaraton Award as the nation's best player and the 2004 and 2005 Lt. Donald McLaughlin Jr. Award as best midfielder. *Jay Van Rensselaer*

6

Individual Offense

There are five basic skills that all offensive players should continually practice in order to achieve maximum effectiveness in attacking the goal. The proper techniques for catching, dodging, shooting, cutting toward the goal, and feeding (passing the ball to an open teammate) are essential for every midfielder and attackman. Goalies and defensemen must also be able to execute basic dodges, because they frequently receive considerable pressure from riding opponents, whom they must dodge past. Defensemen must also know how to shoot properly for those occasions when they clear the ball to the offensive half of the field and have an opportunity to take a shot at the goal. (Clearing is the movement of the ball from the defensive to the offensive half of the field; riding is the countermove to prevent a clear.)

DODGING

Dodging is the skill that every player on the team must master in order to beat a defender. Five types of dodges define that skill: split dodge, face dodge, freeze dodge, bull dodge, and roll dodge. These five dodges enable the player with the ball to run past his opponent and advance the ball toward the goal. An attack on the goal often begins with a dodge. A dodge may also occur because of an opponent's mistake, such as an overcommitment in one direction by the on-ball defender (the man who is opposing the player with the ball) or because the on-ball defender is incorrectly positioned on the field.

Creating space between the dodger and the on-ball defender is critical to executing any type of dodge. Having this space will allow the dodger to catch the ball and plan his dodge without pressure from a defender. As in basketball, the player receiving the ball should be in the triple-threat position described in chapter 5—a position that always will allow him to dodge, pass, or attempt a shot.

After receiving the ball and planning his dodge, the offensive player should face the goal squarely (or "square the goal") and attack his defender directly by running right toward him (or going at him "north-to-south"). Usually it is best to force a defender to retreat, or backpedal. Remember: A dodger can run faster going forward than a defender can run when moving backward. By making his initial attack move north-south, the dodger should get a step or two ahead of his defender and give himself enough space to make a quality shot or a good feed. Attacking east-west usually will carry the dodger away from the goal, which can lead to a poor-angle shot or a difficult pass.

Protection of the stick by the dodger is probably the most important factor in completing a successful dodge. The simple rule for protecting your stick when beginning a dodge is to carry your stick somewhat parallel to your head and away from your body. This allows the dodger to cradle the ball and control it and the stick while protecting the stick at the same time. A defender who tries to check the ball carrier's stick when it is held in this position runs the risk of hitting the dodger in the helmet and committing a foul.

Several other points should be made about dodging. When beginning his dodge, the ball carrier should go for an open area, a place that already has been cleared ("cleared through") for him by his teammates rather than a space on the field already occupied by one of his offensive teammates or an opposing defender. If the dodger moves into an already-occupied area, this not only limits the space he can use to beat the on-ball defender but may also allow another defender to slide easily over to support his teammate and double-team the ball carrier. Most defenses are designed to support the on-ball defender fairly quickly, so it is critical for the ball carrier to realize that once he has beaten his defender and a slide (defensive support) is made, he should shoot if he is within range of the goal or move the ball forward by passing it to a teammate who is in the open. The dodger should not try to beat the defender who is sliding, or supporting, the on-ball defender. The odds of beating both the defender playing the ball and the slider are not good. When a dodger draws a slide and does not have a quality shot right away, he should pass the ball as quickly as possible. This may lead to a higher-percentage shot for another teammate. Finally, once the dodger gets past his defender, he should turn his hips toward the near pipe of the goal, or the goal pipe to which he is closest. This ensures that his momentum continues toward the goal, not off toward a sideline where he could take only a poor-angle shot. Maintaining your momentum toward the goal will help add more power and accuracy to your shot than you would get if you were shooting across your body while fading away from the goal. When the ball carrier moves directly toward the goal, it also puts more pressure on the defense to slide toward him, which takes pressure off his offensive teammates and puts more pressure on the defense. That improves his chances of making a good shot or passing the ball to one of his teammates.

Let's take a look at the four basic dodges. For simplicity's sake, the explanation and the illustrations are for a right-handed ball carrier. The moves for the left-hander are the same but to the opposite side.

Split Dodge

The most commonly used dodge in today's game is the split dodge. In the past, the split dodge was used more by midfielders than attackmen, but with the growth of the game and changes in tactics, the split dodge now is used almost as often by attackmen. The reason for this is that a split dodger never turns his back to the goal, as a roll dodger must do.

In the split dodge, creating space between the offensive player and the defender opposing him is more critical than in any other dodging maneuver. When the offensive player receives the ball, he should face the goal squarely and sprint at the defender head-on, building forward momentum. The split dodge is executed with both hands on the stick, held in the triple-threat position. The dodger should create the impression ("sell the defender") that he is going one way by faking a move in that direction, then quickly switching to move in another.

The split dodge has several variations. One is the

Figure 6.1 Two phases of the face dodge with sidestep.

right-to-right or left-to-left split dodge. (This also could be called a same-hand split, or one in which the ball carrier moves in the direction of the hand in which he is carrying his stick.) In this version, when the ball carrier attacks his defender, he tries to sell the defender on a quick move to the left but breaks to his right, with his stick in his right hand. In the left-to-left version, you sprint at the defender and fake a quick step to the right and then break back to your left. A right-to-left (or opposite-hand) split dodge involves a sprint toward the defender, a fake move to the right, and then a quick transfer of your stick across your face from your right hand to your left hand. By selling the defender on the move to the right, prompting him to step in that direction, you switch your stick to your left side and move that way instead. A left-to-right split is the exact opposite.

A split dodge can incorporate a portion of the face dodge (moving the stick in front of your face to transfer it from one hand to the other) but does not involve the crossover movement of the feet that is common to the face dodge.

Face Dodge

The face dodge is best used when an opponent rushes toward the ball carrier, has his stick in the air, or delivers a slap check to the ball carrier. As soon as the ball carrier sees the defender rushing at him or beginning a slap check, he should pull his own stick across the front of his body. Actually the stick goes in front of his face, hence the name "face dodge." It is more difficult to execute the face dodge against an opponent's poke check, because such a check generally is aimed toward the middle of the ball carrier's body and can block the movement of the dodger's stick. A slap check does not block the movement of the dodger's stick as much because its aim is to check the stick while the ball carrier is holding it to one side, and so it is less effective when the ball carrier moves his stick to his other side.

The ball carrier can help set up the face dodge in several ways. He can fake a pass to a teammate, fake a shot, or fake a dodging move toward a specific area. He should have two hands on the stick when faking a pass, shot, or dodge to make it more realistic. To fake a pass, he can use a head-and-shoulder fake and look in the direction of the anticipated pass; he even can call out to a player in that area by name. If the opponent raises his stick in the air to block the faked pass or to check the fake shot or dodge, this will open up the opportunity for the face dodge just as effectively as when the defender rushes toward the ball carrier or uses an aggressive

Figure 6.2 Face dodge with a crossover step.

slap check. To fake a shot, the ball carrier can look toward the goal and make a quick pump fake, as if he is about to shoot. To fake a dodge, he can make a quick, one-step motion toward one area of the field, then quickly change direction.

Figure 6.1 shows a right-handed player executing a face dodge. In one simultaneous motion, he pushes off with his right foot, steps to his left with his left foot, pulls the stick across his face, and moves his right foot in the same direction as his stick. This right-foot step across the dodger's body provides stick protection and also puts the defender behind the dodger, or "on the dodger's back." It is important to remember that when pulling your stick in front of your face to the other side of your helmet, you want to keep the stick almost parallel to your body. This will allow you to move your stick from one side to the other without losing control of either the stick or the ball. When the face dodge is done with quickness and agility, the dodger gains at least a step or two on his opponent when moving in the new direction.

Once driving to his left, the dodger should stay with a right-handed grip on the stick for at least the first two or three steps. If he changes to a left-handed grip too quickly after making the face dodge, his opponent may be able to reach around him from the rear and check his stick. The dodger should also avoid bringing his stick back into the normal right-handed position, to the right front of his body, too quickly after the sidestep. He should keep his stick in his right hand but still hold the stick on the left front of his body with the head of it near his helmet and away from his opponent. This will ensure stick protection. When the dodger is certain his opponent cannot make a successful check, he can either bring the stick back for a right-handed shot or pass or change the stick to his left hand.

Remember that to use the face dodge you must begin it first by using faking movements to create the impression that you are going to pass, shoot, or dodge. By creating this impression, you are forcing the defender to react in the way *you* want him to move. Once you have executed the face dodge, do not slow down. Instead, continue to sprint forward in order to run past your defender. If you slow down, you may give the on-ball defender an opportunity to recover his position or check you. By sprinting out of the face dodge, you may create

Figure 6.3 Two phases of the bull dodge.

enough space between yourself and the defender to permit you to make a quality pass or shot without being pressured by a defender (figure 6.2).

Bull Dodge

Whereas the split dodge, face dodge, and roll dodge often have the dodger changing his direction and going in a way opposite to his original path, the bull dodge starts in one direction and continues that way. The name of the dodge indicates the use of speed and brute strength to overpower the defender. When an Adam Doneger-type (6'2" and 225 pounds) matches up against a Kevin Boland-type (5'9" and 155 pounds), it is likely that the bigger player will use his physical advantages to bull past his smaller defender. Although the Doneger-Boland matchup is extreme, there are many instances when a bigger, stronger, and faster offensive player will drive by the defender into the prime shooting area (known as the slot), ten to twelve yards to either side of the goal. When executing the bull dodge, the attacker can hold his stick with either one or two hands. When dodging with two hands, which is preferable, the dodger should keep his stick in a passing-and-shooting position, but a

little farther back, in order to protect it. The lower hand is held near the hip to guard against a poke or slap check directed at the stick handle. When dodging one-handed, the offensive player protects the head of his stick by keeping it even with his own head and extends his free hand straight out in front of his body to guard against stick checks. He must be sure not to move his free arm to the side, because that will result in a warding-off call by the referee and a loss of the ball possession (figure 6.3).

The bull dodge is most effective when sheer strength and speed are used to beat the defender. It does not rely on finesse. When an offensive player has the advantage of size and strength, he can use a burst of speed for approximately ten yards to gain a step on his man and consequently get a good shot at the goal. Since the attacker has the advantage of knowing when he is going to start his burst, he will even be able to beat a defender who is as fast as he is. A dodger with greater size should have no trouble gaining the advantage if he runs at full speed throughout the dodge. Indeed, it is important to remember that *all* dodges should be done at full speed.

If the defender has similar or greater speed and size compared to the attacker, the attacker can

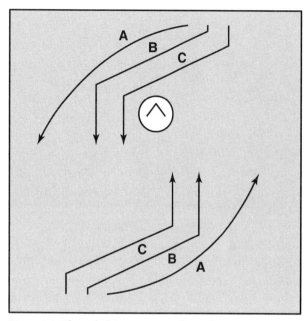

Figure 6.4 Three dodging routes to the goal.

make use of change-of-pace maneuvers, head fakes, and stick fakes to throw the defender off balance. By driving hard and using one of these techniques, then bursting full speed in the original direction, he can gain a jump on his man.

The path that the attacker takes to get into the prime shooting area is very important. Figure 6.4 shows three routes to the goal:

Route A. The dodger goes in an east-west direction, taking him more toward the sideline than toward the goal. It is a roundhouse path that does not place pressure on the defender through most of the route.

Route B. The most effective path is for the dodger to go directly at the defender and, once he is beaten, to move toward the near pipe of the goal.

Route C. This is also a direct path toward the goal. The dodger goes directly at his defender, north-south, but then makes his move by turning his hips toward the middle of the goal, or the far pipe, thus putting himself in a position where he could easily be double-teamed (played by two defenders). In the case of the drive from behind the goal, the ball carrier can be shoved into the crease.

The same principles apply to dodges from behind the goal. The perfect dodges are not executed on an arc but on direct lines and angles. In route A, the offensive player dodges on an arc, which takes him toward the sideline and too wide of the goal. In route B, the offensive player moves on a sharper angle toward the goal, and once he approaches the goal line he seeks to place himself in an area five yards above and five yards wide of the goal. In route C, the path taken is too sharp and too tight to the goal. It does not give the ball carrier much space or time once he gets above the goal line and will enable the defense to double-team him easily.

Freeze Dodge

The freeze dodge is commonly used today at all levels of lacrosse. It combines a same-hand split, a bull dodge, and a fake shot. It is used when a defender senses that an offensive player who is receiving a pass can catch the ball and generate a shot.

To execute this dodge, the offensive player who catches the ball will fake a shot as the defender rushes forward to check him. It is common that the defender, who sees what he thinks is going to be a shot, will stop or at least slow down or hesitate—in other words, freeze. When the defender freezes, the offensive player will execute a fake shot, or pump fake, then run past the defender for a shot or a feed. It is important for the dodger to keep his stick in the same hand he used to fake the shot, as he would in a bull dodge or a same-hand split dodge. For this dodge to be successful, it is critical to prompt the defender to stop or hesitate for a moment. Making a good, hard pump fake or fake shot should do the trick. The freeze dodge is similar to the bull dodge or same-hand split once the shot fake has been executed. After executing the freeze dodge, don't forget to protect your stick as you run past the defender. Once you are by him, you again should move your hips toward the near pipe of the goal so that you can continue your momentum toward the goal, increase your angle, and put more pressure on the defense to slide. The dodger should be ready to shoot or pass once he beats his defender. The freeze dodge may be used today more by a mid-

Figure 6.5 Three phases of the inside roll dodge.

fielder than an attackman, because the placement of midfielders in front of the goal often puts them in a shooting position. Attackmen often are behind the goal and aren't able to use a fake shot to freeze the defender. An attackman would use a freeze dodge if he receives the ball when he is moving above the goal line, or if he receives the ball when he is on a wing or out in front of the goal.

Roll Dodge (Quick Change-of-Direction and Inside Roll Dodges)

The traditional roll dodge, once the most common in lacrosse for both midfielders and attackmen, has evolved along with the game. It now comes in two versions: the quick change-of-direction dodge, used at the midfield, and the inside roll, used by offensive players dodging from behind the goal (figure 6.5).

As sliding has become a frequent aspect of team defense, the old roll dodge move for players in the midfield has become more of a quick change-of-direction dodge. At Hopkins, we do not teach our players to use the old roll dodge at the midfield because when doing so, the dodger momentarily turns his back on the whole offense, loses sight of the entire field, and leaves himself more vulnerable to a double-teaming by the defense. With a change-of-direction dodge, the offensive player sprints one way, stops quickly, then turns and sprints the other way. It is a great dodge for a quick offensive player to use against a slower-moving defender.

In addition to being used at the midfield, a quick change-of-direction dodge can also be executed behind the goal, where attackmen often use the back of the goal to their advantage, charging hard toward it and forcing the defender to get over the point of the goal in order to beat the attackman to that spot. To do so, the defender may have to take a wider step or even jump over the point of the goal net. As the defender is doing that, the attackman will stop suddenly, change direction, and go the other way. This compels the defender to switch his own direction and once again go over the back of the goal.

The only roll dodge commonly used today is the inside roll, which is used by offensive players—either midfielders or attackmen—dodging from behind the goal. It is called the "inside roll dodge" because the offensive player actually is rolling inside of the defender and finishing his move with a point-blank shot at the goal. It is, without a doubt, one of the best offensive maneuvers in the game.

When making his move from behind the goal, the offensive player sprints toward the side and aims for an area we call "the island," five yards above and five yards wide of the goal. This imaginary line from the goal pipes to either side of the field is a great spot. From this position, the offensive player can see quite a bit of the field and has the opportunity just to turn and shoot the ball or make an inside roll against his defender. When the offensive player reaches that area and sees that his defender is overplaying his move to the goal by placing his body in a position that is square to the end line or is overchecking his move to the front of the goal, he runs directly at his defender, executes either a split dodge or a bull dodge one way, plants his lead foot (the left foot, if he's a right-handed player), and crouches down. He then executes an inside roll by swinging his other leg around toward the front of the goal, puts the defender on his back, and takes a shot.

If the offensive player fails to drive to at least the five-yard mark, he will be vulnerable to the defender pushing him into the crease after he has made his pivot and roll. He also will decrease the effectiveness of his shooting angle if he drives to less than five yards in front of the goal. He can put the greatest pressure on the defender by getting to this point with a hard drive. When he arrives at this spot, he must strongly threaten a forehand shot. He may move to this point with one hand on the stick, but he should then put his other hand on the stick to fake the shot. In most cases, the defender will respond with a hard check, and when it is delivered, the offensive player will pivot and roll tight to his man. He does not want to make contact with the defender, because he could be knocked off stride. He goes right for the goal and does not change hands but keeps his stick directly in front of his head in the complete pivot and when taking the shot itself. If he were to change hands, the left-handed shot would give him a poorer angle, along with exposing him to a reach-around move by the defender.

SHOOTING

Since games are won by the team that scores the most goals, shooting plays a vital role in any team's success. Although being able to shoot the ball with power or speed is important, the two most crucial factors in effective shooting are shot selection and accuracy. One of the shocking statistics in lacrosse is the high percentage of shots that miss the goal completely. This statistic can be determined by adding the number of goals scored by a team and the number of saves by its opponent's goalie to give the total number of shots on goal. The remainder of a team's total shots obviously have missed the goal.

With dedication to practice, a team can increase its shooting percentage dramatically and improve its chances for winning more games.

In basketball, many of the great teams that have won NBA and college championships are those that have had solid shooting percentages. For instance, consider Larry Bird. He was a player who was not as gifted athletically as many others, but he was a tremendous shooter. He became a tremendous shooter because he practiced it. Many times after a regular practice was over, he would stay on the court to shoot an extra 150 jump shots. Similarly, on my 2001–2004 teams, Conor Ford was not a superior athlete with great size or speed—but Conor was a great shooter whose statistics improved every year. He arrived at Hopkins with a solid background in shooting, but because he invested so much time in practicing his shots, he became an outstanding finisher, putting the ball in the net time and again. Conor scored 101 goals in his career on 306 shots, for a shooting percentage of 33. When he played attack as a freshman and a senior, he scored 66 shots on 154 shots, for a shooting percentage of 42.9.

Shooting a lacrosse ball is much like shooting a basketball. How much time you put into it is how much you will get out of it. In 2001, my first year as head coach at Hopkins, we took 444 shots and scored 128 goals (28.8 percent successful shots). That year we made the NCAA quarterfinals. In 2002, we increased our shots to 481 and had 138 goals (28.7 percent successful shots). That year, we made the NCAA semifinals. In 2003, we had a huge increase both in shots and goals. We took 706 shots and scored 224 goals (31.7 percent successful shots). That is the year we went to the national championship game. In 2004, we had 632 shots and 299 goals (28.8 percent successful shots) and went to the national semifinals again. In 2005, we took 610 shots and got 186 goals (30.5 percent successful shots) and won the national championship.

These statistics don't lie. In our best shooting years so far this century, we went farthest in the national play-offs.

When my assistant coaches and I arrived at Hopkins to lead the lacrosse program in 2001, among the first things we did was to define and help our players understand exactly what constitutes a quality shot. As mentioned earlier, shot selection plays a critical role in team success. You can be an accurate and powerful shooter, but if you take shots from too great a distance or a poor angle, then your level of accuracy or power won't matter much. The end result most likely will be a save by your opponent. At Hopkins, we think the worst turnover in lacrosse results from a poor shot. A poor shot often ends with the opponent's goalie making a clean save—and gaining possession of the ball.

Along with emphasizing good shot selection, we focus on accuracy. Many believe that being able to shoot the ball hard or fast is the most important factor in shooting. Nothing could be further from the truth. After shot selection, accuracy is the next most important thing. The best way to achieve greater accuracy is to take some speed off the shot. It is much easier for a shooter to control his shot or aim the ball more accurately if he does not wind up and try to overpower the goalie with speed or velocity. For example, in baseball, you frequently will find a young pitcher who tries to throw the ball as hard as possible but lacks control. He becomes known as a "wild pitcher." If he practices, however, and learns how to take a little speed off of his pitch and concentrate more on control, in time he will pitch with much greater accuracy and achieve a far better strikeout rate. Shooting a lacrosse ball is no different.

Bobby Benson, a captain of the 2003 Hopkins team that went to the national championship game, was not considered by many to be a great athlete. He was not extremely fast; he was not very strong; and he certainly did not shoot the ball hard. In fact, Bobby rarely shot the ball outside of a ten-yard radius of the goal. But one of the gifts Bobby possessed was his understanding of his own strengths and weaknesses. He was keenly aware that he did not have great speed or velocity on his shots, so he took many of his shots from the "hole" area, which is ten yards in front of the goal and eight yards wide of it. Although he lacked a speedy shot, he had a remarkable knack for finding an open space and for placing the ball in good spots.

While players such as Gary Gait or Conor Ford beat goaltenders with the tremendous velocity of their shots, Bobby Benson beat them with his accuracy. His success came not only from being a superb lacrosse player but more so from his exemplary work ethic. Often, even the day after a game, you could find Bobby out on Homewood Field, shooting 150 to 200 practice balls—developing special skill in the kind of shots he knew he could do best. He recognized the importance of shot selection and understood that a key to scoring is not how hard you shoot the ball but how accurately.

When a shot ends up on target, inside that six-by-six-foot area, four things can happen, and three of those are to the advantage of the offense.

1. The goalie makes a clean save and catches the ball in his stick.
2. The goalie stops the ball with his body or stick but is unable to gain control of the ball. This leads to what we call a "50–50 ball," which means the offense has a 50 percent chance of regaining control of the ball in an unsettled or broken situation. Such situations actually account for a large percentage of the goals scored in lacrosse and can be advantageous for the offense.
3. The goalie does not save or stop the ball, and a score results.
4. The ball misses the goal but is backed up by the offense, which then retains possession.

Obviously the first event is to the advantage of the defense, but the other three favor the offense. When the goalie stops the ball but fails to make a clean save and get the ball in his stick, he still is in a vulnerable position because the ball often rebounds directly in front of the goal, where an offensive player can scoop it up and shoot it into the goal. Many times the defense is caught out of position, and this allows an offensive player around the crease to get an open shot. This type of score often is called a cheap or "garbage" goal, but with every score being crucial, there is nothing cheap or trashy about throwing the ball in the back of the net. The offense simply has capitalized on an opportunity. It puts a point on the scoreboard, the same as a spectacular dodging or passing play that brings the crowd to its feet.

One problem that plagues all shooters is their desire to take fancy but wild shots at the goal. Although these shots may be fun to practice and bring loud acclaim from everyone watching when—and if—the ball goes into the goal, they frequently do not result in a score. These low-percentage, fancy shots from too far out or from poor angles can do more harm than good. Remember: The worst turnover in lacrosse is a poor shot. A player shouldn't shoot the ball to get gasps of astonishment from the spectators. He should shoot the ball to get a goal. That is what counts.

In team practice sessions, offensive players should concentrate only on the shots they will use in the game. Emphasis should be placed on shot selection, technique, and accuracy, taking only the good shots and keeping them on target, inside the six-by-six.

Too often, players—young ones, in particular—do not understand the importance of generating a quality shot. They may take the first available shot, not the best available shot. There is a difference. The first available shot may be a good one, but if the offense takes its time, shows some patience, and gets more players involved, there's a very good chance they'll create a better, or higher-percentage, shot. At Hopkins, we have a motto: Pass up the twelve-yarder for a ten-yarder; pass up a ten-yarder for an eight-yarder; pass up an eight-yarder for a five-yarder; and pass up a five-yarder for a layup. We believe it is important for us to try to generate the highest-percentage shot we can. Often there are shots that are available from twelve yards, but if we work a little harder, and play unselfishly, there's a chance we can get a ten-yarder or a nine-yarder, which will increase our ability to score because it is a closer-in shot.

It is important for a coach to recognize a player's individual abilities and just as important for the player to recognize his own abilities—and limitations—too. Some players on the Johns Hopkins team have a green light to take a thirteen- or fourteen-yard shot because they shoot the ball hard and accurately enough to have the ability to score

from that distance. We have other players, however, who are very talented but simply do not possess the ability to score from what we call "the porch"—that area outside of twelve yards. These players need to show more restraint and not take those shots for fear that they will give the goalie an opportunity to make an easy save and turn over possession of the ball to the defense.

For an offensive player, the three most important aspects of lacrosse are the ability to catch the ball, throw the ball, and shoot the ball. These skills do not take great athletic skill, nor do they take great size; it doesn't matter if you're big, tall, short, or strong. Catching, throwing, and shooting the ball require practice, and therein lies the most important part of shooting: practice.

At Hopkins, our daily practice plan includes fifteen to twenty minutes of shooting. We have designed all our shooting drills to fit within the framework of our offense. That means Associate Head Coach Seth Tierney focuses on our general offensive patterns. We don't practice taking fourteen- or fifteen-yard shots, because we don't want those used much in our games. We practice taking shots off of two passes more often than one, because in our offense, the ball usually is moved around more than once. We will take a lot of shots from the slot area, which we described earlier. We practice taking shots while moving away from where the ball was passed, because in our offense, we prefer attacking the defense that way—opposite of the direction from which the ball is coming. It is critical for coaches to insist that players practice the shots that they are going to get in the game. Too often, players want to step up and just rip that high-and-hard shot or shoot the behind-the-back shot—all the flashy stuff that looks fancy and draws the oohs and ahs from the crowd. But the shots that are important to take are the fundamental ones. They're the shots you get off a dodge in a game. They're the ones that you'll get with time and room to shoot.

It's important to remember, however, that every team shoots the ball in practice, and a player probably will not become a much better shooter in practice. The fifteen or twenty minutes that a team uses to practice shooting isn't enough to help a young person—or a college-level player, for that matter—to become a great shooter, in part because the repetitions in practice are limited, based on how many other players are there to shoot. A player becomes a better shooter before practice or after practice. He has to put in the extra time.

In addition, it is a natural human tendency to want to do what we're good at, not what we're not good at. The same holds true for shooting in practice. Most times, you'll see young lacrosse players practicing the right-handed shot, the one they're good at. But how many times will you see them out there taking the left-handed shot, the one they're not so good at? During the summer of 2003, Kyle Harrison of Hopkins took the opposite—and more difficult—approach.

Kyle was coming off a breakout season in which he earned All-American honors, but the knock on him from other coaches and commentators was that he couldn't shoot with his left hand, so all you had to do was force him left to be successful. Many, many days that summer, when I would leave my office to go to my car, I would walk along the side of Homewood Field, and who would be out there every day, on his own, without the prompting of his coaches? Kyle Harrison. He had a bucket filled with about a hundred balls, and all summer, the first 150–200 shots were left-handed, with time and room and on the run. And his last shot always was left-handed. That summer, he put in the extra time at what he was not good at and became a quality left-handed shooter.

In the first game of the 2004 season, Kyle was forced to his left hand. He sprinted at his defender, split right to left, and buried a left-hand shot in the goal while on the run, from ten yards out. He became a much more difficult player to defend because he developed the ability to shoot the ball on the run, right-handed and left-handed, and with time and room, right-handed and left-handed. He became a more complete player because he put in extra time practicing what he had not been good at doing as well as the shots that he was going to get in the games.

Of course, it's okay to practice all different kinds of shots. It's fun, it's creative, and there is a place in the game for them. In the first edition of this book, Coach Scott described some of these: the three-quarter arm or over-the-shoulder shot, the sidearm shot, the underhand shot, and the one-handed shot. The most important shot, however, is the fundamental overhand, high-to-low shot—directing the ball from a high position over your head to a low position in the goal. It's the shot that no one thinks looks pretty, but it's the one that goes in the goal most often. It is the most difficult shot for a goalie to stop.

Many youngsters believe that it is important to shoot for corners. Talented players such as Mike Powell and Gary and Paul Gait of Syracuse, Adam Doneger and Conor Ford of Hopkins, and Jesse Hubbard of Princeton had the ability to really wind up and stick the ball in the corners. In order to develop that skill, however, they first practiced the fundamentals of shooting and became great at them before moving on to doing the fancier things.

Time-and-Room Shot

When shooting the ball with time and room, it is important to have good technique. We have discussed earlier the fundamentally sound way to catch the ball. Much of that applies to preparing to shoot the ball. Shooting the ball involves different phases: preparing to shoot it, catching it, and shooting it.

Preparing to Shoot

Too often, players wait until the ball is in flight to them to prepare to shoot. Preparing to shoot requires the player to assume a comfortable yet athletic position, setting his feet so that they are a little staggered and about shoulder-width apart. Next, a shooter must give his teammate a target. Unlike merely catching the ball, however, the shooter's target is not created by placing the stick head in the box area, right by your ear. Instead, the shooter's target should be extended a little farther away from his body and a little higher from the box area. That is because when the player does shoot the ball, he wants to be able to begin his shooting motion with his hands as far back as possible to generate velocity on his shot. It's important for the would-be shooter to communicate to the passer by using his name and the "one more" call: "Kyle, one more," meaning make one more pass to me.

When making the "one more" call, the shooter wants to be sure he is facing the goal rather than facing the sideline. If he is facing the sideline, it will take a lot more energy for him to generate a shot with velocity.

Catching the Ball

As the ball flies through the air toward the shooter, he should prepare to catch it with his stick located almost behind his head. This will allow him to protect his stick from a check and also gives him an opportunity to generate a shot quickly. Too often, players hold their sticks out in front of their bodies as the ball is being passed to them. A player then will catch it in front of his body, cradle it, and have to reach back to shoot the ball. This can take too much time. The catching and shooting should be in one fluid motion, if possible. As the ball approaches the shooter's stick, he should reach back and catch it almost as he would if someone were throwing an egg to him. He does not want to catch the egg in a stationery position, for fear that it might break. If he catches the ball behind his head, his stick will be closer to the area from which he will generate his shot.

Shooting

As the shooter prepares to take his shot, he should step into it, rotate his hips toward the goal, get his hands up high and away from his body, look at his target, and shoot the ball overhand, sending it down to the lower portion of the goal. He is shooting for net, not for a corner. We encourage our players to shoot for net so that if the shot is not perfect, which most shots aren't, it still has an opportunity to go into the goal. Shooting for corners takes a very precise and extremely talented shooter. Unless the player is in that special category, such a shot often misses.

On-the-Run Shot

Shooting the ball on the run probably is the most difficult thing to do in lacrosse. Often as players shoot the ball on the run, they make the mistake of shooting it while moving away from the goal rather than toward it. To avoid this, the first thing an offensive player needs to do when he's shooting the ball on the run is to make a good, strong dodge to create space between him and his defender. This will allow him to get his hands free.

Once the offensive player has created space between himself and his defender and is on the move, he needs to turn his hips toward the nearest pipe in the goal. This will force him to focus his momentum toward the target—the goal—rather than away from it toward the sideline.

Just as he would do in a time-and-room shot, the offensive player wants to make sure his hands are way back, away from his body and the box area. This again will enable him to generate velocity on the shot. As he approaches the goal, the shooter wants to make sure that he steps with his front foot toward his target and follows through, as a pitcher would in baseball.

FEEDING AND CUTTING

In today's game, feeding almost has become a lost art. For many years, lacrosse was dominated by great passers, or "feeders," such as Tim Nelson and John Zulberti of Syracuse, Joe Cowan and Dave Marr of Hopkins, Tim Whiteley of Virginia, John Hess of Princeton, and Tim Goldstein of Cornell. They and many others like them were able to put a ton of pressure on defenses because of their ability to pass, or feed, the ball. These feeders were directly responsible for the success of some of the game's greatest crease men, such as John Wurzberger of Cornell, who worked with Tim Goldstein; Terry Riordan and Brian Piccola of Hopkins, who worked with David Marr; or Michael Watson and Doug Knight of Virginia, who worked with Tim Whiteley.

For the most part, however, feeding the ball in today's game is not quite the same as it used to be. A key reason for that has been the evolution of the stick. The great feeders of the past, such as Goldstein and Marr, played with sticks that were very different from what is available today in the age of the offset head. The pockets in the older sticks were not as deep. Now, with the offset heads, most players' ability to shoot the ball with velocity has improved, but the ability to pass the ball accurately has decreased. Many coaches today firmly believe that the evolution of the stick has given all players the opportunity to develop improved stick skills in terms of handling the ball and shooting but has led to decreased passing skills.

Nevertheless, occasionally there are players in today's game who, like a point guard in basketball, take great pride in distributing the ball and quarterbacking the offense. Ryan Boyle, who graduated from Princeton in 2004, was an outstanding feeder, and his skill at passing was a big part of Jason Doneger's success.

A great feeder must have the ability to handle the ball, good enough stick skills to pass it accurately, and a keen understanding of offense. He must see plays develop before they actually happen. A great feeder must think two passes ahead and realize that as an offensive player is dodging from out top, he will have an opportunity to be open for a shot if the ball could be in his stick after two more passes. The passer cannot wait and react at the moment he receives the ball. He must be thinking about what he will do with the ball way ahead of time. Figure 6.6 shows the prime feeding areas on the field.

A talented feeder also must have the ability to dodge. Players who are strictly feeders have greater pressure put on them by defenders, who tend to play them a little more aggressively and tightly because they do not respect their dodging ability. If a defender is worried about the dodging ability of an offensive player, however, he may not be as aggressive and instead play a bit farther away from that offensive player in order to defend him as a dodger. This will create time and space for the feeder to pass the ball freely.

Cutting is a job that most offensive players don't want to do. It is an aspect of lacrosse in which most offensive players don't excel. Yet off-ball cutting is a critical part of our game, and many goals can be generated or scored by a player who is willing to work without the ball. Indeed, the cutting game can give the offense its best scoring opportunities, because

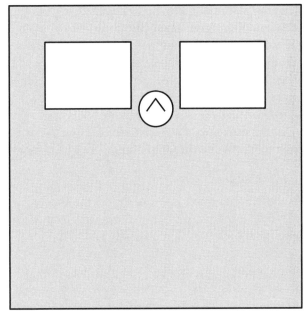

Figure 6.6 Prime feeding areas.

the cutter normally receives the feed right in front of the goal and is shooting at point-blank range. The goalie is in a disadvantageous position, looking at the ball when it is behind the goal with the feeder, and then with the pass he has little time to react to the cutter's shot. Since the pass by the feeder and the catch and shot by the cutter all take no longer than about two seconds, the goalie and his defensive teammates are placed in a precarious position.

Much like a feeder, a great cutter must have the ability to see the play developing and anticipate a few passes ahead. He needs to understand when to time his cuts and when not to cut too early or too late. It is important for a great cutter to play his defender "on offense," meaning he moves every time his defender turns his head. When the defender positions himself a specific way, the cutter will move in the opposite direction. When the defenseman turns his head to find the ball, the cutter will make a back-side cut or move behind his defender. Developing the skills to do this takes patience, understanding of the game, and a little bit of savvy.

There is an art to cutting, and it isn't as simple as running toward a player who has the ball, having him pass it to you, and shooting. The cutter's art is developed every day in practice by watching the defender and responding to the things that he does. For example, various fakes can throw the defender off stride. By looking one way and holding his stick on that particular side as he moves, the cutter can cause the defender to anticipate a feed there. The cutter then will gain a step or two on his defender when he breaks to the side opposite his fakes.

If the cutter does not receive the ball after making his cut, it is important for him to get back into the offense by balancing the field. This may mean moving back out top or replacing another player on the crease. The one thing the cutter does not want to do is stay in the crease area for too long, for fear that he may jam it up. The opportunity to feed the crease is better when the action of cutters is continuous. The offensive player who has made his cut must recognize that if he is not available to receive a feed, someone else may be executing a cut to create an open shot.

Hopkins midfielder Paul Rabil cocks for a shot against UMass in the second-round game of the 2005 tournament. *Jay Van Rensselaer*

Midfielders Joe Malo (JHU '05) and Steve Peyser (JHU '08) celebrate a Blue Jay goal.
Jay Van Rensselaer

7

Team Offense

The structuring of a team's offense is vital to its success. Games are won by scoring goals, and a team must utilize the talents of its ballplayers to give them the opportunity to score. This requires detailed organization by the coach and a thorough understanding of the offensive strategy by each attackman and midfielder. A disorganized offense can completely demoralize a team. Confusion will reign when there is little coordination between attack and midfield units and when players are allowed to freelance (or "do their own thing") without their teammates' awareness and cooperation.

Traditionally, teams have scored more than half of their goals in unsettled play. These goals would be created in situations varying from a failed clear, an intercepted pass, taking the ball away from a defender, or creating a transition at a team's defensive end. The goals scored in these situations are the easy ones, because the opposing defense may have a numerical disadvantage or may not have had the opportunity to set up completely. The more goals a team can score this way, the better its chances of winning.

In today's game, however, more and more emphasis is being placed on the half-field offensive and defensive alignments, or "sets." Teams are trying harder not to allow the opponent to score the easy, unsettled-situation goals. More time and preparation are being put into the clearing game, with midfielders being given more responsibility for moving or "converting" from the offensive end of the field to the defensive end to prevent their opponents from creating opportunities for any type of transition.

Consequently, teams must be well schooled in both their half-field offense and half-field defense.

An offensive team has to work with persistence and patience to score in these situations. Different teams have different ways of doing this. Some offensives are attack-oriented, while others are midfield-oriented. The capabilities of the players determine the emphasis. To be successful in any offensive play, all six players must be involved. Some of them may have to be role players, with their teammates carrying out the primary effort to score. However, no player can just stand around and watch the play unfold. That will allow his defender to help stop the offensive drive.

Great national collegiate championship teams have been well balanced in scoring ability from both the attack and midfield positions, although some focus their offensive power in different ways. Syracuse University's teams, while well balanced, have thrived on the transitional game rather than the half-field set. Other championship teams have had tremendous success through their half-field offense. Hopkins's 1987 championship team comes to mind. We had an attack with big names and midfielders who, although very talented, were far less heralded by comparison. Lining up in our starting attack was Brian Wood, a two-time World Teamer and All-American; Craig Bubier, a one-time World Teamer and All-American; and Michael Morrill, a two-time World Teamer and All-American. Our first midfield line was made up of Brendan Kelly, a sophomore; Larry LeDoyen, a transfer and fifth-year senior from the University of Virginia; and John Dressel, younger brother of Del Dressel. All were very capable players but certainly did not command the same level of attention as Wood, Bubier, and Morrill.

Another reason Hopkins's offense in 1987 was very attack-driven and our style of play was more half-field offense than run-and-gun or transition style was that we had a very young and inexperienced starting defense. It consisted of three sophomores who had never started a Division I game prior to the 1987 season—myself, James DeTomasso, and Greg Lilly—and a freshman goalie, Quint Kessenich. Recognizing this, Coach Don Zimmerman and his staff, including Fred Smith, knew that it would be better for us to control the pace of the game and

have the ball on the offensive end of the field more than the defensive end. Had we been a run-and-gun team, we likely would have wound up having to play defense more, and our opponents would have been able to capitalize on our inexperience and youth on the defensive end. By playing a slower, more deliberate style of game and by utilizing the talents of Wood, Bubier, and Morrill, we were able to control a game's tempo and control time of possession, and our chances of scoring were greater than our chances of giving up goals. This outstanding coaching plan—using our attack and playing a half-field set—enabled us to win the semifinal and championship games in the 1987 play-offs, the first versus a Maryland team that had beaten us in the regular season, and the other against Cornell University, the number one seed heading into the tournament.

Unlike the 1987 team, the 2003 Blue Jays initiated the majority of their offense through the midfield. Players such as Kyle Harrison, who had the innate ability to break down our opponent's defense and create a slide, and Adam Doneger, who at 6'2" and 220 pounds commanded a lot of attention, made life a little easier for our attackmen. The attack for our 2003 team featured Peter LeSueur, Conor Ford, and Kyle Barrie. Ford and Barrie were two of the best finishers in the game. Conor possessed a rocket shot and could score goals not only from in close but also from fourteen to fifteen yards out, and Kyle Barrie was a sharpshooter from twelve yards out and closer in. Peter LeSueur, on the other hand, was more adept at the little things: riding, picking up loose balls, passing the ball, and finishing from in close rather than from out on the perimeter. With Harrison, Doneger, and other midfielders breaking down the opponent's defense and forcing them to slide, our team was able to move the ball quickly and find Ford and Barrie in positions that allowed them to do what they did best, which was shoot the ball and score.

Unfortunately, we came up a little short in the 2003 championship game against a very talented University of Virginia team that also was very midfield-dominant. Virginia was much like Johns Hopkins that year in that a lot of what they did was initiated with their midfielders. Chris Rotelli, Billy

Gladding, and A. J. Shannon were three seniors who all possessed tremendous athletic ability and, like Harrison and Doneger, were able to break down a defense and put their attack in a position to finish the ball.

There are different styles of offense. Some teams will use the fast-break, up-tempo style; others will use a half-field, slow-down set alignment style; and some will combine both. Regardless of style, each player must know his responsibilities within the system and carry them out to the letter.

THE DODGE

One of the easiest ways to get a goal is to give the ball to a talented dodger and clear out an area of the field so that he can get to the goal for a shot. The clear-out, or isolation, maneuver gives the dodger an entire area of the field in which to beat his defender. As soon as the defender commits himself, the dodger gains at least a half step and moves in for what we hope will be a medium- to close-range shot. If a team has talented dodgers, it should make maximum use of their skills.

In any offense, the first option for the dodger is to go for the goal and try to create a shot for himself. In today's game, however, it has become more difficult to generate a quality shot on the initial dodge. Instead, what often happens is that the initial dodge will take place and, as the dodger approaches a dangerous area, the defense will execute a slide to force him to make a decision: shoot or pass. Often the dodger will not be close enough to the goal to generate a quality shot, so a pass becomes his best option. This is okay. The dodger has done his job even if he has not been able to take a quality shot. He has forced the defense to slide and rotate. Compelling the defense to do this will create a potential opportunity for one of his teammates to take a quality shot.

When the first dodger does not get to shoot, he passes the ball to another dodger, who moves it around. On the second pass, another player has an opportunity to dodge and go to the goal because the defense still is rotating and not completely set up. This series of maneuvers is called the "dodge, pass-pass, dodge."

An especially effective way to create space for a dodger is by using the "motion offense," one of the most basic in lacrosse. It is very similar in philosophy to that of the motion offense in basketball, with the exception that in basketball the players cannot go behind the basket, as players go behind the goal in lacrosse.

MOTION OFFENSE

The motion offense creates confusion for the defense because it involves all six players on the offense and makes it difficult for the defenders to know who should slide, since so many offensive players are moving around constantly. Once one player dodges, all five of the others move, too.

The motion offense is set up in two triangles. In the midfield triangle, two middies are up top and one is on the crease. In the attack triangle, one attackman is at X-behind (directly behind the goal) and two attackmen are out on the wings. Dodges in this offense can be initiated from the attack or the midfield, which allows a team to take advantage of its strengths and still involve the players who are not dodging. It teaches the basic principles of team offense and combines all the skills of individual offense.

When we begin fall practice at Johns Hopkins, the first offense that we teach is the motion offense. It shows our players the importance of understanding movement without the ball. It is natural for a player with the ball to want to move, but players without the ball have a tendency to stand around, watching and waiting to get the ball. Standing around is not what lacrosse is all about. Because the motion offense includes every offensive player and involves considerable movement without the ball, it teaches players without the ball how to clear space for the dodgers so they won't move into an area where a defender is already standing. Because it has specific patterns, the motion offense is not a complicated one to learn or to execute, but it nevertheless is one of the more difficult offenses for the opposing team's defense to handle. That is because it forces five defenders to play off-ball defense. As will be noted in chapters 9, 10, and 12, off-ball defense is far more demanding for defenders to play.

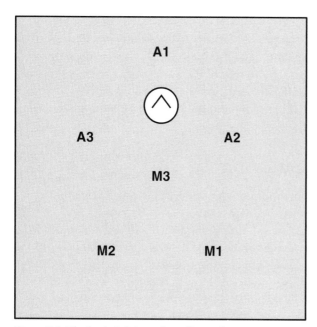

Figure 7.1 The basic 2-3-1 motion offense alignment for midfielders.

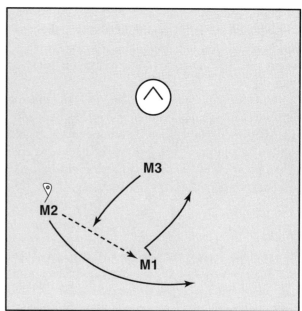

Figure 7.3 Further movement of the midfielders, "balancing the field."

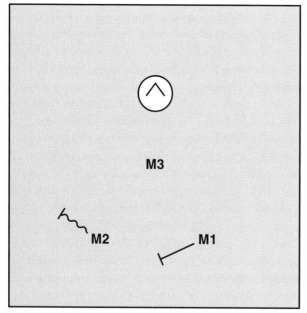

Figure 7.2 The midfielders' position as ball moves counterclockwise.

Figure 7.1 shows the basic 2-3-1 alignment for the motion offense: two out top, three across, and one behind the goal. Out top will be player M1 and M2, who will dodge when the ball is out top. A3, M3, and A2 will align themselves across the face of

the goal, with M3 being a midfielder. A1 can be a dodger from behind the goal.

As the ball moves down the field and crosses the midfield line, the offensive players will communicate with each other what alignment they will form, with all six players shouting "Motion!" and passing on the call from one player to another. It is critical that every player on the field knows what offense will be used.

The Midfielders

Figure 7.2 shows the position of the midfielders as the ball is being moved counterclockwise around the perimeter by the attack. When the ball is one pass away from M2, he will move over to the ball side to receive the pass. Since the ball is being moved counterclockwise in this case, it would come from the right-handed wing.

As M2 receives the ball, M1 moves to the middle of the field. He moves there so that when he does receive the ball, he has additional space to dodge right-handed. Another reason for M1 to move to the middle of the field is that once he begins his dodge and moves toward the goal with his right hand, he has a good angle from which to shoot the ball.

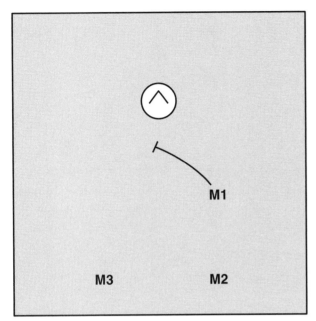

Figure 7.4 Final positioning of midfielders in basic 2-3-1 motion offense alignment.

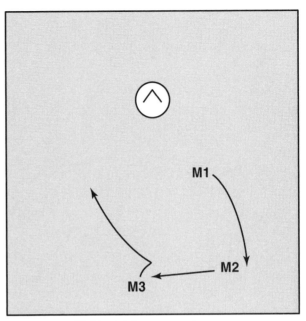

Figure 7.5 Midfielder 2-3-1 movement in reverse.

In figure 7.3, M2 has received the ball. He passes it to M1. M1 wants to have his hips facing the goal ("square to the goal") when he catches the ball. Upon receiving the ball, M1 makes a right-handed dodge, using a split dodge, a bull dodge, or whatever dodging move with which he feels most comfortable. When M1 makes his right-handed dodge, M2 moves to replace M1 in his original position. M3 rotates off the crease and moves toward M2's original position. All three midfielders are moving at once. The reason M2 moves to M1's original position is to provide M1 with an easy, adjacent outlet to pass the ball back should a defensive slide force him to turn away from heading toward the goal.

M2 and M3 are also charged with "balancing the field," or positioning themselves so that they not only can play offense but also can get back to the defensive end quickly if the ball is lost because of either a failed shot or a successful move by the opposing team's defense to take away the ball.

This alignment enables M3 to put a lot of pressure on the opposing team's defense. When the dodge occurs and M3 leaves the crease, the crease defender has a very quick decision to make: Does he slide to help his teammate, who is defending against M1, the dodger, or does he go with M3? If he decides not to rotate off with M3 and slides, then he does support his team's on-ball defender, but he allows M3 to rotate off the crease into an open area with no one on him.

Figure 7.4 shows where the midfielders will wind up. Once the dodge takes place, each midfielder rotates one spot in their triangle. Having dodged, M1 can shoot the ball or pass it to M2 and move immediately to the crease area. M2 has replaced M1 to provide defensive balance, rotating from one position to another to ensure that we do not give up a fast break or allow the offense to get over the top of us if we lose the ball or the ball is saved. This movement also offers an easy, adjacent outlet for M1 if he is forced to roll back. M3 has rotated off the crease to provide defensive balance and force the defense to make a decision on whether to stay with him or slide to support the on-ball defender.

If M1 is forced to roll back, the same movements would be used, except in the opposite direction (figure 7.5). M1 would roll away from the pressure and pass the ball to M2, who would move over to the ball side to provide an easy outlet. M3 would rotate

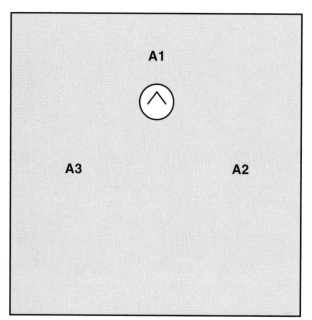

Figure 7.6 Alignment of attack players in motion offense.

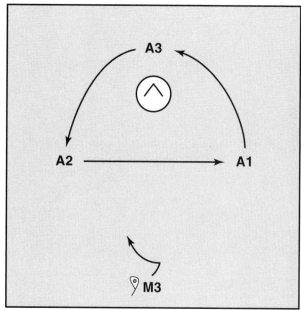

Figure 7.8 Reverse rotation of attack in motion offense.

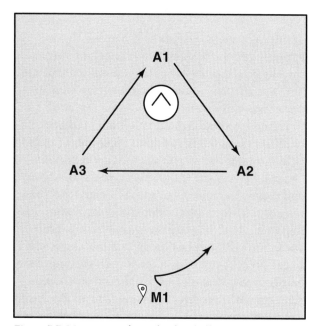

Figure 7.7 Movement of attack when ball is in the midfield during motion offense.

this situation, would rotate out to replace M2. M3 would dodge, and M2 would replace M3. Again, our midfielders have rotated one spot in their triangle. This offense gives the midfielders the option to go any way they want.

The Attack

Figure 7.6 shows the alignment of the attack, which also plays an important role in the motion offense. A1 is located at X-behind, or right behind the goal (see chap. 9). A2 is located on the wing. A3 is on the opposite wing. When the ball is in the midfield, the attackmen must understand when the dodge is taking place and execute their motion patterns to create space for the dodger, as indicated in figure 7.7.

When M1 executes a right-handed dodge, all three attackmen will rotate one position simultaneously, moving into the ball. A2 is responsible for clearing space for the dodger. He will rotate across the face of the goal and replace A3. This move ensures that the dodger always will have two adjacent outlets for a pass—one out top, which is M2, and one on the attack, which in this situation would be A1. A1's responsibility in this triangle rotation is to move toward the position where A2 had been to

to the middle of the field to put himself in a good position from which to dodge. Once the ball has been moved from M1 to M2 and then from M2 to M3, M3 would execute his dodge left-handed. M1, who would be considered the crease midfielder in

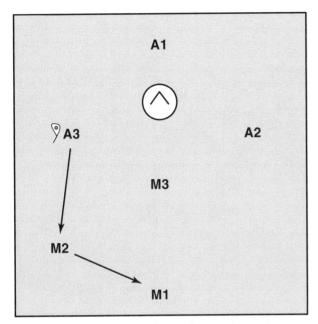

Figure 7.9 Midfield and attack triangles in 2-3-1 motion offense, moving counterclockwise.

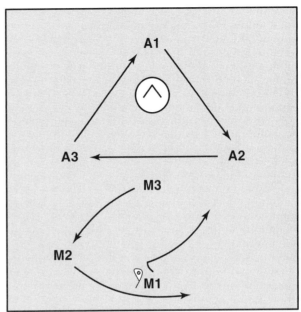

Figure 7.10 Second phase of the rotation of midfield and attack.

provide M1 with an easy outlet. Once A1 has vacated the X-behind position, A3 will rotate behind the goal to cover that spot. Each attack player thus has rotated one position, moving into the ball. A3 will be available for a pass from A1 if A1 receives the ball. A3 also is in a position to back up and run out any shot taken by a dodging midfielder. If A3 does not hustle to the X-behind position, it's possible he may not be in position in time to back up that shot, thus creating a turnover and a clearing opportunity for the defense.

If each player has rotated one position and M1 happens to roll back and moves the ball up top, as he did in figure 7.5, then the responsibilities of the attack are simple, as shown in figure 7.8. They just reverse their rotation on the second dodge. In that situation, M3 will have rotated off the crease and received the pass and will be dodging left-handed. A2 is responsible for creating space for M3, A3 is responsible for providing an adjacent outlet, and A1 is responsible for replacing A3 at X-behind, so that we have backup and a player to move the ball to behind the goal.

Figure 7.9 shows the midfield and attack triangles put together. As the ball is moved around,

counterclockwise, A3 receives it in the 1½ position. M2 moves over to the ball side to receive the pass from A3. M1 rotates to the middle of the field so that he creates an area in which to dodge. M3 is located on the crease. As the ball is passed from A3 to M2 and from M2 to M1, the offense then gets triggered when M1 begins his dodge.

In figure 7.10, M1 dodges right-handed. M2 rotates over to replace M1 and balance the field. M3 rotates off the crease, again gaining defensive balance as well as forcing the defense to make a decision whether to stay with him or slide off of him. A2 clears space for the dodger and rotates across, replacing A3. A1 rotates to A2's position, providing an adjacent outlet, and A3 will rotate behind the goal, being responsible for backup and giving the offense the ability to pass the ball behind the goal.

Figure 7.11 shows the last step of the motion. M1 has dodged and passed the ball to A1, who is an easy, adjacent outlet. M1 then quickly moves to the crease, putting the offense back in its two triangles. A1 then passes the ball to A3. Now the offense executes its dodge, pass-pass, dodge tactic. At this point, it is hoped that the offense's movements have forced the opponent's defense to slide and now rotate to recover

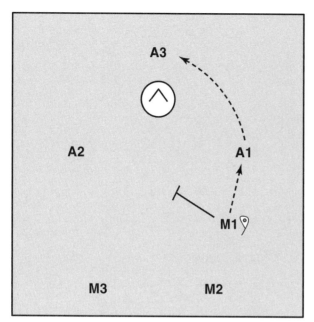

Figure 7.11 Final phase of the counterclockwise motion offense.

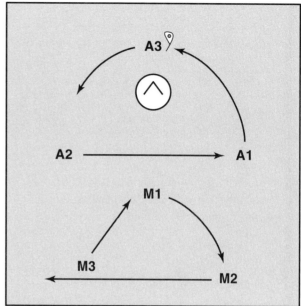

Figure 7.12 Alignment after second dodge, reversing the rotation of attack and midfield.

its previous positioning. Figure 7.12 shows the alignment once A3 receives the ball, triggering the motion again. Because he is the second player to receive a pass since the first dodge was initiated, A3 should dodge right-handed, away from where the ball came, as A2 clears space for him and rotates across to replace A1. A1 is responsible for rotating to X-behind, where he will give A3 an easy adjacent outlet for a pass and provide backup for a shot. M1, the crease man, is responsible for rotating off the crease, away from the ball. He rotates out and replaces M2, thus forcing the defense, if they are sliding from the crease, to decide whether to go with him or to stay and slide to provide support for the on-ball defender. M3 will cut to the crease and replace M1. Someone must always be moving into the crease because it's the most dangerous area of the field. M3 also will provide the dodger, A3, with an easy adjacent outlet up top. With these movements, the rotating roles of the attack and the midfielders have been reversed, with attack rotating away from the ball and the middies rotating into the ball. Before, when the ball was in the midfield, the attack rotated into the ball and the middies rotated away from it.

Each one of these moves is designed to create a

quality shot opportunity and can put a lot of pressure on the defense. These types of offense can also be used against any type of defense. If it is a crease-sliding defense, a lot of pressure is put on the crease defenseman to decide what to do. If it is an adjacent-sliding defense, which will be discussed in chapter 10, a lot of pressure is put on the adjacent slider, who also must decide whether to stay with his man, who is vacating an area, or slide. The motion offense aims to force all six defensemen to scramble around to make sure they cover their men. It takes advantage of both on-ball or dodging principles and off-ball play.

The following summarizes the basic principles of the motion offense:

• Align the offensive players in two triangles. The first option is to dodge and shoot the ball. If a quality shot opportunity does not exist, execute the dodge, pass-pass, dodge maneuver.
• Rotate to clear space for the dodger.
• Always provide easy, adjacent outlets for passes, both in front of and behind the dodger.
• Maintain offensive balance by always having someone at X-behind to back up a shot.

- Maintain defensive balance by having two players out top so that they can immediately get into riding positions in case a shot is taken and the ball is turned over to the opposing team.
- With only one offensive player located behind the goal, this offense can help with riding because the five players in front of the goal will be able to drop back quickly and get into the ride, and the player behind the goal can move to confront the opposing team's goalie.
- The motion offense works against any kind of defense, whether it is a slide-adjacent defense, a crease-sliding defense, or even a zone defense.

TWO-MAN PICK PLAY IN MOTION OFFENSE

Several tactics can be used to add a little wrinkle to the basic motion offense. One effective maneuver is designed for just two players: the two-man pick play involving two midfielders, located out top.

In this play, proper use of the pick depends on both the man setting the pick and the man with the ball. The pick man places himself in a position that will impede the progress of the defender playing the ball carrier. As he sets the pick, he tries to get as close to the defender as possible without moving into him and committing a technical foul called a "moving pick." He faces the defender squarely and places his feet a little farther apart than shoulder width. This position places the middle of his body directly in the defender's path and forces the defender either to run into him or to maneuver around him. If contact is made, the pick man should be ready to move back rather than give an impetus into the defender that could be interpreted by the official as a moving pick. This is the most common error in using the pick. Another routine mistake is to set the pick in front of the defender, where the pick serves no purpose because the defender will run by it. The pick man wants to pick the defender, not thin air.

After a successful pick, which could necessitate a switch of men by the two defenders, the pick man rolls away from the play and replaces the dodger, always providing an easy, adjacent outlet for the ball carrier. It is critical that the dodger utilize the pick.

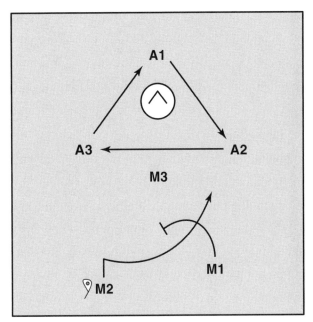

Figure 7.13 Setting a pick.

In this instance, the dodger should drive his defender backward toward the goal, then make his move toward his teammate. As the dodger approaches his teammate setting the pick, he must almost rub shoulders with him. Doing so will force the defender playing the pick to make a decision. In this instance, if the on-ball defender cannot get through the pick, the defender playing the pick must execute a switch. This compels the defense to communicate "A pick!" and then execute proper defensive pick play. If the defense does not execute the proper pick play, the dodger may find himself moving past the pick and being wide open for a shot.

Figure 7.13 shows this maneuver. M2 has the ball. M1 moves a bit toward the goal and then toward the middle of the field and sets a pick. M2 will drive his defender backward and make his move right-handed, coming right off the shoulder of the pick. Once the pick is set, M1 then will roll back to the side the ball is on to provide the dodger with an easy adjacent outlet. A2 will clear through; A1 will provide the adjacent outlet; A3 will rotate behind. M3 will remain on the crease. The attack's responsibility is the same as in the regular motion offense: A2 will rotate across; A3 will rotate behind; and A1 will provide an

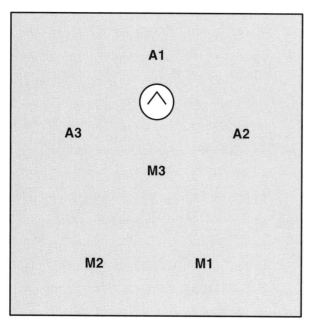

Figure 7.14 Motion pick play for the attack.

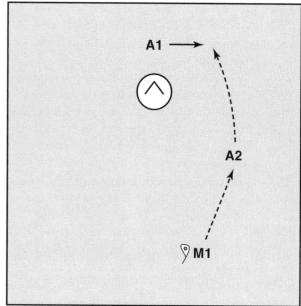

Figure 7.15 Setting up a dodge.

easy, adjacent outlet for the ball carrier. The triangle motion has been executed, but this time with a pick.

A problem with this offense is that it is not as balanced as the regular motion offense. What is lost in balance, however, is gained in forcing the defense to play the pick correctly. This pick-and-roll maneuver is identical with the one basketball players use as one of their key offensive weapons. Essentially, it compels the defense to deal with just another problem. Not only do they have to worry about playing off-ball defense and about sliding and supporting, now they have to worry about playing a pick correctly as well.

It is important for a coach to have consistency in the concepts that are taught. The basic motion offense enables a coach to teach his players how to play the game rather than just run plays. They learn about spacing, dodging, and off-ball movement. In the previous paragraphs, the motion offense philosophy was used to design a midfield-oriented play that involved a pick. A little thing like that really can create havoc for a defense. The next play we're going to describe is consistent with what we have done with the motion offense and the motion pick play, but instead will be attack-oriented.

MOTION PICK PLAY FOR THE ATTACK

In figure 7.14, the alignment of the players is exactly the same as it is in our motion offense set. The players are set up in a 2-3-1: two middies up top, a middie on the crease, two attackmen on the wings, and an attackman at X-behind. This can be an effective play in creating a quick shot for an attackman, or at least in forcing the defense to make a quick decision about whether or not to slide. It's important to remember that if we don't generate a shot right away but do force the defense to slide, we have done a good job on offense.

As the ball moves around, counterclockwise, it is passed from M1 to A2. A1, who is located at X-behind, drifts toward A2 to receive the ball. This creates some space for A1 to catch the ball and square up toward the goal so that he can attack his defender (figure 7.15). When A1 receives the ball, he will initiate a dodge.

Figure 7.16 shows the movement of the attack. As A1 receives the ball, squares up, and attacks toward his defender, A3 immediately moves toward the area just around X-behind, about two or three yards from the crease, setting a good, fundamental pick.

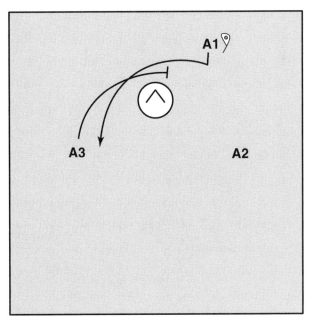

Figure 7.16 Movement of the attack with question mark dodge.

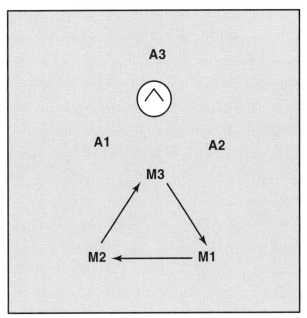

Figure 7.17 Midfielder movements during attack motion pick play.

A1 uses this pick to dodge at his defender, moving toward his right and almost rubbing shoulders with A3. Once A1 runs past A3, A3 will roll so that he is facing A1, providing him with an easy outlet at X-behind if the defense slides to cover him. A1's job is to get to the island, the area that is five yards above and five yards wide of the goal line extended (see p. 118). If he can get to this spot on the field, he may be able to execute a question mark dodge. Starting at what would be the bottom of the question mark, he will circle or arc away from the defender, turn when he reaches the end of the question mark loop, and shoot. He also may execute an inside roll or even be able to beat his defender to the topside. A2 remains in the 2½ position, the wing shooting area. He is not required to clear any space, just make himself available for a pass and a shot.

Figure 7.17 depicts the midfielders' responsibilities in this motion pick play for the attack. It shows A1 getting to the island, A3 at X-behind, and A2 on the left-hand wing at the 2½ position. Just as they would in the regular motion offense, the midfielders will use their triangle rotation to occupy the attention of their defenders. M3 rotates off the crease, away from the dodger, and replaces M1. This will force his defender to make a decision: Does he stay with M3 and move off the crease with him, or does he remain on the inside of the defense and stay as a slide man? M2 rotates into the crease to replace M3, and M1 rotates over to replace M2. M1 also becomes an easy outlet for A1, the dodger. Once this rotation takes place, A1 will have two easy, adjacent outlets, with A3 behind the goal and M1 out in front of it. Once M3 rotates off the crease and M2 rotates in, we have a balanced offense. Two players are out top and can rotate quickly back to defense to prevent the opponent's defense from creating a fast break, and we have an attackman behind the goal for an easy outlet as well as backup.

Once A1 has used that pick to get to the island, if he finds that he does not have a quality shot opportunity, he very easily can move the ball back to A3, and A3 can utilize a pick from A2, moving the other way. The offense also has the option of moving the ball up top to M1, who can rotate the ball over to M2, and the offense can move right into its motion offense alignment. M3 can dodge, A2 can clear through, and both groups can run their triangle motion offense out of this little pick variation.

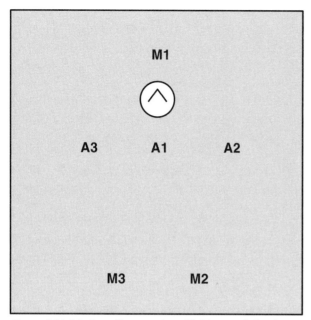

Figure 7.18 Motion offense with midfielder at X-behind; attack on the crease.

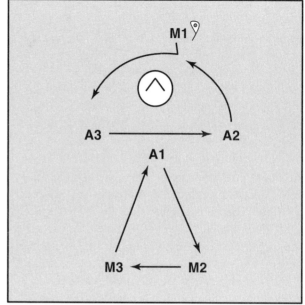

Figure 7.19 Motion invert offense.

MOTION INVERT OFFENSE

Inverting the offensive personnel by placing a midfielder or midfielders behind the goal and an attackman where a midfielder should be can create additional headaches for the defense. Defensemen normally are not as comfortable playing attackmen at the midfield as behind the goal. More important, midfield defenders are not comfortable or confident defending both on- and off-ball behind the goal because in normal practice sessions they rarely train at defending there. They also do not have the advantage of the longer defense stick to put pressure on their man and keep him from getting close to the crease for the point-blank shot. In addition, defensive coaches will react differently when an opponent's midfielder is dodging from behind the goal. He may change his defense and decide to have his player slide from a different position, thus possibly creating confusion for the defense.

Along with the advantages that might be gained by using the invert—possibly creating a mismatch behind the goal or making a defenseman uncomfortable—disadvantages also can result. With an attackman positioned in a midfielder's spot, an offensive coach must be concerned if a shot is made and saved or if the ball is turned over. The defensive midfield position now is occupied by an attackman who is not as well-prepared as a midfielder would be for switching to a defensive role to prevent a clear. At Hopkins, if such a situation develops, we often try to get the attackman off the field and have two midfielders drop back to execute the ride. Another option simply would be to have the attackman who is playing in the midfield drop back and have the midfielder hustle to his spot as quickly as he can. Basically, the attackman is buying time for the midfielder.

Figure 7.18 shows our basic motion offense alignment with a subtle difference: there is a midfielder at X-behind and an attackman on the crease. Our alignment is a 2-3-1. In figure 7.19, the ball moves counterclockwise and is received by M1, who is square to the goal. He then attacks or dodges at his defender. As M1 makes his move, right-handed, hoping to get to the island, A3 rotates across and replaces A2. In turn, A2 rotates behind, for balance and to create an easy outlet and backup. A1 backs out of the crease and rotates to replace M2. M2 rotates across to provide balance and an easy outlet for the dodger, and M3 rotates to the crease.

Several advantages can be created by doing this. First, the midfielder has an opportunity to attack a midfield defender, who may not be as comfortable or confident behind the goal. This can force the defense to have to slide more quickly and readily than they otherwise might if an attackman was back there. A1, rotating off the crease, is putting even more pressure on the crease defenseman to make a decision if he is going to stay on the crease and slide or rotate off and stay with his man. This alignment also puts pressure on A3's defender, because as M1 dodges right-handed, A3 leaves the adjacent position. What does the defender do? Does he slide to the dodging M1, leaving A3 wide open? Or does he go with A3, leaving the defense with no adjacent slide on M1?

Clearly, the invert offense can create difficulty for the defense. Should M1 dodge and find that he may not be able to get to the goal, he simply can circle away or roll back and pass the ball to A2, who then can dodge in the opposite direction. Those three players in the base of the offense will run their triangle motion, and the three players out top will again execute their triangle motion. This tactic forces an opponent's midfielder to play defense off the ball in an area where he may not be comfortable doing so.

ZONE OFFENSE

For many years it was thought that a team could not play the offense it used against a man-to-man defense when facing a zone defense. Since a zone defense has each defender covering a specific area of the field and the player who happens to be in that area, rather than covering a specific offensive player wherever he goes, it was thought that the principles used for man-to-man offense wouldn't be successful against a zone. In today's game, however, it is possible for a team to utilize its basic offense versus a zone, provided it is executed properly and run well.

The motion offense has been successful against a zone. A team should have other specific offensive strategies to attack a zone, but it is not necessary to scrap the motion offense when confronted by a zone. It may not be the most effective tactic, and

other offensive strategies may be more appropriate, but it can work.

In attacking a zone defense, it is important to have good stickwork and put your best shooters on the field. As will be explained in chapter 10, the zone defense is designed to force the offense to limit itself to taking long-distance, low-percentage shots from the perimeter. Understanding how the zone defense works is essential to finding the appropriate way to attack it. One tactic is to move the ball around the perimeter quickly to generate perimeter shots. Therefore, it is helpful to have a few players who can shoot the ball from that area. It makes no sense to shoot the ball from the perimeter without people who are capable of scoring from that distance. If your team does not have such players, then it will be even more critical to be extremely patient and work very hard to generate shots from closer in.

Perhaps the best way to defeat a zone, however, is to force the defenders in the zone to rotate from one area to another. Doing so may allow the offense to catch the defense rotating incorrectly, not being able to rotate quickly, or missing rotations. The following example will describe this tactic.

It is critical to understand what kind of zone a defense is running. For the sake of this brief discussion of zone offense, we will assume that the defense is using a perimeter-sliding tactic, with one man responsible for the crease. One tactic would be for the offense to focus on producing perimeter shots. Another tactic would be to put multiple players on the crease to put extra pressure on the one defender solely responsible for that area and then employ a lot of off-ball movement there.

At Johns Hopkins we have tried to combine both, since we have had the luxury of having some quality players who could score from the perimeter and others who were expert at scoring from the inside. We had Adam Doneger, who had a rocket shot and could score from fifteen yards; Conor Ford, another player who was well known for his long-distance shooting abilities; and Bob Benson, who was a great inside player. They allowed us to attack the zone effectively from both the perimeter and the inside.

If a team has the ability to shoot from the perimeter, the zone defense is going to be forced to stretch and extend, thus opening up opportunities on the inside. If the offense is able to get a couple of goals on the inside, the defense becomes a little more worried about the crease area, and it opens up things from the perimeter. Another example of these tactics would be the outside-inside game of a perimeter player and a post man in basketball. The big, talented post man forces the defense to worry a great deal about him, thus opening things on the perimeter. If the offense tends to make some shots from the perimeter, then that forces the defense to extend and open up things for the post man.

The 1-4-1 set is the one with which we at Johns Hopkins feel most comfortable attacking the zone. It allows us to put our best shooters on the wings and out top, our best feeder behind the goal, and our two best crease players, or off-ball players, on the inside. This enables us to create scoring opportunities from both the perimeter and the inside of the defense. We also like the 1-4-1 because it allows us to rotate a crease player out to the perimeter, thus essentially forcing the defense to have to rotate. One tactic that we have used very effectively is to run with the ball from one area of the zone to the other while rotating offensive players off of the crease and then passing the ball back to the very area we just vacated. This single movement normally forces the zone defenders to rotate.

If an offense can force the zone defenders to rotate, a big step has been taken in achieving success versus the zone. If the zone is rotating, an opportunity always exists for a player to miss his rotation or be late rotating to a specific spot. The offense may inhibit a player's ability to rotate, or the defense may be overly concerned with rotating their perimeter players and not as worried about supporting the single crease defender as he tries to guard against the two or more offensive players on the crease.

Senior attackman Peter LeSueur in action against Virginia in the 2005 men's tournament semifinal game. *Jay Van Rensselaer*

Midfielder Matt Rewkowski (JHU '05) dodges past
a Princeton Tiger. *Jay Van Rensselaer*

8

Extraman Offense

When an opponent commits a foul and has to serve time in the penalty box, the unpenalized team is given a golden opportunity to score. To make the most of having an extra man, the offensive unit must be highly organized, well drilled, and able to move the ball with precision around the goal. It waits for the defense to make a mistake or to fail to cover the extra man, and then it takes a high-percentage shot with a good angle and from close range. Since most college teams will average anywhere from three to six fouls per game, the team that is more successful in handling extraman situations often will be the winner.

At Johns Hopkins, extraman offensive opportunities—and man-down defensive situations—are a major priority in practice and game strategy. We now call the players who handle these assignments our "special teams," much like the special teams units in football. And like their gridiron counterparts, they have played a huge role in our success.

We spend a great deal of time practicing these special teams situations. During a game week, when there are five days of practice, we spend at least fifteen to twenty minutes on extraman four times a week, at a bare minimum. The one goal we get—or the one goal we keep off our opponent's side of the scoreboard—often makes the difference between winning or losing. Although the best offensive players often are selected to play on the extraman offensive unit, that isn't always the case. Of primary importance is the ability of the players to handle the ball and exercise good judgment in determining who is the open man.

During the 2003 season, our extraman unit had a phenomenal 50 percent success rate. Out of every four penalties, we scored two goals; out of every six, we scored three goals. Although Seth Tierney, our associate head coach, kept it very simple, he did a wonderful job of putting our players in positions where they could take advantage of their greatest strengths. Much of that season was spent using a 3-3 extraman offense. In the top center was Kyle Barrie, who had great vision and the ability to shoot from the perimeter. In the top right was Conor Ford, whose low-to-high shot from the perimeter was unforgettable. In the top left was Adam Doneger, who could unleash a rocket at any time. He made a living off of time-and-room shots from the 3 position. In the lower left was Peter LeSueur, four-year starter and lone lefty on our extraman unit. Then there was Kevin Boland, all of 5'9" and probably lucky to be 155 pounds wet. He was a true powerhouse, however, and the leading assist-getter on our extraman that year. Playing in the low right, he often fed Conor Ford in that top right position or Bobby Benson on the inside. Bobby will go down in Hopkins history as one of the greatest inside crease players ever. This six-player extraman unit consisted of five All-Americans, three of whom later were named to the all-time Johns Hopkins University lacrosse team. Coaching certainly is very important in these situations, but it sure helps to have talent like that on the field.

Many days during practice, our extraman offense and the man-down defense would go against each other, strength versus strength. I like to think our man-down unit was responsible in part for helping our extraman unit become a better group. I certainly know our extraman was very helpful in developing our man-down unit. It's nice to know that every day in practice, you're facing as good or better a man-up unit as you'll be facing on game day. For all their personal strengths, however, this unit was just that: a unit. They were well drilled. They were unselfish. They had a good understanding of what the man-down defense was trying to accomplish. And they were passionate about this special teams group. They knew they could make a difference for our team, and our ability to get to the national championship game against the University of Virginia in 2003 was directly affected by the 50 percent success rate of our extraman unit.

At least nine to ten players should be taught extraman offense. Six of these players will be the starters, and three or four of the next-best offensive players will be the substitutes. These substitutes are extremely important because of the possibility that a starter may be sidelined with injuries.

Every starter and substitute learns at least one, perhaps two, positions on each extraman play. Often the three starting attackmen and the three best midfielders will constitute the extraman unit. It makes no difference whether the midfielders play on the same midfield unit or not. Sometimes a team will have a fourth attackman, however, or a second-line midfielder or a reserve who may not be the greatest athlete but is an outstanding shooter or feeder, and he will be on the unit along with the other players. In fact, it really does not matter who is used on the extraman; they need not be three attackmen or three midfielders. It could consist of five attackmen, provided all are drilled in playing defensively as midfielders whenever the man-down defense gains possession of the ball and clears it to the offensive end of the field. This does happen occasionally, and all the extraman players must be geared to playing defense. The most important thing is that the six best offensive players be in the game.

In order to get the most effective extraman offense, a team must make maximum use of the talents of its players. If a team has superior stick-handling, it can employ a considerable number of passes and a more intricate play. If its stickwork is limited, it should have a simple play with a minimum of passes. If a team has an excellent feeder, it should gear its offense to a variety of cuts and maneuvers in different areas of the field to give him the opportunity to pick out the open man for close-range shots. If there are several outstanding midfield shooters, the play should revolve around action that gives them shots at the twelve-yard mark or closer to the goal. If the crease attackman is a potent scorer, such as Bobby Benson was, he should be set up for shots in the crease area.

For organizational purposes, extraman sets or alignments are identified according to the number of players who are out top, across the face of the goal (including the crease and the wing areas), and behind the goal. For example, the 2-3-1 alignment in figure 8.1 shows two offensive players out top, located in the 3 and the 5 positions; three offensive players located across the face of the goal, in the 6 position (the crease) and the ½ position (the wings); and one player located at X-behind. Some teams reverse the numerical order and count first the player behind the goal, then the crease area, and then the players out top. At Hopkins, we count from the top down.

There are two basic styles of extraman offense. One style makes use of set plays, and the other uses freelance moves from various offensive alignments. Often teams favor the set-play style, which gives specific assignments to each player and takes advantage of the strengths of specific players. If carried out properly, a close-range shot could result. The set play is designed with a series of passes and often includes several cuts to cause the defenders to make adjustments. Each player knows every step of the play and is ready to capitalize on a defensive mistake at any time. The freelance style gives the players more freedom to move the ball in any manner from a basic alignment. There is no special sequence of passes. Since the offense has an extra man, it should be able to get a good shot just by moving the ball sharply, forcing the defense to rotate, and looking for a defensive lapse. A set play usually is more effective than a freelance play when less than ten seconds remain in a penalty and the ball goes out-of-bounds. In this instance, a coach would design a simple play that can be executed in a very short period of time.

At the collegiate level, there probably is a variation in the number of plays each team has in its extraman arsenal. At Hopkins, we will have as many as ten plays prepared for any specific game. That does not mean we will use all ten, however, and a number of those ten plays are not overly complicated. They may just be a subtle variation of the same play, such as one that we run to the right and a variation of it that we run to the left. Some may consider having ten extraman plays excessive, but when you consider the variety of techniques a man-down defense can use, it is important that the extraman offense be prepared for everything. A team must be ready to attack an aggressive man-

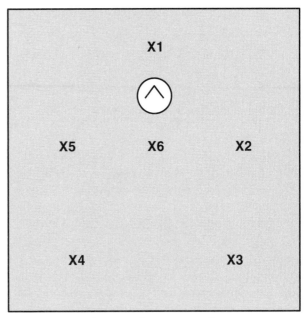

Figure 8.1 2-3-1 alignment for extraman offense.

down defense that is putting pressure on the perimeter, shutting off the best shooter, shutting off the best feeder, or playing a four- or five-man rotation man-down. Those are simply four options that a man-down defense can use. That is why it is important for the extraman unit to be well schooled and prepared for each one of them.

After the team practices its extraman plays for the opening game of the season, it is advisable to install some new plays at various times throughout the season. If a team does not vary its extraman plays, its opponents will be able to scout the extraman offense and prepare their man-down units for those specific plays. Seeing familiar plays on game day boosts the opposing defense's confidence more than anything else. Seeing plays that the man-down defense is familiar with provides them with an advantage when defending against the extraman offense. This advantage could be the difference between scoring a goal and not scoring a goal, between winning a game or losing a game. It is a sound strategy to prepare a new play, similar to one of the offense's regular plays but with several subtle changes in it. It takes a clever man-down unit to make the proper adjustments to defend against these subtle changes. A simple variation in moving

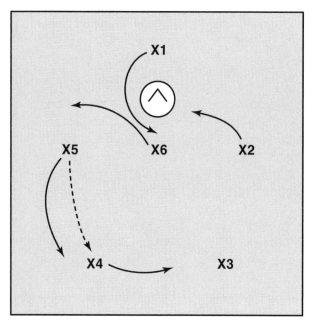

Figure 8.2 Beginning movement from 2-3-1 alignment to 3-3 alignment.

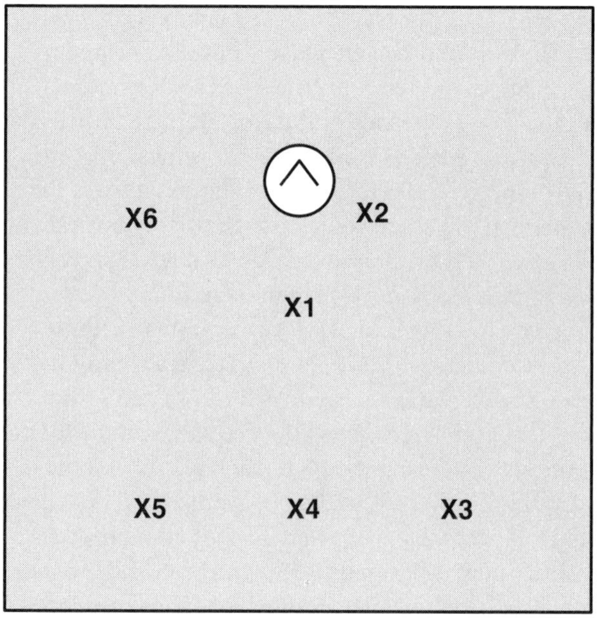

Figure 8.3 Movement continues toward a 3-3 alignment.

two players can confuse a man-down defense. Initiating a play from a different place on the field can also confuse a man-down defense.

When a foul occurs, it is the responsibility of the coach to determine which play to use. He will inform his offensive players or often choose one leader of the extraman to inform him, and that player will then share the extraman play with his offensive teammates. It is imperative that all six players know which play has been called. Usually there is no problem in doing this at the outset of an extraman play. However, confusion can reign in the latter part of a play when a shot is taken and the offense regains possession of the ball either inbounds or out-of-bounds. At this time, in particular, the coach must signal what extraman play will be used. The offense should identify its plays without tipping off the type of play to the defense. Often, a coach and an extraman team will use code names for different alignments or different plays. Our extraman unit and coach actually have had a little bit of fun conjuring up our extraman play code names. The guys sometimes have used the names of characters from popular television shows. We also have had "Mustard" and "Ketchup," which were similar

plays but just run in different directions. We had "Lion" and "Tiger." We used the nicknames for players on our team. We even designed plays that were given the nickname of one player but actually were for another guy—to confuse our opponents.

After a play has been called and the whistle blows, there is a need for a signal to initiate the action. While the ball is being passed around the perimeter to get the opponent's defense moving, a designated player can call out, "Let's go!" Or a coach can predetermine when the play will start by yelling from the sideline, "Second time, Jim!" or "Second stick, Jim!"—meaning the second time Jim touches the ball, the play will begin. No secrets are being given away, other than when the play will start.

Most of our extraman offenses at Hopkins combine set plays with freelance. This means that we organize ourselves in a specific set and run a play out of that set, and if we do not create a quality scoring opportunity out of that specific play, we will move quickly to a freelance extraman offense. Usually our basic strategy is to start our set plays with one alignment and then, by cutting or just adjusting our personnel, move into another alignment. For example, figure 8.2 shows our extraman

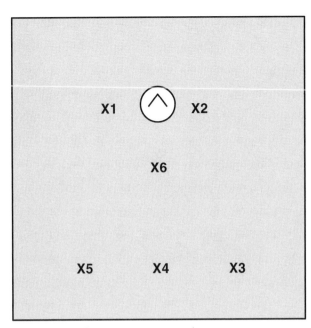

Figure 8.4 Final positioning in a 3-3 alignment.

but within it are many options—as our 2003 extra-man special team proved dramatically. There are several reasons for the effectiveness of the 3-3. One is that all six players are located in front of the goal and have the ability to shoot the ball at any particular time, unlike any other extraman alignment: with a 2-3-1, there's a player behind the goal; with a 1-4-1, there's a player behind the goal; with a 2-2-2, there are two players behind the goal. In a 3-3 set, everyone is a potential scorer. Ideally, it certainly helps to have at least two left-handers in the 3-3. Unfortunately, even though we've been able to do a wonderful job of recruiting here at Hopkins, so far we have never had two left-handers on the left-hand side of the 3-3. That, thankfully, has not proven to be a problem. A team can more than make do with a right-hander—as we did with Adam Doneger. Adam played the left-hander spot right-handed and was terrific. Another reason the 3-3 is effective is that if a team does not have a great feeder from behind the goal, a 3-3 keeps everyone out in front and there is no need to have anyone behind the goal.

THE 3-3

In figure 8.4, X1 is aligned five yards wide of the goal and a yard or two above the goal line. X2 mirrors him on the opposite side. X3 will play the top left-handed position and be the lefty shooter. X4 will be the top-setter player. Ideally, he will be a big-shooter, a player who can shoot and pass. X5 will be the top right-handed shooter. X6 will be the best inside player. All six players are located in front of the goal and put a lot of pressure on the defense.

Figure 8.5 has X4 starting the movement of the ball. He has a number of options. His first options are to throw the ball to one of the two adjacent players, X5 or X3. Another option would be for X4 to skip-pass the ball to the corners, meaning he bypasses his adjacent players and throws the ball to either X6 or X2. Skip-passing the ball can put a lot of additional pressure on the man-down defense. This is a viable option if the defense, lacking a man, is not covering the skip-passing lanes or is extended too far or sucked in too much. X4 also has

offense in a 2-3-1 alignment. We may call this alignment "Blue Jay." As the ball moves around the perimeter, counterclockwise, the play is designed to begin when X4 touches the ball the second time. Figure 8.3 shows us moving from one set to another. As X4 receives the ball the second time from X5, moving counterclockwise, the play will begin. When X4 receives the ball, he runs with it to the middle position, which is called the 4 position. X5 will move into X4's previous position. X6 will leave the crease and rotate to the lower right spot in a 3-3. X2 will cut to the lower left shooter spot in a 3-3. X1 will delay his cut for one second, then move directly to the crease, cutting with his strong hand. By utilizing this movement, the play forces the defense to move as well as to recognize what set we have moved from and what set we are moving to. Moving from a 2-3-1 alignment to a 3-3 alignment usually compels the defense to defend each set in a different manner. Figure 8.4 shows our final alignment after X4 initiates the play by carrying the ball to the middle of the field. We have now moved our 2-3-1 "Blue Jay" set to our 3-3 "Hopkins" set.

With the right players, the 3-3 set is the most dangerous. It is a very simple extraman alignment,

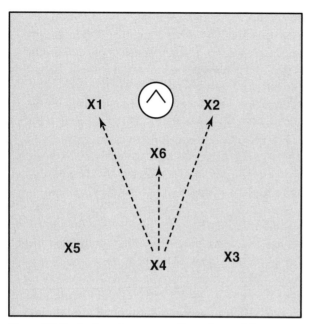

Figure 8.5 Beginning of extraman offense from a 3-3 alignment.

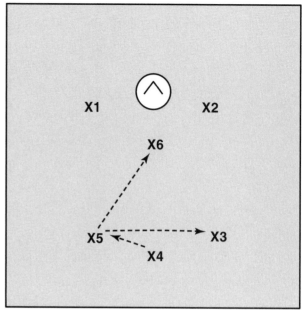

Figure 8.6 Second phase of extraman offense from a 3-3 alignment.

the option to skip-pass to X1. These options may also be available not only because the defenders on the wings are stretched out too far or sucked in but also because the two base defensemen may be helping their crease defender teammate to cover X6. A defender who is covering X1 but sloughed in a bit to support X6 will have a difficult time covering X1 if the ball is skip-passed to him. A fourth option for X4 is to pass inside to X6. He would be available to receive the ball if the defense is so concerned with the perimeter shooters, X5 and X3, that they don't do a good job of covering the inside. That will leave X6 with some time and room to shoot. Of course, if you have a quality inside player in X6, such as we at Hopkins were fortunate to have in Bob Benson, your opponents will always be concerned with him, too. That has the potential of forcing the perimeter defensemen to sag in a little bit more so that X6 does not have quality opportunities, thus opening up shots for the players on the perimeter.

In figure 8.6, the ball is being moved from X4 to X5, who also now has various options. X5 certainly can pass the ball to his adjacent teammates (to X1 or back to X4), or he can skip-pass the ball to X3. Every time the extraman offense skips the

ball, it puts tremendous pressure on the man-down defense. The defense's aim is to force the offense to make the next easy pass. Skipping the ball will force the defense to have to rotate very quickly, which they will be unable to do at times. X5 also has the option to pass the ball to X6. A pass to X2 probably would be the most difficult and the lowest-percentage one to do. Remember that although it is preferable to skip-pass the ball as much as possible, it is also important to play the percentages and not take too many risks to avoid squandering the extraman opportunity.

Figure 8.7 shows the ball being moved down to X1 in the lower right position. Keep in mind that as this is taking place, X6 does not just play a stationary role. It is important for him to be very active. By moving, he may be able to draw the attention of the perimeter defensemen, which can result in creating open skip-passing lanes. As the ball is passed from X5 to X1, X6 should move a little higher so that he has the ability, as X1 receives the ball, to cut toward X1 for a quick pass and a shot. X1 has different options as well. He has the option to throw the ball back to the adjacent player, X5, but this would probably result in just moving the ball

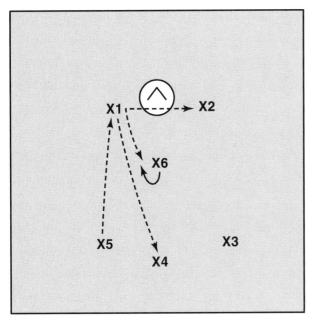

Figure 8.7 Possible movements of the ball.

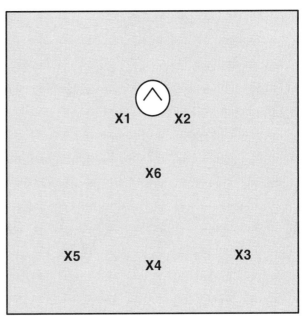

Figure 8.8 Adjustments to 3-3 extraman movement strategy to put pressure on the defense.

around the perimeter. He also can pass the ball inside to X6, who now is facing the goal. X1 also can feed the ball across the crease to X2 if the defense is playing soft on the back side. And he can also skip-pass the ball to X4. Again, that skip-pass will put a lot of pressure on the defense. If the ball were reversed to the other side, X3 and X2 would have the exact same options as X5 and X1.

Two subtle adjustments to this extraman strategy can also put a lot of pressure on the defense. X1 and X2 could pinch in a little higher and a little closer to the crease, as shown in figure 8.8. The extraman offense here is not as spread out as it once was in the 3-3 set. However, by moving in, X1 and X2 will become much more dangerous threats to score and will force the base defenders to spend more time being concerned with them, and possibly less time being concerned about X6, the crease man. This could open up some quality opportunities for X6 on the inside. In this situation, and in the 3-3 in general, backing up the goal is essential in case there is a shot. When the ball is on one side of the field, the opposite low player must be responsible for backup if the ball is shot and misses the goal. In figure 8.8, X1 and X2's job is a little more

difficult than that in figure 8.7, because they are located a little bit more above the goal and a little farther in, making it more difficult for them to get to the end line and back up a shot.

In figure 8.9, X1 and X2 have gone behind the goal. These two players now have the ability to move both behind and out front. If they are out front, our alignment is exactly as it was in figure 8.7. They will move behind only to pass the ball from one side of the field to the other between themselves. This is another subtle change that can put a lot of pressure on the man-down defense. With the traditional 3-3, the defense only had to worry about the ball being passed from one side of the field to the other around the perimeter out top. Now they have to be concerned with the ball going from one side of the field to the other by being passed behind the goal. Once the ball is passed from X2 to X1 or from X2 to X1 and then moves out front, these players again can move in front of the goal and position themselves for a shot.

Figures 8.8 and 8.9 are just subtle wrinkles in the 3-3. During the 2003 and 2004 seasons, Hopkins did exceptionally well with the alignment in figure 8.9. We found that moving these two players below

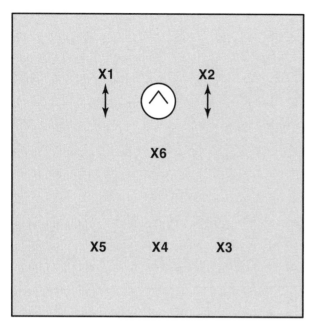

Figure 8.9 Adjustment to 3-3 extraman, putting two players behind the goal.

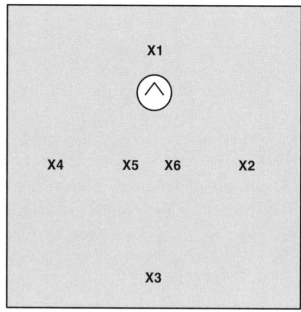

Figure 8.10 1-4-1 alignment of extraman defense.

the goal line extended to exchange the ball put a ton of pressure on teams to cover the crease, thus creating excellent opportunities for our extraman.

THE 1-4-1

Figure 8.10 shows the extraman unit aligned in a 1-4-1 set. The one player behind the goal should be the team's best feeder. The three players in front of the goal—X2, X3 and X4—should be the best perimeter shooters. Inside, X5 and X6 should be the best off-ball players and inside finishers. Ideally, X5 should be a left-hander and X6 a right-hander. The 1-4-1 puts a lot of pressure on the man-down defense because it places two offensive players on the crease, thus forcing the man-down defensemen to be even more concerned than they would have been if there were only one crease offenseman. The alignment that the man-down defense will use versus a 1-4-1 is a 1-3-1, with one specific player trying to move between and cover the two crease players. He will get some support from the perimeter players, but they also have the responsibility for covering the perimeter shooters and the skip-passing lanes.

In figure 8.11, the ball is being moved counterclockwise. For the sake of this example, as X3 moves the ball to X2 and X2 passes it to X1 for the second time, the play will begin. As X1 receives the ball, he will carry it right-handed and X4 will set a screen on the wing defender. A screen occurs when an off-ball offensive player moves into position to impede the progress of an off-ball defender. What is known as a "slip screen," as shown in figure 8.11, occurs if the off-ball defender succeeds in getting around the screen or simply moves to another area on the field. Then the off-ball offensive player cuts to the ball. In other words, as X4 moves in and sets that screen, X5 will execute what is called a "high C." He will do a little curl between the crease and where X4 had been, looking to receive a quick feed from X1, and generate a quick left-handed shot. Once X4 has set the screen and X5 executes a high C, X4 will execute a "slip screen," meaning he will slip or cut to the ball-side pipe, looking for a quick feed as well. X1 then has two options off of this quick-hit play: feed X5 for a quick left-handed shot, or feed X4 on the slip screen. This play can work very effectively if X4 is able to screen the wing defender well or if the wing defender fights around

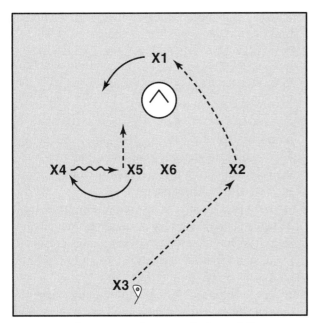

Figure 8.11 Slip screen with counterclockwise ball movement in a 1-4-1 extraman offense.

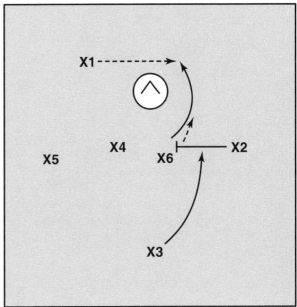

Figure 8.12 Second phase of the slip screen.

the screen and gets out to X5, thus possibly leaving X4 open on his little slip screen.

If no good shooting opportunities are available, the second part of this play (figure 8.12) shows X6 rolling off of the crease and cutting to the 2 position behind the goal. X5, who executed a high C off of the crease, will balance the field and replace X4 out on the wing. When X1 realizes there is no quality shot available from close range on his side, he will pass the ball across X-behind to X6, who will catch it right-handed. As X6 receives the ball, X2 will move in and screen the wing defender on his side, and X3 will cut off that screen to receive a pass from X6 for what could be a good right-handed shot.

It is always important for the extraman sets and plays to be fluid so that if one play doesn't work, it is possible to flow into another one. This will force the defense to recognize what you are doing and react accordingly several times. If no quality shot is available after both of these cross-screens have been executed, then the extraman can move to a 4-2 alignment, with four players across the face of the goal and two players behind it.

Figure 8.13 shows the players positioned as they would be after the previous play was executed. X2,

who came in to set a screen on the wing defender, now is located on the inside. X4, who set the original screen on the right-handed side of the field, is located on the inside. X5 and X3, the players who utilized the screen, now are located on the wings. The alignment now is four across the front of the goal and two behind. The two players behind the goal will become feeders, and the four players out in front of the goal will continue to be shooters. X1 and X2 will move the ball back and forth between the two of them. Whenever the ball comes to a side, it will be possible for a cross-screen and a high C to be executed. For example, should X2 realize that he doesn't have a quality opportunity to pass the ball on his side, he will immediately pass it across to X1, who will look for X5 setting a screen for X4, doing a high C. Then X5 will execute a slip screen. If no quality shot opportunity is available, the ball will move back across to X2, and on the opposite side, X3 and X2 will mirror what X5 and X4 did.

The biggest concern with this offense is if a bad shot is made and saved or the extraman offense somehow loses the ball and the defense quickly picks it up. With the majority of the extraman play-

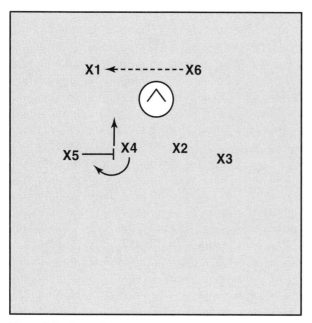

Figure 8.13 A 4-2 slip screen.

ers positioned very tight to the goal, no more than ten to twelve yards above the goal line, it will be difficult for them to get back to the midfield line and ride.

ADDITIONAL GUIDELINES

Do not rush the play and try to score in ten seconds or less when operating with a one-minute penalty.

As the ball is moved around the horn, make sharp and accurate passes to the outside of each player. If the pass is thrown to the inside, a sliding defender has an opportunity to intercept the ball or check the attacker's stick as he is catching it.

Keep the offensive players spread far enough apart so that one defender cannot guard two attackers. This does not apply to the players in the crease area.

The ball carrier should force a defender to guard him by moving toward the goal.

Back up every shot with at least one man behind the goal.

Back up every feed to the crease with at least one man in the midfield area.

Use at least two extraman plays against the opponent's basic defense during the course of a game. This makes the defense adjust to different plays instead of allowing it to get comfortable seeing the same play again and again.

When only ten seconds or less remain in a penalty, be ready to use a set play or freelance maneuver that may provide a quick opening and a close-range shot after just several passes and a cut or back-side sneak.

Don't be discouraged if unable to score on extraman plays in the early stages of a game. As long as close-range shots are being taken, the percentages will work in favor of the offense eventually scoring goals.

Should the man-down defense gain possession of the ball with the play being stopped by the official's whistle, the extraman unit must ride all five defenders and the goalie with a tight man-for-man coverage.

Extraman offense is such an important part of team play that it is normally practiced for ten to fifteen minutes per day, four days a week. When inclement weather forces a team to practice indoors, extraman offense can receive an intensive workout, even in a gymnasium. A team with a well-organized, well-prepared, and confident extraman unit will capitalize on average 30–40 percent of its opportunities, and this often will be a decisive factor in the outcome of the game.

First-team All-American defenseman Tom Garvey (JHU '05) applies pressure to a Virginia Cavalier. *Jay Van Rensselaer*

9

Individual Defense

A complete understanding of the basic skills of defending against an opponent with the ball is essential for every player on the field and is a key to any team's success.

Naturally, each defender and midfielder takes responsibility for neutralizing his man when he has possession of the ball, but even attackmen should understand the basic principles of on-ball, or one-on-one, defense in case they must cross the midline into the defensive end in order to oppose a defenseman who is trying to clear the ball up the field. Another reason for an attackman to learn these principles is to gain a better feel for defensive tactics in general. As an offensive player, he then will find it easier to attack what he understands. Similarly, goalies occasionally find themselves out of the cage, where they must defend against an offensive player who has the ball. Goalies must also be able to assist their defensive teammates with positive verbal instructions.

The technique for playing one-on-one defense in lacrosse is similar to that used in basketball. The major difference is the lacrosse player's ability to use his stick. Unfortunately, often too much emphasis is placed on use of the stick, especially at the youth and high school levels. Far too many players feel that they must check their opponent or take the ball away from him in order to catch a coach's eye or appear to accomplish something. At Hopkins, we call that playing defense "in a hurry." Such an aggressive style may be impressive versus a less-talented offensive player, but against a top-notch offensive player, taking too many risks to try to take the ball away could lead to some very poor results, such as getting bypassed by a dodger or fouling him. Although there is a time and place for this type of defense, the overall philosophy at Hopkins and in many other programs is to avoid taking the risks such play often involves and thus becoming easy prey for the opposing offensive players.

As I think back over my career, I can recall only a few great take-away defenders. These guys could take the ball away because they excelled at positioning themselves properly on the field. On the other hand, I can think of a host of outstanding defenders who took far fewer risks but got the job done exceptionally well at the highest level. Among these players were Johns Hopkins University's John DeTomasso, a four-time All-American and Defenseman of the Year in 1985; Princeton University's David Morrow, two-time All-American and National Player of the Year in 1993; Hopkins's Steve Mitchell, the first long-stick middie ever to be named a first-team All-American in 1987; Brian Kuczma of Hopkins, three-time All-American and Defenseman of the Year in 1997; Hopkins's Shawn Nadelen, another All-American in 2001; Mike Peyser, a two-time Hopkins All-American from the Class of 2003; and Tom Garvey, a two-time All-American from the Class of 2005. These were just a few of the great players who kept their defensive tactics simple but helped their teams achieve considerable success.

Different defensive recipes are used at every level of lacrosse, and each has its merits. For instance, at Johns Hopkins, Princeton, Navy, and Cornell, you'll find defenses that have been quite successful using a less aggressive, on-ball philosophy, whereas teams such as Syracuse and Virginia have had success being more aggressive. Much depends on the style of play the coaches want to employ and the type of players they have available to put it into practice.

One reason that Hopkins and many other successful programs prefer the less aggressive on-the-ball philosophy is that we believe the odds are in the offensive player's favor if our defenders take too many risks trying to check their opponents or take the ball away. Imagine that a defender challenges a dodger one hundred times. During these one-on-one battles, an aggressive defenseman may successfully knock the ball to the ground seventy-five times

out of a hundred, for a success rate of 75 percent. But that also means the defender will be beaten twenty-five times, or 25 percent of the time. For our defense and teams to be successful at the highest level, this is not an acceptable percentage. The odds will favor the attacking team because of the excellent scoring opportunities that result in those twenty-five chances.

Usually, when a defender tries to take the ball away, the following things can happen, all but one of which are negative:

1. He knocks the ball out of his opponent's stick. This creates what we call "a 50–50 ball," with either team having a 50 percent chance of picking it up. As mentioned in chapter 6, the majority of goals are scored in such broken or transitional situations. These can be dangerous.

2. The defensive player knocks the ball out of the offensive player's stick and picks it up.

3. The defender fouls his opponent but does not take the ball away and gives up a quality shot. If a goal is scored after a defender has committed a foul, he still must serve time in the penalty box, thus penalizing his team not once, by giving up a goal, but twice.

4. The defender may not take the ball away and gets beaten for a quality shot.

5. The defender does not get beaten for a quality shot but gets penalized for a personal foul.

At Hopkins, the primary objective of our on-ball defender is to *contain* the offensive player with the ball, forcing him to take a low-percentage shot, make a low-percentage pass, or just to pass the ball on.

In order to explain better how a defender can contain a dodger, I have separated our defensive tactics into three categories: positioning, stance, footwork.

POSITIONING

It is critical to the success of an on-ball defender to be in the appropriate position on the field when an offensive player receives the ball. As the ball is in the air on its way to an offensive player, the defender who will be playing the ball must work his way out from his team's defensive position to the player he will be covering and position himself in a way that will force the ball carrier or dodger to a specific area of the field that we choose. We call this "addressing the ball." To address the ball correctly, a defender first must understand what areas of the field we want to make available to the dodger and which ones we want to take away.

Positioning Out Top, or Positioning in the Midfield

When defending against an offensive ball carrier out top or in the midfield, our rule of thumb is to take away the middle of the field and to force the ball carrier down the side. This decreases the ball carrier's vision of the field and his shooting angle, which often leads to a low-percentage shot or a low-percentage pass. If the middle of the field is left open to this offensive player, his field vision and shooting angle will increase, which could prove to be costly to our defense—and our team.

While moving toward the offensive player while the ball is in flight, the defender should be careful not to rush out too quickly, which can cause him to become unbalanced and lose control. This could lead to his being dodged successfully. When the defender approaches the ball carrier, he should slow down and stop about one to three yards, or a stick's length, away from the ball carrier. The distance could differ, depending on whether the defender is using a short or a long stick. Allowing for this room will provide the on-ball defender with a cushion so that he is able to react appropriately to the offensive player's dodge. The positioning of the on-ball defender's body and feet is an integral part of addressing the ball. Since the defender is attempting to take away the middle of the field, he should try to overplay that area with his body and his stick. This means that the defender should be more to the middle of the field than the offensive player is, thus deterring him from moving toward the middle and encouraging him to take the path down the side, or "down the alley."

Figure 9.1 shows the numbers that we at Hopkins apply to each area of the field. The lower right portion of the goal, the back right, is the 1 position.

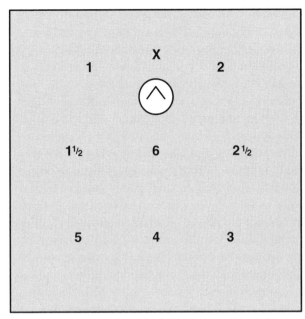

Figure 9.1 The numbers applied to each area of the field.

Directly behind the goal is "X-behind." The lower left position behind the goal is the 2 position. The wing left is 2½; the wing right is 1½. The top left, in front of the goal, is the 3. The top center is X-up top, or the 4. The top right is the 5. The crease is the 6. If the offensive player receives the ball in the 3 position, our defender will be addressing the ball correctly if he can force the offensive player toward the 2½ or the 2 position, thus cutting down his shooting angle and field vision.

Another reason we want to force the ball carrier to specific areas of the field is to make it easier for the on-ball defender's teammates to lend support by sliding if he is beaten by the dodger. Imagine how much more confident an on-ball defender will be if he always knows that should he be beaten by his man, that offensive player would be moving into a designated area to which his defensive teammates are prepared to slide. This portion of team defense will be discussed in chapter 10.

Positioning behind the Goal

When a defender positions himself against a ball carrier behind the goal or below the goal line extended, his tactics are a little different than when the dodger is out top. The way the defender addresses the ball carrier, however, is much the same. When defending a ball carrier below the goal line extended, or in the 1 or 2 positions, our objective always is to take away the area of the field we call the topside, or the area above the goal line extended. In order to do so, the on-ball defender should attempt to overplay the topside with his body and stick and force the ball carrier to the area behind the goal, the X-behind. In forcing a dodger behind the goal rather than allowing him to dodge to the front or topside, the defender has achieved a great victory. In order to score goals, a dodger must be in front of the goal. If he is forced to stay below the goal line extended or toward X-behind, he can never score. He can only feed. He is also forced from one side of the goal toward the other. This longer path to the topside will allow the defenders in front of the goal line to adjust their own positioning and to prepare to slide if necessary. It also will allow the on-ball defender to use the crease area to make up some ground if, by chance, he has gotten a step behind the dodger.

The only difference in playing defense when the ball carrier is in the X-behind area, rather than at top center, or the 4 position, is that our aim no longer is to take away the middle of the field or force the ball behind. It is to take away the offensive player's strong hand. Since the dodger is in the middle of the field and can move to a dangerous area on either side, the most effective tactic is to take away his strong hand and force him to play the game with his weak one. This is accomplished with the same methods the defenseman uses to overplay an area of the field and force his opponent into the area where we want him to go. You overplay the ball carrier's strong hand and force him to play with his weak hand.

STANCE

The stance of an on-ball defender is vital to his effectiveness. The proper on-ball stance helps enable the defender to force the ball carrier to the areas of the field we choose. When the ball carrier is out top, the defender attempts to take away the middle of the field by using a staggered stance that places

Figure 9.2 On-ball stance, with heel-to-toe alignment.

his inside foot forward and his outside foot back in what we call a heel-to-toe alignment (figure 9.2). His legs should be about shoulder-width apart. The defender should be on the balls of his feet. Comfort is critical, and balance is very important. The defender does not want to be on his tiptoes or on his heels. He wants to find a level of comfort that will allow him to be in what we call an athletic position, which permits him to react quickly. The defender should bend at the knees and just slightly at the waist, almost as if he was about to sit down in a chair.

This stance allows the on-ball defender to maintain balance, athleticism, and explosiveness. When the ball carrier is in the top center, or the 4 position, the on-ball defender should position his feet based on the offensive player's strong hand. If the dodger is a right-hander, then the defender will place his left foot forward and his right foot back; if the dodger is a left-hander, he will do the exact opposite. This enables him to take away his opponent's strong hand when he is in the middle of the field; when the ball carrier is in other areas of the field, it enables the defender to take away the middle of the field.

Below the Goal Line Extended

The stance used to defend against a dodger from out top is similar to that used when defending below the goal line, with the exception of where the feet are positioned. Since the defenseman's aim when behind the goal is to take away the ball carrier's path to the topside, the defender will always put his outside foot forward and his inside foot back. This holds true on either side of the goal. The stance of his legs and upper body should be exactly the same as elsewhere: legs bent at the knees, and upper body slightly bent at the waist. If the dodger is at X-behind, then we will defend the exact same way we do when the ball is located in the top center. We will take away the offensive player's strong hand by placing the outside foot forward and the inside foot back.

FOOTWORK

Once an offensive player is prepared to dodge and the defender covering him has gotten into the correct position to take away an area of the field, the defender must then be prepared to react to the ball carrier's initial move. He can do so by using the proper footwork. A player running forward can do so at a much faster rate than one moving backward. Since the defender has to run backward initially when responding to the offensive player's first move, it is important for the defenseman to have his stick out in front of him to provide the cushion mentioned earlier. This also forces the dodger to make his move farther away from the defender's body.

When the dodger begins his move and starts to run toward the defender, the defender should begin to run backward, or backpedal. Defenders often are taught to shuffle their feet in response to their opponent's first move, but it is nearly impossible

Figure 9.3 Hip-to-hip position of defenseman vs. dodger.

to shuffle quickly enough to cover a dodger, so we recommend running backward. This is very similar to the movement or footwork a defensive back in football uses when covering a wide receiver. Moving backward and keeping the stick out in front enables the defender to respond to the initial thrust of the dodger and continue to force that dodger to a specific area.

Once the dodger chooses which way he wants to run—and we hope the defenseman has done a good enough job addressing the ball and using the proper stance to force the dodger to the area of the field where we want him to go—the defender should drop-step (swing his leg to the side the dodger has chosen), turn, and run with the dodger. The defender should try to stay alongside the dodger, as if they were connected at the hip. We call this a "hip-to-hip position" (figure 9.3). This allows the defender to contain the offensive player by maintaining the proper position between his man and the goal.

DRIVING

While running hip-to-hip with his man, the defender needs to try to drive him away from the goal. As the dodger makes his move closer to the goal and gets in a more threatening position, the defenseman wants to begin applying pressure on him by gradually making contact with his body. A right-handed defenseman, for example, should keep his left hand on the butt end of his stick, his right hand a little farther up the stick, and move close enough to his man to have his forearm make contact with the offensive player's body around the waist area. The reason the defenseman places his hands in the area of his opponent's hip is that wherever you put pressure on an offensive player's hip, the rest of his body has to follow. There's no strength in a player's hip. There's strength in his legs and upper body. If the defenseman places his hands in the area of his opponent's shoulders or chest, the dodger has the strength of his legs to continue his forward momentum. By placing his hands on his man's hips, the defenseman can begin to drive him away from those threatening areas of the field. Each time the offensive player lifts his foot to take another step to run, the defenseman wants to apply driving pressure—not by pushing his man but simply by maintaining contact. When the dodger is on one leg he is not balanced, so each time he lifts his leg to step, the defenseman applies pressure and tries to drive the dodger a step farther from that dangerous area.

Should you hook the offensive player with your stick as he dodges, you very easily could be called with a hold penalty. If you place your stick out in front of him, however, and you are driving him away from the goal with your body and not hooking him with your stick, then you will be executing a clean play. In the past, such defensive moves often were called holds because the defenseman was holding his man back from advancing. We don't use the word "hold" at Hopkins now because it is identical to the name of a penalty we want our players to avoid. Our goalie won't yell, "Hold, hold, hold!"

to encourage his defensemen. He'll yell, "Drive, drive, drive!" because that defines what we want to do in this situation. We want to drive the offensive player away from the threatening area.

If the offensive player is left-handed and the defenseman is right-handed, a different driving technique is used. When the defender gets in the hip-to-hip position with his man as he moves toward the threatening area on the field, the defenseman should keep his stick out front, making gradual contact around his opponent's hip or waist area but bringing his hands closer together on his stick so that his hands are on the offensive player's hip. The defenseman in this situation should avoid putting his hands wider apart, because if he places the shaft of his stick on his opponent's hip he could be called for an illegal cross-check hold. Once the defenseman has his hands close together on his opponent's hip, he can use the same technique for driving him away from the threatening area.

Yet another driving technique is used behind the goal. When an offensive player approaches the topside on either side of the goal, the defenseman's foot and body positioning are more important than where he places his stick. It doesn't matter whether the stick is in front of the offensive player or behind him. As the offensive player is dodging from behind the goal and approaches the goal line extended, the goalie should shout out a drive call when the dodger is about a yard to a yard and a half below the goal line extended. By the time the defenseman gets to the goal line, he should have beaten that offensive player to a spot that blocks his path to the topside. The defenseman wants to have his top foot positioned toward the corner of the field so that he can do what we call "closing the gate" (see fig. 9.8). If the defenseman were to swing his right foot and face the sideline, he'd open an easy path for the offensive player to get to the topside. To close the gate, he instead swings his top foot toward the corner of the field and positions himself so that he is almost square with the end line. In order for an offensive player to get to the topside, he has to run through not only the defenseman's stick but his body. When the defenseman is in that position, he should assume the slightly bent posture described earlier (almost as if he were about to sit down in a chair), put his hands on the offensive player's hip or waistline, and drive the offensive player away from the goal each time he tries to take a step toward it.

A great example of outstanding containment defense that always comes to mind when I think of this tactic involves the 2004 regular-season game matchup between Tom Garvey, an All-American defender I had the opportunity to coach on the Hopkins teams of 2002–2005, and Syracuse's Michael Powell, a four-time, first-team All-American and one of the finest players in the history of the game. Mike Powell possessed great quickness and speed and was an attackman who rarely had the ball taken away from him. Most defensemen who tried to do so put themselves out of position and their team at risk. Tom Garvey, as fundamentally sound a defenseman as you will find, took tremendous pride in playing Mike Powell. In that game on Homewood Field before 6,519 fans, Tom did what he always does—stuck to the basics and played good, solid on-ball defense. Tom so effectively contained Mike Powell that he did not score a goal or an assist for only the second time in his career.

Mike Powell always presented an enormous challenge not only to Hopkins but to any defense. In Syracuse's first offensive possession that afternoon, Mike got the ball in the back right position, and it was obvious that he was determined to make a statement early in the game. Tom ran out to cover Mike and did such a great job of containing him by taking away the topside and forcing him into the area of the field where we wanted him to go that Mike had to use an inside roll in an effort to advance toward the goal. As soon as Mike rolled inside, however, Hopkins's All-American midfielder, Kyle Harrison, executed a well-timed slide and we were able to double-team Mike quickly, knock the ball down, scoop it up, and clear it down the field to our All-American attackman, Conor Ford, who scored the first goal of the game. That was a great way for us to set the tone for the day in our defensive end. Tom and the rest of the Blue Jay defensemen went on to hold Syracuse to its lowest scoring effort in thirteen years as we beat the Orangemen 17–5.

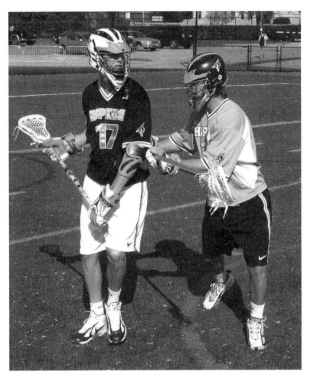

Figure 9.4 Forehand or open-stick technique.

USING THE STICK

As I mentioned earlier, using the stick too much to check the ball carrier or try to take away the ball reduces your ability to contain your man. The stick can be used, however, as a cushion or as a source of pressure to the hands of a dodger as he tries to feed or shoot. In all instances, when the defender has addressed the ball and gotten into the appropriate on-ball stance, he should place his stick directly out in front of him, at the waist level, and pointed at the dodger's midsection. Doing so will help the defender to guard against a split dodge and a face dodge, which we discussed in chapter 6.

Forehand or Open-Stick Technique

The forehand or open-stick technique is used when a right-handed defender is running hip-to-hip with a left-handed dodger, as shown in figure 9.4. To stop the offensive player's momentum toward the cage and to drive him away from the goal, the defender places his butt-end hand onto the hip of the dodger. The defender should then place his top hand about

Figure 9.5 V-hold or backhand stick technique.

Figure 9.6 Two phases of the poke check.

a foot or foot and a half apart from his lower hand and just underneath the rib cage of the dodger. This puts the defender's stick at about a forty-five-degree angle. Placing the defender's hands in these two areas will force the defender to crouch down a bit and get in a very solid and fundamental posture around the goal line extended. The stance is similar to what we used when we initially defended the ball.

The V-Hold or Backhand Stick Technique

When a right-handed dodger goes against a right-handed defender near the goal line, he can use the V-hold or backhand stick technique, as shown in figure 9.5. He places his stick straight out in front of him, with his forearm parallel to his body and his butt-end hand around his hip or waist area. This forms a "V" between his stick and forearm. As the offensive player approaches the goal line and the goalie gives the drive call, the defenseman tries to make contact gradually with the ball carrier so that by the time that player reaches the goal line extended, contact has been made. The defenseman then crouches in the athletic and fundamental posture described earlier; places his forearm on the hip or waistline of the offensive player or the dodger;

keeps his stick out in front, impeding the offensive player's progress not only with his body but with his stick; and uses the power in his legs to drive the dodger away from the goal.

It is important to remember that feet and body positioning are the most crucial parts to successful on-ball defense. Using the stick is not.

BASIC CHECKS

So far, we have discussed how to contain an offensive player and have not mentioned much about taking the ball away or checking, for the reasons stated at the beginning of this chapter. Nevertheless, a team may find itself at a point in a game

Figure 9.7 Two phases of the slap check.

when it is down a goal, its opponent is holding the ball, and an effort needs to be made to get the ball back. In this instance, checking can play an important role in a team's success. Two commonly used checks are the poke check and the slap check.

The Poke Check

The poke check consists of a thrust of the stick, propelled through the upper hand by the lower hand (fig. 9.6). This technique is similar to the billiard player's handling of his cue stick. The lower hand draws the stick back slightly just prior to the stroke to give more power. It is important for the upper hand to remain in contact with the handle as it slides through the fingers to give better control. If the upper hand loses its grasp, the lower hand will not be able to control the stick, thereby giving an advantage to the attacker. If the attacker is holding his stick with one hand, the thrust can be directed at any part of the handle that is showing. If he has two hands on the stick, it can be aimed at the cuff of the glove holding the butt end of the stick. The defender must guard against an overaggressive poke that will cause him to step into his opponent and give him an opening to roll by on the side opposite his check.

Although the poke check is a commonly used

technique and may appear simple, it actually can be troublesome because often a defender tends to slow down when doing it.

The Slap Check

The slap check, as the term implies, is merely a short, slapping blow directed at the attacker's lower gloved hand or the handle of the stick just above it (fig. 9.7). It is used mainly when the attacker either has both hands on the stick or is about to put his lower hand on it. The slap check will not be effective if the attacker is holding the stick in one hand and protecting it well with the other. The wrist action of the upper hand on the stick delivers the check, and it should be as quick as possible. The head of the stick will be directed at the target anywhere from a horizontal position up to an angle of approximately forty-five degrees above the horizontal. The check should not cover a distance any greater than approximately eighteen inches. In fact, the shorter the check, the less it is telegraphed. When the defender hauls back with his stick as if to bludgeon his opponent, he not only tips off his maneuver but also begins a check that generates so much power it gets out of control and exposes him to a face or roll dodge. The head of the defender's stick should not go beyond a position horizontal to

Figure 9.8 Positioning of defenseman vs. dodger to "close the gate."

the ground when it is in the downward motion. If it does, it can cause a foul by hitting the attacker on the lower part of his body or can even trip him. When making the slap check with the stick moving in a horizontal path, the defender must guard against using too vigorous a check, which will give the attacker an easy roll dodge.

In the first edition of this book, Bob Scott wrote that he hesitated even to mention other checking manuevers such as the over-the-head and wraparound checks—and I am even more reluctant to do so. They are, as Scotty said, dangerous—both physically and tactically—and require extreme caution. They still exist but are not good checks to use.

HIGHLIGHTS OF INDIVIDUAL DEFENSIVE PLAY

Be patient and play position first—the percentages favor this style of play over the aggressive, take-the-ball-away approach.

Put pressure on the dodger's hands to deny him a good-angle shot and impede his feeding ability.

When your man makes his initial offensive move, your first step is to run backward, keeping your stick out front and in your strong hand at all times to provide a cushion between yourself and the dodger.

Run hip-to-hip with your man when he has the ball and is going at top speed.

Keep your stick in the same hand when playing your man.

When executing a driving maneuver, keep your stick in front of the number on your opponent's jersey, crouch, and drive by applying pressure to your man's hips; be ready to check his stick.

Don't step into your man when using poke and slap checks.

A check that travels a short distance is the most effective.

The defender must keep his legs spread to provide a strong base when driving against his man.

Driving tactics should be used only when the attacker is in front of the goal—ten yards or less from the crease for a midfielder, five yards or less from the crease for an attackman.

Hopkins midfielder Benson Erwin takes a swipe at a Loyola
player during the 2005 season. *Jay Van Rensselaer*

Long-stick midfielder Brendan Skakandi (JHU '07) and defenseman Chris Watson (JHU '05) execute effective team defense in the 2005 NCAA Tournament semifinal game. *Jay Van Rensselaer*

10

Team Defense

Today, when flash often appears to outweigh substance, many lacrosse fans seem only to want exciting offensive plays, with acrobatic passes and electrifying shots, rather than good, solid defense. At Johns Hopkins, we work extremely hard to be productive in the offensive end and to allow our players freedom to be creative. In my opinion, however, the bottom line in lacrosse is that defense wins championships. When you look back at the many great Hopkins teams that have won championships, it's no accident that they played great defense. The Princeton Tigers of the 1990s were no different from these Hopkins teams. Both of these programs, although rich in offensive talent, made producing strong defensive teams their staple. Even the Syracuse Orange championship teams, despite being loaded with offensive stars—some of the game's greats—always played their best defense at the end of the year, come tournament time. Again, it should come as no surprise that these three programs have combined for the most championships in lacrosse.

The success of any lacrosse team normally depends upon its mastery of the fundamentals as well as the players' ability to work together. The ingredients for playing successful team defense are no different. Each player must lose himself in the team concept. Here at Hopkins, we talk about the *we* being more important than the *me:* the team always is more important than the individual. In defense, the goalie, three defensemen, and three midfielders must work together to form a well-coordinated group that presents a solid and unified front to the opposition. Each member of the defense must understand and be able to execute the responsibilities of playing his man as well as supporting his defen-

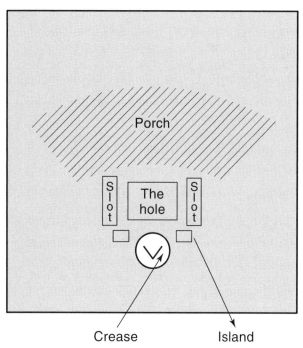

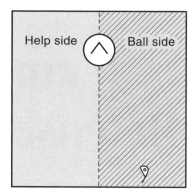

Figure 10.1 Defensive areas of the field.

sive teammates. The aim is not to make playing defense a one-on-one battle but rather to force the opposing team's offense to beat not only the on-ball defender but also his six defensive teammates—the five other defenders and the goalie. The support of these other defenders is paramount to playing successful defense.

The philosophy for our team defense follows the pattern established for individual defense. We call this the "part-whole principle": unless the parts fulfill their responsibilities, the whole will suffer.

DEFENSIVE AREAS

Before we discuss the specifics of team defense, it will be helpful to identify certain areas of the defensive end of the field. In chapter 9, we gave individual numbers to specific spots on the field. We will continue to use that numbering system but now apply additional terms to describe particular portions of the defensive end of the field. As shown in figure 10.1, these areas are the crease, the hole, the defensive box, the porch, the slot, the island, and ball side and help side.

The Crease

Around each goal is a plainly marked circle known as the crease. It has a radius of nine feet around from the center of the goal line. An attacking player may not enter the goal crease at any time. A defensive player may run through the crease as long as he does not have possession of the ball. He may gain possession of the ball while he is in the crease, but if he already has the ball, he cannot enter the crease from the outside. Should the goalie gain possession of the ball in the crease, he—or the ball—must leave the area within four seconds, meaning he either must get out of the crease or pass the ball within that period of time.

The Hole

The area eight to nine yards directly in front of the crease and four yards wide of it is the hole. It is the most dangerous area of the field, because any offensive player in this area, with or without the ball, is a potential scorer with a high-percentage shot. The defense must give this part of the field the highest priority for protection. In the hole, expect to see quite a bit of hard stick checking, physical contact, double-teaming, and sliding. Shots in this area usually are generated off of a feed—a pass either from out top or behind the goal.

The Slot

Just outside the hole area, about eight to ten yards above the crease and five to seven yards wide of it, are the areas we at Hopkins call the slots. As in hockey, shots that come from out in front and to the side of the goals are said to come from the slot—and they are quality shots. Another way to identify this area is to look at the hash markings on a football field. The slot is the area just inside and just outside the hash marks. Many shots from this area often are what we call "time and room" shots: the offensive player receives the ball with time to set up his shot and room to follow through on it, without having a defender on him. In addition, it is an area in which many shots are taken off a dodge, with a midfielder often executing a split dodge, running toward the goal, and firing a shot from the slot.

The Porch and the Perimeter

The area thirteen to twenty yards in front of the crease and eight or nine yards outside of the slot is what we at Hopkins call the porch. Beyond twenty yards of the crease, the area is called the perimeter. If our individual defenders do a good job of containing the ball carriers and if quality team defense is used, shots from the porch or beyond are all that will be available to the opposing offense. These are the low-percentage shots our defense is designed to encourage the other team to make. Shots from the porch and beyond (see chapters 6–8) are ones that can lead to the worst ball turnover in lacrosse—a weak attempt to score that usually hands the ball over to the defense. In the perimeter area, offensive players move the ball around a lot as they position themselves to initiate a dodge. They are not closely guarded there because they are too far from the goal to be effective. If they were to be played, they have so much running room that the defender will have difficulty maintaining his position. Also, the de-

fender may get overanxious and try to take the ball from his man, get dodged, and create a six-on-five scoring opportunity for the offense. In today's game, given the sophisticated development of the stick and the size and strength of many players, it is rare to see defensive players taking the ball away from their opponents in the porch or perimeter areas. The defense might try to go after the ball in the perimeter area only when their team is behind in the latter stages of the game and must gamble to get the ball.

The Island

The area five yards above the goal line and five yards wide of it is called the island. It is very dangerous to allow an offensive player to dodge from behind the goal and get to this area. Any offensive player in this area has several options: he can move toward the topside and shoot the ball, turn and shoot, or pass the ball. Both shots are high-percentage ones. If the defensive players allow a ball carrier to get to the island, they should be prepared for him to dodge before his shot.

The Ball Side and the Help Side

The term *ball side* refers to the area of the field that the offense with the ball is trying to penetrate. The term *help side* refers to the side of the field where the players who will help support the defensive players on the ball side are located.

DEVELOPING A TEAM DEFENSE

Under the Blue Jay lacrosse program's part-whole principle, our on-ball philosophy is designed to fit the needs of our team defensive plans. The part each player performs contributes to the whole. In addition to having a consistent defensive philosophy, our plan requires each defensive player to have a complete understanding of the what, the why, and the how. In other words, every individual must know *what* it is we are trying to accomplish on defense, *why* we are trying to accomplish these things, and *how* we can meet our specific individual and team defensive responsibilities.

We believe it is just as important to play solid

off-ball defense as on-ball defense. Indeed, I believe it is more difficult to play off-ball defense, because the player is responsible not only for playing his man but also for lending support to the on-ball defender. The on-ball defender has a single, simple responsibility—containing his man and forcing him into the areas of the field where we want him to go. Off-ball defenders have more responsibilities. They have to worry if their own man will get the ball and, if he does, where he might try to cut. They also must be concerned about what amount of support to provide if the on-ball defender is beaten by the ball carrier and he heads their way.

So when does a team begin to play defense? From our perspective at Hopkins, defense starts the moment our offense loses possession of the ball, whether it is through a shot, a save, an opposing player picking up a ground ball, or the ball going out-of-bounds. When we begin to ride, or attempt to block the opposing team from moving the ball into their offensive side of the field, that is the beginning of our team defense and our effort to get the ball back. We will discuss riding in chapter 15.

If the opposing team succeeds in bringing the ball across the midline into its offensive area of the field, our seven defensive players now must play team defense. We want to make sure our three midfielders, our three defensemen, and our goalie are in place, with each player positioned to cover his man. The first rule of defense is to stop the ball's penetration of that area. As we observed earlier, attackmen also must know the defensive plan and techniques in case they have to go over the midline and are forced to play defense.

Once the ball enters the defensive end, we must remember that the first responsibility is to stop the ball—stop penetration. Each defender should position himself according to where the offensive player he is covering is located on the field. It is imperative that the defensemen communicate with each other. At Hopkins, whenever we discuss defense, we talk about communication. That is because whenever the ball comes into our defensive end, we want to know who is stopping the ball; what defense we're in, whether it's man-to-man or zone; and who each player is covering. We never

want to have two defensemen playing one offensive opponent. Consequently, communication is paramount the moment the ball crosses the midline and the defense positions itself on the field.

This communication begins with the goaltender. He is our quarterback. He identifies where the ball is located and says who should stop the ball. He tells the defense what it should be doing. He calls out what the situation is, whether it's transition or six-on-six. He tells each of his teammates "Check up"—focus on their men and call out their jersey numbers. Then he will call out a defense, letting his teammates know if they should adopt a man-to-man defense or a zone defense. The defense then reacts accordingly.

The second phase of team communication begins once the defensive players know what defense they should adopt. They have to determine who will be the slide man (at Hopkins we call this the "hot player"); who will be the second slide man, or the person who supports the first slide man; who will be the third slide man, or the person who supports the second slide man; and so forth.

When the opposing team clears the ball into the offensive half of the field and the three midfielders and three defensemen drop back inside the perimeter to pick up their men, the defender playing the man with the ball should meet him just outside the porch. The other five defenders should "slough in" or "sag off" their men at varying distances, which are determined by the location of the offensive players to the goal and to the ball. The terms *sloughing-in* and *sagging-off* describe how an off-ball defender distances himself far enough from his man to lend the appropriate support within the team defense but is close enough so that if his man receives the ball, he will be able to move quickly to cover him. A defender can slough in only to the point where he can effectively guard his man if he were to receive the ball. The farther the offensive men are from the ball, the farther the defensive players can be from their men.

The sloughing-in technique is a vital part of team defense because it places the five defenders in a position to help out their teammate who is playing the ball.

To simplify the identification of men on the field,

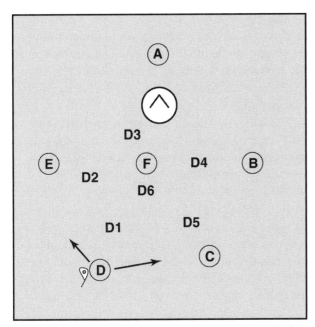

Figure 10.2 Positioning of defensive players on the ball side and help side.

an imaginary line can be drawn down the middle of the field from the midline through the center of each goal. As explained earlier, the half of the field where the ball is located is the ball side, and the other half of the field where the ball is not located is the help side.

In figure 10.2, the offensive players are depicted as circles and the defensive players are identified by letters. Players A, D, E, and F are on the ball side; players C and B are on the help side. The help-side defenders are sloughed farthest from their men because those offensive players are the least dangerous when they are so far from the ball. The ball-side defenders are sloughed off their men, but not quite as far as their help-side teammates.

The five defenders who are playing the opponents without the ball must use their peripheral vision to locate both the ball and their man. They cannot afford to take a long look at the ball and let their man cut by them toward the goal. Then again, if they play their man eye-to-eye, they will not be in a position to assist the teammate who is playing the ball and in need of their support. Therefore, quick turns of the head, as well as use of peripheral vision, will assist the defenders in locating both their man and the ball. At Hopkins, we call this

technique "big eye, man–little eye, ball," a phrase coined by coaching great Fred Smith. This means that an off-ball defender wants to give the majority of his attention to his man, but since these defenders are in a supporting role, they must also give some of their attention to the ball. Another way to describe this is "two-to-one": the defender wants to have his head on a swivel and give two looks to his man and one look to the ball.

Another basic rule for defenders who are playing men without the ball is that they can give more of their attention to their men when the ball is moving around the perimeter or when the player with the ball is not attacking the goal. However, when the player with the ball begins to attack the goal, the off-ball defenders must give more of their attention to supporting the on-ball defender than worrying about their own men.

A rule of thumb is that when the ball is in the midfield, the defenders who are guarding men behind the goal should always position themselves in front of the goal to enable them to lend support within the team defense. There is no reason for them to go behind the goal and cover their men there, because opponents who are behind the goal are in an area where they cannot score. On the other hand, if a dodge is not imminent and the opponent's attackmen exchange positions behind the goal, the defenders must stay with them and move from one side of the goal to the other.

MAN-TO-MAN AND ZONE DEFENSE

Although there are two basic types of team defense, the man-to-man and the zone, these often have many variations to them. The most popular basic defense is man-to-man. In man-to-man defense, each defender is responsible for his man, although he remains involved in a team-defense concept. If your man leaves a specific area, you will go with him. In a man-to-man defense, teams often will put pressure on the ball and extend a little bit on the perimeter. A man-to-man defense will be used to stretch the opponent's offense—to force the offensive players farther away from the goal. A man-to-man defense can be used if the defensive team wants to pick up the tempo of the game and force the offense to stretch, dodge at more inopportune times, and make longer passes, thereby perhaps creating more turnovers. You will want to pick up the pace of the game if you have a clear athletic advantage.

In a zone defense, a defender is charged with playing whichever offensive player enters his area, or zone. If his man leaves that area, the defender passes him off to a teammate and continues to protect his area. In a zone, the areas that are most crucial to protect are the dangerous ones where quality shots are generated. It makes no sense to protect areas that are not dangerous. A zone defense is used when a team feels that it may be inferior athletically and that to go out and cover offensive players farther away from the goal only ensures defeat. The zone is used if you want to slow down the pace of the game. Because you're just defending the most dangerous areas, the offense has to work more methodically to attack those parts of the field. A coach might use a zone if the opposing team is not so good at shooting. They may have an athletic advantage, but they don't shoot the ball well from the porch. And if they don't shoot well from the porch, it may make sense to defend those areas inside the porch and let the opposing team shoot from the area outside of it. A team with a superior goaltender might also use the zone, whereas a team with a goaltender who is not that effective facing shots from the perimeter may choose to employ the man-to-man defense.

Although we employ multiple defensive plans at Hopkins, our basic go-to defense is a man-to-man. Our man-to-man defense, however, is a sloughing man-to-man and combines some of the principles of zone defense.

This can be seen in figure 10.2. Our defensive players are not extended all over the perimeter to try to take the ball away, thus forcing our opponent to go to the goal. Instead, our philosophy is to play the ball and slough in on the perimeter to protect the more dangerous areas of the field—which is much like a zone. While we play the ball, with each man responsible for an offensive player, the concept of sloughing-in is more compatible with the zone principle. Although the defenseman has his man, he also

will slough off of him when he is not in a dangerous area in order to lend more support to the on-ball defender. If his man moves into a more dangerous area, the defenseman will move closer to him. If he leaves an area, we will follow him. In this way, we combine zone and man-to-man defenses.

The Hopkins man-to-man team defense is very play-oriented, meaning we often use it against an opponent who runs set plays. By using an aggressive man-to-man defense, you may throw off the timing of those plays, force your opponent's passes within those plays to be longer, or force the player with the ball to have to run by you because you're pressuring him. Similarly, if a team uses set plays designed to combat a man-to-man defense and you employ a zone defense, those plays may not create the quality shots the offensive team is seeking.

The man with the ball is the most dangerous player on the field, and the defender opposing him must know his strengths and be prepared to stop him. A scouting report can be of tremendous help, but if one is not available, the defender will just have to size up his opponent during the course of play. It is critical to remember, however, that our on-ball, team defense philosophy is guided by where the ball is located on the field and not by whether the ball carrier's strength is as a right-handed or left-handed player, with the exception of when he is in the middle of the field. Since most offensive players today are capable of going to the goal both right-handed and left-handed, the most important factor for the defender is his awareness of his opponent's position on the field. As we explained earlier, our focus is to try to encourage low-percentage shots from specific areas of the field. This being the case, we have to remember that how we play the ball is determined by where the ball is located, not by what might be the offensive player's strong hand.

When the offensive player is located behind the goal anywhere in area 1 (see figure 10.3), the defender must primarily be concerned with his opponent's attempts to drive toward the topside (the front of the goal) for a right-handed shot. The goalie identifies area 1 as "right behind" or "back right," and this call helps condition the defender to think, "I'm on the right-hander's side—take away the topside and force him

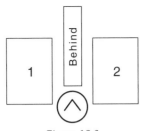
Figure 10.3

back behind the goal." A key reason for being primed to stop the right-handed shot in area 1 is that the offensive player's route to the goal is shorter. If the offensive player goes from area 1 to area 2, the defender has the ability to go through the crease to shorten his own distance to that dangerous spot just below the goal line, beating the offensive player there while still maintaining his position and taking away the topside.

When the ball is in area B, which we call X-behind, the goalie will call "Center behind" or "X-behind." This is the most difficult area for the defender, because the offensive player can make his move to the front of the goal by going either right- or left-handed. The attacker's route to the goal is almost a straight line, compared to his following the arc of the circle when moving from area 1 to area 2 and vice versa. The defender still may cut through the crease to get to the front of the goal, but he doesn't have as much advantage as when the attacker is in area 1 or area 2. Area X-behind is the toughest spot to defend behind the goal, and therefore, as we said earlier, the defenseman must take away the offensive player's strong hand and force him to advance with his weak one.

Sliding (Backing Up)

As lacrosse has evolved, sliding—or backing up—has come to play a much more important role in team defenses. In today's game, many teams play a man-to-man defense that involves quite a bit of sliding. In years past, team defense involved more of a "I have my man, you have your man" philosophy than is the case in today's game. Now, although every player has his man, each defensive player also has an important role in supporting the on-ball defender. Few teams in today's game will allow a dodger to beat them for a goal. The ability to

slide or support correctly is central to executing a successful team defense.

There are several locations from which a defenseman can slide to support the on-ball defender. One location involves the defensive players directly beside, or adjacent to, the on-ball defender. The other involves the defenders on the crease. Although there is merit to using both of these defenses, the simpler of the two is the one that employs the adjacent slide. At the college level, both the adjacent-sliding and the crease-sliding defense are used throughout a game. How the offense is attacking or where specific offensive players may be located on the field often determines which defense is used.

At Johns Hopkins, we use both the adjacent-sliding defense and the crease-sliding defense, but when we begin to teach team defense to our players, even at the highest level, we always start with the adjacent-sliding defense. Not only is this the most basic of the two defensive maneuvers, but it also helps our defenders to understand and learn how to rotate. Understanding how to rotate correctly will help them when we move to a more complicated defensive strategy, such as the crease-sliding defense.

Sliding or backing up is the key to establishing the necessary support for the on-ball defender. Each member of the defensive unit is responsible for backing up the on-ball defender in case he gets into trouble or is dodged successfully by the ball carrier. The defensive players adjacent to the man playing the ball carrier will let him know loud and clear that they are supporting him on either side.

In figure 10.4, player D5 will call out to D1, "I have your help, left." That tells the on-ball defender that if he is beaten to his left, D5 will slide to help him. D2 has D1's right and will call out, "I have your right." D3 will tell D2, "If you slide, I have your back." D4 will call out to D5, "If you slide, I have your back." As the ball is passed around by the offense, the defense will slide, or rotate, toward the ball, or "into the ball," not away from it. If D1 is beaten to his left, D2 will be the first to slide; D3 would rotate to cover D2's man. As D3 vacates his initial area, D4 moves to cover D3's man, and D5 moves to cover D4's man. Ul-

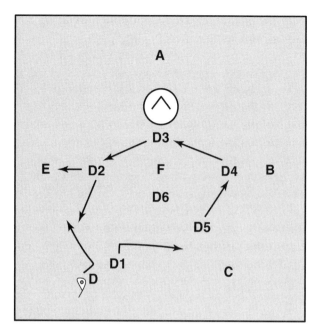

Figure 10.4 Adjacent sliding defense.

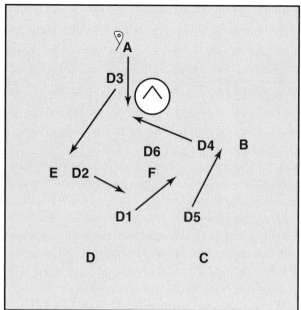

Figure 10.5 Adjacent sliding against a dodge from behind the goal.

timately, the only offensive player left open is C, who is the farthest player from the ball, and the defenseman who will go cover him is D1, after D2 slides to support him.

When employing the adjacent-slide defense, it is important for the adjacent defenders to be sloughed in and not too close to their own men. This is because whenever you execute a slide, you want to slide from "inside the ball," or from the inside of the defense out rather than from the outside of the defense in. Our main defensive aim when we slide is to stop the ball carrier. Our next aim is to force that player to move toward the perimeter or some similar, less-dangerous area, such as the sideline or the end line. In order to force the offensive players away from the goal, the defense wants to align itself so that it can slide from inside of the defense, or from an area closer to the crease, and prevent the offense from penetrating the more dangerous areas closer to the goal. By sliding from the inside out, the defense seeks to force the ball carrier and his teammates away from the goal. If the defense is aligned "outside the ball" when the players begin their slides, the ball carrier actually can be driven toward the more dangerous areas rather than away from them.

A full defense always involves seven players—the six defenders and the goalie. If the defensive players coordinate properly to support each other, play the ball correctly, and force it to the less-dangerous areas of the field, they should be able to stop the offense.

Figure 10.5 shows how to slide adjacent against a dodge from behind the goal. Player A has the ball. D3 is the on-ball defender. As explained earlier, when playing the ball out top, you want to force the ball carrier down the sides, as shown in figure 10.4. In figure 10.5, the defense's aim is to ensure that if the ball carrier beats the defender, the dodger only can do so by going underneath. The defense's aim on any dodge from behind the goal is to make certain the ball carrier cannot beat the defender to the topside.

In the adjacent-sliding defense shown in figure 10.5, defender D4 is D3's backup to his right. D2 is his backup to the left if he is beaten to the topside. Should D3 be beaten underneath—as we would prefer—D4 then moves to stop the ball carrier and cover D3's man. D5 rotates over one spot to cover D4's man. D1 rotates over to cover D5's man. Since the ball carrier has moved underneath, D becomes the offensive teammate of his who is farthest from the ball and the most difficult to whom he could make a pass. Offensive player E remains dangerous. Consequently, D2 is going to have to cover both D and E until D3 rotates from the ball carrier and moves to E. Then D2 can rotate to D. As a result of these moves, all of the defenders have rotated one spot into the ball. Each man in this defense is supported by the adjacent defender.

To make an effective slide involves a specific technique. A common mistake made by defenders executing a slide is to try to hit the ball carrier when making contact with him. By doing so, the defenders very easily could be knocked out of position. That will give the dodger a clear path to the goal for a shot, without any defenseman directly on him. Instead, in a properly executed slide, the adjacent defender will meet the ball carrier in an area of the field where he does not yet have a shot and force that offensive player away from the goal into a less-dangerous area of the field. A defenseman sliding toward a dodger also should have his stick out in front of him. This will allow him to reach the ball carrier sooner, given the length of his stick, and to position it in the area of the offensive player's gloves or the numbers on his jersey. This will inhibit his man's ability to shoot or to pass the ball. The defender wants to force the ball carrier to either take a poor shot or pass the ball to a teammate. Should the defender meet the ball carrier in an area that is too close to the goal, there's a good chance that by the time the defender gets there, the ball carrier will have an opportunity to take a shot and possibly score.

PLAYING THE CUTTER

When playing off-ball defense, one of the most difficult things to do is to defend against a cutter. Offensive players can make two types of cuts: toward the ball or toward the goal. In both instances, the defender must keep himself between the player with the ball and the player who is cutting.

Once an offensive player begins to make his cut, it is important for the defensemen to keep themselves between the ball carrier and the man they are guarding. Consequently, their attention changes from concentrating on where the ball is and where their

man is to focusing specifically on where their man is located. This enables them to check their man if he is the cutter to whom the ball will be thrown. The defenders will rely on the goaltender to alert him with "Check!" when the ball is fed to his man.

The position of the defender's stick is also important when defending against a cutter. When a cutter is moving toward the ball carrier or toward the goal, the defender must keep his stick in the ready position—held in the air, parallel to his body—so that if the ball is passed to his cutter, he can execute a check immediately to keep that player from catching the ball or shooting it. A common mistake among defenders covering cutters is to keep their sticks down around their hips. When the ball is passed to their cutter, they then have to bring their stick up to the ready position before they can execute a check. This takes too much time and easily could provide an offensive player an excellent opportunity to catch and shoot the ball. If defensemen have their sticks in the ready position, they will be prepared to make the check quickly.

When executing a check, the defender wants to aim for the area between his opponent's gloves and forearm, or between his elbow and bottom hand. Doing this will hamper or impede the offensive player's ability to catch, pass, or shoot the ball. The defender never wants to aim for the offensive player's pole or the head of his stick, because the offensive player's pole or stick head usually is located close to his helmet. Should the defender throw a check to the pole or stick head and miss, he very easily could hit the offensive player in the helmet, causing a foul and drawing a penalty.

DEFENDING THE CREASE

The offensive player who is on the crease or in the hole area is especially dangerous. It is simple to understand why. Because he is located directly in front of the goal, when he catches the ball he possesses a better angle to shoot it than anyone else. He must be played extremely tightly by his defender.

When the ball is behind the goal, the responsibilities of the defender covering the man on the crease will be much the same as those of the defender playing the cutter. Although he wants to maintain his position between the man with the ball and the player he is covering, he also wants to make sure he remains face-to-face with his man and not be concerned with locating the ball. A crease defender who spends too much time looking for the ball may lose sight of his man, allowing him to break for an open space. Simply put, the crease defender wants to follow his man and forget about the ball. The goalie, who is always watching the ball, acts as the eyes for the defender on the crease. The crease defender's ears help to compensate him for not being able to see the ball. He listens intently for the goalie's calls giving the location of the ball behind the goal—"Right behind," "Center behind," or "Left behind"—as well as the goalie's call to "Check." When the defender hears "Check!" he will take his stick, which he has been holding in the ready position, and follow through with an aggressive stick check to the gloves or forearm of the offensive player on the crease.

As mentioned earlier, there are several types of sliding defense. The adjacent-sliding defense puts very little pressure on the crease defenseman. A crease-sliding defense, however, puts much greater pressure on the crease defender because he has the responsibility not only for covering his man but also for supporting the on-ball defender. The crease-sliding defense is much more difficult because of the greater pressure it puts on the defender covering the player who is in the most dangerous area of the field.

In figure 10.6, the defender on the crease (D6) is positioned between his man and the ball, with his back to the ball-side sideline. This allows him to see his man and keep an eye on him if he moves, as well as to see the ball and know when he may have to slide to support the on-ball defender. The most difficult thing for a crease defender to do in this position is to maintain his ability to fulfill both of his responsibilities well. Often, the crease defender spends too much time watching the ball and loses sight of the offensive player on the crease. Yet if he spends too much time watching his man, he may not be able to slide quickly and support the on-ball

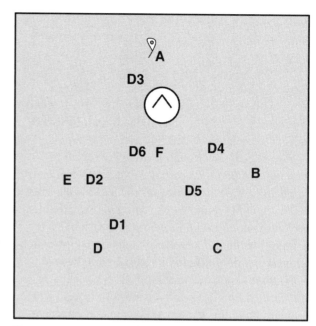

Figure 10.6 Positioning of a crease defender.

defender if he is dodged successfully by the ball carrier. The crease defenseman must play with his head on a swivel, constantly moving to see both his man and the ball. In the crease-sliding defense, it also is critical for the crease defenseman to have the support of his defensive teammates, who must sag toward the crease to help him out.

PLAYING PICKS

The pick is an offensive technique that is used in lacrosse in just about the same manner as in basketball and several other team sports. A pick is a simple yet effective way for one offensive player to block the defense in order to free another offensive player.

The defense can be presented with two different challenges when playing against a pick. One is defending against a pick that has been set to enable the offensive player with the ball to break free and head toward a dangerous area; the other is to defend against a pick that has been set for an offensive player without the ball—but who may be a prime candidate to receive it. Playing a pick on the ball involves defending against two offensive players—one who has the ball and another who is try-

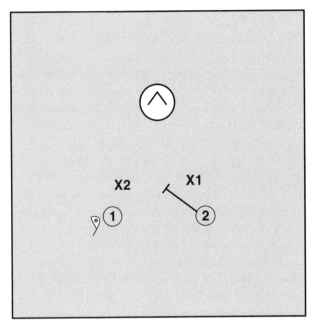 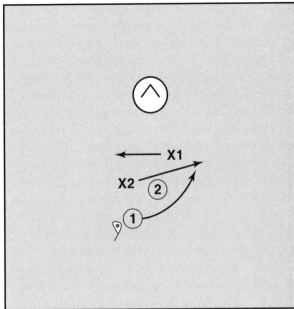

Figure 10.7 and Figure 10.8 A defender playing a pick on the ball.

Picks On the Ball

Playing a pick on the ball can involve two different defensive philosophies. One favors switching men automatically, and the other favors keeping our matchups and sliding the defender past the pick whenever possible, switching only when the defender who is playing the ball has difficulty getting through the pick. The approach at Hopkins is to avoid the automatic switch when defending on-ball picks and to emphasize trying to have each player stay with his own man. As a basic rule, the switch is used only when the man playing the ball has difficulty getting through the pick, or is "bumped off."

As in every aspect of defense, communication between the two defenders handling the pick is essential. It should include a preparatory warning and a command. Since the defender who is playing the ball normally doesn't concentrate on the offensive player who is setting the pick, he must receive help from his teammate who is defending the pick man. The

ing to free him. Playing a pick off the ball involves defending against two offensive players who do not have the ball, but one is trying to free the other to enable him to get in a position to receive the ball.

defender playing the pick man does most of the communicating, since he does not have the responsibility for playing the ball carrier. He is able to see the pick developing, whereas the on-ball defender does not. As he sees a pick being set up, it is his responsibility to make the call to the on-ball defender.

In figure 10.7, player X1 will call to X2 by his name, warning, "Watch the pick on your left; get through." X2 then is alerted to the pick and understands that he is responsible for maneuvering through it. If the pick is executed poorly and O1, the offensive player with the ball, does not utilize the pick correctly, X2 can go over the top of the pick. This is not the preferred route, but it is a viable option. If the pick is set properly, however, X1 will call to his teammate, by name, "Pick on your left; get through," and X2 will move underneath the pick, or between O2 and X1. This is the preferred method. If X2 tries to get through over the top against a good, solid pick, he will either get bumped off or end up trailing behind the ball carrier. This will affect his ability to keep the ball carrier from getting to the goal. See figure 10.8.

The on-ball defender must listen carefully for his teammate's call that a pick is being set. When he is alerted to the pick, the on-ball defender, for a split second, must locate the pick so that he knows exactly where it is and can make a smooth transition getting through it. He can do this simply by quickly lifting his head, locating the pick, and then swiftly bringing his attention back to the ball carrier. As the on-ball defender approaches the pick, he should lift his stick to a straight up-and-down position in an effort to keep it from making contact with the player setting the pick. Failing to do so could impede his ability to get through the pick or possibly result in a penalty if the on-ball defender's stick hits or makes contact with the pick man. Once the on-ball defender gets past the pick, he immediately should bring his stick down and direct it toward the gloves of the ball carrier.

If X2, the on-ball defender, gets bumped off by the pick and a switch is necessary, X1, the defender who is playing the pick, will take advantage of where he has set himself—about two yards wide of his man and two yards back, in what is called a "hedging" position. If the pick defender does not hedge and places himself directly behind the pick man, he will end up trailing the ball carrier to the front of the goal when the switch is made. Because it takes a second or two to determine whether a switch is necessary and react accordingly if it is, hedging is critical.

As soon as the defender playing the pick man decides that the switch is necessary, he must shout "Switch!" loud and clear to his teammate to leave no doubt that they are to exchange men. The switch call must come from the defender playing the pick, because he is the one who sees the entire play developing. In some instances, the switch can be made aggressively by defender X1, who will try to turn back the ball carrier as he comes off the pick. If X1 is able to do this, X2 has a golden opportunity to double-team the ball carrier and knock the ball to the ground. However, if on the switch the pick man cuts to the goal, X2 must react quickly and position himself between his man and the ball. He should hold his stick in the ready position, listen for the goalie's check call, and be ready to break up a return pass from the ball carrier (O1) to the pick man (O2). This maneuver is the same as one used by basketball players defending against a pick-and-roll play.

Picks Off the Ball

The technique used to play a pick that is set off the ball is similar to what was described for picks on the ball. The difference, of course, is that neither offensive player has the ball. The two offensive players who are executing the pick are doing so to confuse the defense, create mismatches, and potentially free an offensive player—"spring him open"—so that he can catch and shoot the ball or head toward the goal without a defender on him. The off-ball picking game most often is used in the crease area. Since this is such a dangerous part of the field, creating confusion or springing a teammate open often can lead to quality opportunities for the offense.

As explained earlier, the defense has two basic ways to play picks. One way is to get through the pick, and the other is to switch. When defending picks on the ball or on the perimeter, it is much easier and far less dangerous to try to get through. When playing against a pick on the crease, however, it is more dangerous to try to get through, because should an offensive player free himself for a split second, he very easily may have a chance for a pass, a shot, and a goal.

Consequently, when defending against a pick on the crease, it is best to use the switching technique. This will ensure that the defenders will be positioned in such a way as to never trail behind the offensive players—remain between them and the man with the ball—and thereby prevent them from getting quality opportunities to receive a pass and shoot the ball. No matter where the ball is located, the two players on the crease will switch whenever the pick is set. Communication between the defenders is critical, as always, and the defender whose man is setting the pick will do the majority of the communicating. In figure 10.9, as offensive player O1 approaches X2 to set a pick, X1 will call to his teammate that a pick is being set on his right and will tell him that they will play the switch. As offensive player O1 sets the pick on X2 and offensive player O2 uses that pick, X1 will switch to O2 and X2 will switch to O1. By doing this, both defenders maintain their position between the man with the ball and their man. It is important for the defenders playing the switch on the crease always to keep their sticks

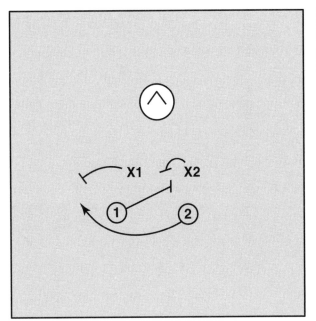

Figure 10.9

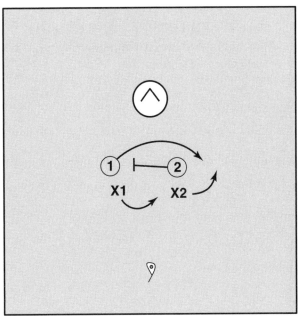

Figure 10.10 Playing a pick when the ball is out top.

in the ready position, so that if the ball is passed to the crease, they will be prepared to check their man and prevent him from taking a shot.

In figure 10.10, the ball is located out top—but the location of the ball does not change how picks on the crease are played. As offensive player O2 sets a pick for O1, X2 will call to X1 that a pick is being set on his left and that they are going to switch. Once player O1 comes off that pick, X2 will switch and position himself between the man with the ball and his new man, and X1 will position himself between the ball and his man.

HIGHLIGHTS OF TEAM DEFENSE

Communication is critical.

Defense is teamwork. It is not about one individual.

Know the responsibilities of being a defender on the ball as well as those of being a defender off the ball. Playing off-ball defense is more difficult than covering the ball carrier.

Good team defense consists of six players who work together as a unit. No player is left without backup.

The aim of on-ball defense is to force the ball carrier to the least-dangerous areas of the field.

The farther your man is from the ball, the farther you can be from your man.

The closer your man is to the ball, the closer you should be to your man.

Off-ball defenders always should use the big eye, man–little eye, ball technique (two looks to your man, one look to the ball).

When defending off the ball, always maintain a position between your man and the ball carrier. The aim of the defense is to contain, not take away, the ball. Attempting to take the ball away can put you out of position. Such a risk can lessen your ability to contain the offense.

When playing picks on the ball or on the perimeter, maintain the defender-opponent matchup and strive to get through the pick.

When defending picks on the crease, switch the defender-opponent matchup always to maintain your position between the ball and your man.

When sliding adjacent to the ball carrier, execute the slide from the inside out, not the outside in.

When playing a cutter, always stay between your man and the ball.

The defender playing the pick does most of the communicating and coordinates how the pick will be played.

The aim of this type of defense is to force the offense to take low-percentage shots.

The goalie is the quarterback of the defense. He will communicate where the ball is located and what defensive technique will be used.

Never rush out to cover the ball carrier. Approach him carefully, and use the appropriate on-ball stance when you reach him.

Hopkins midfielder Benson Erwin breaks upfield against Virginia
in the regular-season match of 2005. *Jay Van Rensselaer*

Benson Erwin (JHU '05) and longstick middie Greg Raymond
(JHU '05) move out with a loose ball. *Jay Van Rensselaer*

11

Transition

Some of the most thrilling action in lacrosse takes place during transition plays. A team gains possession of the ball in its defensive half of the field, moves at top speed to bypass a lagging defender, quickly gains a numerical advantage, and sprints toward its opponent's goal to capitalize on its superiority in numbers. The defensive players must scramble to get back into the hole area and form a tightly knit unit to handle the offensive thrust. Swift, pinpoint passing by the offense can lead to a high-percentage shot, a goalie's spectacular save, or a breakup of the scoring by quick-reacting defenders who are outnumbered by the offense.

Transitions, or unsettled situations, actually can be created anywhere on the field. They can come off of a face-off win or off of a ground ball. Most often, however, a transition originates in a team's defensive end of the field and moves rapidly to the offensive end.

Throughout the 1980s and 1990s, transition goals may have accounted for almost 40 percent of all the scoring in games. In today's game, however, there is a greater emphasis on six-on-six play, half-field offense, and half-field defense. This has caused a decrease in the number of transitions that take place in a game. Nevertheless, perhaps more than 30 percent of goals scored today still come from some type of transitional or unsettled situation, whether it be a four-on-three off of a face-off, a five-on-four, or a six-on-five. In every game, transition opportunities do occur, and it is critical for a team to know how to handle these situations from both a defensive and an offensive perspective. We will treat each phase of play separately, starting with defense.

TRANSITION DEFENSE

Before we explain exactly how to defend each type of transition, let's outline a number of key components to transition defense that apply in every unsettled situation. At Hopkins, we call them collectively "the RCR" (recognition, communication, and reaction).

1. The team's defense must *recognize* when their opponent's offense is gaining a numerical advantage.

2. No defense can be successful without *communication,* and the goalie is the chief communicator. He must alert his defense to the fact that they will be defending against a transition and what type of unsettled situation it is.

3. How a team *reacts* is determined by how many defenders it has available in the unsettled situation. *The number of the opponent's offensive players does not matter.* The key is to realize that they have an advantage.

4. Never slide up the field.

5. Stay tight. Force the offense to shoot from the perimeter.

6. One defender must always be responsible for stopping the ball carrier from penetrating the defense.

7. "Step to the hat" on all slides made in an unsettled situation. At Hopkins, we put an imaginary hat in the middle of our defensive formation. If we're in a triangle or a box, the hat's at its center. What "step to the hat" means is that each time a player executes a slide, the first thing we want him to do is step toward the middle of the field. Stepping to the middle ensures that rather than getting spread out on all our slides, the defenders will get tighter and tighter. As we will explain later in this chapter, each offensive player is taught to move to the ball as it is passed to him. Stepping to the hat by the defense will allow us to improve our angle to defend against passes and shots by sliding to where the offensive player is moving rather than sliding straight up the field to where he may have been.

8. Everything we do is from the inside out. This tactic is very similar to our adjacent-sliding defense, in which we want our defense to be inside the offense and working to push the offense farther out on the perimeter.

9. Keep your sliding disciplined and under control to ensure that you break down the offense and are not dodged successfully by it.

10. Buy as much time as you can. You want to force the offense to make as many passes as possible so that a defender who is hustling to get in the hole to help has the time to do it and have an impact on the play.

11. When the extra defender has gotten into the hole and the defense now has the same numbers as the offense does, look away. This means that everyone other than the man who is playing the ball should look away from the ball and find a person to cover.

We're now going to describe the types of transitions, beginning with the simplest—the two-on-one.

The Two-on-One

A two-on-one can occur at any time or any place in the defensive end. It can happen if a defender slips. It can happen off of a ground ball. It can happen off of a failed clear, when defenders are arranged in different areas of the field, a pass is intercepted by the offense, and only one defender is close enough to get into the hole to play defense. In a two-on-one, a defender finds himself in real trouble. Obviously, it is very difficult for one defender to play two offensive players. Still, there are certain things he can do to successfully defend a two-on-one. Look at figure 11.1. First, D1 wants to buy time to allow a teammate the opportunity to recover into the defense. Second, he wants to be sure he splits the two offensive players. If D1 gives too much attention to the player with the ball, there could be a quick pass to the second offensive player for a layup, or a high-percentage shot. If D1 gives too much attention to the off-ball player, or O2, and does not stop the ball, the ball carrier could just go right past him for a layup.

The lone defender confronted with two attackers moving toward the goal must drop into position no farther than seven or eight yards from the goal.

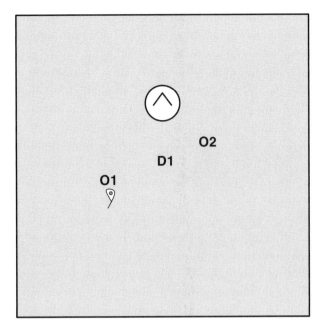

Figure 11.1 The two-on-one transition defense.

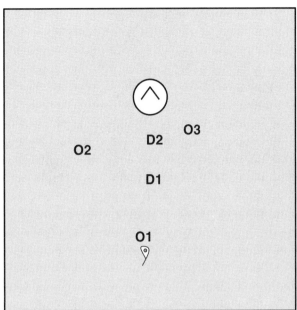

Figure 11.2 The three-on-two transition defense.

Here, his main aim is not only to buy time to allow another defender to recover but also to knock down a pass if possible, check an offensive player as he shoots, or force the offense to throw a poor pass. As players O1 and O2 move toward the goal, it is critical that D1 plays with his stick in the passing lane between them, ready to knock down a pass. D1 can play a cat-and-mouse game with O1 and O2. By faking a slide to the player with the ball (O1), he hopes to force that player to pass the ball to O2 or to make a low-percentage shot. If O1 passes the ball to O2, the defender tries to knock the pass down. If he is unable to do so, he then moves with the pass and plays O2. If O2 passes back to O1, D1 moves back to cover O1. The defender attempts to make O1 and O2 pass the ball as many times as possible, with the hope that one of these passes will be a poor one and possibly go out-of-bounds or that he can knock the ball down or buy enough time for a teammate to recover to the defensive end.

The Three-on-Two

When two defenders are confronted with three attackers moving toward the goal, these defenders must drop into position no farther than eight to ten yards from the goal (figure 11.2). The two defenders

position themselves in an "i" formation. D1 will be the closest to the ball carrier, and D2 will be about a stick's length behind D1 so that D1 is dotting the "i" of D2. The first priority for D1 is to stop the player with the ball from penetrating the defense, keeping him about ten yards from the goal. When he does so, O1 will pass to one of his teammates. In this case, D1 will attempt to knock this pass down. As soon as O1 passes the ball to O2, D1 will turn and face the ball—or "open to the ball"—and never lose sight of it. He then will slide into a position where he can cover O1 and O3. In this situation, he will be splitting two offensive players.

It is important that D1 gives more of his attention to the player who is closer to the goal and less of his attention to the player who is farther from the goal. In figure 11.3, you can see that O3 is more dangerous, or closer to the goal, than O1. Once the ball is passed and D1 opens to the ball and splits the two offensive players, D2 will slide from his position toward O2 in order to stop O2 from shooting or penetrating the defense. He will not extend any farther than ten yards from the goal and six or seven yards wide of the goal. D2 must be careful not to rush out too hard at O2 and give him the opportunity to dodge past for a point-blank shot. If O1

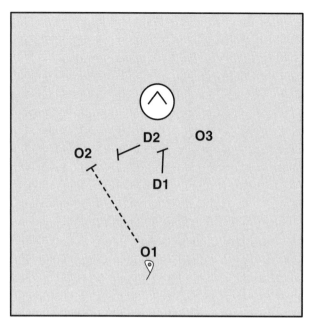

Figure 11.3 Second phase of the three-on-two transition defense.

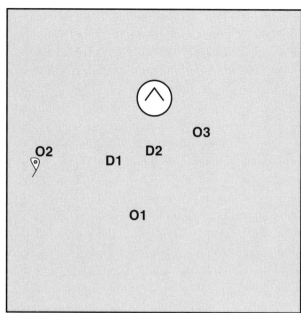

Figure 11.4 The three-on-two defense if offensive player approaches from the side instead of the middle.

should throw his initial pass to O3, then D2 should slide toward O3, and D1 would split O1 and O2.

If the three-on-two transition approaches the goal from the side rather than the middle of the field, as shown in figure 11.4, the two defensemen again will arrange themselves in an "i" formation facing the ball. D1 is responsible for stopping O2, the man with the ball, no father than eight or nine yards from the goal, and D2 is responsible for playing both O1 and O3. If O2 passes the ball to O1, D2 will move toward him, not extending past ten yards, trying to force him to pass the ball to O3 or shoot while being checked. D1 will then slide toward the middle of the field in an effort to split O2 and O3. In figure 11.5, as the ball is passed from O2 to O1, D2 will slide toward the ball to stop O1 from shooting or penetrating the defense, and D1 will slide toward the middle of the field in an effort to split O2 and O3. It is important to remember that each time D1 or D2 slides, they first step to the hat so that they don't rotate too far away from the goal.

The Four-on-Three Fast Break

The four-on-three fast break is probably one of the most exciting plays in lacrosse. The defense must

meet the challenge of an opponent racing ahead of his man toward the goal. This places the three defensemen in a difficult situation, because they must defend against four attackers. The key to an effective fast-break defense is training the three defensemen to form a closely knit triangle within eleven yards of the goal. By forming a tight triangle, the defense is covering the hole area and preventing openings on the crease, which would give the offense point-blank shots at the goal.

The goalie, as always, is the director of the defense. In fact, he and his defensemen must anticipate a fast break occurring and prepare their strategy for it in advance. If the ball is in a team's offensive end, the three defenders and the goalie must always be communicating and preparing for a fast break, determining before it ever takes place who is going to cover the point position (closest to the restraining line), who is going to cover the left, and who is going to cover the right in the triangle. Should a fast break take place, the goalie identifies it by shouting instructions to his defense. An example of his commands to the defense would be "Fast break, fast break, four-on-three, drop in." At that time, each defender again will communicate his po-

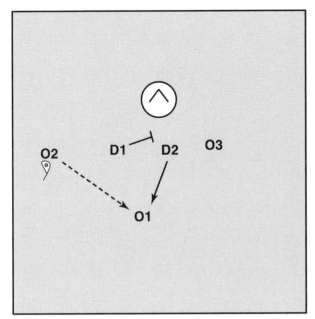

Figure 11.5 Second phase of the three-on-two defense on approach from the side.

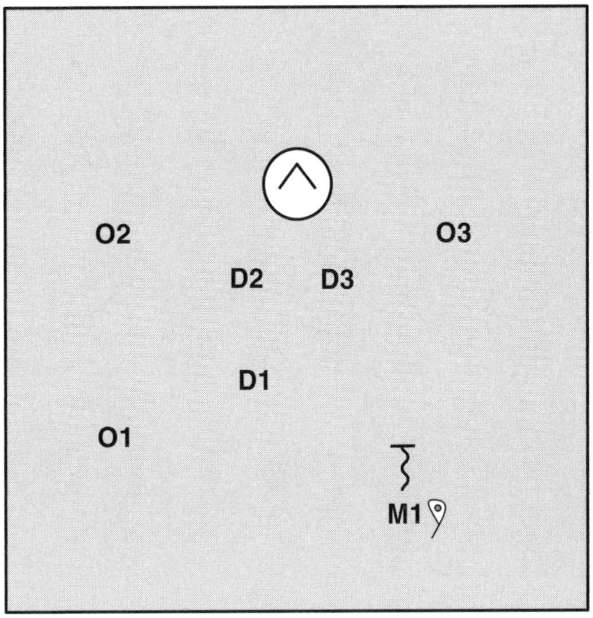

Figure 11.6 The four-on-three fast-break defense.

sition in the triangle and shout, "I have the point," "I have the left," "I have the right," as shown in figure 11.6. Communication helps to minimize any uncertainty or hesitation by the defenders. It is imperative that each knows which position he will be manning and the responsibilities of that position.

Before analyzing these responsibilities, let us consider the general principles that apply to all three defensemen:

1. When a fast break is identified, all three defenders immediately run at full speed to their positions in a tight triangle. As they are running into position, they should turn their heads and try to keep the ball in sight. When we had two defenders, we were aligned in an "i" formation. When we had one defender, we were in a dot. As you'll later see, when the defense has four defenders, they will form a box; when the defense has five defenders, they will form a box-in-one.

2. Once in the tight triangle, the defenders are more concerned with watching the ball than their man. Since the offense has an extra man, zone principles are in effect, not man-to-man defensive principles. In this situation, we use big eye, ball–little eye, man, unlike in our six-on-six defense.

3. All three defenders should hold their sticks in the passing lanes and in position to block the offense's passes.

4. A keen sense of anticipation of the next pass will aid the defense tremendously and often help in defending a break.

5. The defender covering the man with the ball must move quickly to him, but under control. He must be careful not to rush at him and overcommit. If he does, the attacker has an easy opportunity to either face dodge or split dodge the defender and take a point-blank shot at the goal.

6. If a shot is taken and successfully blocked, the goalie and all the defensive players should be ready to follow the ball, and if it is headed out-of-bounds, they should race to run it out. The man closest to the ball when it goes out-of-bounds will gain possession of it. Often attackmen are not in a favorable position to back up a shot when on a four-on-three because all four offensive players are above the goal line. They can be beaten to the boundary line.

7. Once the fast break is stopped and the defense becomes all-even, the last defender getting into the hole area must communicate to everyone, "All even, all even." At this point, each defender will

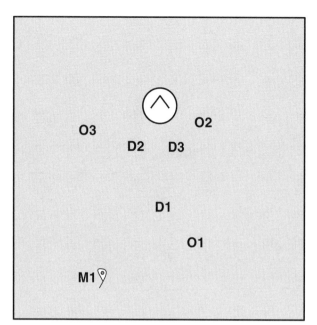

Figure 11.7 Positioning of point defenseman.

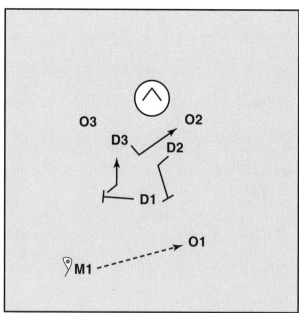

Figure 11.8 Rotation of defenders responding to a fast break.

identify the player he is covering by calling out his opponent's jersey number. Frequently defenders end up playing a different man than the one they originally were guarding. The identification of men is referred to as "checking up" and is very important because it avoids the common error of two defenders playing the same man.

Figure 11.7 shows the fast break coming down the right side of the field with the point attackman (O1) on the left side. As stated earlier, the goalie should predetermine the point defenseman—normally the man closest to the ball—as it is advanced by the opposition on a fast break. In figure 11.7, the middle of the three defenders takes the position. The point man places himself about two yards from the center of the field on the side opposite the ball and no more than eleven or twelve yards between the restraining line and the goal. The most crucial mistake on fast-break defense occurs when the point defenseman, whose responsibility is to stop the ball, commits to the ball beyond this eleven- or twelve-yard mark. When he plays the ball at the eleven- to twelve-yard mark, he assumes an athletic position and is ready to move. As the ball carrier approaches the eleven- to twelve-yard mark, the defender slides parallel to the restraining

line toward the offensive player with the ball, thus stopping this player from penetrating the defense. The point defender should be careful not to make his move too aggressively by sliding up the field beyond the eleven- to twelve-yard mark, which would take him out of position once the ball is passed and leave the passing lane open.

About 90 percent of the time, if the point man is in a good position, the ball carrier will pass off to one of the attackmen. At Hopkins, we teach our defenders to stop the ball carrier with their stick pointed to the ball carrier's glove, not in the air. Placing your stick in the air may give the ball carrier an opportunity to dodge past you. Playing with your stick in front of you, aiming it at the offensive player's gloves, will enable you to extend beyond the eleven- to twelve-yard mark without physically leaving that location and may also allow you to get a poke check on the offensive player with the ball as he either passes or shoots.

Once the ball leaves the stick of the offensive player initiating the break, the point man must open to the player receiving the ball and run at full speed to his passing lane. He should keep his stick up, toward the goal and in the passing lane.

Figure 11.8 shows the player initiating the break

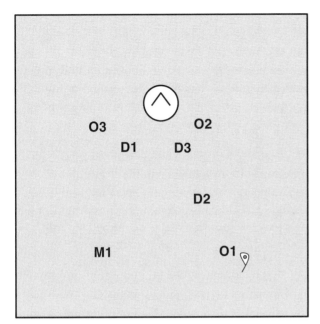

Figure 11.9 Location of defenders after one rotation in response to a fast break.

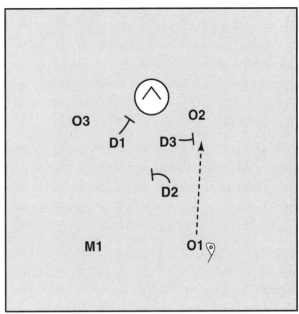

Figure 11.10 Defensive response to ball being passed down the side.

and passing the ball to the point attackman. Once D1 rotates parallel to the restraining line, stops the ball carrier, and forces the ball to be passed from M1 to O1, he will open up toward the ball, step toward the middle of the field, and then rotate down the back side to cover the passing lane from O1 to O3. As O1 receives the ball, D2 will step to the middle and rotate up toward O1. D2 will not stretch any farther than ten or eleven yards from the goal. He will play O1 with his stick out in front of him in an effort to deter a dodge and to get a check on the gloves of O1 if O1 attempts to make a pass or a shot. Upon D1 and D2 rotating, D3 will follow suit. He will step to the middle and rotate across from O3 toward O2. By following this scenario, each defender has moved toward the ball by rotating one spot.

Figure 11.9 shows where the defenders will wind up when they have rotated once. If the offense reverses its movement of the ball, the defense simply reverses its triangle's rotation. D1 would step to the middle and rotate up, D3 would step to the middle and rotate over, and D2 would step to the hat and rotate down the back side in the passing lane between M1 (the midfielder bringing the ball down

the field) and O2, thus bringing each one of these players back to their original spots.

Figure 11.10 shows the ball being thrown down the side after it was passed to the point man. On the pass from O1 to O2, D3 will play the ball. D1, who was covering the passing lane between O1 and O3, now will cover the passing lane between O2 and O3. D2 will be responsible for two players at this point. He will open up to the ball and split O1 and O2, putting his stick in the passing lane from O2 to M1.

The Five-on-Four and Six-on-Five Breaks

All of the key principles used when defending against other unsettled situations also apply when defending a five-on-four or a six-on-five break. As we stated earlier, the number of offensive players is unimportant; the number of defensive players is critical. With four men available, we defend a five-on-four with a box alignment. What will happen in this situation is very similar to the fast break. In order to form the box alignment, the first midfielder into the hole area will fill in the spot opposite the point man at the top of the box, thereby forming our square. The point defender's main responsibil-

Transition 139

ity is still to stop the ball. He should be no farther than ten or eleven yards from the goal. The two base defenders will be in the same positions as when defending the four-on-three.

A significant difference between defending a four-on-three and a five-on-four break, however, is that in a five-on-four, the offense often will move the ball down the side of the field and behind the goal, whereas in a four-on-three, all the offensive players are located above the goal line. The five-on-four offensive alignment, which has one player behind the goal, will force our defenders to turn their backs briefly to the offensive players out top when the ball is passed behind the goal. The defense then finds itself having to be concerned not only with the ball behind the goal but also with the players in front of the goal.

A simple yet effective way of defending a five-on-four is to make sure that the player farthest from the ball assumes the most responsibility for the crease, as he would in a man-down situation (which we will describe in chapter 12). As the ball is moved behind, each defenseman should rotate one spot into the ball. While the player farthest from the ball concentrates primarily on the crease, all of the players on the defense must make sure they each give some of their attention to this vital area.

The six-on-five is very similar to the five-on-four, but with one additional defender. Unlike in the four-on-three or five-on-four, however, the responsibility of the point defender is different. Although his primary role in the other situations was to stop the ball, now he is assigned to play the crease, and his sole responsibility will be to defend it. The two midfielders, who are hustling to get to the hole to help play defense, now will fill in the two top spots, no farther than eleven yards from the goal in our box. As the ball moves down the side and behind, our defense will rotate, just as our man-down does.

Effective transition play is important to any successful team offense. It is difficult to defend against a good transition, and the best way to do so is to prevent your opponents from creating fast-break situations. For example, in 2003, Hopkins had to play an explosive Towson University team twice—not only at the end of the regular season but shortly afterward, on their home field, in the play-offs. We had to defeat them in order to move on to the Final Four. That year Towson had a high-powered offense that relied a great deal on transition and fast-break play. Heading into each game, we were very concerned about being able to slow Towson down and take away much of their transition. Our success in both of those games was a direct reflection of our team's ability to do a good job of getting into the hole, playing half-field defense, and preventing Towson from running.

During a critical point in the play-off game, Towson was just beginning to go on a run and came down on a four-on-three fast break. As the ball moved downfield, our defenders aligned themselves perfectly. When the ball was passed to Towson's point man, all three of our defenders rotated very quickly, took away the passing lanes, and forced the Towson offensive players to make a bad pass. The ball went out-of-bounds. Hopkins got the ball back, cleared it, and went down and scored a goal. That was a turning point in the game. Successfully defending Towson's fast-break offense allowed us to keep them from scoring a goal and going on a run that could have changed the momentum—and the outcome—of the game.

TRANSITION OFFENSE

In chapter 7 on team offense, we noted that the ultimate aim of an offense is to create a numerical advantage over the defense in some way. Often this is done by drawing a slide, beating a defender, and moving the ball forward as quickly as possible to the open man *before* the defense can recover.

Transition offense is no different. It is just a variation of six-on-six offense. The aim, as it is in half-field offense, is to beat the defense before we lose the numerical advantage.

As we explained earlier, quite a bit of transition play is created in a team's defensive end and moves to its offensive end. However, many unsettled or scrambled situations can develop elsewhere on the field, creating a two-on-one, a three-on-two, a four-on-three, or possibly a five-on-four off of a failed clear, a ground ball, a shot's rebound that squirts out to the perimeter, or simply because of a defenseman falling down. Whatever the case, the offense wants to push the ball as quickly as they can to capitalize on their numerical advantage.

It is important, however, to make good decisions on when to push up the tempo of play and capitalize on numerical advantage and when to "pull it out," or recognize that the defense has done a good job and there is no longer a numerical advantage. Then it is time to hit the brakes, pull the ball back out to the perimeter, make substitutions, and set up the offense. This is the most difficult part of transition or fast-break offense. Teams that push the tempo must rely heavily on the decision making of their offensive players. If these players make quality decisions, then the offense can thrive in this style of play. However, if the offensive players make poor decisions, the results can lead to bad passes, bad shots, and many turnovers—which obviously leads to playing a lot of defense.

There are a number of basic principles and stages that apply in all transition or unsettled situations:

1. It is as important, if not more important, for the players who do not have the ball to sprint as fast as they can to get ahead of the defense to create an unsettled situation. At Hopkins, we call this "running without the ball," or "running without it."

2. Recognize when a transition situation has been created.

3. Keep it simple. Don't do anything fancy.

4. Get in the proper alignment. The alignment will be determined by the number of offensive players the team has available in the transition.

5. Communicate. There is defined terminology that is used in each transition situation.

6. Execution. In an effort to force the defense to rotate and open up passing lanes, the ball carrier should always make a defender commit to him.

7. Stickwork is critical. Since the offense does not have much time to take advantage of these unsettled or transition situations, it is important that passing be pinpoint. An offensive player can ill-afford having to take the time to catch a bad pass, gather himself to shoot, make a pass, or make a decision on where to go.

8. When preparing to receive the ball, each offensive player should give the passer a target with the head of his stick in the box area so that he can receive the ball and be able to do something with it quickly.

9. Each offensive player should always move toward the ball when it is passed to him rather than waiting for it to come to him.

10. Complete the unsettled situation by generating a quality shot, scoring a goal, or deciding that the unsettled situation no longer is available and pulling the ball out to the perimeter to set up another offense.

At one time, perhaps the most common transition in lacrosse was the four-on-three fast break. Today it is actually the least frequent of all the unsettled situations in the game—although it certainly remains the most exciting. We'll get to it, but first we will describe other transitional opportunities, beginning with the two-on-one.

The Two-on-One

Of course, the two-on-one is the most difficult for the defense to handle, because there is only one player left to cover two offensive players. In this situation, the offensive players must maintain good spacing between themselves and not get too close to each other. It is critical to create passing lanes by not allowing the defender to play between the man with the ball and the man without it. It is important that the player with the ball make himself a threat by moving toward the goal in an effort to force the lone defender to concentrate more on him than on the player without the ball. Once the offensive player with the ball has drawn the defender's attention, he then will look to pass the ball to his open teammate. If the defender is fortunate enough to be able to recover to the offensive player who is receiving the ball, the offense then will repeat this scenario. The player receiving the ball will attempt to draw the majority of the defender's attention, while the off-ball offensive player will put himself in an open passing lane so that he can catch the ball and shoot.

Figure 11.11 shows the offense with a two-on-one advantage. The defender positions himself relatively close to the goal. O1, who has the ball, will move toward the goal in an effort to draw that defender and

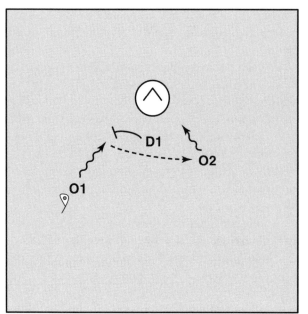

Figure 11.11 The two-on-one transition offense.

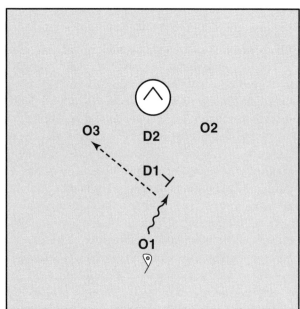

Figure 11.12 The three-on-two transition offense triangle.

will pass off to O2, whom we hope has done a good job of creating an open passing lane. Once the ball is passed to O2, he will continue to move toward the goal. If he is uncontested, he will proceed to shoot the ball. If D1 is able to close in on him, O2 will look to move the ball back to O1, who has created an open passing lane, for a possible shot.

The Three-on-Two

In the three-on-two, the offense may find itself having to pass the ball a few more times, since there are more defenders to beat. The offensive alignment in a three-on-two usually is that of a triangle. Like in a two-on-one and all other unsettled situations, spacing is important. The offense's ability to make good, crisp passes depends on the spacing. In addition, one of the aims of the offense is to force the defense to stretch. The more distance there is between offensive players, the more area the defense is forced to play and the greater the chance that they will overextend themselves.

In this situation, the same tactics hold true as in the two-on-one. The first job of the offensive player with the ball is to draw the attention of the point defender. Once he does this, he should pass the ball to one of the two open players. In doing so, we hope to

transform the three-on-two to a two-on-one. Figure 11.12 shows the ball coming in from O1 in the top center. O2 is located to his right, and O3 is located to his left. D1 is the point defender; D2 is the second defender. As O1 moves down the field, he will draw the attention of D1. Once he does that, he will pass off to either O2 or O3. If he passes to his left, to O3, as shown in figure 11.12, O2 then positions himself to create a passing lane for O3 to pass the ball to him. As O3 receives the ball, D2 will now become responsible for covering him, and D1 has the difficult job of covering two players, O1 and O2. In this situation, it is clearly more important for D1 to focus his attention on O2, because he is in a more dangerous area of the field. Figure 11.13 shows how it is critical for O2 to create an open passing lane to receive the ball from O3. We do not want O3 to be forced to pass the ball through a defender's stick. If D1 does a good job and O2 is not open, O3 then will throw the ball back to O1, and the offense will restart its maneuvers.

The Four-on-Three Fast Break

Occasionally, a four-on-three fast break can be created when a team is on offense and the ball is knocked to the ground or when the defense fails to clear the ball. However, the majority of four-on-

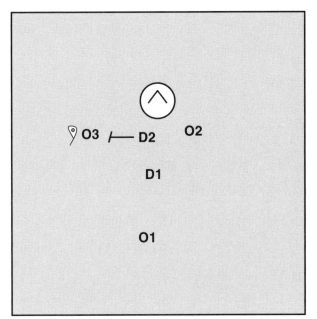

Figure 11.13 Creating an open passing lane.

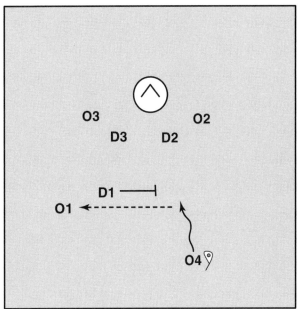

Figure 11.14 The four-on-three fast break.

three situations will occur off of a face-off—which is one of the most exciting plays in our sport—or from the defensive end of the field. In these situations, a player from the defensive end will carry the ball on the fast break.

A number of offensive patterns can be used in a four-on-three fast break. The most common and simplest is the box or rectangular alignment. Since the defense normally will use a triangular setup, the box offense makes use of a two-on-one situation against the point defenseman. Once the ball is stopped by the point defenseman and a pass is made, the defense then will be forced to rotate. This offensive alignment is spread in such a way as to take advantage of the offense's numerical superiority. Simply put, the aim in this situation is to go from a four-on-three to a three-on-two to a two-on-one to a one-on-none. Each time the offense passes the ball, the players seek to create a greater numerical advantage by taking one defender at a time out of the play.

Since each of the three attack positions on the fast break requires special skills, it is advisable to identify which position each attackman will play. As is the case with the defense, the offensive players can determine in advance who will be the point man and who will be responsible for the left and the right.

Practice sessions should give each man the opportunity to perfect the skills necessary for his position. However, there are occasions when the attackmen will not be able to get to their regular positions, so a small portion of practice time should be set aside for playing the other fast-break positions.

Let's look at the responsibilities of each of the four men involved in the four-on-three fast break. In figure 11.14, the man carrying the ball on the fast break (O4) must run at top speed because an opponent will be trying to catch up to him to stop the break. It is important for O4 to choose quickly on which side of the field to carry the ball so that the attack can align itself appropriately. Once over the midfield line, O4 will listen for the point attackman to communicate to him. One of two calls can be made: "Early!" or "Draw!" If the point attackman yells "Early," he wants the midfielder carrying the ball to pass it early, before the point attackman draws the attention of the point defender. If the point attackman shouts "Draw," that means he wants the midfielder carrying the ball to draw the point defender before he passes the ball. Then it becomes the job of the middie carrying the ball to force the point defender to commit to him. If O4's penetration is not stopped by the point defender, he

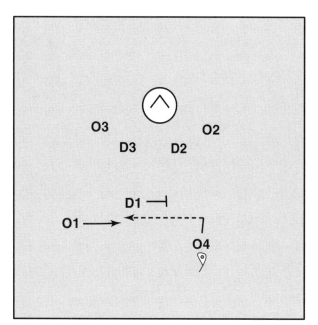

Figure 11.15 A second stage of the four-on-three fast break.

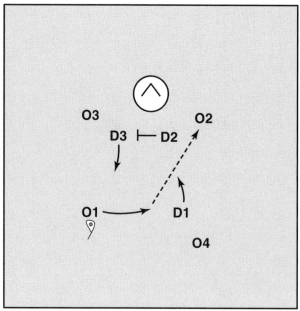

Figure 11.16 A third stage of the four-on-three fast break.

should continue forward and shoot the ball. Most well-coached defenses, however, will react properly and stop the initial penetration of the ball.

If the defense reacts properly to the break and drops into a tight triangle, the break man will carry the ball to a point several yards inside the restraining line, at which time the point defenseman will start to move toward him. In figure 11.14, O4 is carrying the ball down the left side. As he gets inside the restraining box and draws the attention of D1, O4 immediately passes the ball to O1, the point attackman. O4 then will stop rather than continue toward the crease. If he were to move toward the goal, he would get in the way of a passing lane to one of the other offensive players. However, if O4 sees D3 anticipating the pass to O1 and getting too far away from O2, then O4 can fake a pass to O1 and skip-pass the ball to O2, throwing it behind D2's back. If O4 notices D2 starting to move across the front of the crease and getting too far from O2, then O4 can fake a pass either to O1 or O3 and throw the ball directly down to O2. Once O4 has passed the ball to any of the other three attackmen, he should stop and become the last person forming the offensive rectangle.

The alignment of the attack is critical to the success of any four-on-three fast break. The point

attackman is the quarterback of the offense. He should be the smartest of the attackmen and have the ability to react quickly under pressure in determining the open man, and his stickwork should be excellent. It is also common for a team's best shooter to take the point attackman position in an effort to force the opposing team's defense to honor him and stretch to cover him.

As soon as a fast break begins, the point attackman moves to the side of the field opposite the man carrying the ball. If the break comes down the left side of the field, he moves to the right side about four to five yards inside the restraining line and about seven to eight yards inside from the center of the field. This position allows him to attack the defense most effectively. If he receives the ball at the restraining line or beyond it, he is too far from the goal and his diagonal pass to O2 has a greater chance of being blocked or intercepted. He also is not in a good position to gain a three-on-two advantage on D2 or D3. If he receives the ball at the fourteen-yard mark or closer to the goal, he is too close to the goal and is vulnerable to D3's slide. If he does catch the ball before being checked by D3, he simply does not have enough time to make the right decision. His position of seven to eight yards

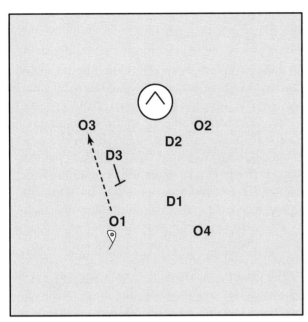

Figure 11.17 A fourth scenario for the four-on-three fast break.

from the center of the field gives him better vision of both O2 and O3 than he would have from the center of the field.

The point attackman has the following options after he receives the ball:

1. If no one picks him up, step in and shoot to score.

2. Make a diagonal pass to the lower left side to O2.

3. Make an onside pass to the right side to O3.

4. Make a return pass to O4.

5. If a defender charges at him out of control, dodge the defender and go to the goal.

Player O1 must always give the ball carrier a target with his stick, and when he receives the ball, his body should be positioned so that he can read the defense's reaction quickly and determine where the next pass will go. As he catches the ball, O1 should move toward the player who passed it to him in an effort to force the defense to change the angle of its slide. Often, a defensive player will slide to where an offensive player has been rather than to where he is moving. O1's move will create a difficult situation for D3 to cover O1 as he slides up the field.

Figure 11.15 shows O4 carrying the ball, draw-

ing the point defenseman, and O1 catching the ball as he moves toward O4. Once O1 receives the ball, it is his job to read the reaction of the lower left side defenseman, which in this situation is D2. If D2 has rotated across the face of the goal, there is a very good chance that O2 is open. If D2 is still covering O2, then there is a good chance that O3 is open, because D3 already has started to slide toward O1, who just has received the ball.

In figure 11.16, O1 is reading the fact that D2 has rotated across and O2 is his open man. In this situation, D1 has a very difficult responsibility. He not only is charged with stopping the initial penetration of the ball but, once it is passed, also becomes responsible for covering both O4 and O2. This slide down the back side is one of the most difficult to make in lacrosse. If O2 catches the skip-pass, the chances are that D1 was late getting down the back side, which will leave O2 open to take a shot.

In figure 11.17, O1 has moved toward the ball, received it, and now has read D2. In this scenario, D2 has not rotated quickly enough—or "stayed at home," as we put it—and is slowly rotating across to O3. This leaves O3 open as D3 rotates up to cover the ball. O3 will look for the shot first, and if D2 happens to rotate across, he can quickly pass the ball across the crease to O2 for a layup.

Figure 11.18 shows the defense having done a good job, rotating well and taking away all of the passing lanes. In this situation, O1 will pass the ball back to O4, and we will run the break once more. O4 will try to play the "draw-and-dump" game again—drawing the defense away and passing (or "dumping") the ball to another offensive player, who can either shoot the ball or pass it to another offensive player.

On a fast break, the lower right attackman, O3, is usually the team's best right-handed finisher. He positions himself on the goal line about four to five yards from the center of the field. When the ball is thrown to him, he moves toward it rather than waiting for it. By doing so, he will be in a position about three to four yards in front of and four to five yards from the center of the goal. This will give him an excellent shooting angle while at the same time providing a little cushion from D2, who will

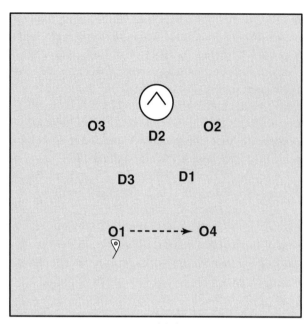

Figure 11.18 Reacting to a good defense on the four-on-three fast break.

be making the slide across the crease to play him. If he were to remain too close to the crease, D2 might be able to check him when he receives the pass.

When receiving the pass on the fast break, O3 should be facing the ball. As soon as the ball hits his stick, his head and upper body should turn toward the goal. He then will be able to get off the shot quickly, since he will be looking at the goal. The shot will also have power because when shooting right-handed, the body weight initially is on the right leg and then transfers to the left leg as the ball is being released. O3 should be in this position and ready to receive the ball as soon as the ball carrier nears the restraining box.

The lower right offensive player has the following options after he receives the ball:

1. Shoot the ball with power, aiming for an open area on the goal. *Don't rush it.* If he has time, he should take it.
2. Make a pass to the left side to O2, who is moving into position for a left-handed shot.
3. Make a pass to either O1 or O4, out top, cutting for the goal.
4. If D2 slides across and is charging at him, out

of control, he should run through the defender's check and go to the goal.

If the ball is passed to O2 from either O4 or O1, the lower right attackman can cut toward the back-side pipe, looking for a feed from O2 and a point-blank, right-handed shot, or he can pop up the field a little to create an open passing lane for a two- to three-yard shot. If O1, O4, or O2 takes a shot, O3 must be ready to race to the back line if the shot misses the goal and goes out-of-bounds. If he fails to move quickly in backing up the shot, the goalie or a defenseman may beat him to the ball and gain possession of it. It is important for the attack to maintain control of the ball.

On a fast break, the lower left attackman, O2, has the same responsibilities and assumes the same relative position as the right-handed attackman except that he does so on the left side of the field. He is primarily a shooter and should have an excellent left-handed shot. When he is receiving the ball, his feet should be staggered—right foot back and left foot forward. His head and upper body turn toward the goal once the ball is in his stick. The lower left attackman has the same options with the ball as the lower right attackman except that the pass across the crease will be directed for a right-handed reception by O3, who will be looking for a right-handed shot. Player O2 also must always be ready to back up a shot by O1, O3, or O4.

The Five-on-Four and Six-on-Five Fast Breaks

Although, as we stated earlier, four-on-three fast breaks are not as big a part of lacrosse as they once were, transition situations still occur quite frequently. They are not always perfectly organized and can happen at different times throughout a game, yet they still are an exciting part of the sport.

A five-on-four fast break can occur under a variety of circumstances. One might be off a save; another could follow a scramble for a ground ball in the defensive end of the field that the team on the defense wins, enabling them to get out ahead of the riding team and develop a clear-cut five-on-four fast break. More often, these opportunities will happen in what we call "broken" situations, meaning off of a failed clear or off of a loose ball in an offensive team's end of the field.

In a five-on-four, the attackmen will be aligned as they are when the ball is down in the opponent's defensive end of the field. They are positioned at equal distances across the field, with one attackman in the middle, located closest to the midfield line, and the other two attackmen dropped back a little bit from the midfield, basically in a 1–2 formation. When the attack recognizes that an opportunity exists for a five-on-four fast break, they should get into position quickly. For the purposes of this example, assume that a shot has been taken and the goalie has made a save. At this point, one of the players on the offense quickly drops back toward the defensive end of the field. Two of the defensive players break out quickly, and the goalie passes the ball to one of them. The five-on-four is developing as five players—the three attackmen and the two defensive players—are breaking out to clear the ball.

The team that is moving to the offensive end must choose a side of the field on which to proceed. Figure 11.19 does not include the defenders so that it will more clearly show how the offensive players will set themselves up. A1, A2, and A3 are in their positions when the ball is in their defensive end. As the goalie makes the save, M1 and M2 will break up the field. In this example, the goalie will pass the ball to M1. The three attackmen will move quickly into position and will sprint toward their opponent's goal, never losing sight of the ball. A1 will break to the wing area just outside of the restraining box. A3 will sprint to X-behind. A2 will fill in the position opposite of A1 in the wing area outside the box. This will provide M1 with an outlet down the side of the field to A1. If the goalie were to pass the ball to M2, his outlet would be A2 on the other side of the field.

In figure 11.20, M1 has crossed the midfield line with the ball. Always remember that in transition situations, the ball can move faster than the players. This means that the ball should be passed more than it should be carried. As soon as M1 crosses the midline, he should get the ball out of his stick and pass it down the side to A1. On that pass, M2

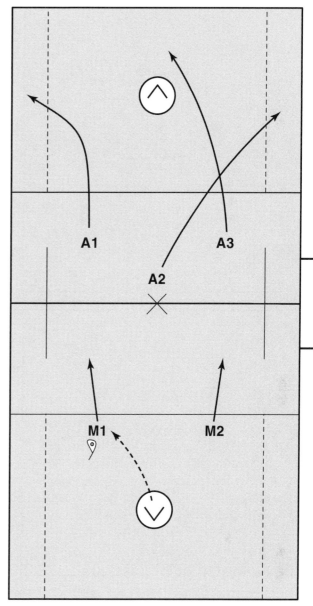

Figure 11.19 Offense for the five-on-four fast break.

should begin to make what we call a "selfish cut" toward the crease. We call this a "selfish cut" because M2 is looking for a pass so he can generate a quick shot. As soon as A1 receives the ball, he should pass it quickly to A3 in the X-behind position. As this happens, A2 begins to move in a little closer to the goal from the wing area.

A1 passes the ball behind the goal to A3 because doing so will now force the opposing defense to

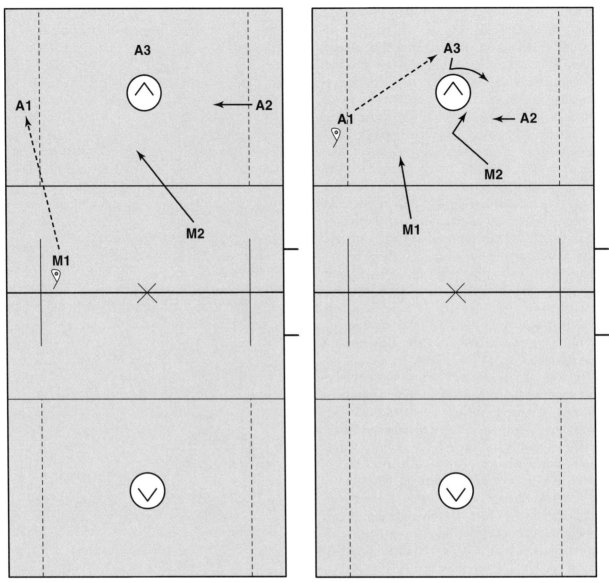

Figure 11.20 Second stage of offensive movement in five-on-four fast break.

Figure 11.21 Offensive options in five-on-four fast break.

turn and look at the ball, which will make it more difficult for them to see the offensive players in front of the goal. This may allow the offense an opportunity to open up passing lanes, make a quick cut, or otherwise improve its opportunities.

When A3 catches the ball, he should always move in the direction opposite from where he received the ball (figure 11.21). As A3 drives toward that side, M2 will make a selfish cut toward A3. By doing so, he forces the defenders who are playing up top to col-

lapse toward the middle to respect him as a shooter. That, in turn, will open up an area for M1 who, as A3 drives aside, will fill high and opposite from where A3 drives. He will locate himself in a shooting area, about fourteen to fifteen yards high and opposite of the area to which A3 is moving. The final formation the offense will wind up in is a 1-3-1.

Upon receiving the ball and driving opposite, A3 has several options. He can quickly pass the ball to M2, who is making a selfish cut. He can pass the ball

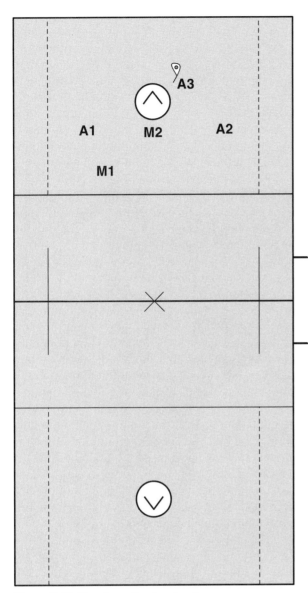

Figure 11.22 The six-on-five fast break.

has one more player, giving them five, and the offense has one more offensive player, giving them six. The attack's responsibility and formation are exactly the same as in a five-on-four, but a subtle difference lies in the midfield. As the ball is passed down the side of the field, as in a five-on-four, the first midfielder down the field will make a selfish cut to the crease. In this situation, however, the next player down the field, rather than filling high and opposite as he did in a five-on-four, will make a cut to the crease as well, usually cutting off the back of the midfielder who has made the first cut. In a six-on-five, the midfielder who makes the first selfish cut is making what we call a "dummy cut." He is trying to gain the attention of the defense, and as the ball is passed to X-behind, the second midfielder down the field cuts right off the back of the first midfielder, almost utilizing him as a pick. Basically, he is cutting toward the area in which A3 is carrying the ball. The last midfielder down the field will fill high and opposite. The final formation of a six-on-five is a 1-4-1.

It is critical to remember that the offense does not have to force the issue simply because a transition or fast break has occurred. Once the players execute a fast break and make their cuts, if no quality shot presents itself it is absolutely fine to pull the ball back out and set up a traditional offense. Forcing the issue can lead to turnovers and fast breaks or transitions going the other way.

to A2, who has moved closer to the goal on the wing and is prepared to step in for a quick shot. He can skip the ball diagonally to M1, who has moved down an area fourteen or fifteen yards from the goal and is prepared to catch and shoot the ball. Or he can throw the ball back to A1, who has begun to creep into a shooting position after having passed the ball to A3.

Figure 11.22 shows the six-on-five, which is very similar to a five-on-four but with several differences.

The most obvious difference is that the defense

Scott Smith (JHU '06) in the goal. *Jay Van Rensselaer*

12

Man-Down Defense

Whenever a player is sent to the penalty box and his team must operate with one fewer man than its opponent, a great challenge is presented to what we call the man-down defense. However, if the unit has a thorough understanding of the situation and complete confidence in its ability to handle any extra-man play, it can consistently thwart the offense. On average, teams will defend against three to five penalties per game. Naturally, in some games there will be more fouls, and in some games fewer extraman situations arise. No matter how many extraman opportunities occur in a game, each one of them can make the difference between winning or losing.

Developing pride in man-down defense goes a long way toward ensuring the success of any team—and specializing in man-down defense long has been a tradition at Johns Hopkins. When Bob Scott wrote the first edition of this book thirty years ago, he noted that his teams practiced man-down defense twenty to thirty minutes a day for three days. Today, we devote as much time—perhaps even more—to man-down defense. Our special man-down and man-up units practice at least four times a week. We believe that this part of the game is so crucial that we are willing to concentrate more on it than on some other aspects of play. Our won-loss record, particularly in critical one-goal games, indicates that the importance we place on man-down defense is well deserved.

From 2000 to 2005, Hopkins won twenty-one out of twenty-five one-goal games, which is an impressive result. In 2005 alone, we went 5–0 in one-goal games, including the semifinal and the championship games. Winning one-goal games comes down to doing the little things right, and one of those "little things" is playing effective man-down defense. In each of the one-goal games that we were fortunate to win, we were man-down at least once, and in all of those games, we were able to thwart our opponent's extraman offense and preserve our one-goal edge. On average, most teams set a goal of turning back their opponent's extraman offense 80 percent of the time, or of being beaten only 20 percent. The man-down unit on our 2003 Hopkins team, which went on to play for the national championship, had a man-down percentage of just 14 percent—the best in the country.

At Hopkins, we focus on preparing our man-down units just as a football team would concentrate on its special teams units. In fact, when training our man-down unit in 2003, we actually borrowed an idea from the University of Nebraska football team. Its defense is considered a special group and wore special black shirts during practice. We gave our man-down specialists similar black practice shirts with the number "19" printed on them. That was meant to remind them of how important they were and of how we wanted to keep our opponent's extraman offense success below 20 percent—to 19 percent or better. Our players more than met that challenge.

For example, the captain of our man-down unit that year was Kevin Conry. Although not a starter at the close defense, Kevin was a backup, long-stick middie and a major contributor to the success of our man-down efforts. He put endless hours of preparation into practicing man-down, because it was his primary job and he understood how critical it was. Toward the end of that season, we were involved in an important game with Towson University. Towson's players were known for their crisp passing, their inventiveness on extraman, and their high-powered shooters. As we prepared that week for Towson's extraman, we noticed in game tapes that Towson would occasionally throw a bounce pass. Of course, it is extremely difficult to knock down a bounce pass, which skips by down around your ankles, not in the box area that we have discussed throughout this book. Not only our coaches but all the extraman players were aware of this bounce pass and discussed how to prepare for it. In the third quarter of our game against Towson, we were penalized for a slash. As Towson's extraman offense, con-

sidered to be one of the better units of its kind in the country, took to the field, our man-down unit set up in our basic formation. As the Tigers moved the ball around the perimeter, changing from one offensive alignment to another, our defense reacted accordingly. When the ball was passed from the left-hand wing, from the 2½ position to X-behind, a Towson offensive player began to move toward the goal. As he did, one of our defenders was prepared to play him as he approached this dangerous area. An important part of man-down, as you'll learn in this chapter, is covering skip lanes, or the potential routes for diagonal passes. As the Towson player carried the ball from X-behind to the right side of the cage, he quickly threw a bounce pass that was intended to skip the adjacent player and reach their best shooter, who was located out top in the 5 position. Had this player received the ball, he would have generated a high-quality shot. As the ball bounced off the turf, however, Kevin Conry was ready for it. He was able to stab at the ball and actually pick it off. He then passed the ball to an open teammate, enabling us to clear the ball and end Towson's opportunity to score on the man-down. This was a critical point in the game, because had Towson scored a goal, it would have taken the momentum from our team and given it to the Tigers. Kevin Conry's intense preparation really paid off for us that afternoon.

The same qualities needed by defensemen to play all-even are required for handling man-down situations. Mental alertness, or the ability to recognize a developing situation, and physical agility, or the ability to react quickly, are the most essential qualities for any man-down player. Many times those players who have the ability to play good off-ball defense are important role players in the man-down. Their skill at anticipating helps them react swiftly to the movement of the ball. Talk helps even more. The most important aspect of man-down defense is communication, because everyone on the unit must know which offensive alignment, or set, they are defending against and how their teammates plan to react to it. Peripheral vision also is fundamental, since each defender must see not only the ball but the player or players in the area for which he is responsible. This is different from all-even play, during which a player uses split vision to locate both his man and the ball but places primary emphasis on his man, unless the ball carrier has moved into a dangerous area and is threatening the goal. In man-down defense, seeing the ball and the man are of equal importance.

Today, most teams will teach their man-down concepts to eight to eleven players. At Hopkins, we teach man-down to eleven men. We have two man-down units, one our starting man-down, the other our second man-down. Each of these units consists of four defensive long-stick players and one short-stick defenseman. We include at least one face-off specialist in this group of eleven. The reason for this is that sometimes we may find ourselves facing off in a man-down situation. Although that doesn't happen often, we believe it is necessary to have someone at the face-off point who not only has the ability to win the face-off but also knows man-down and how to play it, just in case he loses the ball. Of course, it is much easier to play man-down when you have the ball than when you do not.

We teach so many players our man-down concepts at Hopkins for several reasons. Should we have a starting man-down player who is injured, it would be difficult to replace him with someone who has little knowledge of our concepts and has not practiced them. We also could find ourselves in a situation where one of our man-down players is the person who has committed the penalty and has to be replaced by another player, who should also understand the man-down. Finally, we teach the man-down to so many players because, at the college level, we graduate members of our team each year. Rather than have to reteach our man-down concepts to a whole new group of players, we instead are able to increase the roles of those who may not have started on the man-down unit but have had experience playing it in practice and know our concepts well.

THE FIVE-MAN ZONE

A number of systems can be used to play the man-down defense. Which system is employed will depend ultimately on a coach's preference as well as on the talents of his players. No matter which style is used, a coach looks for several important qualities in his players when choosing his man-down personnel. Players who have one or more of these qualities may be perfect candidates for your man-down unit. They should:

1. Possess good communication skills.
2. Play good off-ball defense.
3. Understand and play good team defense.
4. Have good stickwork and be able to knock balls down or pick off passes.
5. Have top athletic skills.

The ability to play one-on-one, on-ball defense is not as important in man-down defensive players. Since the offense has a numerical advantage and the man-down defensive unit will be playing areas rather than a man, it is not necessary to have the most talented one-on-one defenders on the man-down defense. It is more important to have good team defensive players who communicate well and play solid, off-ball defense.

Although in today's game the man-down defense has to protect the goal against more offensive cutting and screen shots, the basic way the extraman offense sets up its alignments and varies them remains largely as it has been for a long time. Despite the increasing complexity of the man-up offenses, there really are only so many variations that can be used. The same applies to the movements of the man-down defense.

Many teams employ a pure zone man-down defense, which is similar to the 2-1-2 and 2-3 zones used in basketball. The five defenders are given certain areas of responsibility, and they try to jam up the prime shooting area and prevent close-range shots. The pure zone defense can vary by how it deals with attackmen behind the goal. The most important difference between the zone man-down and the rotation system is how the crease is played. Essentially, the zone man-down is a 2-1-2 setup, just like a zone in basketball. The defense wants to prevent the offense from generating shots from high-percentage places on the field. In the zone, one player is responsible for the crease, whereas in a five-man rotation system, everyone has a level of responsibility for the crease. That changes, however, if your opponent adopts a specific offensive set, which probably will require the defense to place more responsibility for the crease on a specific defender.

In chapter 11 we discussed how to defend against the offense when it has a numerical advantage. These advantages may be five offensive players versus four defensive players or six offensive players versus five defensive players. In an effort to maintain a certain level of consistency in our defense, we have designed our Hopkins man-down around concepts similar to those that we use when defending transition. These similarities in philosophy and concepts help to eliminate confusion and enable defensive players to grasp the man-down concepts more readily.

The man-down defense that most resembles our transition defense is the five-man zone. In this man-down defense, the alignment of our defensive personnel is exactly the same as when we are defending a six-on-five transition. The numerical advantage the offense holds is exactly the same. When playing this type of man-down defense, we have one defender whose sole responsibility is to protect the crease, the most dangerous area of the field. Once the man-down unit's crease defender is positioned, the other four defenders will align themselves in a box around the crease. This alignment resembles a box with one inside, or five-on-a-die (resembling the dots on dice), with four on the outside and one in the center.

A few simple rules apply to playing man-down defense:

1. The defenders should always play with their sticks in the box area—not up in the air or down by their hips—in the position described in chapter 5 that enables them to be ready to knock the ball down should it be thrown through the passing lane between one offensive player and another.

2. Do not allow the man-up to make diagonal passes or skip-passes. Force the ball to be passed to the adjacent offensive players.

3. Recognize the offensive alignments or sets against which you are defending and call them out every second or third pass.

4. One defensive player should play two offensive players as much as possible. This will keep the man-down from constantly having to rotate.

5. Sprint to the ball; sprint off the ball. In other words, when the man in your area receives the ball, sprint out to play him. When the man in your area passes the ball, sprint back in to resume the team defense alignment. If you do not do this, you will miss taking away those skip lanes we want to guard.

6. Look around. All defenders on the perimeter should play with their heads on a swivel, turning them as often as possible, in order to locate the ball and to see the area they are defending.

7. Do not extend too far. Only defend the dangerous areas of the field.

8. When an offensive player carries the ball from one area to another, the defender playing him will stay with him, and the other defenders will rotate around in an effort to support. We call this maneuver "carry with a carry." If your offensive player is carrying the ball, you will stay with, or carry, him.

9. The crease defender is responsible for the player in his area. If there is more than one offensive player on the crease, the defender's chief responsibility is to defend the player nearest to the ball.

At Hopkins, we believe that the most dangerous man-up alignment to defend against is the 3-3, because in it all six offensive players are located above the goal and are a threat to score.

Figure 12.1 shows this offensive alignment, positioned against the five-man defensive zone made up of four long-sticks and one short-stick. This is in keeping with the rules, which say that at no time is a team permitted to have more than four long-sticks on the field. Since we want to use as many long sticks as possible—given the long stick's obvious advantage for intercepting or blocking feeds and passes—we use four long-sticks and then select one of our best team defenders to fill the fifth spot of the man-down with a short-stick. The short-stick is in the 3 position—for a reason. Most lacrosse players are right-handed, and the majority of quality shooters are right-handed. Because of this, we want to place the short-stick in the area where a less-powerful shooter would be located and place our long-stick in

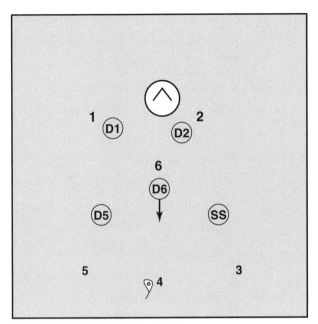

Figure 12.1a Five-man zone defense for man-down.

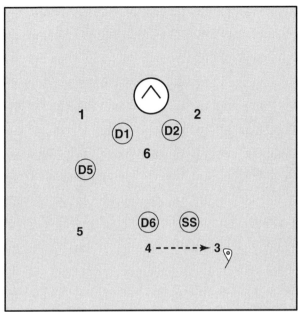

Figure 12.1b Alternate movements in five-man zone defense.

an area where we may face a more dangerous shooter. This alignment, with D2 being a long-stick, responsible for the crease area, allows us to better cover the area in which a dangerous shooter is likely to be.

In phase one (see figure 12.1a), our man-down defense is in a 2-1-2 setup. When the defense recognizes that the offense is in a 3-3 set, our crease defender realizes that he must become more involved on the perimeter. If the crease defender just covers the crease, we are at a disadvantage, having five offensive players versus four defenders on the perimeter. The offense simply will force us to rotate around, and we're going to wind up getting beat. In an effort to defend against this, we will utilize what is called a "string defense." When O4 is located at the top center with the ball, D6, who normally covers only the crease man, will "string," or rotate up to cover the ball. He will extend no farther than eleven or twelve yards. As this happens, the crease now will be open—but the ball carrier is limited to taking a shot from the porch, which is a low-percentage location. The short-stick assumes responsibility for covering the skip lane, or the passing lane between O4 and O2. D5's responsibility is the skip lane between O4 and O1. D1 and D2 will be responsible for O1, O2, and O6, the three offensive players located on the crease.

The hand in which O6 holds his stick will determine whether D1 or D2 will cover him the most. In our man-down defense, we try to provide coverage, or help, to the crease with the defender who is farthest from the ball. In phase one (see figure 12.1a), however, D1 and D2 are the same distance from the man with the ball. Consequently, how we will defend O6 will be determined by whether he is a righty or a lefty. It is best if the defender guarding a player near the crease who is receiving the ball will rotate toward him—what we call "fill"—from the back side. If O6 is a righty, D1 would be responsible for covering him and D2 will pay more attention to O2. This is because if the ball is passed to O6 on the crease and he is a right-hander, he will have to turn to shoot. If O6 has to catch and turn to shoot and D2 is covering him, O6 would just be able to throw the ball to O2, who isn't being covered. Of course, the opposite tactics apply if O6 is a lefty. D2 would then have more responsibility for him, and D1 would concentrate on O2.

Phase two (figure 12.1b) shows O4 passing the ball to O3. When this happens, the short-stick becomes responsible for playing the ball. D6 is responsible for the skip lane between O3 and O5. D2 will begin to rotate his way out a bit toward O2, thereby inhibiting O2 from receiving the ball and

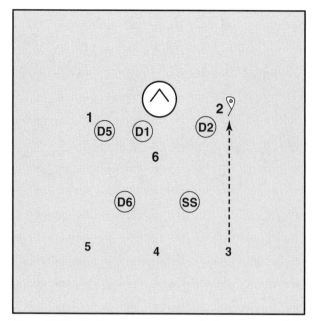 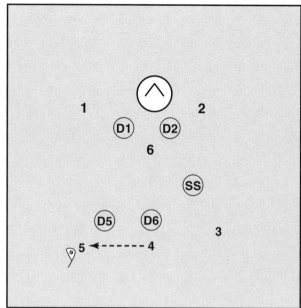

Figure 12.1 (c,d) Alternate movements in five-man zone defense.

shooting. D1 will rotate from his man toward the crease, and D5 will rotate down the back side to support D1.

In phase three (figure 12.1c), as the ball is passed from O3 to O2, D2 will rotate out to play the ball. The short-stick is responsible for the skip lane between O2 and O4. D6 will cover the skip lane between O2 and O5. D1 will rotate from his position to cover the crease man, thus guarding the most dangerous area of the field. In order to support D1, D5 will rotate down the back side and cover the man in area 1.

In figure 12.1d, the offensive players in phase one move the ball in the other direction, passing it from O4 to O5. D5 is responsible for covering the ball, and D6 covers the skip lane between O5 and O3. The short-stick begins to rotate down the back side, because D2, being the farthest man from the ball, is beginning to rotate in. D1 is going to begin to rotate out to cover his man.

In phase two (figure 12.1e), the ball moves from O5 to O1. D1 will play the ball, and D2 will rotate in from his back-side position to cover the crease. The short-stick will slide down the back side to help. D5 covers the skip lane between O1 and O4, and D6 covers the skip lane between O1 and O3.

Basically, the man-down defenders want to force the offense to move the ball around the perimeter by making the next easy pass to their adjacent teammates. If the defense allows the ball to be skip-passed, the most dangerous areas of the field will not be covered properly. Therefore, every defender is responsible for a skip lane, and one defender is also responsible for the crease.

Again, communication among the defenders is vital. Each time the ball is moved, the defenders will call out their new position, and every second pass, the defenders will call out what set they are defending. For example, in phase one (see figure 12.1a), D6 is responsible for covering the ball and will call out, "I have the ball." The short-stick is responsible for the skip lane between O1 and O2, and he will shout, "I have the left." D5 will communicate, "I have the right." D1 and D2 will communicate, "I have down low; we're helping to the crease." As the ball moves, the defenders alert their teammates to their new responsibilities. If the ball moves from D6 to the short-stick, he will call out, "I have the ball." D6 is going to say, "I have the right"; D2 is going to say, "I have the left"; D1 is going to say, "I have the crease"; and D5 is going to say, "I'm down the back side."

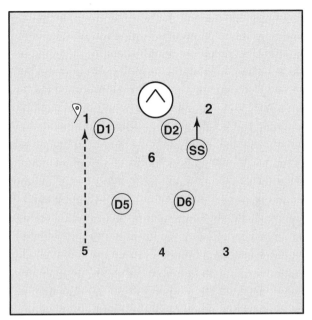

Figure 12.1e Alternate movements in five-man zone defense.

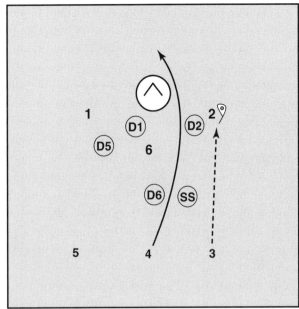

Figure 12.2a Man-down defense vs. a 2-3-1 setup, phase 1.

Naturally, the man-up offense often will change its alignment. A 3-3 will move to a 2-3-1, with one player located behind, and a 2-3-1 often can move to a 1-4-1. Of course, the extraman offense does not have to change its alignments this way. They can move from a 3-3 to a 1-4-1 or from a 1-4-1 to a 2-3-1. The illustrations in this chapter are meant to show merely a simple progression, demonstrating alignments that go from having no offensive player behind the goal and three offensive players out top, to one man behind the goal and two men out top, to one man behind the goal and one out top. These diagrams by no means represent the way such movements always happen but rather offer examples for which the general man-down defense rules apply.

Figure 12.2a shows phase one of the development of a 2-3-1 setup. On the pass from O3 to O2, the offensive player O4 cuts and rotates behind the goal. D6, whose original job is to cover the crease, has to stay with that cutter, or "carry with him" into the crease, and then as O4 rotates off the crease and behind the goal, D6 will pass the responsibility for covering him to D1 and resume his original role of covering the crease. Since there is no longer a player in the top center and there are only five players located in front of the goal, we will then realign ourselves to where we were when we started defending, in the 2-1-2.

In phase two (figure 12.2b), the offensive players now have aligned themselves in a 2-3-1 set. D2 is responsible for the ball. The short-stick is responsible for the skip lane between O2 and O5. D5 is responsible for the skip lane from O2 to O1. And D1 is responsible for covering O4, if he were to cut—what we call "sneak"—on either side of the goal for a pass. D6 is solely responsible for the crease.

Phase three (figure 12.2c) shows the change in alignments on a pass from O2 to O4. D1 will rotate behind the goal to play the ball. His aim is to keep the ball on the side from which it just came. When D1 rotates behind and vacates his area, D5 will replace him. D6 remains responsible just for the crease. The short-stick will rotate to the middle of the field and will be responsible for O3 and O5, and D2 will be responsible for the back side and playing O2. This diagram shows the defense beginning to rotate around the perimeter.

In phase four (figure 12.2d), on the pass from O4 to O1, D5 will play the ball. D1 will return to his original position, always traveling on the side of the ball, because if he goes on the opposite side, O4 could sneak in for a shot and possibly a goal. The

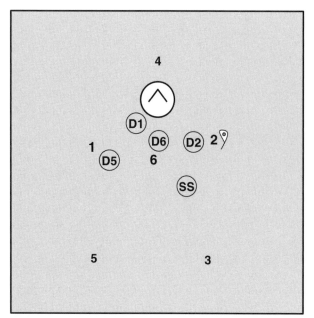

Figure 12.2b Man-down defense vs. a 2-3-1 setup, phase 2.

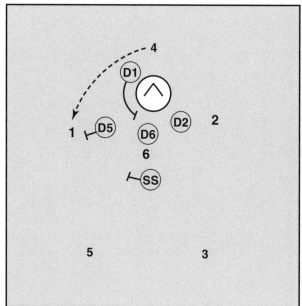

Figure 12.2d Man-down defense vs. a 2-3-1 setup, phase 4.

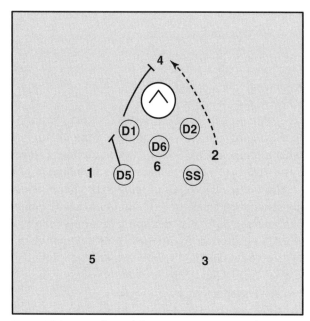

Figure 12.2c Man-down defense vs. a 2-3-1 setup, phase 3.

O5. The short-stick will rotate out to play the ball. D2 will begin to rotate up and will cover the skip lane between O5 and O2. D5 will slough or sag in just a little bit to cover the skip lane between O5 and O4. If O4 were to sneak toward the crease, D1 would rotate over just a little bit and share responsibility for covering both O4 and O2. As the ball moves around the perimeter, the defense continues rotating its four players against the offense's five, always maintaining one person on the crease to ensure that the most dangerous area of the field is not left open.

In man-down defense, the crease man is responsible not only for any offensive player who is located on the crease but for any and all cutters who come from the perimeter to the crease. If an offensive player leaves the perimeter and cuts to the crease, the defensive player initially covering him is responsible for keeping with him, or "carrying him," as he moves toward the crease and then passing him on to the crease defender. If one offensive player is already on the crease and another offensive player cuts in, then the crease defender will be responsible for both of them, concentrating on the man on the side closest to the ball.

Figure 12.3a illustrates phase one of the defensive maneuvers of a 1-4-1 set. Facing a 2-3-1 alignment

short-stick begins to rotate over to O5 and cover the skip lane from O1 and O3. D2 is going to cover the skip lane between O1 and O2, knowing that he also is responsible for covering, or "splitting," the two players farthest from the ball, now O2 and O3.

Phase five (figure 12.2e) shows a pass from O1 to

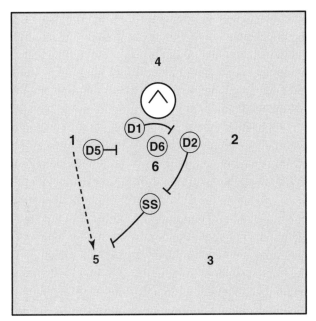

Figure 12.2e Man-down defense vs. a 2-3-1 setup, phase 5.

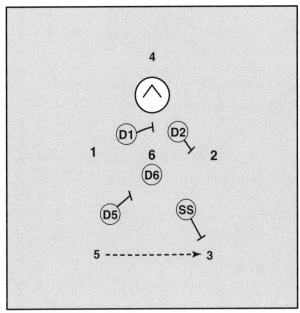

Figure 12.3a Man-down defense vs. a 1-4-1 setup, phase 1.

our defense will maintain its box-in-one positioning, or five-on-a-die setup. As the ball moves from O5 to O3, defenseman D5, who was originally on the ball, will sag in to cover the skip lane from O3 to O1. The short-stick will rotate out to play the ball. D2 will begin to rotate up a little bit toward O2 to cover him as a potential shooter, and D1 will rotate toward the middle of the goal and cover both O1 and O4. D5 will be helping D1 by taking away the passing lane between O3 and O1.

In phase two (figure 12.3b), the ball moves from O3 to O2. On that pass, D2 will rotate up and cover O2. The short-stick, who was originally playing the ball, will sag in and cover the skip lane from O2 to O5 and also share responsibility for covering both O5 and O3 out top. D1 begins to work his way over and prepare to go behind if the ball is passed from O2 to O4. D5 slides down the back side and covers the skip lane from O2 to O1, making the easiest passes available to the offense from O2 back to O3 or from O2 back to O4. As stated earlier, what we are aiming to do is force the offense to pass the ball to the next adjacent player, never skip-pass it through defense.

In phase three (figure 12.3c), the ball is passed from O2 to O4. D1 will rotate behind the goal, going in on

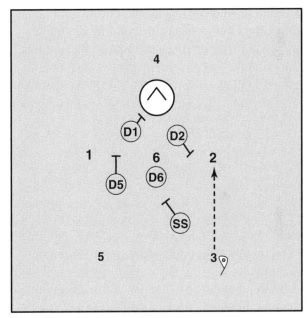

Figure 12.3b Man-down defense vs. a 1-4-1 setup, phase 2.

the side opposite the one from which the ball came. If possible, he wants to try to keep the ball on the side from which it was passed. As D1 rotates behind, D5 will now drop down and cover the man in area 1 as well as the skip lane from O4 to O5. D2 will sag in a little bit and cover O2 along with the skip lane

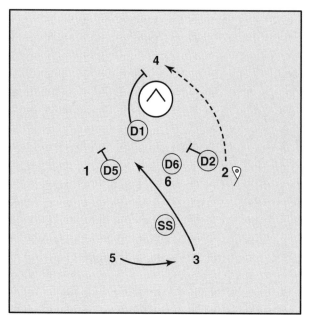 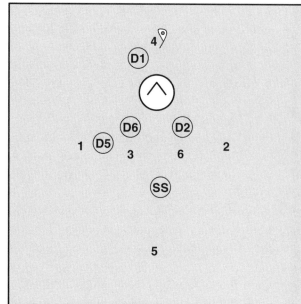

Figure 12.3 (c,d) Man-down defense vs. a 1-4-1 setup, phases 3 and 4.

between O4 and O3. As the ball is thrown behind, O3 makes a cut to the crease area. The short-stick will carry O3 in, moving along with him toward the crease, while alerting D6 that a cutter is coming by yelling "Cutter! Cutter! Cutter!" D6 now becomes responsible for both O3 and O6 on the crease, concentrating most on covering the player closest to the side on which the ball is located. The short-stick then assumes responsibility for O5, who has rotated to the middle. Our alignment has now changed defensively from a 2-1-2 box to a 1-3-1. Whenever we play against a 1-4-1, we align ourselves in a similar formation, meaning we go from a 2-1-2 to a 1-3-1; the 1-3-1 is a similar formation, less one man.

Phase four (figure 12.3d) shows D1 behind the goal, playing the ball. D5 is covering O1 in his area and helping on a skip-pass up top. D6 is now going to share responsibility for covering O3 and O6. D2 is covering O2 and helping to cover a skip lane up top. The short-stick is going to slough in to about ten or eleven yards from the goal, but his responsibility will be to cover O5, if the ball is thrown to him, out top. In this 1-4-1, D6 has a great responsibility. He is covering two people on the crease, the most dangerous area.

In phase five (figure 12.3e), although we would

like D1 to keep the ball on the side from which it was passed down, that won't always happen. If O4 receives the ball and carries to his right, O3 becomes the closest crease man to the ball. D6 will then give the majority of his attention to O3, while O6, the back-side creaseman, will be covered by D2 on the low side and by the short-stick on the high side. That is how best to cover a 1-4-1.

BASIC RULES

1. All defenders keep their sticks in the passing lanes of the extraman offense. Many passes can be blocked or intercepted if the defenders' sticks are properly positioned.

2. The defender playing the crease attackman concentrates on the location of the ball as much as on the position of his man. In all-even play, the crease defenseman plays his man almost completely eye-to-eye, but this is not so in the man-down situation, because he must enter into the overall team defense and help out even more.

3. A defender on the crease, whether the crease defenseman or any of the man-down defenders, should leave the crease to play the ball when it is passed from behind the goal to an attacker in a dangerous

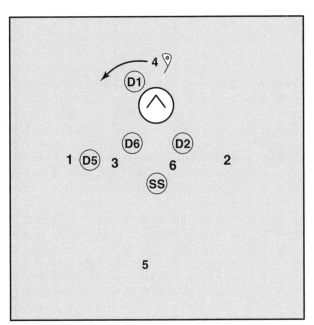

Figure 12.3e Man-down defense vs. a 1-4-1 setup, phase 5.

shooting position in the midfield about twelve yards or closer to the goal. If there is no defensive teammate between himself and the ball, he leaves the crease area and hustles to the shooter to prevent him from moving in even closer to the goal for a point-blank shot. To avoid being dodged, the defender must also be under control when he reaches the shooter.

4. A defender on the crease should be reluctant to leave a man on the crease to play a man behind the goal because he is moving away from a potential scorer to play a potential feeder, who is obviously less dangerous. There are times when he does make this move, but he must be covered by a teammate before going.

5. An onside crease defender never leaves the crease to play the ball behind the goal.

6. The defender playing the ball carrier behind the goal must respond quickly to a pass from his man to an attacker in front of the goal. As he follows the flight of the ball with his eyes, he sprints to the crease area. He is ready to move toward the offside crease, because the extraman offense normally tries to move the ball with speed and take advantage of a slow-reacting defense.

7. The defender playing the cutter not only makes his call that a man is cutting but also tries to read the play in order to determine whether the cut is meaningful or not. Often the extraman offense will use a cutter just to cause confusion in the defense and to make a defender play him. Granted, the cutter must be covered when he breaks for the goal, because an open stick in the crease area can result in a goal, but as soon as the feeder passes the ball to another attacker, the defender releases the cutter to get into the regular rotation. Often the defense makes the mistake of staying with the cutter too long in man-for-man coverage.

8. The defender playing the ball carrier can afford to be considerably more aggressive in the man-down situation than in the all-even, because the extraman offense is not geared to dodging. However, a certain amount of caution must prevail to avoid a second foul.

9. After a shot is taken and the offense regains possession of the ball, whether inbounds or out-of-bounds, the man-down defense must regroup. Frequently the extraman offense will set up another play in this situation, and the defense must be ready to adjust to it.

10. When time has elapsed on a penalty, the defender entering the game runs at full speed to get inside the defensive perimeter. He plays the nearest man who is unguarded and calls out, "All even." Players entering the game from the penalty box frequently make the mistake of calling too soon, and this causes the defense to relax, thinking all the men are covered when actually they are not.

11. The distance from the center of the field to the defensive perimeter is shorter than the distance from the penalty box to the defensive perimeter. Therefore, the player entering the game from the penalty box usually should head toward the attack half of the field, releasing a fast midfielder at the center of the field to take the shorter route back to the defense.

TWO- AND THREE-MAN-DOWN SITUATIONS

When two members of a team are in the penalty box, the offense has a tremendous six-on-four advantage. It is quite likely that they will generate a shot. However, if the defense does a good job, the offense

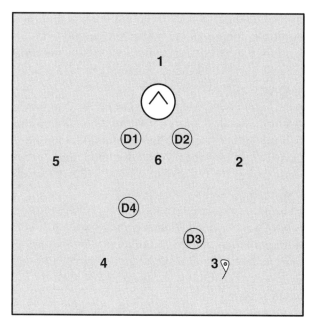 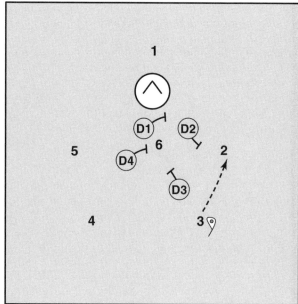

Figure 12.4 (a,b) Man-down defense vs. a 2-3-1 setup, phases 1 and 2.

may only have an opportunity to shoot from the perimeter, not from the crease area. No matter what alignment the offense adopts, the defense will play in a box, with four men around the perimeter. *Every defender shares responsibility for the crease as well as for trying to cover two offensive players.* Even the defender playing the ball does not concentrate fully on the ball carrier; rather, he tries to anticipate where the ball will be thrown so that he can react quickly and adjust his position. The ball carrier is not played until he is at about twelve to thirteen yards in front of the goal. By jamming the crease, the defense hopes to encourage the offense to take low-percentage shots from the porch area.

Because the rules state that a team is permitted to have four long sticks on the field at one time, when the defense is two men down, the four remaining defenders all should have long sticks, providing the defense with the greatest chance for knocking down or intercepting passes. Although being able to cover two offensive players is important for every man-down defense, it is never more so than now. If the defense does not have the ability to do that, quick and effective rotation becomes essential.

As illustrated in figure 12.4a, the extraman offense has aligned itself in a 2-3-1 set (phase one). In

this situation, D3 will cover the ball and is responsible for stopping at twelve to thirteen yards from the goal. D4 is responsible for the skip lane between O3 and O5 as well as for covering O4 if the ball is thrown to him. Since D1 is farthest from the ball, he will help cover the crease and also cover O6. D2 will cover the skip lane from O3 to O1. If O1 were to sneak left-handed toward the goal, D2 must be prepared to rotate out to O2, should the ball be passed to him.

In phase two (figure 12.4b), the ball is passed from O3 to O2. D2 will rotate up to play the ball, not extending too far. D1 now has two responsibilities. He will rotate to the middle of the field, not far above the crease, so that he can still help out with guarding the offensive player on the crease, and he will position himself to cover O1, should he make a cut, or "sneak," either left-handed or right-handed toward the goal. D4 is responsible for helping to cover the crease more on the high side as well as covering the skip lane from O2 to O5. D3 will sag in and be responsible for the skip lane from O2 to O4 and also for covering O3 if the ball is thrown back to him. D3 can also help cover O6 on the high side. It is important for the defenders not playing the ball to remember that when playing

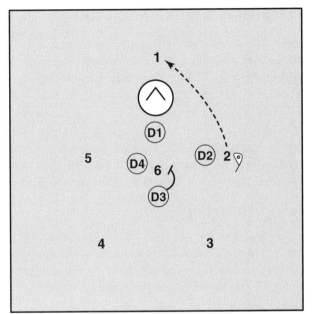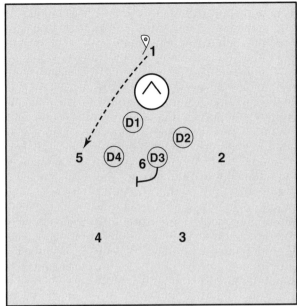

Figure 12.4 (c,d) Man-down defense vs. a 3-2-1 setup, phases 3 and 4.

two men down, their sticks should be held toward the inside of the field, or toward the crease; this will help them either knock down a pass or check the crease man if the ball is passed to him.

Phase three (figure 12.4c) shows the ball being passed behind, from O2 to O1. D1 is responsible for O1, but he will not rotate behind the goal as he would in a regular man-down situation. That is because such a move would create an ever greater opportunity in front of the goal for the offense, giving them a five-versus-three advantage. In addition, remember that O1, being behind the goal, is not an effective scorer from that location. He is a feeder. We want to give more attention to the players in front of the goal who have an opportunity to score. As O1 receives the ball, D1 will play in front of the goal, around the top of the crease. If O1 were to drive toward the goal, D1 would meet him at the goal line extended. D2 then will sag in and be responsible for helping cover the crease; he will also cover the skip lane from O1 to O3 and cover O2 if he receives the ball. D4 has multiple responsibilities as well. He will help cover the crease on his side, with his stick held to the inside; he will help on the passing lane from O1 to O4; and he will be prepared to play O5 if he receives the ball. Since D3 is the farthest from the ball, he will slough in and help cover

the crease. D4 and D2 will help D3 by taking away the skip lanes out top. If the ball is thrown through or lobbed over the top, D3 should have enough time to react and leave the crease to play whichever offensive player receives the ball, be it O3 or O4.

In phase four (figure 12.4d), if the ball is passed from O1 to O5, D4 is responsible for covering O5. D3 will begin to rotate up a little, still helping to cover the crease on the high side but understanding that he will be responsible for covering a pass out top as well as the skip lane from O5 to O2. D2 will help cover the crease, and D1 will be responsible if O1 sneaks toward the goal either left-handed or right-handed.

In phase five (figure 12.4e), the ball is passed from O5 to O4. D3 will rotate out and be responsible for covering the ball. D2 will rotate up a little to help cover the skip lane between O4 and O2 while also being prepared to play O3 if the ball is thrown to him. D1 will position himself toward the middle of the crease, where he will be responsible for covering both O1 and O2. D4 will sag in to help cover the crease and the skip-pass from O4 to O1, should O1 sneak right-handed to the crease. Since D1 is the farthest from the ball, he will provide the most help in covering the crease. Our aim is always to leave

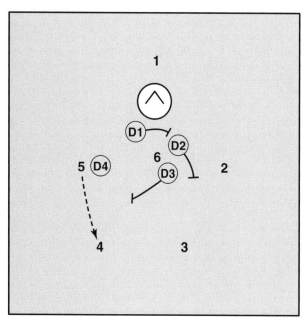

Figure 12.4e Man-down defense vs. a 3-2-1 setup, phase 5.

the least-dangerous offensive player more open than anybody else, and usually the least-dangerous offensive player is the one farthest from the ball—which is why the defensive player farthest from the ball provides the majority of support to the crease. It is also crucial to prevent the offense from executing successful skip-passes in every man-down situation, but particularly when the defense is two men down.

If a team finds itself with three men in the penalty box, the man-down defense is obviously in a very difficult situation. The same basic principles that apply to the two-down defense can be adapted to the three-down situation. The man-down unit should align itself in a triangle and rotate three players against their five opponents—again remembering that one defender should try to play two offensive players as much as possible. The point man, the defender closest to the restraining line, should not go any farther than about ten to twelve yards from the goal. The other two defenders jam the crease. If the ball goes behind the goal, all three move in close to the crease, trying to entice a shot from the wing areas. The offense almost always gets a good shot at the goal. However, with a little bit of luck or a spectacular save by the goalie, the defense can prevent the score.

CLEARING IN MAN-DOWN SITUATIONS

When the man-down defense gains possession of the ball, it must try to clear the ball to its offensive half of the field. This is especially difficult to do, because the defense has one less player to clear the ball than they are accustomed to having. However, it is important to remember that the extraman team, or the riding team, does not have a numerical advantage when clearing the ball, because the clearing team, the man-down team, is able to use its goaltender, giving them six players to use in clearing the ball rather than just five.

In this situation, it is not uncommon for a defenseman or a short-stick who either picks up the ball or receives it on a pass to have to beat a riding player. Some teams instead use specific clearing patterns if the defense gets the ball. They may spring their short-stick to a specific area of the field and look to lob the ball to him, or they might have a predetermined drop area in the offensive end of the field. The defenders know that their teammates on the offense, down at the other end of the field, will be aligned in a specific formation. When the goalie makes a save, he throws the ball down to a specific area, a drop area, at the other end of the field, and the attackman will go fight the opponent's defenders for the ball. Sometimes the opposing defense is not prepared for that.

The best bet for the goalie who makes a save during a man-down is to look to pass the ball quickly to one of his defenders. If the defender can pass the ball to an open man, he should do so. If not, chances are he's going to have to run by a rider, thus breaking down the ride. If no one is open and the goalie makes a save, he can go behind the goal in an effort to use the crease to gain an advantage over the riding crease attackman. If the crease attackman follows him behind the goal, the goalie goes to the opposite side from him. If the crease attackman stays in front of the goal, the goalie can merely stand behind the goal and wait for the crease attackman to make the first move. When he does, the goalie moves to the opposite side and just keeps going around the goal with the attackman chasing him.

It is critical to remember, however, that unlike

many years ago, the rules of today's game place a time limit on a team that is clearing the ball. In recent years, the defending team had to move the ball from inside its defensive restraining box to outside of it in ten seconds. A new rule now states that the clearing team has twenty seconds to clear the ball across the midline. It is important for the man-down unit that is clearing the ball to keep this in mind. Although they do have to clear the ball as quickly as possible, twenty seconds is a *long time*, and they should do their best to use that amount of time wisely.

When the man-down defense gets the ball in an out-of-bounds situation, the team's fastest and best-dodging midfielder should bring the ball into play. If this person is not in the game when the whistle blows, the coach must have him enter as a substitute. Under no circumstances should a slow defenseman or a slow goalie bring the ball into play from out-of-bounds, because he will probably lose it. As soon as the ball is given to the dodger, all other defenders should move to positions away from him. When the official blows his whistle, the man with the ball drives at his defender and either dodges him or uses sheer speed to go by him. This is the easiest and most effective clear in the book when a team is operating with a man in the penalty box.

Another way to handle the situation if the ball goes out-of-bounds during a man-down penalty would be to have the short-stick player on the man-down unit pick up the ball. When the official whistles the resumption of play, the short-stick can attempt to run by a riding attackman. If the opposing team's coach decides to put two offensive players on the ball, this will leave one of the man-down unit's players open. In that case, the short-stick passes the ball to the open man, who aims to carry it up the field.

SPECIAL DEFENSES

Earlier in this chapter, I mentioned that there are several different philosophies that can be utilized when playing man-down. In the previous paragraphs, we have discussed the 2-1-2, or the five-man zone. Another effective way to play man-down is the five-man rotation.

The five-man rotation system differs from the five-man zone in that all five defensive players are involved in playing both the crease and the perimeter, whereas in the five-man zone defense, one defender has sole responsibility for the crease. In a five-man rotation, all five players are used to cover the crease. As the ball moves around the perimeter, the players covering the crease will rotate from the crease to the perimeter and be involved in covering the ball as well. This is unlike what is done in the five-man zone. There are several reasons for using a five-man rotation:

1. It provides a man-down defense with the opportunity to be more aggressive.

2. When the five-man zone has to rotate, we are rotating only four players around the perimeter. The five-man rotation allows us to rotate five, which in turn will give us a greater ability to defend against shots from the perimeter. The five-man zone provides a greater ability to defend against shots from the crease.

3. If a team has an athletic group of man-down players, the coach may want to employ the five-man rotation, allowing those players to be aggressive and use their athleticism.

Another man-down defense tactic is known as the "shutoff." This can be used if a man-down unit feels that the opposing team has one specific player for whom their plays are designed or who is a tremendously talented scorer. In order to execute the shutoff, the man-down defense will have the short-stick go face-to-face against the man-up's best player to shut him off. This enables the four long-sticks to play a four-man box, just as they would with two men down—although in this case, the defense is only playing one man down because they have shut off the offensive's best player.

Regardless of the style of man-down defense a team uses, it must continually strive to improve its effectiveness. A man-down unit that prides itself on meeting the extraman challenge can bolster the overall attitude and morale of a team. It is especially reassuring to every team member to have the confidence that its defense can handle not only the all-even play but also the man-down play.

Jesse Schwartzman (JHU '07) Most Valuable Player in the
2005 NCAA national championship game. *Jay Van Rensselaer*

13

Goaltending

The goalie is the backbone of a team's defense and carries more responsibility on his shoulders than any other player on the field. He has the greatest opportunity to affect the outcome of the game—positively or negatively. There have been few championship teams with an average goalie. To the contrary, almost every championship team has had a goalie whose performance has been either above average or superior. Recent examples of hot goaltenders who made the difference in winning a championship are Virginia's Tillman Johnson in 2003, Syracuse's Jay Pfeifer in 2004, and Hopkins's Jesse Schwartzman in 2005.

Although the qualities of a good goalie are described in chapter 4, they should be repeated briefly here. The most important is courage—or just plain guts. It takes a special kind of person to place, without flinching, his head and body in point-blank range of a powerfully thrown lacrosse ball. Regardless of the protective equipment worn, getting hit with the ball stings, at the very least.

Along with courage the goalie must have a number of other qualities, the most important being superb reflexes and agility. Quick reactions inside the six-by-six-foot goal are of primary importance, because the goalie must try to get both his stick and his body in front of every shot. Good stickwork is essential, because it minimizes the number of shots that rebound out of his stick or off his body, giving the opponent additional opportunities to regain control of the ball and score. In addition, the goalie must exercise positive leadership in directing and controlling his teammates on the defensive half of the field. When a goal is scored, he must be careful not to overreact. If there has been a defensive breakdown that results in a goal, it is up to the goalie to talk to his teammates in a tactful manner. His job is not to criticize his teammates but to unify them. The goalie must also keep his emotions from running wild when he misses a ball that he feels he should have saved. A goalie should always be thinking about the *next* shot, not his last save or the last goal that got by him. Concentrating on the next shot keeps the goalie focused on the present moment and on his job and will block out distractions. Dwelling on a mistake does nothing for his own steadiness or the general morale of the team. The most telltale sign of a goalie's composure is how he reacts after a goal has been scored on him. A goalie who throws his equipment or scolds his teammates is a goalie who is losing control of his position in the game. The goalie should act positively toward his defense and not blame them if a goal is scored. When Quint Kessenich was in Hopkins's goal, he often shouted briefly "My fault! My fault!" to reassure his defense if the opponent scored. Occasionally, however, a goalie must also be forceful in addressing any shortcomings or misplays by his defense.

Size and speed are bonus qualities for the goalie (as in any other position) but are not essential. There is no prototypical size for a goalie. A goalie who, with his cleats and helmet, is six feet tall or more has the advantage of having his head extend above the top crossbar on the goal. The broader he is, the more of the goal he covers. Bigger goalies, such as the University of Massachusetts's Sal Lo-Cascio and Hobart's Guy Van Arsdale, have been successful. Smaller goalies, such as Quint, Hopkins's Brian Carcaterra, and Navy's Matt Russell, were more active in and out of the goal but also enjoyed great success. Although it helps to have size in the goal, quickness is more beneficial.

Other important qualities of successful goalkeepers are concentration, patience, footwork, and quick hands. It is imperative that as the goalie directs the defense, he pays primary attention to the ball. A patient goalie does not overreact to fakes, gives himself more time to read the shot, and frustrates shooters who aim at areas where the goalie moved his stick or body after a fake. Good balance enables a goalie to handle shots more easily, move to the ball on shots

more directly, give up fewer rebounds, be prepared for rebounds, and cover a greater area of the goal. It is crucial for a goalie to have top-notch stickhandling skills to enable him to pass accurately, dodge when necessary, and participate in the field aspect of the game as it occurs in the defensive half. Goalies are required to make a wide array of passes and be proficient in all of them. Short-touch passes to defenders and long-leading passes to breaking midfielders or long-stick defensemen on clears frequently are required and must be practiced regularly. Goalies must have superb vision and be able to scan the field to detect open teammates as well as be aware of the position of riding opposition players. Finally, and possibly just as important as courage, quick reflexes, and all the rest, the goalie must have confidence in himself. This is important to meet the challenge of the opponent's shooters and to command his own defense.

COACHING GOALIES

One of the main jobs of the coach in developing a goalie is to instruct him in the proper position in the goal; teach proper hand, feet, and stick positioning; and instill confidence. The coach cannot give a player the fearlessness to stick his nose into a hard shot, the quick reflexes to react to the ball, or the speed to move outside the crease. These qualities must come naturally to him. With proper handling of a young player who basically is not afraid of the ball, however, a coach can develop his skills through training to give him the confidence to become a first-rate goalie. The goalie realizes that he will receive a certain amount of physical punishment from the ball, but the coach can help him to minimize this by teaching him to make as many saves as possible with his stick rather than his body. If the goalie is not given intelligent and meaningful direction, his confidence can be affected, and he may fail. This often happens when the goalie picks up bad habits doing what comes naturally to him or when just listening to advice from other players who really don't know the fine points of playing in the goal.

In working with a beginner who has the desire to be a goalie, the first step is to concentrate on the fundamentals of handling the stick—catching, throwing, cradling, and scooping. Once he has confidence in handling the ball in the big pocket, he is ready to be instructed in the basic movements to the ball. The coach should have a bucket of balls ready and maintain a steady number of shots on goal. Some will go in, some will go wide, and some will be stopped. If the goalie becomes either frustrated or tired, the coach can have him shag the balls from behind the cage and in the net—or give the goalie a rest and retrieve the balls himself. Emphasize with young goalies that the important thing at the beginning is not necessarily stopping the ball. They must first get their mechanics and technique down correctly. Once that is accomplished, the saves will happen.

To help the beginner get the feel of proper footwork and movement into the ball, a coach might give him a midfielder's stick instead of a goalie stick for the first few workouts. If he learns to hold the stick properly, stand properly, put himself in the right position, and stop the ball with that stick, doing so later with the larger goalie stick should be easier.

After the goalie learns to move properly, the coach can begin throwing balls at him at about half speed and from a distance of about twelve to fifteen yards. The coach makes all his shots with an overhand throwing motion. Rather than starting with bounce shots, which are more difficult to catch, he should keep the ball in the air. The shots are directed first to one side of the goalie's body and then to the other side, with emphasis on movement of his body behind every shot. Once the goalie handles these shots with reasonable confidence, the coach can move to bounce shots near the feet, then high bounce shots. The coach lets the goalie know that the shots will be thrown only on one side. The goalie then gets the rhythm of moving into the ball on that side. After the goalie experiences reasonable success, the coach switches to the other side. The coach can use this format for the first three or four sessions with the goalie and then, according to his progress, begin to shoot harder. The coach should correct mistakes immediately to reinforce proper footwork, stick positioning, and body positioning. As the goalie handles these shots effectively, the coach can work

him on high shots without telling him on which side they will be thrown, then on bounce shots to either side, and finally on a mixture of both high and bounce shots to either side. If a young goalie still is not stepping to the ball properly, however, and just basically throwing his stick at it, the coach may try to correct that problem by replacing his stick with a lacrosse handle minus its head and use a tennis ball for part of the workout. This technique can help the goalie react to the ball properly.

The coach will probably not want to open up with full-speed shots at the twelve- to sixteen-yard mark until the goalie has had at least several on-field practices and is ready for them. Once the goalie has confidence in handling hard shots at this distance, he is over the hump in his development in the goal. The coach can then proceed to teach him how to play the various types of shots other than the overhand shot and also shots that are taken from different locations on the field, including the point-blank shots on the crease. Next the coach can work with the goalie on the vocabulary he uses to direct the defense, on playing screen shots, on handling ground balls around the crease, and on clearing the ball. All these areas will be covered in this chapter, with the exception of clearing, which will be covered in chapter 14.

EQUIPMENT

Aside from a helmet and gloves, the goalie wears an athletic supporter and cup and a chest and throat protector, all standard equipment required by the rule book. Rarely do goalies wear arm or elbow pads, which interfere with maneuverability. Some goalies wear sweat pants to reduce the sting of shots, but few, if any, wear shin or leg protectors.

According to the rule book, the goalie's stick may be of any length and the pocket of any depth. A goalie should use a stick with which he is comfortable and feels adept at handling. This will help him make crisp clearing passes, reach for ground balls outside the crease area, and maintain proper position in the goal. Goalies often do this by hitting the pipes with either the head of the stick or the handle. This movement should be limited. Although the length of a goalie's stick is generally between forty-six and sixty inches, some goalies prefer a stick shorter than forty-six inches because they can dodge more easily with it. Nonetheless, the majority of collegiate goalies use a stick in the range of fifty to fifty-six inches. The pocket of the stick should definitely be deep enough for the goalie to be able to keep even the hardest shot in his pocket. If his pocket is too shallow and the ball bounces out, the attackers have an excellent chance for a rebound shot and possibly a goal. Controlling the ball is the primary consideration regarding the depth of the pocket, although a pocket with an excessive sag will cause the goalie trouble with his throwing. The pocket should be big enough to handle bounce shots and loose enough to give on hard shots so as to eliminate rebounds.

BODY AND STICK POSITIONING

Ball in Front of Goal

When the ball is in front of the goal, the goalie places himself in a direct line between the ball and the center of the goal. Since the ball leaves the shooter's stick about one to two feet from the side of his body, the goalie actually lines up between the center of the goal and the ball carrier's stick side. This places him in a more advantageous position to stop the shot than if he were lined up with the center of the ball carrier's body. His feet are about shoulder-width apart, and his weight is carried in his legs and on the balls of his feet. For stability and balance, his heels are just barely touching the ground. His knees are bent, his upper body leans slightly forward (not too much), and his eyes never leave the ball. Although he is responsible for directing the entire defense, he will not try to do so at the expense of taking his eyes off the ball. Figure 13.1 shows the goalie in his basic stance when the ball is in the midfield area near the restraining line.

The goalie grips his stick in a different manner than the other players on the team, because the head of his stick is considerably bigger and heavier. To control it properly and to move it quickly to the

Figure 13.1 Goalie's position when shooter is located near the restraining line.

ball, he grasps it with his upper hand on the handle next to the head of the stick or just an inch or two from it. A goalie should keep his hands about six to ten inches apart, but he needs to position them in a way that is comfortable for him. The grip is relaxed with both hands, although the upper hand is the dominant one and controls stick movement. A relaxed grip helps the goalie relax his body. A firm grip at the throat tends to make the goalie tense, which can often cause him to give up rebounds when the ball hits the pocket of his stick.

The position of the goalie's stick will be determined by the location of the ball. Since the most common shots are taken at the ten- to twelve-yard range, the goalie holds his stick so that the head is located slightly above his shoulder and away from his body. This stick placement, along with the appropriate foot positioning discussed earlier, will allow the goalie to react quickly to a shot that is taken either high or low (see figure 13.1). The goalie should never drop his stick below the level of his waist unless he is moving to the ball to make a save on a low shot.

The key to the goalie's position is his readiness to attack the ball as soon as it leaves the shooter's stick. He can't let the ball play him; he must go after it and "play the ball." With his body weight centered in his legs and the balls of his feet, he is ready to spring at the ball like a panther at its prey. Some goalies bounce continuously in place while waiting for the shooter to release the ball. Such movement can in fact be a handicap, because the goalie could be in the upward motion of the bounce when the ball is shot and thus lose a split second in reacting to the ball. To help keep their legs in a ready-to-move position, some goalies continuously shift their body weight just slightly from the ball of one foot to the other, but overdoing this is not recommended. Economy of motion and as little movement as possible before a shot bring the best results.

As the ball changes location in front of the goal, the goalie must adjust his position accordingly. He moves with short, lateral steps, first with one foot and then the other. His feet never get closer together than about three inches as he moves, and he definitely does not hop with both feet leaving the ground at the same time. Figure 13.2 shows the path on which the goalie travels as the ball moves in front of the goal. When the ball is directly in front of the goal, the goalie is positioned at the outer edge of the arc that runs from one goalpost to the other. The maximum distance from the goal is three feet. As the ball moves away from the center of the field, the goalie moves with it. When the ball is even with the plane of the goal, he is next to the post.

The speed and accuracy of today's shooters often make it difficult for many goalies to get their stick on the ball. Body position and the ability to deflect the shot simply by being in the right place at the right time can enhance save percentages. A number of philosophies exist on proper body positioning, but no consensus on them has ever been reached. For example, when the ball is out front, some goalies prefer to play very high in the goal, close to the front portion of the crease, to reduce the shooter's angle. Shorter goalies, such as Navy's 2004 first-team All-American Matt Russell, play with this style. As effective as it was for him, such a method has the potential of putting the goalie out of position on quick passes across

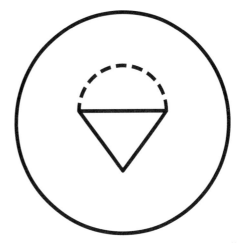

Figure 13.2 The arc on which the goalie travels as ball moves in front of the goal.

the face of the goal line extended, making it more difficult for the goalie to "find the pipe," or become properly positioned as the ball moves more toward the side of the goal. In contrast, some goalies choose to play deep in the goal, with their feet almost on the goal line as it extends between the pipes. This allows them to "take up" more of the goal and gives them more time to react to shots. Trevor Tierney, the former Princeton All-American, was very successful with this technique. This method also makes it easier for the goalie to move from pipe to pipe and protect against back-side feeds, but it does not enable the goalie to cut down the angle as well.

The goalie can maintain proper position better by making several marks on the ground with his stick. The first one is on the crease and directly in front of the center of the goal. He can also draw an arc on the ground with the butt end of his stick in order to check his positioning on it during practice sessions. Since the ball often moves rapidly from one position on the field to another, the goalie must use his stick as a feeler while keeping his eyes on the ball. A right-handed goalie moving from the center of the goal to his left uses the butt end of his stick to hit the left goalpost. When moving from the center to his right, he uses the head of his stick to hit the right goalpost. This contact helps to keep the goalie on his arc and in the best position to make the save. If he doesn't use the stick as a feeler, he will probably stray from the arc and lose position. If he turns his

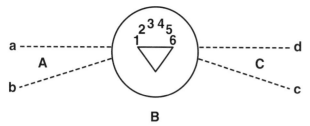

Figure 13.3 Goalie's position in the crease when the ball is behind the goal.

head even for an instant to look at the goal instead of using his stick, he may sacrifice the save. Once the goalie finds the pipe, he should put his foot closest to the pipe right next to it. He will know where the pipe is without having to bang his stick against it and lose his stick position.

Ball behind Goal

When the ball is behind the goal, the goalie takes a position about 1½ to 2½ feet from the goal and approximately in the middle of it. He is primarily concerned with maintaining the position that will give him maximum coverage of the goal when a feed is made to the crease area. Close-range shots often will be stopped by the goalie just because he is in the right position and the shooter hits him with the ball. If he lines up closer than 1½ feet or less from the goal, he is too close to it and will give the shooter too much room on either side of him as well as make himself vulnerable to shots that may ricochet off his body and go into the goal. If he is farther than 2½ feet from the goal, he may give the shooter too much room to shoot around him. The optimum position is 1½–2½ feet from the goal. Since he must protect the entire goal when the ball is fed to the crease area, he must be in a position near the middle of the goal most of the time. In figure 13.3, the goalie is in either position 3 or 4 when the ball is located behind the goal in area B. When the ball crosses line b moving from area B into area A, the goalie will move into position 2. When the ball approaches line a (the goal line extended), which is even with the plane of the goal, the goalie moves into position 1. The same adjustments take place on the other side of the field when the ball

moves from area B to area C and then from area C to line d (the goal line extended). The goalie moves from position 4 to position 5 and finally to position 6. Figure 13.4 shows the goalie in position 3 with the ball behind the goal.

As is often the case with goaltending, some coaches and players have a different philosophy on positioning when the ball is behind the goal. Some would prefer that the goalie play closer to the goal line, believing that this positioning gives him more time to react, always places him between the pipes, and makes it easier for him to go pipe-to-pipe and protect against a back-side feed. In some respects, however, positioning when the ball is behind the goal follows the same philosophy as positioning when the ball is in front. If the goalie prefers to play in close with the ball in front, then he probably should do the same with the ball behind so that when he turns to follow the feed, he is in his preferred position. If he prefers to be farther out in the goal when the ball is in front, then he may be better off playing farther out when the ball is behind.

When the ball is behind the goal, the goalie is primarily concerned with calling out the location of the ball to help his defensive teammates in front of the goal who may not be able to see the ball. He also tries to intercept feeds to the crease area. He watches the feeder's eyes and stick, trying to get a jump on the whereabouts of his pass. The goalie holds the head of his stick above his own head and in or near the feeding lane of the attackman. This enables him to get to the ball more quickly than if he were to hold the stick at shoulder level or lower. The goalie must be careful in blocking a feed not to bat the ball into the goal. He should not extend himself to catch a feed unless he is 99 percent sure of getting the ball. If he misses, he will not be able to get in position to play the shooter's quick shot.

The goalie must always remember that the basic rule of goaltending is to keep his eyes on the ball at all times, even when it is behind the goal. The exception is when there is a feed from behind. The goalie should momentarily take his eye off the ball on feeds from behind so that he can see how the recipient of the feed catches the ball. By seeing the

Figure 13.4 Goalie's position when the ball carrier is even with the plane of the goal.

cutter catch the feed, the goalie gets an invaluable tip-off on the type of shot he can anticipate from the shooter. If the ball is thrown anywhere to the right of the center of the goalie's body, he turns to the right, trying to follow the ball in its entire flight. If it is thrown to his left, he turns to the left. He never turns his back to the ball, because he then cannot see the ball, will not see it caught, and will have to move a greater distance to get to where he wants to be. When he makes the turn, he pivots on one foot, always keeping one foot on the ground and maintaining his balance. This will place him in good position to stop point-blank shots from the crease. Sometimes a feeder may be deterred from passing the ball to the crease if the goalie's stick is in the proper position for fear of having the pass intercepted.

When the ball carrier gets to the goal line extended, the goalie moves to a position where his body is against the goalpost. Figure 13.4 shows the goalie with his left foot and the entire left side of his body next to the post. His feet should be apart and balanced. His stick is placed six to ten inches away from his body so that he can cover shots on either side of his head. The goalie holds this position until the ball carrier is past the plane of the goal by three to four feet. At this point the goalie starts to inch away from the post in order to as-

sume a position that will minimize open area for the shooter. It is vital that he does not move too far from the pipe too soon. If he does, he exposes himself to an easy shot by the ball carrier.

Making the Save

The goalie's prime responsibility is to stop the ball. Both proper positioning and movement into the ball are the keys. To get his body to move in the proper direction, the goalie must concentrate on the ball in the shooter's stick and follow it completely from the instant it leaves his stick. The goalie's critical movement is stepping first with the foot nearer the ball and pushing off with the other foot. If the ball is shot to the goalie's left side, his left foot is obviously nearer to the ball than his right foot, and he should step first with that foot. Figure 13.5a shows the goalie in his initial move on a shot to his left side. His first step is always toward the ball and forward at approximately a forty-five-degree angle, not to the side and definitely not back toward the goal. As he pushes off with his right foot and steps with his left, he brings his stick in a sweeping motion from his right side to a position where the head of the stick is directly in front of his body and his body is directly in front of the ball. It is important that the entire head of the stick is opened up to the ball to facilitate the catch.

Figure 13.5 (a,b) Goalie's initial move and save on a bounce shot to his left.

The handle is in a position almost perpendicular to the ground. Figure 13.5b shows the goalie completing his save on a bounce shot to his left side. The goalie should end up in essentially the same ready position he held when waiting for the shot. In other words, he should end up with his feet shoulder-width apart, balanced, and with his hands out and away from his body. Once the ball is in the goalie's stick, he should scan the field for an outlet pass. Often the first place to look is where the shot came from, since the shooter is usually closer to the goal than his defender.

On a bounce shot, the goalie must rotate the head of his stick toward the ball with the top of the stick head close to the ground. Since some outside bounce shots will skim close to the ground instead of rising, the goalie must guard against this possibility first and then be ready to raise the level of his stick to play the higher bounce. If he fails to do so and the ball gets under his stick, there is a good chance

of a goal resulting because he has only his ankles and feet to stop the ball. On the contrary, when the ball bounces over the stick, the goalie still has a reasonable chance to stop it because he has his entire midsection and upper body in front of it. The goalie should bend at his knees more than at his waist when reaching for a bounce shot.

The sweeping motion of a right-handed goalie moving to his left, and a left-hander to his right, is very natural and normally much easier than a right-hander going to his right and a left-hander to his left. To illustrate this point, a right-handed pitcher or quarterback throws the ball with his weight transferring from his right side to his left side. The same thing applies to a batter hitting a baseball right-handed. A right-handed shortstop usually feels more comfortable playing a ball on his left side because he gets that natural push-off with his right foot. Although this also applies to the right-handed goalie, both he and the right-handed shortstop must be able to move as

Figure 13.6 (a,b) Goalie's initial move and save on a bounce shot to his right.

effectively to their right side. The motion may not be as smooth, but it must be made quickly to get the body behind the ball. Figure 13.6a shows the goalie in his initial move, pushing off his left foot and stepping with his right. Instead of sweeping his stick, he merely directs it toward the ground and in line with the path of the ball. He especially wants to make sure that the head of the stick gets close to the ground so that the ball does not get under it. This move is somewhat awkward for many goalies and, in fact, is one of their vulnerable areas—a low bounce shot on their stick side. Figure 13.6b shows the completion of the save with the handle of the stick close to a perpendicular position with the ground and the trailing (left) foot just several inches from the right foot.

On shots that do not bounce and are at a level between the goalie's feet and shoulders, the goalie makes the same move with his body and stick as he does on bounce shots. He even makes the same move on high shots on his stick side, as shown in

figure 13.7. However, on high shots at shoulder level or above and on the side away from his stick, he does not normally use the sweeping motion because it is awkward at this level. Rather, he merely pivots the head of his stick in front of his face and in line with the path of the ball. Figure 13.8 shows the goalie making a save of a shot over his left shoulder. The goalie should try to keep the head of his stick out and away from his body and make the most direct stick-to-ball movement as possible, with little wasted motion.

Making a save on one-on-one shots can be more difficult and dramatic—and more rewarding. When a shooter becomes open underneath the defense and one-on-one with the goalie, he has a distinct advantage. He controls where the ball will go and what amount of time the goalie has to react. A goalie has tricks, however, with which he can try to equalize the odds. As in every situation, proper positioning is essential, and not giving up that position when the shooter fakes is difficult but criti-

Figure 13.7 Goalie's moves on a high shot to his right.

cal. The goalie should try to keep his stick mobile, not rigid, to allow for a quick, reflexive reaction to the ball. Sometimes the goalie can try to bait the shooter by, say, holding his stick in a very high position to make a low shot look like the best choice, then reacting quickly to drop low when the shooter takes the bait.

When the shooter is at close range, the goalie relies primarily on being in the proper position and moving toward the ball once it leaves the shooter's stick. He tries to anticipate where the shooter will be aiming his shot, and it's amazing how often a shooter will tip off his shot. The goalie mirrors the head of the shooter's stick with the head of his own stick. Often the shooter carries his stick high and shoots high, which makes the goalie's job easier (figure 13.9). Similarly, a shooter who decides to shoot low may conveniently lower the head of his stick prior to the shot. The goalie has the toughest time against a shooter who either holds his stick

Figure 13.8 Goalie's moves on a high shot to his left.

Figure 13.9 Goalie's position on a high shot at close range.

high and shoots low, and vice versa, or has enough time to fake one way with his stick and eyes and then shoot in the opposite direction. In such situations, concentration on the ball is paramount. When the offensive player fakes high and shoots low, the goalie may try to stop the ball with his feet, and it is surprising just how many times during a season he will succeed.

Rarely should a goalie leave the crease to play an offensive player who is moving in for a close shot. When the offense has a break situation, whether two-on-one or any other advantageous combination, the goalie may try to anticipate a particular pass. If the receiver is close enough to the goal, the goalie may leave the goal to check him, but only if he is certain to arrive in time to make the check. The shooter will have a wide-open goal if the goalie is late. If there is any doubt in the goalie's mind as to whether or not he can reach the attacker in time to check him, he should not make the move. Rather, he should stay in the proper position and play the percentages on the shooter either hitting him with the ball or missing the goal completely. Because the pressure is on the shooter to score, he will often make a poor shot.

Using the Crease

The crease is the goalie's "home," and he has complete protection within it. After a save, the goalie has four critical seconds of protected time in the crease, according to the rules. The opposition cannot check him or his stick, regardless of whether the ball is loose on the ground or in his stick. The goalie

must be as quick as a cat, pouncing on a ball that lies on the ground inside the crease, because it is a potential goal if the attackman gets his stick on it. In almost every case he uses his stick to control the ball, rather than dive on it with his body. If the ball is bouncing at a height of about six inches or higher, he catches it in the air. If it bounces to a height of less than six inches or is just rolling on the ground, he clamps the ball to the ground with the back of the head of his stick. The entire stick is flat on the ground or certainly at an angle no greater than ten degrees. This position prevents the attacker from poking at the ball when the goalie rakes the ball into his pocket. Once the goalie has made his clamp, he must rake the ball immediately or else he will be penalized for delay of the game, a technical foul that gives the ball to the opposition. When the goalie rakes the ball, the handle of his stick points outside the goalposts rather than inside, where he could inadvertently rake the ball into the goal.

If a loose ball is on the ground outside the crease and within several yards of it, the goalie tries to get possession by keeping one foot in the crease and stepping out with the other (figure 13.10). His move is like that of a first baseman in baseball who keeps one foot on the base and stretches out with the other to reach the ball. The goalie does not have protection of the crease, however, when the ball is loose outside of it. If he gets the ball under his stick outside the crease, the rules now allow an opposing attackman to try to sweep his stick under the goalie's stick in an effort to dislodge the ball. About the only time it

Figure 13.10 Goalie clamping a loose ball outside the crease.

is desirable for the goalie to dive on a loose ball with his body is when the ball is outside the crease in front of the goal and the opposition has a dangerous crease attackman who is skillful at flicking ground balls into the goal. Once he decides to go for the ball, the goalie must be absolutely certain he will gain control of it, because the goal will be wide open if he fails. If the loose ball is more than several yards from the crease and too far for the goalie to reach it, he merely maintains his position in a direct line with the ball and the center of the goal. His stick is kept close to the ground, because a low shot is most likely if an attacker can direct the ball toward the goal. In this situation the goalie's position is about a foot or two from the front edge of the crease.

When a loose ball is on the ground behind the goal, the goalie can move to the rear of the goal but remains in the crease. If he cannot reach the loose ball with his stick, he calls for a defensive teammate to bat the ball with his stick or to kick it with his foot toward the goal, giving the goalie the opportunity to get possession inside the crease. The defensive teammates should direct the ball toward the goalie on the ground, however, because if they flip it into the air, an attacker may pick off the pass and break for the front

of the goal. With the goalie behind the goal in this situation, he is usually caught trailing the attacker to the front of the goal and gives up an easy score.

Some goalies are bold ones. Quint Kessenich, Matt Russell, Brian Carcaterra, and Greg Cattrano all liked to run around out of the goal. At times they nearly gave heart failure to everyone in the stadium, in particular their coach. All of these goalies were extremely athletic, however, and few goalies have that level of athleticism. Most goalies should stay at home in the crease and be somewhat cautious—certainly not reckless—about leaving it to make a play for the ball. This applies to attempts to play ground balls that are more than several yards from the goal and to other situations, such as checking dodgers or potential shooters and intercepting passes. Before leaving the crease, the goalie must be absolutely certain of either getting the ball or checking it out of his opponent's stick. If he fails in his attempt, he leaves the goal wide open and subjects his team to giving up an easy goal.

GOALIE'S VOCABULARY

As the director of the defense, the goalie must talk continuously to his teammates, giving commands and instructions that are invaluable to them. Since every member of the team must know the exact meaning of each command, the coach must take time to explain these expressions at the start of the season. The goalie's words of encouragement and reassurance are also very helpful to his teammates. Nonetheless, he does not want to get so carried away with hearing his own voice that he is more concerned about giving orders than he is with stopping the ball. The goalie also should not become a cheerleader, constantly talking and mixing important commands for the defense with unimportant chatter. If he does that, the good will be lost in the bad. The goalie acts as the eyes of the defense. Often off-ball defensive players do not know exactly where the ball is, or even where their own position is relative to the goal. They rely on the goalie for that vision. Therefore, the goalie must call out the ball's position and his teammates' positions relative

Figure 13.11 Goalie's position as he looks around a screen to locate the ball.

to the goal so that all of his defensive players know where the ball is and where they are at all times.

The following commands are used by the goalie:

"Ball left front." Giving the location of the ball in the various defensive positions on the field.

"Who has the ball?" Getting the defender to tell his teammates that he is playing the ball.

"Who has the two?" Getting his defensive teammates to respond that they have the second sliding player (as described in chapter 1) covered.

"Drop in, Chris." Telling the defender that he is playing his man too far from the goal.

"Move out, Tom," or "Get up on him." Telling the defender that he is too far from his man and should move out to play him.

"You're good, Matt." Telling the defender that his position on the ball carrier is fine.

"Check up." Telling all defenders to identify their men.

"Get up on his right (left)." Telling the defender that he is not in the proper position on the ball carrier and should adjust his position to favor the side to which he is moving.

"Drive." Telling the defender to make contact with the dodger and drive him away from the goal.

"Slide." Telling all the defenders that a teammate has been dodged and they must now move to stop the offensive thrust. The nearest man plays the dodger, and the other defenders move to new men. (Some teams use different words for this alert, such as "Red.")

"Check." Telling the defenders in the area of the crease to check the attackers' sticks.

"Ball down." Telling all defenders that the ball is on the ground and to be ready to play it.

"Bodies." Telling the defenders whose men are on the crease that a ball is loose in the area. They should check their opponents' sticks and use their shoulders to drive them off the crease.

"Here's your help." Telling the defender who has the ball in his possession to pass the ball to the goalie.

"Clear." Telling all defenders that the goalie has made a save and now wants them to move into their clearing lanes, looking for a pass.

WARMING UP THE GOALIE

It is imperative for the goalie to receive a proper warm-up before each day's practice and obviously before every game. The coach should be the only one to warm up the goalie. However, if he is handling the team by himself, he may need the assistance of his most reliable offensive player to work with the goalie during some of the practice sessions. This player should receive specific instructions concerning the techniques of warming up the goalie. No other person should ever shoot at the goalie unless the coach is there to supervise. If players are allowed complete freedom to shoot at the goalie without supervision, they will often do more harm than good. They are more concerned with scoring than with giving the goaltender the proper warm-up he needs. A warm-up is for the goalie, not for the shooters.

Every coach and team does warm-ups in their own way. At Hopkins, we believe that about twenty minutes are needed to give the goalie a complete warm-up with practice against all types of shots. Since most teams have either two or three goalies, the coach may be able to give a thorough workout to only his number one goalie and a modified workout to his other one or two. He does not want to slight any of his players, in particular his second-string goalie, because he becomes an important player if the regular goalie gets hurt or is having a bad day. But time is a critical factor at practice, and the coach cannot afford to spend one hour working with three goalies. However, if he uses time both before and after each practice session, he should be able to give about fifteen to twenty minutes to his number one goalie, ten to fifteen minutes to his number two goalie, and five to ten minutes to his number three goalie. Since an intense warm-up can be demanding physically on the coach as well as on the goalie, he may want to receive help from some of his best offensive players. Along with the starting goalie, his backups also should be given practice on six-on-six and extraman situations. This not only gives shooters a different challenge but ensures that the goalies have experienced varying situations and don't feel as if they are being used as target practice. In addition to utilizing the time before and after practice, the coach can frequently squeeze in about fifteen minutes' work with a goalie when the rest of the team is doing calisthenics or basic stickwork drills. Designated team leaders or an assistant coach can supervise the team at this time.

The following sequence describes the warm-up procedures at Hopkins and can be used as a guide in warming up the goalie:

1. High shots at three-quarter speed from ten to fifteen yards.
2. High shots at full speed from twelve to sixteen yards.
3. Bounce shots at three-quarter speed from ten to twelve yards.
4. Bounce shots at full speed from twelve to sixteen yards.
5. Mixture of high shots and bounce shots at full speed from ten to sixteen yards. The mixture should include shots on the run to try to make the goalie move in the crease while maintaining good stick and body position.
6. Mixture of high shots and bounce shots at three-quarter speed from ten to fifteen yards.
7. Mixture of high shots and bounce shots at three-quarter speed from five to fifteen yards.
8. Feeds from behind, from the side, and from out front to the shooter, who takes a mixture of shots in the air and bounce shots from all areas of the crease.
9. Dodges from behind the goal by attackmen, who take a mixture of shots at slightly less than three-quarter speed from three to four yards off the crease.

After the goalie makes a save, he should concentrate on making a sharp, accurate pass to the coach. Once he has had about ten to fifteen minutes of warm-up and is reacting well to the ball, the coach can simulate a clearing situation after the save by breaking out and giving the goalie a target with his stick. He can also use midfielders in the right- and left-front positions and have them do the same thing alternately. The coach doesn't want to overemphasize the clearing aspect of the goalie's job, so he may call for the clearing pass on every third or fourth save. But the goalie must be ready for it on every save and respond with an accurate lead pass when the coach or midfielder makes the break.

PREPARATIONS FOR THE GAME

Since the goalie is the one player on the team whose performance has the most significant impact on the outcome of the game, special attention must be given to his complete preparation, both physical and mental. A scouting report on the offensive capabilities of each opposing player, including his hand dominance, favorite shots, and where he tries to shoot them, is very important. The goalie also must be aware of the opposing team's offensive and extraman strategies and who the likely shooters may be in those situations. If the coach or one of his best shooters simulates the various shots of the opponent's star players in the warm-up during the practice sessions before the game, the goalie becomes so familiarized with their techniques that he is completely confident when he faces them on game day. The coach should call out the name and jersey number of the player he is simulating and then unload one of that player's most dangerous shots.

If the team is playing an away game on a field different from its home field, it should try to simulate the field conditions during the practice sessions prior to that game. For example, if the crease area on the home field is completely bare of grass but the team is traveling to a school that has grass in its crease area, the goalie should receive his warm-ups on grass during every practice before that game. This will just require the goal being moved from its normal position to a grassy location. If it is raining hard the day before the game and rain is forecast for game day, the coach should take his goalie out in the rain and give him a warm-up on the wet field. The rest of the team does not have to practice outside, but the goalie must feel confident in the goal, regardless of weather conditions. The goalie may want to use an old stick while practicing in the rain and save his best stick for game day.

Since the ball takes varying bounces depending on the playing surface of the field, the goalie must be fully aware of what to expect in each case. On a dry artificial surface the ball will take its truest bounce, but when the surface is wet, the ball will tend to skim along the ground. On a dry grassy field the ball may be somewhat cushioned and not bounce as high as on a dry dirt field. When the grass is wet, the ball will skim even more than on a wet artificial surface. On a dry dirt field, the ball will bounce very high; when wet, the dirt may turn into mud, and the ball will stay right on the ground or possibly just get stuck in the mud. The bounce of the ball is also affected by the distance from the goal when it hits the ground. If the ball hits close to the goalie's feet, the bounce will obviously be limited. Generally, the farther away from the goalie the ball hits the ground, the higher the bounce, except in wet field conditions.

The confidence that the team has in the goalie and the goalie has in himself is vital to the team's success. At Hopkins, we believe that this confidence can be bolstered by the type of warm-up given to the goalie on the day before the game. On that day, our starting goalie takes part in all of the basic drills—clearing the ball and the like—but otherwise has a light warm-up. We do not try to score on him or bring as much velocity to our shots as we would during practices earlier in the week. We don't want the ball going in the goal. The goalie also spends less time in the goal than during other practices to make sure he doesn't get injured. He sees fewer shots on the day before a game than at any other time in the week.

At Hopkins, we believe that the goalie's warm-up on game day should be the same as in a regular practice. The coach shoots the ball with power and accuracy because he wants to sharpen the goalie's reactions. He may not try quite as hard to score on him, because he does not want to affect his confidence. The coach takes him out on the field about fifty to sixty minutes before game time. He may first warm up the number two goalie for about ten minutes and then follow with the starting goalie for about ten minutes. The coach will then move to the other goal to give the goalies the feel of operating in it. This is important, because there may be a slight difference in both the area in front of the crease and the location of the sun. The coach will give the number one goalie another ten to fifteen minutes of warm-up in this goal. Since he will be overheated and somewhat tired after this workout, the goalie can move to the sidelines to relax for about five minutes while the coach is finishing with the second goalie. If a team has three goalies, the third one may not get a warm-up or, at best, may get just a limited one by the coach. The goalies should complete the warm-up in the goal on the side of the field their team will be using for the pre-game activity. The goalies should be involved with the defense in making both long and short clearing passes to them. After doing this, the goalies may want to relax for another five or ten minutes; then the coach may want to give the goalie another two or three minutes in the goal right before the start of the game. The goalie now is ready to man the nets. He is prepared both mentally and physically to meet the challenging responsibilities of his position, knowing he has the backing of all his teammates and coaches.

Nick Murtha (JHU '02), first-team All-American and winner of the Ensign C. Markland Kelly award as the nation's top goalie, scans the field for a clear. *Jay Van Rensselaer*

14

Clearing

Once the defense gains possession of the ball, whether it be off of a ground ball or a save, it has accomplished a major part of its responsibility, which is to prevent the opponent from scoring. However, before a team can score, the defense must move the ball from its defensive half of the field to its offensive half, which is known as clearing.

Clearing can be accomplished either by passing the ball from player to player or by just running with it. Since the defense has the advantage of an extra man—its goalie—it should be able to be successful on a high percentage of its clearing attempts. Failure to clear the ball with consistency can be both frustrating and demoralizing to a team, because the opponent is afforded opportunities to score easy goals. These are called "second chances." When the defense loses the ball in its clearing effort, most of its players are away from the goal, and the opponent frequently gains an advantage in attacking. We discussed this advantage in the offense portion of chapter 11. Clearing, therefore, is a very important phase of the game.

In fact, the statistics for a team's success at clearing frequently reflect the outcome of a game. The team that succeeds 80–85 percent or more of its clearing attempts often will put themselves in the position to win the game, whereas the team that clears in fewer than 80 percent of its attempts will have greater difficulty. In 2003, the Hopkins team that played for the national championship against the University of Virginia cleared the ball at a rate of nearly 85 percent. Although our clearing percentage in our previous two years had been over 80 percent, it had never been as high as it was in 2003. Our coaching staff believed that getting to the national championship game was directly affected by our ability to clear the ball.

Several factors facilitate the clear. Of primary importance is the complete organization of the various types of clears a team employs against the different rides used by its opponent. A thorough understanding of each clearing pattern is essential for the entire team. Although the goalie, clearing defensemen, and midfielders handle the bulk of the work in clearing, the players on attack are also involved in their own way. In fact, they play a critical role as the ball is crossing the midfield line. It is also important that the attackmen know the role of midfielders in clearing, because there may be times during a game when an attackman must move into the defensive end for a midfielder who is caught behind the play and has to stay back in the midfield. In such situations, the attackman will be playing defense, and he has to know how to clear the ball. Continual practice of various clears is imperative. Good stickwork and a solid understanding of where to pass the ball—what we call where "the looks" are—help considerably.

Speed, or the ability to run past a rider, is also important. It is difficult to beat speed in almost every phase of the game—as it is in almost every sport—and especially in clearing in lacrosse. Some of the most effective clearing takes place when a defender simply runs by his man, not using any fancy footwork or tricky dodges, just sheer speed. This is breaking the game down to its simplest form. Some of the game's best clearers have been good athletes with limited stickwork but outstanding speed and a strong understanding of the clearing game.

The goalie is the director of the clears, much as he is the quarterback of the defense. Since he always keeps his eye on the ball, he knows exactly when one of his defenders gains possession and sets the clear in motion by shouting "Clear!" This tells every defender to move to his assigned position on the field for the clear. Since the majority of clears originate with the goalie off of a save, he must have a complete understanding of each clearing pattern, be well drilled in carrying out his responsibilities, and know exactly where his looks are.

In the years since Coach Scott published the first edition of this book, the rules regarding the clear have changed dramatically. When the first

edition was written, there was no time limit put on a clearing team, meaning they did not have to clear the ball from their defensive end in any specific amount of time; once they did clear the ball across the midfield line, they did not have to move the ball to a specific area in any specific amount of time and indeed could pass the ball back into the defensive box. In the 1990s and early 2000s, the rules were changed to require the defense to clear the ball from its defensive box within ten seconds. If they failed to do so, they committed a technical foul and lost possession of the ball. In addition, the new rules required that once the ball was cleared from the defensive box, it could not be passed back there. And once the ball was cleared over the midfield line, the clearing team had ten seconds to move it into their offensive box. For the 2005 season, the clearing rules were changed again. In today's game, the defense now has twenty seconds to clear the ball out of the defensive half of the field and over the midfield line. They also have the ability to go back into the defensive box, as long as the ball is cleared within twenty seconds. However, once the ball crosses over the midfield line, they are still required to move the ball into their offensive box within ten seconds.

The intent of the original rule change—having to move the ball out of the defensive box in ten seconds and not being able to go back—was to increase the speed and the pace of the game to make it more fan-friendly. Television coverage probably has played an important role in some of these rule changes, as coaches, officials, and administrators have tried to make the game a more fast-paced and exciting one for the viewers at home.

The following guidelines are helpful to the clearing team:

1. The ball moves faster than the body. Never run with the ball when a teammate who is farther down the field is open. The ball will arrive more quickly at its destination when passed than when carried in the stick.

2. If no one is open to receive a pass, the ball carrier should run past the pressure of his opposing rider to an open area, normally—but not always—

toward the offensive end of the field. Sometimes the best way to alleviate the pressure is to move away from it, which may mean moving back toward the defensive end of the field for a brief period of time.

3. When a ball carrier who has either speed or clever stickhandling or both is confronted by a riding opponent, he can just run by him or dodge him, as long as he has enough room to do so and doesn't have to be concerned about another defender double-teaming him. Midfielders are able to dodge much more easily than defensemen because their smaller sticks present less of a target to the riders' checks.

4. Every member of the clearing team must keep his eyes on the ball at all times. If a player does not know the location of the ball, he is unable to help out in the clear.

5. When a breaking defender is open and wants the ball, he must first call the ball carrier by name to get his attention. For example, "Kyle, Kyle! Here's your help!" Since everyone responds more quickly to the sound of his own name than to any other words, this is the most effective way to gain his attention. This point applies to any situation during a game when an open man wants the ball immediately. It is especially helpful in clearing the ball against a hard-riding opponent.

6. Before calling for the ball, the defender must be sure he is open. The player who continually calls for the ball, even when he is partially covered, will soon find himself being disregarded completely by his teammates.

7. The breaking defender should always give the ball carrier a target with the head of his stick to let him know exactly where he wants the ball. This target is a big help to both the passer and the receiver. The passer has a point at which to aim his throw, and the receiver has his stick in a position to receive it where he can best handle it. This will also allow the defender who is receiving the ball to be able to dodge past an opponent or pass the ball quickly to another open teammate.

8. When a defender gets possession of a loose ball on the ground, he should immediately move toward daylight or move away from any pressure,

listen for a teammate's call for a pass, or look for an open teammate.

9. The ball carrier must never allow himself to be forced out-of-bounds with the ball in his stick and thus lose possession of it. Rather, if he is on his defensive sideline and is being pressured, he should circle away from the pressure and look across the field for an open teammate. The reason he can do so is that, traditionally, riding teams—as in other sports—tend to flow toward the ball. This means that once a ball is on one side of the field, the riding team gives the majority of its attention to the ball, thus leaving a player on the other side of the field open and available to be an outlet if the ball carrier is being pressured.

10. If a defender is behind the goal and about to be forced out on the end line, he should either look across the field to an open teammate, or, if he cannot do that, he should try to clear the ball by making a long, cross-field pass to a teammate on the attack. He should never throw the ball back toward his own goal. It is a cardinal sin in every sport to throw the ball back toward your goal.

11. When the ball goes out-of-bounds behind the goal and the opposing team loses possession of it, play will stop and a clear—known as a "dead ball clear"—will be set up. "Inbounds" clearing is off of a save or a ground ball, and there is no stop in the action. In a dead ball clear, a defenseman or a midfielder should always pick up the ball, depending on what kind of clear will be used. At Hopkins, we never allow our goalies to pick up the ball for this clear because our better stickhandlers are usually our defensemen or midfielders.

12. Have predetermined players assigned to handle this responsibility. Since the riding team normally uses its best rider to play the person bringing the ball into play from out-of-bounds, the clearing team will be in trouble if it has one of its weaker stickhandlers or slower clearers in that position.

13. The player farthest from the ball on the opposite side of the field is usually responsible for preventing his team from violating the offside rule, which requires four players on the defensive half of the field at all times.

14. The attack plays an important role in the

clearing game, and it is imperative that these players not just stand down at the other end of the field. As the ball is advanced up the field and crosses the midfield line, it is important for the attackmen to break away from their defenders to provide an outlet for the midfielder or the defenseman who has carried the ball over the midfield line into the offensive end of the field.

15. When throwing the ball from the defensive end over the midfield line into the offensive end, a clearing player should be very careful not to make what is called a "buddy pass" to a teammate. He must be aware of where the opposing team's riding players are, for fear that if a riding player is near the teammate to whom he is throwing the ball, that rider will slide up the field and put a swift body check on his teammate. Although such a pass is called a buddy pass, in reality the thrower is not being kind to his buddy but is setting him up to be clobbered.

As previously noted, there are two basic categories of clears. One is the inbounds clear, and the other is the dead ball clear. It is important to design inbounds and dead ball clears that are effective against a variety of rides.

INBOUNDS CLEARING

Teams execute inbounds clears much more frequently than dead ball clears throughout a game. Some of this has to do with style of play. Some of it also has to do with the playing surface. For instance, at the collegiate level, you will find that there will be more inbounds clearing on a field that is made of grass, since the ball will stay inbounds more often than it would if play was taking place on an artificial turf field. Inbounds clears originate off of three situations: a save by the goalie, a ground ball, and an intercepted pass by the defense.

Phase One of the Inbounds Clear

Figure 14.1 (see page 189) shows the initial patterns of an inbounds clear. In this example, let's say the goalie has made a save when the opponent's offense was working out of a 2-2-2 set. The goalie, base

defensemen, crease defensemen, and midfielders all have specific responsibilities in this clear.

Goalie

When the goalie gains possession of the ball in the crease, he should immediately look up the field to pass the ball to a midfielder. Ideally, the goalie may be able to gain an advantage in creating a transition by passing the ball to the midfielder who was covering the shooter. Often when a player takes a shot, he tends to stop to watch his shot and see if it goes in the goal. This enables the midfielder who was covering him to gain an advantage by taking off up the field quickly toward the midfield line. If that midfielder is not open, however, the goalie should look first to the other midfielders. The midfielders tend to be a team's best stickhandlers, and the more quickly the ball can be moved up the field, the sooner the clearing team will get it into the offensive end.

If no midfielder is open, the goalie has the option of looking to either of the three defensemen. Often a riding team will put an attackman right at the top of the crease to "get in the goalie's face" and prevent him from making a quick outlet pass to a midfielder breaking up the field. The goalie must anticipate this and try to avoid any contact with the creaseman as he is releasing the ball. If the goalie moves a step to one side or the other of the crease, he can avoid this problem and create a better passing lane to any of the three defensemen.

The goalie is permitted to remain in the crease for a period of four seconds after gaining possession of the ball. Frequently, less-experienced goalies rush things and do not take advantage of the full amount of time they have but instead use only one, two, or three seconds. One way to overcome this problem is to count out loudly four seconds in practice each time the goalie gains possession of the ball. This will improve his awareness of the time element, encourage him to be patient, and allow the clear to develop and the players to get open.

If no one appears open and the goalie is unable to pass the ball to any of the clearing players, he should not panic. Instead, he should move outside the crease, just behind the goal. Since the riding attackman is not permitted to run through the crease, the goalie can use it to put some distance between himself and the riding attackman. He can use the crease to play a cat-and-mouse game with the riding attackman until one of the clearing players springs open or until he feels there is a clear lane he can use to carry the ball up the field himself. A goalie should not be dodge-happy and take too many chances when it is not necessary for him to do so.

Base Defensemen

When the goalie gains possession of the ball and shouts "Clear," the base defensemen (D1 and D2) will "banana out," meaning move on an arc below the goal line and toward the sideline in an effort to free themselves to receive a pass from the goalie (see figure 14.1). There are a number of ways these defensemen can execute their "banana break." They can either backpedal into their break to catch the ball in a forehand position, or, if they are more comfortable doing so, they can run, looking to catch the ball over their shoulder in the backhand position. Executing this type of break can provide an easy outlet for the goalie and also create space between both of these base defenders and any of the riding attackmen. This space will be critical if one of these defensemen receives the ball. For instance, if D1 were to banana out and receive the ball, having this space will allow him time to look over the field without being pressured so that he can determine where the riders are and where an open man is located.

When making their banana break, D1 and D2 should never lose sight of the goaltender, who needs to have them looking at him in order for him to be able to throw the ball to them. It is best for these defensemen to try to catch the initial pass with their strong hand, especially those players at a younger level who have less experience. It is also critical for D1 and D2 to communicate with their goaltender. Communication plays an important role in every aspect of the game. Clearing is no different. When one of these two defensemen feels he is open, he should call out to the goalie by using his name, "Nick, here's your help!" or "Nick, one more!" The "here's your help" indicates that he is open to provide the goalie with an outlet; the "one more" indicates that the defender wants the goalie to make one more pass to him.

Crease Defensemen

When the goalie makes a save on a shot, the crease defenseman (D3) should remain in the crease for one to two seconds to make sure that the goalie actually has made a clean save and not given up a rebound. If a rebound occurs and D3 has moved up the field too quickly, he will not be in a position to help out on defense. If the save is clean and D3 is sure that the goalie has possession of the ball, he should then move to an area about five yards inside the restraining box, almost directly in front of the goal, keeping his eye on the goalie as he moves up the field. He should also give a quick look to the crease attackman and move to either one side or the other of him. This will help create a passing lane for the goalie. It is important that D3 not allow the riding attackman, who will try to get in the goalie's face, to establish a position between him and the goalie.

D3 will usually serve as an outlet valve, or the last choice as an outlet for the goalie, if no other outlets are available. He is usually the last choice because a pass to D3 can often be more difficult than a pass to the base defensemen or the middies who are moving upfield. This is because of the attackman who has positioned himself directly in the goalie's face.

Midfielders

The three midfielders are critical to the clearing game and have specific responsibilities. In figure 14.1, M1, M2, and M3 are the clearing midfielders. Where they actually go on the field will depend on the position from which the ball was shot or where the ground ball was picked up. In this example, M3's man has shot the ball. As mentioned earlier, the easiest and quickest way for the goalie to get the ball up and out in a clear is to look back to where the shot came from, because offensive players tend to watch their shots. Consequently, M3 will immediately sprint up the field, trying to move toward the middle of the field, since that is the area that will give him the greatest amount of space in which to maneuver. Because the shooter most likely is watching his shot, M3's sprint upfield may allow the goalie to pass the ball quickly to him, thus creating a fast break. As M3 moves up the field, he looks over his shoulder to keep his eyes on the goalie and will shout to the goalie by name to call for the ball if he is open.

The remaining midfielders, M1 and M2, will fill the two other clearing spots. They will break toward the area where the sideline meets the midfield line. If they break more toward the center line, they will be moving into the area that M3 has just left. As both of these midfielders break to their spots, it is important that they do so while looking over their shoulder so that they never lose sight of the goalie, and they should call to him by name if they believe they are open and want to receive the ball.

Keep in mind that all of these clearing players are not robots. Although they have definite areas of the field to which they should move, they do not have to move to one little, specific spot. They are not playing lacrosse in a phone booth. If there is a riding player in their area, they should move away from him. They are moving to an area, not a bull's-eye, and they can utilize that entire area in setting up the clear.

Phase Two of the Inbounds Clear

Figure 14.2 shows the second phase of the inbounds clear.

Goalie

If the goalie cannot outlet the ball quickly upon making the save and is being pressured by the crease attackman, he can go behind the goal and look to make a pass to one of the base defensemen, D1 or D2, on either side of the field. If, for example, the goalie passes the ball to D1, he should then position himself almost at the level of D1 and on the side of the defender who is receiving the ball.

Base Defensemen

Once the ball has been passed to D1, he should immediately look up the field. Although D1's first look should always be straight ahead of him, it is impor-

tant for him to understand that such a pass may not be open and that he may have to look to one of the other clearing players. That is why it is critical for him to know the clearing position of each player. D1 also should also be prepared to be pressured by a riding attackman, so it is important for him to be ready to protect his stick once he catches the ball. In this example, once D1 receives the ball, D2 should position himself almost on the sideline opposite and parallel to D1. Doing this will enable D2 to provide D1 with a cross-field outlet in case D1 is pressured. D2 must get as close to the sideline as possible to create maximum space between him and D1. This will also create space between D2 and the riders, thereby allowing him to have time and space to look over the field and find another open man should he be pressured. We call this "stretching the field." Remember, the defense has a numerical advantage when clearing: seven players versus the riding team's six. Stretching the field will not allow one rider to play two clearers.

Crease Defensemen

Sometimes, especially at the younger levels of lacrosse, the defenseman playing the crease may not have the greatest stickwork. As the level of play advances, however, most players have quality stick skills. In this situation, when D1 receives the ball, D3 should have positioned himself about four or five yards from the restraining box, on one side of the goal or the other, to serve as an easy outlet for D1. If D3 receives the ball, he should immediately move up the field, looking to pass the ball to M1 or M3. He may find himself having to carry the ball over the midline. If he does, it is important for M1 and M3 to clear space for D3 to do so.

If D3 does not receive the ball, he should immediately move up the field toward M3, and M3 should stretch, or move down toward his offensive restraining box. This will put three clearers across the bottom of our clear, three clearers across the midfield, and one in the offensive zone.

Midfielders

In figure 14.2, D1 has received the ball. D3, recognizing that he is open, runs on a straight line (or a line parallel to the restraining box) toward the ball.

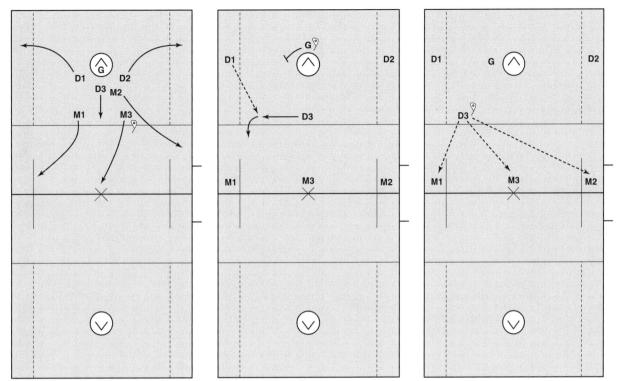

Figure 14.1 Phase one of an inbounds clear.

Figure 14.2 Phase two of an inbounds clear.

Figure 14.3 Phase three of an inbounds clear.

D1 passes the ball to D3, who should try to catch it with his right hand, over his shoulder. When he catches the ball, D3 should move up the field. His looks then are to M3 or, diagonally, to M2. M2 may find himself to be most open, because riding teams are taught to move heavy to the ball side (figure 14.3).

If no one is open, D3 also has the option of carrying the ball over the midfield line himself. Should he do this, the man farthest from the ball, which in this situation would be M2, is responsible for staying back and making sure that the clearing team does not go offsides.

Phase Three of the Inbounds Clear

If D3 does not receive the ball from D1, a coach has several decisions to make, the most important being what he wants to do with D3. The first choice is to keep D3 on the field and available to execute the clear. The second option is to have D3 sprint off the field and put in a substitute known as a designated clearer. This would be a midfielder who would come in from the sideline specifically to help clear the ball. For the purposes of this example, D3 will be kept on the field.

In figure 14.4, D1 has the ball. The goalie has moved to the ball side. D2 has positioned himself parallel and opposite to the ball. M1, M2, and M3 are positioned across the midfield, and D3 is just inside the box. When D3 recognizes that he cannot receive the ball, he should move to replace M3, and M3 should move down the field into the offensive end, toward the restraining box. This creates a 3-3-1 alignment. Moving M3 down the field will force one of the riding midfielders to go with him, which may vacate the area that D3 is entering.

In phase three of the inbounds clear, it is important for the goalie to try to stay almost parallel to the side the ball is on. This gives D1 a shorter distance from which to pass the ball to the goalie and also forces the riders to honor D1 and the goalie, which will create more space for D2 (figure 14.5).

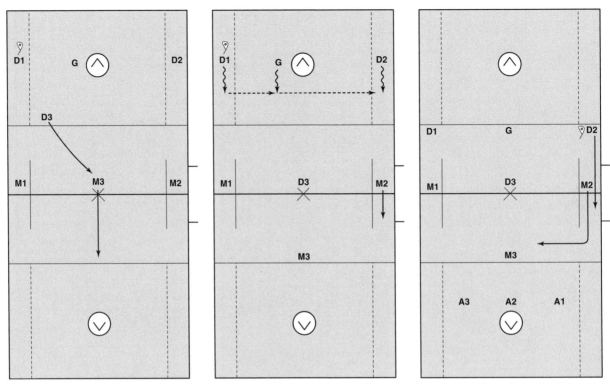

Figure 14.4 Ball and player movement in phase three of an inbounds clear.

Figure 14.5 Goalie position in phase three of an inbounds clear.

Figure 14.6 Phase four of an inbounds clear.

As the two base defensemen and the goalie move up the field, D1 passes the ball to the goalie, who then redirects it over to D2. As D2 carries the ball up the field, he has several options. He can look to pass the ball to M2, who may be covered by a riding attackman and is moving over the midfield line to get open for a pass. D2 can also look to pass the ball to D3, the third defenseman in this phase, who is in the middle of the field and trying to find an open passing line. He has the option of moving toward the ball or over the midfield line to receive it. D2 can also look to pass the ball to M3 or M1.

Midfielders

If M2 is being covered by a riding attackman, he should go over the midfield line, where he will be open to receive the ball. M3, who is already over the midfield line and located by the offensive restraining box, should try to move to an open area and create a passing lane for D2. Chances are, however, that M3 will be covered by a midfielder and may not be open. M1 must make sure he positions himself diagonally across the field, understanding that he is responsible for staying onsides. Being the player farthest from the ball, however, M1 may find himself wide open, because the riders have flowed toward D2, who has the ball. If M1 finds himself in this situation, he should communicate to D2 that he is open by calling him by name: "Chris! Diagonal! Diagonal!" This alerts D2 that he should throw the ball diagonally to M1. If this pass is made, it is important for D3 or M2 to make sure that they move across the midline to remain onsides.

Phase Four of the Inbounds Clear

D2 must remember that the ball has to be cleared across the midline in twenty seconds. The ball can continue to be redirected from one side of the field to the other, and the available passes for D2 and D1 will still be the same.

If D2 is pressured, however, he can carry the ball over the midline himself (figure 14.6). If he does so, M2, who has moved or stretched to the offensive end of the field hoping to receive the ball, should clear through to the middle of the field, creating space for D2 to carry the ball. Because D2, a defender, is carrying the ball over the midline, D3 and M1 must remain onsides, since four players must always be back in the defensive end.

The two midfielders, M2 and M3, can try to find an open passing lane to provide D2 with an easy outlet. It is also important for the attack to remember that they are involved in the clearing game, and at no time are they more important than they would be in this situation, when a defenseman carries the ball over the midfield line. This is because D2 will probably be receiving pressure from a rider, so the attack must provide him with an outlet. Moving the ball from the defenseman's stick to an attackman's stick is what clearing is all about. Once D2 has moved the ball to any of the players in the offensive end, he should quickly sprint back to the midfield line and cross over so that M1 can leave the defensive end and enter the offensive end of the field.

DEAD BALL CLEAR

When the ball goes out-of-bounds, an official blows his whistle, the clock is stopped, and both the clearing team and the riding team have an opportunity to make substitutions, if they wish, to set up their ride and clear. Figure 14.7 shows what is called a "34 alignment" for a dead ball clear. Three clearers (the goalie, D1, and D2) are across the bottom of the alignment, and the four midfielders (M1, M2, M3, and M4) are aligned across the midfield line. Since the ball went out-of-bounds, an advantage can be created for the clearing team by taking the third defenseman, D3, off the field and replacing him with a designated clearer—a midfielder who is substituted for the sole purpose of helping to clear the ball. For youth groups and teams that may not have great defensive stickhandlers, having a midfielder start the clear can be particularly help-

ful. Middies are usually the better stickhandlers at that level of play.

Phase One of the Dead Ball Clear

Goalie

The goalie should never be the one to bring the ball in from the sideline. Instead, he should be positioned slightly on the side where the ball is located. This helps the clearing team to stretch the field and to provide an easier outlet for D1, who will bring the ball into play. D2 will align himself almost parallel to D1, directly across the field and as far to the sideline as possible, in order to stretch the ride—or force the riders to have to cover more of the field. When the whistle blows, D1 will walk or jog the ball up the field. The goalie will mirror D1, as will D2. If D1 is pressured, he can move the ball quickly to the goalie or pass it across the field to D2.

Midfielders

In phase one, the midfielders really do not have much to do until the ball is moved a little farther up the field. Obviously, if D1 sees that one of the midfielders is open, he should quickly call that player's name and prepare to pass the ball to him. If any midfielder finds that no one is covering him, he should move back toward D1 to position himself to receive the ball.

Phase Two of the Dead Ball Clear

In figure 14.8, D1 is receiving pressure from a riding attackman as he moves up the field. He passes the ball to the goalie, who will redirect it across the field to D2. As D2 moves up the field—keeping in mind that the ball must be cleared across the midfield line in twenty seconds—M4 will move down the field into the offensive end, toward the restraining box. M3 will cut, on an angle, over the midline, looking to receive the ball over his left shoulder from D2; and M2 will move toward the middle of the field on a straight line, looking to receive the ball from D2. These movements give D2 four options: He can throw to M4; he can throw to M3, cutting over the midline; he can pass to M1, on the

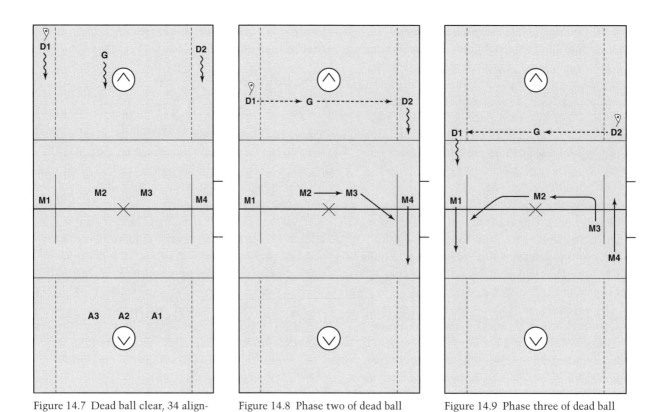

Figure 14.7 Dead ball clear, 34 alignment.

Figure 14.8 Phase two of dead ball clear.

Figure 14.9 Phase three of dead ball clear.

diagonal; or he can pass to M2, cutting down the line. M2 must remember that he has to stay onside, should D2 carry the ball over the midfield line. On the other hand, if M2 realizes he is being covered by an attackman, he can go across the midfield line and receive the ball, since the riding attackman will be unable to follow him over the line. When M2 makes his cut, however, he should remember not to go much farther than the middle of the field. If he goes too far, that will take him out of position for the next phase of the clear.

Phase Three of the Dead Ball Clear

In figure 14.9, D2 has the ball, is receiving pressure, and finds no one open to whom he can pass the ball. Since the new rules allow the clearing team to pass the ball back into the defensive box after having initially moved it from this area, D2 should throw the ball back to the goalie, who will redirect it to D1. D1 will then carry the ball, looking for M1, who will be stretching over the midline. M2

will cut over the midfield line on an angle, looking to receive the ball over his right shoulder. M3 will come back onsides and move down the line toward the middle of the field. M4 will sprint back to his original position so that he can maintain onside responsibility. In phase three, the midfielders' responsibilities are the mirror image of what they were in phase two, just moving the other way. D1 now has the option to pass to M1, M2, M3, or M4. If no one is open, D1 can carry the ball over the midfield line, leaving M3 and M4 responsible for staying onsides.

Clearing is such an important part of the game that it requires special emphasis during practice. Each failed clear will lead to an offensive opportunity for the opposing team, whereas each successful clear will lead to an offensive opportunity for your team. At Hopkins, our practice plan usually contains at least fifteen to twenty-five minutes of clearing every day. Incorporated in all of our defensive stickwork drills are several of the passes that we will use in our clearing game. The same holds true for our midfielders. In addition, we take time to practice several of our clears at every practice. We do this with the understanding that usually our opponents will not execute just one ride against us but will utilize several, thus forcing us to make adjustments and possibly use more than one clear. Remember: It's worth the extra time to practice clearing with your team. Failure to clear the ball will lead to failure to win games.

All-American defenseman Chris Watson (JHU '05) puts the squeeze on a Syracuse Orangeman. *Jay Van Rensselaer*

15

Riding

In the first edition of this book, Coach Scott often cited the accomplishments of one of Hopkins's greatest players, Joe Cowan. I've had the opportunity to see some film of Joe, and he truly was an amazing athlete. Although Joe was known for his scoring and passing ability—he remains the second all-time leading assist-getter at Hopkins—it was obvious to me that one of the best aspects of his game was his ability as a tenacious rider.

During recent seasons, a young man who was incredibly impressive as a rider was Casey Powell, one of three extremely talented brothers who were among Syracuse University's greatest players. Although Casey may be remembered best for his flashy play and scoring ability, it was his riding that stood out as an outstanding part of his game. Once, sitting in the Carrier Dome while scouting a Syracuse game, I had to marvel at this guy who not only was scoring all these goals but also was absolutely the best rider I had seen in ten years. He was a competitor who took great pride in passing the ball and scoring goals as well as in getting the ball back whenever he or his team lost control of it. Casey Powell would continue his ride right up to the midline, which is highly unusual for attackmen. Often they leave the riding in this area of the field to the midfielders, but Casey Powell not only rode to the midline, he caused four or five turnovers with his riding ability, which led to two or three goals. As mentioned in chapter 11, those broken situations or failed clears are some of the most thrilling in lacrosse, and Casey Powell was as exciting a player as I ever saw in this aspect of the game. His athleticism was overshadowed only by his desire to get the ball back.

Riding is the maneuvering by the attacking

team, once it loses possession of the ball, to prevent the defensive team from clearing the ball to its offensive half of the field. Although some aspects of the riding game boil down to one-on-one match-ups, riding primarily is a team proposition. Even though attackmen and midfielders do the bulk of the work in riding, the defensemen and goalie have definite responsibilities, too. Every team member must carry out his assignment if the ride is to be successful. When all ten players function with precision and cohesiveness, the clearing team may get very frustrated because they have difficulty clearing the ball, even though they have an extra man, the goalie. Loss of the ball to the riders can be demoralizing for a clearing team, since transition opportunities often develop when this happens and opponents score easy goals. Frequently the goalie or a defenseman is caught out of position when the ball is lost, and a four-on-three, a three-on-two, or a two-on-one fast break results. This scoring opportunity places an undue burden on the defensive team. Such "second chance" opportunities obviously are very beneficial to the team on the offensive.

The effective rider has a number of attributes. Speed and hustle are probably the most important. Persistence and a never-quit attitude can cover up a lack of speed. The rider must have excellent control of his body and stick when he encounters the ball carrier. He can act aggressively to get the ball and take the risk of being dodged as long as he is quick in delivering his stick checks and in reacting to countermoves by the ball carrier. Mental alertness is essential, because the rider must have a thorough understanding of the riding strategy. The following guidelines will bring success in riding:

1. The basic defensive fundamentals on positioning, as explained in chapter 9, are applicable to the attackman when he rides a clearing defenseman or goalie. He wants to take away the middle of the field, where there is more space, and force the defender up the side, using the sideline as an ally—almost as another defender—since forcing the ball carrier out-of-bounds will cause him to lose possession of the ball.

2. After running at top speed to reach the ball carrier, the rider must bring his body under control and break down to a good riding position in an effort to avoid being dodged.

3. The one-shot rider can destroy the effectiveness of the ride. If he moves aggressively into the ball carrier and makes one hard check or over-the-head maneuver, he either knocks the ball out of the stick or misses it completely and gets dodged. Unless the rider is like Casey Powell or Joe Cowan (and there haven't been too many close to their level), he should approach the clearer with the idea of applying pressure more than of actually taking the ball away. A rule of thumb is the three Ps—pressure, but with position and patience.

4. The riding attackman must be aware that a defenseman using a long stick can offer a tempting target, luring the rider into making a risky over-the-head or wraparound check. Instead, it is important for the rider to maintain good body position, not overcommit, and try to harrass the hands of the dodger or force him into making a bad pass. These moves will be just as effective as trying to take the ball away.

5. A thorough understanding of the opponent's clearing pattern helps the rider anticipate the next pass. A keen sense of anticipation of the pass will allow the rider to make the proper move to break up the clear. Whenever possible, a rider should read the eyes of a clearer. Remember, clearing defensemen do not throw look-away passes. They usually look to where they're throwing. This should give the riding attackman an indication of where the next pass will go.

6. At times the rider can bait the ball carrier into throwing the ball to the man he is covering by sloughing a yard or two farther than normal from him. When the pass is on the way, the rider bursts at full speed and arrives in time to either check the receiver's stick or put pressure on him.

7. Each member of the riding team must keep both the ball and the nearby clearer in his area in sight at all times. He must keep his head on a swivel, continually turning it to see the ball and the man in his area, because he will be in trouble if he follows one and not the other.

8. The midfield riders who are not playing the

ball carrier must maintain a position very close to the player in their area. This will enable them to prevent him from becoming an easy outlet for the clearing team. Too often, a midfield rider will play too far from his man, thus allowing the defense an easy outlet and an easy clear.

9. The proper distance between a midfielder (not covering the ball) and his man is determined by the proximity of the ball. When riding, the midfielders should play heavy to the ball side, meaning they should cover the players closest to the ball, thus leaving the player farthest from the ball open. Often the players closest to the ball can be five, ten, fifteen, or twenty yards away from the ball carrier. The player farthest from the ball carrier, however, is usually thirty, forty, or fifty yards away from him. The clearing defender would have to make a much more difficult pass to reach this man.

10. One of the most disheartening incidents for the riding team is the failure of one of its defensemen to shut off his attackman and thereby allow him to receive an easy clearing pass from a ball carrier who may be under considerable pressure. It is very upsetting to the three attackmen and three midfielders, who are doing an excellent job of delaying the clear and pressuring the ball carrier, to have a teammate on their defensive half of the field "fall asleep" and allow his attackman to receive an outlet or release a pass. This turns an effective ride into an easy clear.

11. Once a rider gains possession of the ball, he looks immediately ahead of him to see if there is a teammate open. If so, he passes the ball to him for what should be an easy shot. If there's no one open, he bursts at full speed for the goal and looks for a fast-break opportunity. However, in this situation, it is important for the attackman to make a good decision, and if nothing is available, he should pull the ball out, enabling the offense to make substitutions and maintain possession of the ball.

12. Considerable talk among the riders is necessary to employ a successful ride. Riding is much like half-field defense except that it is done on a full-field scale. Many of the techniques employed in half-field defense will also be used in the riding game, and communication is critical in both instances.

There are two basic categories of rides. One involves fast action when the ball is inbounds and the goalie makes a save or the defense picks up a ground ball or intercepts a pass. The other type of ride stems from an out-of-bounds situation, when the ball leaves the playing field and an official blows his whistle. In either case, the riding team has time to place its players in specific positions for the various rides. It is important for the riders to sprint to their positions so that they can effectively execute a ride appropriate to each situation.

Within these two categories of rides there are different ways of riding, and the coach must decide how he wants his team to proceed. Because the clearing rules now impose a twenty-second limit on the clearing team for crossing the midfield line, one tactic for riding is a passive one. The riding team drops back, does not apply a lot of pressure on the ball carriers, and tries to use the clock as an ally by preventing the clearing team from crossing the midfield line in the allotted time. Another tactic is to employ a pressure ride. Two riding attackmen can push down on the clearing team and force the clearers to make longer, more extended passes under duress. Unlike the passive ride, this tactic could result in turnovers if these long passes are intercepted or missed. A third tactic is the ten-man ride. In this instance, the goalie of the riding team will come out and act as another defender, and the riding team will utilize all ten players to ride. This is a very risky and high-pressure ride that is often used only when a team absolutely has to get the ball back.

INBOUNDS RUNNING RIDE, FIRST PHASE

The success of the inbounds running ride depends on the quickness of the offensive team in changing from an offense-oriented group to a hustling band of riders trying to prevent the defensive team from clearing the ball. This basic ride places the midfielders across the midline, where they will be responsible for the men in their area, while the attackmen scramble to cover the four clearers—the goalie and three defensemen. This is a safe and effective way to prevent a team from getting a fast break on its clear.

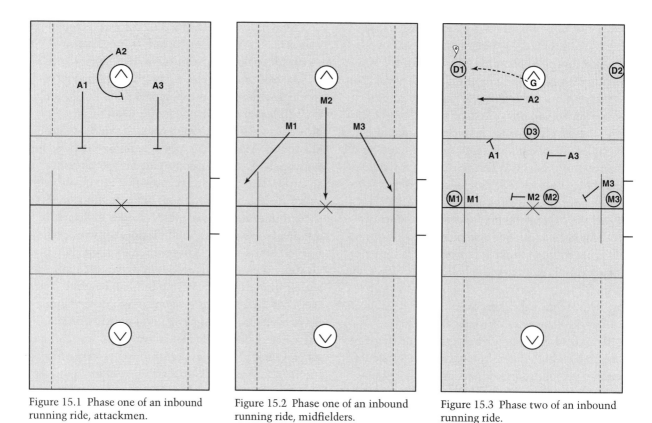

Figure 15.1 Phase one of an inbound running ride, attackmen.

Figure 15.2 Phase one of an inbound running ride, midfielders.

Figure 15.3 Phase two of an inbound running ride.

Attackmen

In this basic ride, the initial responsibility of the attack is to try to keep the ball with the close defense and prevent the clearing team from getting the ball up and out to its midfielders quickly, which could lead to a fast break. In this ride (figure 15.1), the first priority after the goalie makes a save is for A2, the attackman nearest to the goal, to immediately run and position himself two yards in front of the crease, or "in the goalie's face." By doing so, he will prevent the goalie from being able to see clearly and pass the ball to a midfielder who is breaking up the field in an effort to create a fast break. The other attackmen, A1 and A3, immediately position themselves three to five yards outside the restraining box and about six to ten yards wide of the goal pipes. Placing the attackmen in these positions helps the riding team to prevent the clearing team from quickly outletting the ball. They also can cover any opposing player who happens to be open

in those areas. These positions become critical when coupled with the positions of the midfielders, because the clearing team's goalie has been prevented from passing the ball to any of his midfielders; instead, he must pass it to one of the close defensemen or move sideways instead of forward.

Midfielders

Since one of the aims of this ride is to make sure the clearing team cannot move the ball up the field quickly, the role played by the riding midfielders may be the most important. In figure 15.2, all three midfielders have responded to the goalie's save by sprinting to positions in the midfield closest to where they were at the time of the save and at equal distance from each other. Each man is responsible for any opposing player in his third of the field; essentially, he is playing a zone. When a clearing player moves from his defensive half of the field to his offensive half of the field, however, the responsibility of the midfielders will change from playing an area of the field to playing their man, or playing man-to-man, regardless of whether their man has the ball.

At higher levels of the game, it is often critical for the midfielders to cover the area farthest from the box and closest to the middle of the field before covering the area closest to the box. That is because when a save is made, the team on the defensive often makes quick substitutions to improve its clearing chances, thereby creating a lot of congestion in that box area. Since the goalie is unlikely to throw the ball into this congested area and instead will look to pass it to a less-crowded place on the field, it is crucial for the riding team to have its men get to the area farthest from the box first.

INBOUNDS RUNNING RIDE, SECOND PHASE

Figure 15.3 shows the riding players concentrated in the area between the restraining box and the midfield line. This positioning should help the riding team prevent the clearing group—shown as circles—from moving the ball up the field quickly.

Attackmen

Because A2 has impeded the goalie from passing the ball up the field quickly, he normally outlets it to one of his base defensemen, in this case to D1. A2's responsibility in this basic inbounds ride is to chase the ball as long as he can, so, on the pass, he rotates over to play D1. A1, who has positioned himself outside the restraining box, will be able to cover anyone in his area and may move forward a little bit in case D3 cuts to the ball, and A3 will rotate over just a hair to help toward the middle of the field. This enables the riders to take away D3 as an easy outlet and force the clearers to throw the ball back to the goalie or across the field.

Figure 15.4 shows the ball being redirected by the clearing team. As A2 chases the ball as much as possible, the riders may avoid having to rotate. Going from one side of the field to another, however, forces A2 to cover a great distance. If D1 passes the ball back to the goalie and the goalie moves the ball across the field to D2, the area A2 has to cover becomes too large, and he will call to his fel-

low attackmen to rotate. The three attackmen will execute a rotation, moving into the ball. A3 will rotate toward the ball carrier. A1 will rotate over to replace A3 and will cover any clearing midfielders or defensemen in that area, and A2 will rotate back and replace A1. If the ball is redirected again and the on-ball rider does not have the ability to chase the ball in a timely fashion, the attack will reverse this rotation, going in the opposite direction.

Midfielders

Early in the clearing attempt, when the riding midfielders were assigned to covering the man in their area, they played heavy to the ball side. M1 would not have to move to do this; M2 and M3 only would rotate over a little bit, leaving the clearing midfielder farthest from the ball open. A pass to him is one the riding team wants to encourage. Because it is a long pass, the riding midfielders should be able to react as the ball is in flight and move from their positions to either intercept the pass or check the player trying to receive it. Such a pass is inherently difficult to make and could easily be missed and go out-of-bounds.

In figure 15.4, as D2 receives the ball, the midfielders change their positioning and rotate to be heavy to the new ball side. M3 will cover the man in his area. M2 will rotate over toward the ball side, and M1 will rotate over toward the middle, taking a bit of an angle back toward the defensive end. Once more, this will leave the farthest player from the ball open. When D2 has the ball, he often will look to pass it to D3 quickly. A1 should be able to prevent that. If the riding group does a good job, the ball will be passed back to the goalie or across the field again. Often D3 will move out of his initial location in the middle of the field and into another position in the clearing team's formation.

INBOUNDS RUNNING RIDE, THIRD PHASE

Figure 15.5 shows the clearing team in its final phase of the clear. In this example, A3 has been bypassed by D2. If this happens, A3 should turn and chase D2. A2 will rotate or slide over to help A3, and A1 will rotate over to help A2. As the midfield-

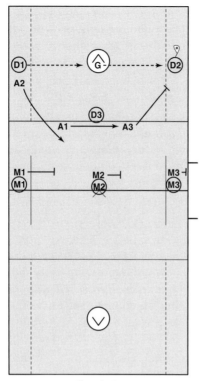

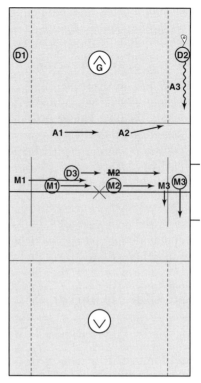

Figure 15.4 Ball and player movement in second phase of an inbounds running ride.

Figure 15.5 Phase three of an inbounds running ride.

ers involved in the clear execute their patterns, our riders will follow suit. When M3 moves down the field to create space for D2 (the clearing defenseman), his rider will follow him. As noted earlier, whenever a clearing player crosses over from his defensive half of the field to his offensive half of the field, the rider will switch from playing a zone to playing the man-to-man principle. As M2 cuts toward the ball to provide D2 with an outlet, his rider will follow him. D3, who had been positioned inside the restraining box, has moved toward the midfield line to create space and to become more involved in the clear. After M2 makes his cut, D3 will cut to the middle of the field. Riding middie M1, the farthest rider from the ball, now must make a choice. Does he follow D3 and just go with him, leaving M1, or does he "split" the two, positioning himself between D3 and M1? The best bet in this riding situation is for him to cover D3 by following him into the area into which he is moving, but doing so on the defensive side of the field,

leaving M1 open and forcing D2 to make a long, diagonal pass to M1 that could go out-of-bounds. By giving more attention to D3, M1 is taking away the shorter, easier clearing pass and forcing D2 to throw the longer, more difficult clearing pass.

During the last part of phase three, if the clearing team rotates the ball to the other side of the field, the riding attackmen will rotate into the ball, and the riding midfielders will go from being heavy to one side of the field to rotating across the field and being heavy to the other side.

This is a fundamental, simple, low-risk ride in that the riding team is not taking chances by trying to slide up the field—a movement that possibly could give the clearing team opportunities to create a transition situation. It is predominantly an attack-driven ride, because the attack is doing the majority of the work with the rotating. It is not a pressure ride, so it is essentially a series of maneuvers aimed at using the clock to the riding team's advantage. This ride is designed to force the clearing players to take their time and work to clear the ball. It is better for the riding team to play the clearers in a half-field defensive set than to give them the opportunity to run or create a transition.

In addition, one of beauties of this ride is that it can be used when facing either an inbounds clear or a dead ball clear. In a dead ball situation, the riders can set up in the same places as they did for the inbounds ride, and their responsibilities will be exactly the same.

DEAD BALL RIDE

The dead ball ride could also be used in an inbounds situation. It may be a little more difficult for the riding players to position themselves to do this for an inbounds ride, but it is possible to do so.

The following dead ball ride is designed to force the clearing team to have to make cross-field passes. The main challenges for the clearing players are maintaining onside responsibility, clearing the ball in the time allotted, and handling the ball well. This dead ball ride tries to force defensemen to handle the ball. Normally, especially at the youth and high school levels, the weakest stickhandlers are the defensemen and the goalie. This ride puts pressure on them. At the collegiate level, it is common to find that many freshmen have never consistently thrown a cross-field pass with either their strong or their weak hand. That is why this ride can be very successful.

In figure 15.6, the clearing team is aligned in a 34-alignment set, which was the dead ball clear described in chapter 14. It is a basic clear with simple patterns. R1 is an attackman. R2 is close to the goalie. R3, R4, R5, and R6 are positioned at equal distances across the midfield. R7, R8, and R9 are defensemen.

Phase One

Attackmen

The attack alignment is two down and one back. R1 and R2 are the two down attackmen in the clearing team's defensive end of the field. R3, the one man back, is located up at the midfield line,

near the box. In this scenario, R1 is responsible for covering D2 when he brings the ball into play. His mission is to prevent D2 from running by him. He wants to force D2 to make a cross-field pass to D1. Depending on the goalie's location, R2 positions himself where he can deter a pass from being made to the goaltender. Essentially, the riding players do not want to give D2 an easy outlet, and taking the goalie away helps to force him to make a cross-field pass to D1. R3 will cover the middie closest to D2 on the ball side, in this case M4. Since R3 is an attackman, however, he has to be concerned with onside responsibility. A well-coached clearing team may recognize this and send M4 over the midline. If R3 does not follow him, M4 could become a very easy outlet for D2. Therefore, R3's responsibility is to cover M4 and, if M4 happens to step over the midfield line, follow him for a brief moment until the ball is thrown across the field.

Midfielders

Since all the clearing midfielders are in their defensive area, the riding midfielders—R4, R5, and R6—will play zone and cover whichever man is located in their area. They should try to position themselves so that the player in the area they are covering cannot receive a quick pass.

Defensemen

The defensemen are positioned in what we call "topside," meaning that each defenseman is in front of his respective attackman at a three- to five-yard distance. The defensemen are located there so that if one of the attackmen chooses to break for a clearing pass, they will be between their man and the ball. In addition, if the ball is knocked loose or passed and happens to cross the midfield line, the defensemen—not the attackmen—will have the first shot at picking up the ground ball.

Figure 15.7 shows what happens when D2, having no one open up at the midfield line to whom he can pass the ball, and finding that the goalie has been shut off, only has the option of throwing the ball across the field to D1. A successful ride has begun. On the pass from D2 to D1, R2 immediately slides across to cover D1. It is important that he

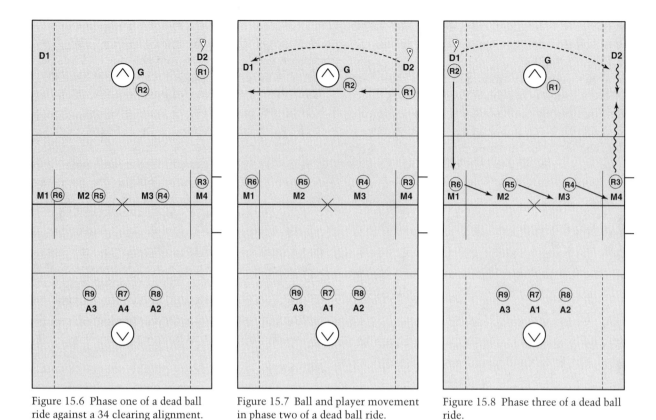

Figure 15.6 Phase one of a dead ball ride against a 34 clearing alignment.

Figure 15.7 Ball and player movement in phase two of a dead ball ride.

Figure 15.8 Phase three of a dead ball ride.

take the appropriate angle and not move to where D1 already is but rather to where D1 might be moving. Once R2 has rotated across to cover D1, R1 will follow him and be responsible for moving toward the goalie and shutting him off from a possible pass. It is almost as if R2 and R1 are attached by a string. R3's responsibility remains the same. If M4 happens to step over the midfield line, looking for an easy outlet, R3 will follow him, with the understanding that he does not have to be concerned with onside responsibility because that will be the responsibility of one of the midfielders.

If R3 has gone over the midfield line to follow M4 when the cross-field pass is thrown to D1, he should immediately return to the offensive end. The reason M4 now can be left open is that, as figure 15.7 shows, D1 would have to make a very long—and risky—pass to get the ball to him. The riding team is happy to encourage the clearing team to try to make that pass.

Phase Two

Midfielders

Phase two for the midfielders is exactly as in phase one. They each are responsible for the man in their area. At this point, the midfielders have not had to rotate at all. Should one of the men in their area cross over the midline to the defensive end, they will follow him.

Phase Three

Attackmen

With D1 in possession of the ball, the responsibilities of R1 and R2 are the same as they were earlier, just reversed (figure 15.8). R2 is responsible for covering D1 and making sure D1 does not run by him. R1 is responsible for taking away the goaltender and forcing the cross-field pass. R3's responsibilities in phase three will increase. As noted earlier, the clearing team has twenty seconds to cross the midfield line. They have to start moving the ball up the field. After D2 throws the ball across the field to D1, he will begin to move upfield. In this instance, because of R2's and R1's positioning, D1 has no one to whom he can pass the ball except to throw the ball back across the field to D2. The riding team has already forced the weakest stickhandlers on the clearing team to throw two quality, cross-field passes.

R3, anticipating the pass from D1 back to D2, will begin to work his way down—or "cheat down," as the expression goes—as soon as the ball is in the air and prepare to play D2. When D1 throws the ball to D2, R1 will maintain his position in front of the goalie and continue to block his view of the field. R2 will sprint back to help R6 with covering M1, leaving D1 open to receive the ball again.

Midfielders

Since R3 has left the area where M4 is located, the other midfielders must move as well. The midfielders should always rotate heavy to the ball side, meaning that as R3 rotates down to D2, R4 will rotate over to cover M4, R5 will rotate over to replace R4 and cover M3, and R6 will rotate to cover M2. Essentially, each midfielder has rotated one spot over to replace another rider in that area of the field. Because it will take R2 a little bit of time to get back to replace R6, this rotation has given D2 two options: a pass back to D1 or a lengthy diagonal pass to M1. If M1 happens to cross the midfield line, it will be important for R2 to call to R6 and alert him that there's a player in the defensive end so that R6 then can give his attention to two players, M1 and M2. Once more, the clearing team's only option is to throw a cross-field pass or a lengthy diagonal pass. It is important to remember that as the riding players rotate one spot, if the clearing player a rider is moving to cover goes over the midfield line, the rider should follow him, switching from covering an area of the field—or a zone—to man-to-man.

Teamwork must be stressed in the riding phase of the game. If everyone does his job, the clear will

be broken often enough to create offensive opportunities. In addition, the riding team gains the big advantage of ball control and continuous offensive pressure. The longer the ball remains on the opponent's defensive half of the field, the less his chance of scoring.

There are several key points to remember:

Plan the ride carefully. It is important that your riding philosophy fit your team philosophy. If your team likes to run a lot, wants to create transitions, and is willing to take some risks, then using a pressure ride, such as the dead ball ride, would be most appropriate. However, if your philosophy is to slow the game down a little and play good half-field defense, then employing a safer, less risky ride, such as the inbounds running ride described earlier in this chapter, is best.

Practice, practice, practice. Areas sorely overlooked in lacrosse are riding and clearing. Riding can create several additional offensive opportunities throughout a game. If a team is forced to clear the ball twenty times, and if you work hard in practice to ensure that your players' riding movements and patterns are automatic, two or three additional offensive opportunities may be created by doing a good job of riding. This can be done by either intercepting a pass, taking the ball away, or forcing the clearing team into an unnecessary change of possession because they haven't cleared the ball in the allotted amount of time or they've thrown it out-of-bounds.

Using multiple rides can be helpful. Not providing a clearing team with a steady diet of the same ride can confuse them and play to the riding team's advantage.

Recognize that a clearing team will be able to clear the ball a reasonable percentage of the time. After all, the clearing team has an extra man on its defensive half of the field. Make it tough on the clearing team, however, by riding hard and intelligently.

Riding does not take great skill. It takes great effort.

Lou Braun (JHU '05) in face-off action against Duke in the
2005 NCAA title game. *Jay Van Rensselaer*

16

Face-offs

Play is initiated at the beginning of each quarter and after each goal by facing the ball at the center of the field. Figure 16.1 shows the face-off men, each in position on the same side of the center of the field as the goal he is defending. Their sticks are resting on the ground with the pockets in a back-to-back position. The heads of the two sticks must be on designated lines on the midfield, four inches apart, with the ball on the ground between them. Both hands must be on the handle of the stick, and the stick must be in contact with the ground. The feet may not touch the stick. No portion of either stick may touch. Both hands and both feet must be to the left of the throat of the stick, and the hands must be at least eighteen inches apart. When the official places the ball between the two sticks and sounds his whistle to start play, each face-off man tries to direct the course of the ball by a movement with his stick and body.

Control of the ball at the face-off is a critical factor in determining the outcome of a game—indeed, it is on a par with the importance of the goalie. In order to score, a team must get possession of the ball, and normally the team that dominates the face-off is the winner. No better example of that would be the record of Virginia's Jack deVilliers. Although the Cavaliers' goalie Tillman Johnson garnered the lion's share of accolades for his thirteen-save performance in the 2003 national championship game against Hopkins, of almost equal importance was deVillier's exceptional work at the X. Taking on a trio of top Hopkins face-off men—Kyle Harrison, Greg Peyser, and Lou Braun—deVilliers won twelve out of nineteen face-offs. Two years later, however, the situation was completely reversed. DeVilliers again faced Harrison,

Peyser, and Braun in the 2005 semifinal championship game and was outmatched decisively, losing thirteen out of twenty face-offs—including the crucial draw against Greg Peyser with just 12.7 seconds left on the clock in regulation time. By winning that face-off, Greg was able to get the ball to Jake Byrne so that he could score the tying goal with only 1.4 seconds remaining in regulation—setting up the overtime period in which we would win the game.

Over the years, the national championship lacrosse teams have had outstanding face-off men. Some of the great ones have been Hopkins's Joe Rzempoluch in 1987, Princeton's Drew Casino in 2001, and Syracuse's Dan Brennan in 2004. The 2005 Hopkins team was fortunate to have not only Harrison, Peyser, and Braun as exceptional face-off men but also Jamison Koesterer and Steve Peyser (Greg's younger brother), who played critical roles as well. We won nearly 60 percent (a remarkable .597, to be precise) of our face-offs in 2005. What a psychological lift is given to the team that has confidence in the ability of its face-off man to get the ball most of the time!

The most essential qualities of a good face-off man are technique, effort, quickness, and strength. Agility is necessary to give body control and balance while contesting for the ball. The face-off man must be the most tenacious and aggressive ground ball man on the field. He has to concentrate fully on the job at hand, and once the ball is on the ground, he must be relentless in his pursuit of it. When size complements strength and quickness, the face-off man has a distinct advantage. This was certainly the case with 6'0", 180-pound Kyle Harrison (who won 39 out of 64 face-offs for a .609 win-lose percentage); 6'1", 205-pound Greg Peyser (75 out of 121 for a .620 win-lose percentage); 6'0", 200-pound Lou Braun (57 out of 98 for a .582 win-lose percentage); and 6'4", 225-pound Jamison Koesterer (26 out of 40 for a .650 win-lose percentage).

If a short man has strength and quickness, however, he can also be an effective face-off man. One of Hopkins's best was Jerry Schnydman, Class of 1967, who was just 5'1¾" but was built like a muscular fireplug. Jerry took great pride in his ability to get the ball on the face-off. He practiced

his maneuvers religiously and thrived on the challenge of competing against larger opponents. In his seven years of playing lacrosse at Hopkins and for the Mount Washington Club, he was successful in more than 80 percent of his face-offs. This is quite a record and would have been considerably higher if it weren't for the day he met his match against Neil Henderson in the 1965 Navy-Hopkins game. In their head-to-head battle, Neil completely overpowered Jerry and controlled sixteen out of seventeen face-offs. It was simply a case of a skillful big man beating a skillful smaller man. Other exceptional face-off men of smaller stature have been Hopkins's Greg Matthews, Class of 1985; the University of Maryland's Brian Haggerty, Class of 1999; and Hopkins's Eric Wedin, Class of 2001.

BASIC POSITION

The face-off player's stance and basic position are the most critical factors affecting his ability to win the draw. The initial stance and positioning of each face-off man are extremely personal, but a proper and well-balanced position over the ball will enable a player to react quickly to the whistle and compete effectively for the ball even if he does not win the face-off cleanly. Often by having positioned himself properly, a player can prevent the opposing team from initiating a fast break and, because he did not take himself out of the play due to poor positioning, perhaps even regain control of the ball after losing the draw. In today's game, the most successful face-off men rely on a variety of moves and their quickness at using them to take advantage of their opponent. Consequently, a player's stance must allow for the use of multiple moves without revealing to his opponent which one will be next.

The basic position of the face-off man is illustrated in figure 16.1. The feet are placed hip-width apart. The right foot is even with the right hand and slightly behind the left foot, in about a toe-instep relationship. This places the right foot in a position from which it can make a natural step forward and toward the top of the stick when the whistle sounds. The right hand grasps the handle at the throat of the stick, right next to the head, and the stick head is then placed in touch with the ground. The left hand is placed in a comfortable position on the handle, normally no farther than eighteen inches from the right hand. The right elbow should be inside the right knee and pushing against the knee. The right knee, in like manner, pushes into the elbow, creating considerable pressure on the right hand and arm. Both elbows should be inside of the knees so as not to limit the player's ability to use a wide variety of maneuvers from the same stance. The body is kept low to the ground in a crouched position, with the body weight distributed evenly, and the right hand and right foot are ready to spring forward when the whistle blows. It is important that the player transfer little to no weight onto his hands while in the crouched position. Although some players feel that transferring weight to their hands may provide additional strength to their moves, this actually hinders their ability to get up and out of the face-off position quickly. Many of the face-off moves in today's game are based upon quickness and the ability to get out of the face-off area rapidly in order to create a transition offense.

GUIDELINES FOR THE FACE-OFF MAN

1. Keep your head down and your eyes on the ball during the entire face-off maneuver, until the ball is under control.

2. Respond immediately to the official's whistle. With experience, a player gets to know an official's cadence—putting down the ball, standing up, moving back—and can try to anticipate the whistle to get a jump on the opponent.

3. Never stand up. Stay low to the ground. Explode out of the stance, but keep your hands and the ball in front of your body at all times.

4. Keep the handle of the stick low to the ground. If it is at an angle greater than forty-five degrees with the ground, this will tend to force you to stand up, weakening your position.

5. Keep turning your body and try to screen off your opponent by placing your body between him and the ball.

6. Don't tip off the maneuver you are planning to use by adjusting your stance. Use the same basic position for all maneuvers.

Figure 16.1 Positioning for a face-off just before the whistle.

7. Scoop the loose ball with two hands on your stick and then protect it with your body. The one-hand maneuver for doing so is often very effective (see figure 5.10, page 57).

8. Communicate with your wing men by using signals to indicate whether you are going to pull forward or backward, whether you want them to ride out and to which side they should do so, or whether they should come in straight for the ball.

9. When you have control of the ball, be ready to pass or flip it immediately to an open teammate as soon as a wing defender moves in to play you.

FACE-OFF TECHNIQUES

There are many more moves in face-offs today than when the first edition of this book was published. A lot of them have colorful nicknames. Two of the most basic and popular, however, are the clamp and the pinch and rake.

Clamp

Figure 16.2 shows the movement of the face-off man as he executes the clamp. When the whistle blows, the right foot and the right hand move simultaneously. The right foot goes to a position next to the top of the head of his stick. The right hand turns the head of the stick flat to the ground with as much force as possible in an effort to cover the ball completely and clamp it to the ground. The left hand lifts the handle about twelve inches from the ground to add more pressure to the clamping mo-

Figure 16.2 Phases of the clamp maneuver.

tion. As the ball is being clamped, the face-off man turns his backside into the opponent and pushes into him with all of his strength. Since the face-off man will have a difficult time scooping the ball at his feet, his backing-in maneuver places the ball in a position from which he can scoop it. If he is unable to drive the opponent back, he pushes the

ball with the head of his stick to a point that is normally to the right rear of his original position. He may also use his foot to kick the ball away from his body. He then scoops the ball with two hands on the stick and is ready to use the one-hand maneuver described in chapter 5 to avoid the opponent's stick check.

Pinch and Rake

The pinch and rake is shown in figure 16.3. The initial movements of the right foot, right hand, and left hand are the same as in the clamp maneuver. However, instead of clamping the head of the stick flat to the ground, the face-off man turns it only about halfway and compresses the head of the stick into the ball, trapping it in the back of his stick. This is done by pulling the left hand up quickly toward the left shoulder. Once the ball is on the ground, the face-off man rakes (or pushes) the ball with the head of his stick to a left-side or left-rear position with a sweeping motion of both hands. The right hand drives across the front of the body to the face-off man's left side, and the left hand moves to his left rear. The entire pinch and rake is one continuous motion. Once the ball has been raked away from his body, the face-off man moves quickly to it and scoops it with two hands on the stick. He is then ready to use the one-hand protective maneuver.

Rake

The rake without the pinch is also a standard maneuver. All of the mechanics are the same as the pinch and rake except that the face-off man makes his raking motion with the head of his stick in its original position.

The Top

This move is easy to learn and execute (figure 16.4). It requires one simple, quick movement that should be in every good face-off player's repertoire. If the player is not successful with the initial move, it still prevents the opposing player from winning a clean face-off. The player places his hands lightly on the ground, with the stick barely resting on the surface. The wrist and hand positions are less

Figure 16.3 Phases of the pinch and rake maneuver.

critical with this move, which makes it easier to master. The hands should be in a comfortable, non-cocked position. On the whistle, the player simply lifts his right hand up and shoves it forward, dragging his knuckles over the top of the ball in a diagonal direction toward his opponent. The closed fist of his hand may contact his opponent's stick and prevent him from cleanly clamping or raking the ball. If this maneuver is successful, the ball should roll toward the player, under him, and can be swept backward by the shaft of his stick.

Flip

For many years the rules required sticks to be touching on the face-off, and this made the flip technique one of the most popular. Now that the sticks are separated by four inches, the flip has become more difficult to execute. However, it can be worked against an opponent who lacks quickness. When the whistle blows, the face-off man delays his movement for just a fraction of a second rather than stepping forward into his opponent. His feet actually remain in their initial position, and he anticipates the opponent pushing the ball into the back of his stick with a clamp or pinch and rake move. As soon as this happens, the face-off man flips the ball by snapping his hands forward and pushing the ball to the left front of his body. The head of the face-off man's stick may be directed either under or over the head of his opponent's stick. His step with his right foot is simultaneous with the flip action. In addition to the front flip, the center can flip the ball back to his right rear by taking a short step in this direction with his right foot and flipping the ball back toward the goal he is defending.

Figure 16.4 "The Top" maneuver.

Figure 16.5 Laser move/reverse clamp.

Counter for Rake

If the opponent has an effective rake maneuver, the face-off man can counter it in several ways. First, his initial step with his right foot helps him use his foot and leg to partially block the opponent's rake. If the face-off man doesn't make the step, the opponent should have little difficulty in completing the rake. The player must be careful not to kick his opponent's stick, which will result in a penalty and automatic loss of possession. Another counter for the rake is accomplished by the face-off man moving at the sound of the whistle to the point at which his opponent has been raking the ball. He makes no attempt to control the ball initially but lets the opponent make the first move and then tries to beat him to the ball. If the face-off man doesn't get to the ball first, he will at least be there to check his opponent's stick and thus prevent him from scooping it.

Counter for Clamp and Duck Under

Against an opponent who uses a clamp with repeated success, the face-off man can counter with another maneuver. When the whistle sounds, he quickly slides his stick under his opponent's stick. This forces the opponent to clamp the ball into the back side of his stick. The face-off man then drives his entire body weight in an upward motion to lift the opponent's stick. He keeps his eye on the ball because it may be flipped into the air or just drop to the ground. Regardless, he is ready to play it immediately.

Counter for Flip

The easiest way to stop the flip action on the face-off is to move the stick back rather than push it forward. The flip is difficult to execute when the ball is on the ground and not in the stick.

Laser Move and Reverse Clamp

Players with quick hands who prefer not to use a pinched or narrow head on their stick have made this move popular in recent years. The stance is slightly different from that used for the clamp. When executing the clamp, a player's feet are angled toward the corner of the field, and his body is crouched as low as possible. His hands are cocked so that he can clamp down with as much strength as possible. In the laser (as in laser-quick) move (figure 16.5), the player's feet are square with the end line, and his right hand should be held high, holding the stick very lightly. No weight at all should be transferred to the hands. On the whistle, the player straightens his left hand and, with a wrist action, rolls the stick forward in the direction opposite what would be used for a clamp, automatically rotating it underneath the opponent's stick and out-maneuvering him for the ball. It is important to remember that the positioning of a player's hands and feet are a dead giveaway that he plans to use the laser move and reverse clamp. It must be executed with the laserlike quickness its name suggests in order to avoid the opponent's countermoves.

Since so many varieties of face-off moves exist, it is vital to practice all of them to determine which are most effective for the player's build, quickness, and strength. Similarly, it is essential to know what moves the opposing players favor. Preparing in advance by using film or video can be extremely helpful. Every move can be telegraphed by a player's hand position, feet position, body position, and the location of the head of his stick. Many teams scout their face-off opponents by watching film of them frame by frame. A single finger drop-off on a player's grip can signal an oncoming jam. A cocked hand can signal a clamp; a rolled hand can predict a laser. Any face-off man who does his homework will be more successful.

ALIGNMENT AND RESPONSIBILITIES OF THE WING MIDFIELDERS

Proper positioning of the two wing midfielders is essential in controlling the ball on the face-off. Figure 16.6 shows the standard positioning of all six midfielders on a face-off, but for explanation purposes we will consider only the moves of wing midfielders O3 and O5. They can line up anywhere behind the wing-area line, which is twenty yards in length. Their legs are primed for the sprint as soon as the whistle blows. Often the face-off man can flip the ball back to the wing midfielder on his left behind. If he is dominating the draws, he can use this midfielder to create two-on-one situations. He can do this by being aware of the opposition team's wingman on the left and communicating with his own wingman to determine if his opponent on the wing is likely to try to prevent a fast break or decide to stay next to his rival. By pulling the ball to strategic places on the field and moving quickly from the X, the face-off man can create a mismatch in his favor.

Wing Midfielder O3

Wing midfielder O3 has defensive responsibilities because he is on the side of the field where the opponent's face-off man (X4) will be trying to control the ball in most cases. The location of O3 is determined by the position on the field where X4 is consistently directing the ball. Player O3 wants to line

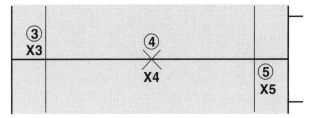

Figure 16.6 Position of the wing midfielders on face-off.

up where he can take the shortest route to the ball. He needs speed to get to the opponent's face-off man before he scoops the ball, and once he reaches him, he must be aggressive and tenacious in the battle for ball control. He can body check his opponent as long as he can keep on his feet and play the ball. However, if he loses his footing and falls to the ground, the body check is useless. Gaining possession of the ball is the primary consideration. If the opponent's face-off man is so skillful that he can get control of the ball before O3 can get to him, O3 should play at the very end of the wing-area line on the defensive half of the field.

The best wing defender at Hopkins in recent years, Corey Harned, was a former high school All-American attackman. We converted him to the long-stick. He had outstanding speed, quickness, and stick skills, but most important, he had a toughness rivaled by few. Not only could Corey scoop up ground balls with two hands in his long-stick, but on occasion, when under duress, he could scoop up ground balls with one hand.

Wing Midfielder O5

Wing midfielder O5 has offensive responsibilities in most cases, because he is on the side of the field where his face-off man (O4) will be trying to direct the ball. Player O5 positions himself closest to the point to which he expects O4 to direct the ball. He starts to move toward the center of the field when the whistle blows but is ready to read the play and react quickly. If O4 can get to the ball before he does, O5 stops and starts to move for the offensive half of the field. If his defender (X5) continues toward O4, O5 calls for the ball. If the ball is on the ground, O4 can either kick it with his foot or push it with his stick toward O5, who should be open.

If O4 scoops it, he can either pass or flip it to O5. Player O5 may have a fast-break opportunity.

If O5 can get to the loose ball before O4 or X4, he scoops it and runs for daylight. He is ready to pass or flip the ball to an open teammate who is calling for it. If the opponent's face-off man (X4) is able to control the ball himself and initiate a fast break, O5 can line up at the very end of the wing-area line on the defensive half of the field, in the same manner as O3. This position will help stop the fast break.

Two outstanding wingmen who graduated with the Class of 2005 were Benson Erwin of Johns Hopkins and Jarett Park of Syracuse University. Both possessed outstanding speed and quickness and were able to outsprint their opponents to balls that were pulled to specific areas of the field by their face-off men.

Responsibilites of Other Players

Every player on the field has certain responsibilities on the center face-off. The three defensemen, the three attackmen, and the goalie must remain in their respective areas until possession is determined by the official or the ball crosses either restraining line. Then they can make a play for the ball. Prior to the whistle, they should gear themselves for a possible fast break from the face-off. The goalie checks with his three defensemen to determine their positions in the event of a fast break. Normally, the defenseman who is in the middle will identify himself as the point man. The man on his left will be the left crease defender, and the man on his right will be the right crease defender. The three attackmen on the offensive half of the field will do the same. The man who normally plays the point position will be in the middle of the field, and the right and left creasemen will be on their respective sides.

Face-off with Player in the Penalty Box

When a team has one or more players in the penalty box in a center face-off situation, it can make an adjustment of its personnel to cover the two wing midfield positions. Normally, a team will move its most athletic, all-round attackman from the attack-goal area to the offensive wing position

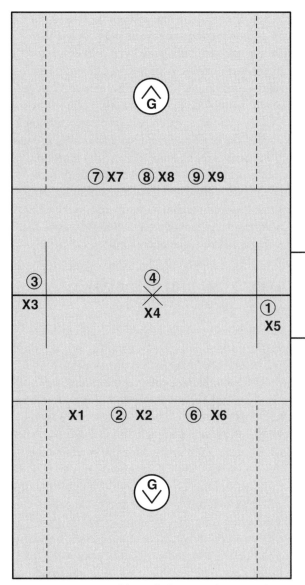

Figure 16.7 Position of face-off players with man in the penalty box.

to battle for the ball, because control of the ball will mean that the opponent cannot make use of his extra man. Figure 16.7 shows the point attackman (O1) lining up in the wing position but on the offensive half of the field. He must avoid going over the center line; if he does go over, his team will be penalized for being offside. This is one of the problems in the man-down face-off situation. Another concern is the need for the face-off man (O4) and defensive wing midfielder (O3) to play man-down defense. If they fail to get possession of the ball on the face-off, they must know how to handle those responsibilities.

A team should have at least two players who are skilled in the techniques of controlling the ball on face-offs. It helps to have one in each midfield unit. They must continually strive to improve and should practice their maneuvers for at least twenty minutes every day. Since strength is so important, face-off men can make use of various weight training exercises to build up their muscles, especially in their wrists, arms, shoulders, and legs. As is the case with every player who wants to be the best, these extra efforts require extra time, on your own, apart from regular workout and practice sessions. Howard Offit, a face-off ace on Henry Ciccarone's championship teams, would take a 2-by-12 wooden board and drill twelve holes in it. Then he would screw in a dozen half-inch screws and take them out to help develop his forearm muscles. He also did many duckwalks, constantly pushing and pulling the ball with his stick. This forced him to stay low to the ground and developed his quadriceps muscles.

The face-off is very demanding, both physically and mentally, and requires complete dedication and concentration for success in this important phase of the game.

Johns Hopkins head coach Dave Pietramala lays down some
fundamentals early in 2005. *Jay Van Rensselaer*

17

Drills

Repetition is the mother of learning, and as you practice, so you play. Never underestimate the importance of well-planned practice sessions that emphasize fundamentals, physical conditioning, and every possible situation a team could face in a game. Drills are necessary to develop meaningful practices that improve individual skills as well as team play. Through repetition in drills, players will develop responses that will enable them to act automatically in game situations. However, it is important to remember to put aside the drills occasionally and simply play during practice. Playing is as important as the repetition of the drills.

It is the coach's responsibility to make use of a variety of drills to condition his players both mentally and physically. The following guidelines can help the coach get maximum effectiveness from his drills.

1. Don't run the same drill for too long a period. Monotony can cause loss of enthusiasm. Each drill should last no longer than ten minutes. You always can come back later and do another ten-minute segment of that drill.

2. Try to avoid long intervals between a player's participation in a drill. If a player spends too much time watching and not playing, he often loses interest in the drill.

3. Then again, don't overwork a player in a drill. Make sure there are enough people so that maximum effort can be demanded throughout the player's time of involvement.

4. Make sure that the drill is explained thoroughly and that each player knows the purpose of the drill. Explain the what, the how, and the why.

5. Some drills can be fun for the players. The coach should try to invent new drills that accom-

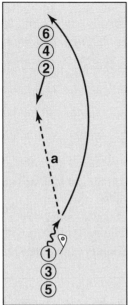

Figure 17.1 Weave line drill.

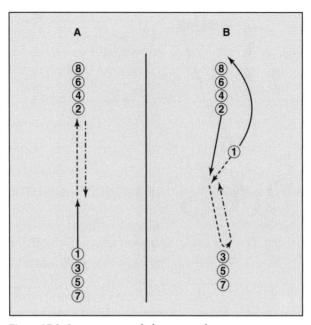

Figure 17.2 Scoop away, and phase two of scoop away.

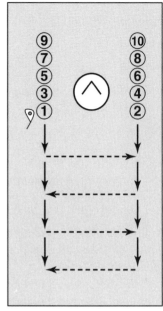

Figure 17.3 Hash-to-hash stick-work drill.

plish the same results as the regular ones but have a different look.

6. Fit the drill to the skill level of the players. Drills that require complicated maneuvers should not be prescribed for players with limited stickwork.

7. Enthusiasm must be shown by all players during a drill—those waiting for their turns as well as those actually playing.

8. Be sure to vary your drills and use a combination of full-field and half-field drills in an effort to cover both aspects of the game.

Coach Scott found some of the following drills to be useful. Most of them are as appropriate for a college varsity team as for a youth league team. However, several may be too complicated for beginners. Added to this list are some of the new drills we use today.

There are drills to hone your basic skills and drills to emulate gamelike situations. When working with players at the youth level on up, it is critical to use line drills, which hone basic skills, but at the higher levels, line drills are not used as often. Many of the stickwork drills at the college level are

up the field and across the field, because that is the way lacrosse is played. As a coach is developing his drills, he should keep this in mind and design drills that reinforce the basics as well as drills that reflect the way the game is played.

LINE DRILLS

Line drills are particularly good for teaching and maintaining basic skills. One such drill is illustrated in figure 17.1.

Six to eight players divide into two lines with three or four players in each line. The first players in each line should be about twenty yards apart. Player O1 starts with the ball, runs several yards, and passes to O2, who initially calls for the ball ("Kyle, here's your help!"), gives a target in the box area with his stick, and moves forward to meet the ball. After he catches it, he passes it to O3. Player O3 must not break for the ball until O2 has control of it in his stick, because forward passes, not lateral passes, are desired. After passing the ball, the player goes to the end of the opposite line. If the players are advanced in their stickwork, they can handle the ball right-handed for several minutes, then left-handed. The coach should be the one to signal for the change.

From this same alignment, the coach can change the drill from catching and throwing to scooping a ground ball. The scooper controls the ball in his stick, making the designated calls "Ball!" as he attempts to pick the ball up and "Release!" once he has possession of it. Then he will pass it to the next player. This drill can be done without passing—just scoop and roll the ball. However, in the real world, a lacrosse player never picks up a ball and rolls it. He picks up a ball and passes it. It is best to keep that in mind when using this drill. The player who is in line behind the scooper should call to him, "I've got you backed." If the ball goes past the scooper, the backer should then play it.

The normal length of time for this drill is five minutes. This drill can be done with six to eight players divided in line, or by position, since many teams do stickwork by position.

SCOOP AWAY

In figure 17.2, six to eight players are divided into two lines (A and B) with three or four players in each line. The first players in each line should be about twenty yards apart. Player 1 will start by picking up a ground ball. He will run several yards and pass to 2, who initially calls for the ball, "Kevin, here's your help." He gives a target with his stick in the box area and prepares to receive the ball in a stationery position. After 2 catches the ball, he will pass it back to 1, who is moving toward him and providing him with a target in the box area. Once 1 gets the ball back, 2 will move toward 1 and 1 will roll the ball away from 2, forcing 2 to scoop up a ground ball as it moves away from him. As he is approaching the ground ball, 2 will make the appropriate call, "Ball!" and as he picks it up will shout the "Release!" call. Once 2 picks the ball up, he will look for his target, 3, who is standing stationary in the other line, holding his stick with the head in the box area, providing 2 with a target. 2 will pass the ball to 3. Once 3 receives the ball, he will immediately pass it back to 2, who is holding his stick with the head in the box area,

providing 3 with a target. As 2 moves toward the ball and receives it, he then will roll it away from 3, who will move to scoop up the ball. As each player rolls the ball away from the scooper, he should advance to the end of each line.

HASH-TO-HASH STICKWORK

Figure 17.3 shows the hash-to-hash stickwork drill. The name of the drill is taken from the alignment of the players on the hash marks of a football field. The coach can make an adjustment of the alignment to reflect the level and abilities of his players. The players can be moved farther apart and can also be asked to move at a slow pace or a quick pace, depending on their skills.

Hash-to-hash stickwork is a full-field drill that simulates gamelike passes as players move up the field. The team splits in half and forms two lines at one end of the field. The players are positioned almost at the hash marks of a football field, about eight yards wide of the goal on each side. Each player in one line will have a ball. The players on the left side of the goal will be catching and throwing left-handed; the players on the right side of the goal will be catching and throwing right-handed.

When the coach blows his whistle, the first two players at the head of each line will begin. Player 1 will start with the ball on the hash marks, jogging up the field, while player 2 jogs up the field remaining parallel with player 1. Each player will hold his stick with the head in the box area to provide his teammate with a target, and they will pass and catch the ball as they move up the field. Each man will be receiving the ball across his body, as he would in a game. Player 2 will be receiving the ball left-handed, and player 1 will be receiving it across his body with his right hand. This repetitive movement will continue as these players move up the field until they get to the other goal line. Once players 1 and 2 get about ten yards from where they started, players 3 and 4 will follow. When players 3 and 4 move ten yards from where they started, players 5 and 6 will go.

In this drill, the players are challenged with throwing quality passes that their teammates can catch. As the drill continues, the pace can be increased. It is best when beginning this drill to start at a very light jog. This drill is great to use as a warm-up, since the players can start off slow and then increase their rate of speed.

When the players get to the other end of the field, they will align themselves as they did before and the drill will repeat itself—except that player 1 will find himself having to catch and throw left-handed, and player 2 will find himself having to catch and throw right-handed. Each single trip up the field should allow each individual player to catch and throw the ball at least eight to ten times, re-creating a gamelike situation with excellent repetition. This drill normally runs five minutes.

HASH-TO-HASH GROUND BALLS

Figure 17.4 shows the hash-to-hash ground balls drill, which begins with exactly the same alignment as in figure 17.3. In this example, players 1, 3, 5, and 7 will start with the balls. When the coach blows his whistle, player 1 will roll the ball out in front of player 2, forcing player 2 to jog forward to pick up the loose ball. He will do so with his strong hand. As player 2 jogs forward to pick up the ground ball, player 1 will mirror his movement up the field so that he and player 2 are moving parallel to one another. Upon scooping the ball with his strong hand, player 2 will roll the ball out in front of player 1 as they move up the field. If player 2 is a strong right-hander, he will switch his stick to the left to roll the ball out in front of player 1; if player 2 is a left-hander, he simply picks the ball up with his strong hand and rolls it to player 1. Player 1 will use the "Ball" and "Release" calls when picking up the ball—signaling that he is making a play for it. He yells "Ball!" as he goes for it and "Release!" once he picks it up, just as he would in a game, so that any of his teammates who were engaging an opponent could release and avoid being called for interference. When player 1 picks up the ball with his strong hand, he will bring the head of his stick to his box area. Having done that, if he is a strong right-hander, he will roll the ball right-handed out in front of player 2. If he is a left-hander, he will

switch his stick from his left to right hand and roll the ball out for player 2. This movement will take place all the way up the field. As in the earlier variation of this drill, when players 1 and 2 approach the ten-yard mark, players 3 and 4 will go, then players 5 and 6, and so forth. Once each pair gets to the other end of the field, they will align themselves in the same positions and be prepared to repeat the drill when everybody has completed it, going the other way.

The purpose of this drill is to practice ground ball work in a gamelike situation, which requires players to pick up a ground ball that is moving away from them. They are doing so on the move and have to pick up the ball immediately. They also get repetition out of this drill. Each player should pick up anywhere from seven to ten ground balls before he reaches the other end of the field. The normal length of time for this drill would be five minutes.

These drills not only involve stickwork and ground ball play but also incorporate conditioning by requiring full-field movement. Jogging up the field however many times in a five-minute period can be demanding. The drill's pace will begin slowly and become faster as the drill goes on, ending, if the coach prefers, with players picking up ground balls or passing the ball back and forth at a full sprint. The distance between the players can also be widened. The speed and distance adjustments can be determined by the skill level of the players.

PRESSURE GROUNDERS

This drill also simulates gamelike ground balls but teaches players how to handle such plays under duress. It also helps to foster a player's competitiveness. At Hopkins, we begin many of our practices with this drill. It is demanding and deals with a critical part of the game. A coach may like to use this drill only after the players have mastered scoop to/scoop away and hash-to-hash ground balls, since it is a little more intense. This drill can also be varied in terms of how many groups of players are involved. The coach can break his team into one group of two

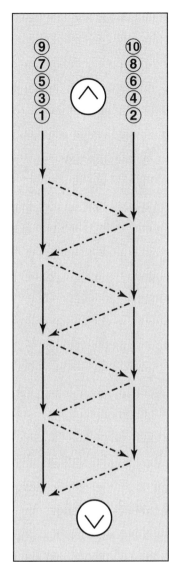

Figure 17.4 Hash-to-hash
ground ball drill.

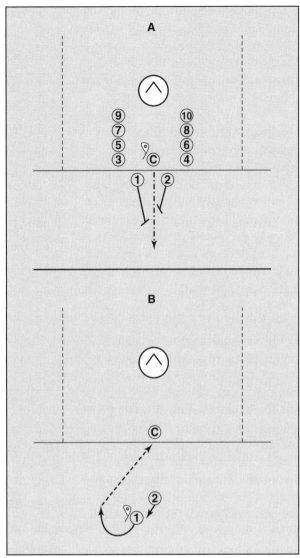

Figure 17.5 Pressure grounders drill.

lines, two groups of two lines, or three groups with two lines. It all depends on how many coaches are available to supervise the players, how much time the head coach wants to devote to this drill, and how much repetition he wants the players to have.

For diagram purposes, figure 17.5 shows one group with the coach positioned by the restraining box, in between two lines of players, about a yard behind the first two players. Since a ground ball can be contested anywhere on the field, however, the drill can also be executed anywhere. It is good to

vary this drill's location so that players can practice picking up the balls in different areas of the field.

To begin the drill, players 1 and 2 will step to the restraining line, placing themselves shoulder-to-shoulder in an athletic position, looking forward. The coach will roll the ball out beyond players 1 and 2. If a coach wishes, he can create an advantage for one player or the other by rolling the ball to one side. If he wants an evenly matched competition, he can roll the ball out directly in the middle of both players.

As soon as the two players gain sight of the ball, their competition for it begins. Each player will move forward, trying to position himself in front of his opponent and preparing himself to pick up the ground ball. The player who succeeds in getting the first shot at the ground ball should yell "Ball!" as he approaches the ball and "Release!" as he picks it up. Unlike the other drills described so far in this chapter, player 1, who in this case has an advantage, must prepare to be checked by player 2. The type of check will depend on the players' respective locations. If player 2 is located behind player 1, he will try to poke check player 1's back hand to deter him from picking up the ground ball. If player 2 is beside player 1, he may check player 1's stick with a slap check or put a body check on player 1, trying to knock him off his path so that player 2 can pick up the ball. This drill is both physical and intense.

Once a player picks up a ground ball, the drill has not ended. He then must make a circular move away from pressure. He may move to his right or to his left, depending on where his opponent is located. He must run to an open area and pass the ball back to the coach. In this example, player 2, who did not pick up the ground ball, will have to play defense on player 1 until he passes the ball back to the coach. If player 2 is able to knock the ball down or take it away, he and player 1 then will compete for the new ground ball. Whoever picks it up will try to circle away from the pressure and pass it back to the coach.

The coach can vary this drill in a number of ways. Once the ball is passed back to him, the coach can roll it out again to the same two players as many times as he wishes, although it is probably beneficial not to do that more than twice. Once players 1 and 2 have completed their portion of the drill, they return to the end of their respective lines. Players 3 and 4 then step up, positioning themselves shoulder-to-shoulder looking forward, and the drill will start for them.

The length and size of this drill depend on how many groups of players are involved. If a coach has a small number of players, the drill should continue for no longer than five minutes. The more groups a coach has, the more repetition his players will get.

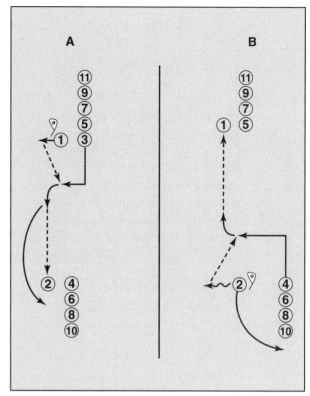

Figure 17.6 Over-the-shoulder drill.

This is a great drill for all players, with the exception of goalies.

OVER-THE-SHOULDER DRILL

The over-the-shoulder drill is designed to simulate a pass and catch as one player moves up the field ahead of a teammate. In the hash-to-hash drill, the players move up the field parallel to one another; in this case, one player will be farther upfield and will be moving away from his teammate who has the ball.

The alignment is similar to the line drills, with one variation. This drill begins with the initiating player not in line with his teammates but standing several yards to the side of them. In figure 17.6, player 1 has the ball, preparing to pass it to player 3. Players 1 and 3 can each handle the ball with their strong hand, or the coach can determine with which hand he would like the players to catch and throw.

When the coach blows his whistle, player 1 moves slightly to his right and player 3 moves straight up the field for about ten yards. Holding his stick in his right hand, he breaks almost on a ninety-degree angle, toward the side on which player 1 is located. Player 3 raises his stick in the air, giving player 1 a target at which he can aim when throwing the ball so that player 3 can catch it over his shoulder as he moves away from player 1. When player 3 catches the ball, he will turn upfield and pass it to player 2. Once player 3 passes the ball to player 2, he will run to position himself behind player 2. Player 1 will remain in his position for one more pass. When player 2 receives the ball, he moves slightly to his left so that he will not be throwing the ball in a stationary position. Player 4 will sprint straight up the field, break to his left at an almost ninety-degree angle, and hold his stick in the air with his left hand so that player 2 can pass him the ball and he can catch it over his shoulder. When player 4 catches the ball, he will turn upfield and pass the ball to player 1. After player 2 passes the ball to player 4, he will go back to the end of his line. Player 4 then passes the ball to player 1, who will move to his right slightly and pass the ball to player 5, who is breaking up the field at a ninety-degree angle. After passing the ball to player 5, player 1 also will move to the end of his line and player 4 will replace him at the head of that line. The only player who passes the ball twice in a row is player 1, because he is the one who begins the drill.

This drill can also be done by position, with defensemen working only with defensemen, middies with middies, and attackmen with attack. It can be run in different areas of the field and is a great way to simulate some of the passing and catching that takes place in the clearing game. The drill should last five minutes.

DODGE THE DEFENDER

This drill can be used to practice a number of dodges: a roll dodge, a face dodge, a split dodge, a bull dodge—whichever dodge the coach decides he wants to work on in that portion of the practice or during the course of the drill. It is the coach's responsibility to signal for the change from one dodge to another. Six or eight players form in two lines with fifteen to twenty yards' distance between the

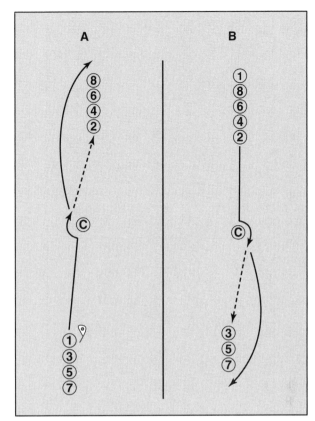

Figure 17.7 Dodge-the-defender drill.

leaders of each line (figure 17.7). Either a coach or a player positions himself in the middle and assumes a defensive role but allows the player with the ball (O1) to dodge. After O1 executes a predetermined dodge, he passes the ball to O2, who is located in the opposite line. After catching the ball, O2 moves toward the defender and uses the same dodge. The defender doesn't give the ball carrier much pressure. In fact, he is playing token defense and tries to help the ball carrier through the dodge. Once the dodger gets past the defender and throws the ball to the opposite line, he can replace the defender, thus keeping the drill moving and giving everybody an opportunity to be the defender as well as the dodger.

THREE-MAN WEAVE

The three-man weave is usually a full-field drill (figure 17.8). It is like a drill commonly used in basketball and simulates a gamelike situation in

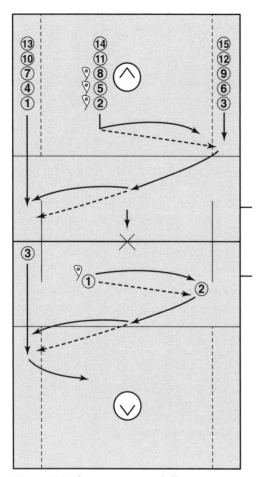

Figure 17.8 Three-man weave drill.

sticks on the outside, which means that the players in group 3 will have their sticks in their left hands, on the outside, and the players in group 1 have their sticks in their right hands. The players in group 2 will hold their sticks in the hand opposite to the one of the player to whom they will be passing the ball. For example, a player in group 2 will hold his stick in his right hand if he will be passing the ball to a player in group 3, who is holding his stick in his left hand. Simply put, a player in the middle group will always be throwing the ball across his body.

When the coach blows his whistle, the players at the head of each line will begin moving up the field simultaneously. Once the player in the middle decides to which side he will throw the ball, he passes it to that player as they both move up the field. In this example, the first player in group 2 will pass the ball to the player in group 3, then jog or sprint behind that player in group 3. The player in group 3, who has caught the ball left-handed, will jog or sprint toward the middle and pass the ball left-handed to the player in group 1, who is jogging up the field. The player in group 3 will then jog or sprint behind the player in group 1.

Each player who throws the ball will follow his pass, and the player catching the ball will move to the area from which he has received the pass, looking to move the ball on to the next player. This movement requires the players to weave in behind each other. Every player who is preparing to catch the ball should call to the passer by name: "Here's your help, Steve!" Using the teammate's name when calling for the ball always helps.

The pace of the players moving up the field can be as quick or as slow as the coach determines. It is probably best to begin slow and then pick up the pace. When the first three players reach the opposite goal line, they should fall in behind the line to which they are nearest. Because the weaving motion has continued as the players run up the field, it is unlikely they will find themselves in the same line as the one in which they began.

When the players who started the drill get ten yards from their teammates, the next group will go.

This drill helps players learn how to catch and

which players move up the field while passing the ball across it. As is the case with the other full-field drills, this exercise may be a little more advanced for youth teams and probably is best done after a team has spent time practicing line drills, the drills for hash-to-hash stickwork, and over-the-shoulder passes.

In this drill, the players all begin at the same end of the field, at the goal line extended. The coach positions the players in three evenly numbered groups at equal distances apart, with each group taking a third of the field. Group 1 is at the restraining box, group 2 is just on the side of the goal, and group 3 is on the other side, at the restraining line. The balls are given to group 2, in the middle, with each player having a ball.

The players in groups 1 and 3 will hold their

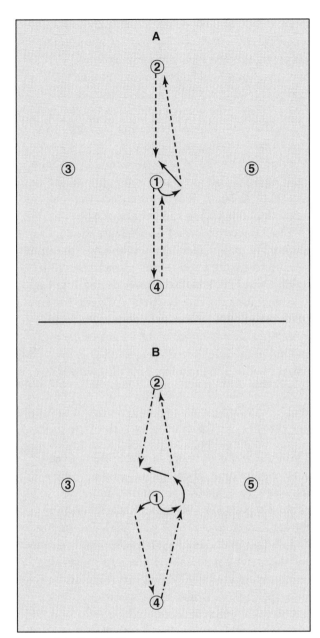

Figure 17.9 Circle drill.

CIRCLE DRILL

The circle drill is very helpful to beginners (figure 17.9). Five or six players form a circle with a diameter of fifteen to twenty yards. A player (O1) moves into the center of the circle. The action starts when O1 makes a break and calls for the ball, and a player on the rim of the circle passes it to him. When O1 catches the ball, he passes it to any of his teammates, who in turn passes it back to him. About four or five circles spread over the entire field can be in operation at the same time. The coach blows his whistle when he wants to change the middle man. The players on the circle can also roll the ball to the middle man and make him scoop it. Thus, for a minute or two a player gets a vigorous workout of catching, scooping, and passing from many different angles. All the appropriate commands are given during this drill. The normal length of time for this drill is ten minutes.

MAZE STICKWORK

The maze stickwork drill, like most of these exercises, aims to involve as many players as possible while trying to simulate a gamelike simulation. It incorporates ground ball work, passing, and catching. The passes it uses are like those that take place in a game. Often players have to pick up a ground ball that is moving on an angle. Rarely, if ever, does a player pick up a ball and roll it, so this drill gives the players an opportunity to practice picking up a ground ball and passing it quickly to a teammate. The drill provides a lot of repetition and many touches in a short period of time.

Maze stickwork involves eight lines, four on each side, located about ten yards in from the sideline, stretching up the field. Each line is staggered from the one opposite it, with each line having an equal number of players in it. In figure 17.10, the drill begins with line 1 and line 2 staggered on a diagonal from each other. Line 3 is staggered on a diagonal from line 2, and so on.

When the whistle blows, the first player in line 1 will roll the ball on a diagonal toward line 2. The first player in line 2 will sprint toward the ball and

throw on the move. It teaches them to move toward their target as they are passing and toward their teammate as they are catching. The drill also involves repetition, so players get a number of catches and passes—or "touches"—before they get to the other end of the field. This drill can be done for five to ten minutes.

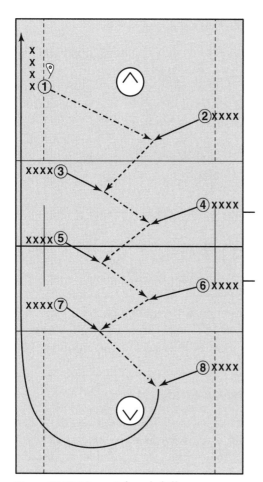

Figure 17.10 Maze stickwork drill.

move to the back of the line of the player who is receiving the ball. Basically, each player is following either his pass or his roll. For example, the first player in line 1 will go to the back of line 2, the first player in line 2 will go to the back of line 3, and so forth. After the first player in line 1 begins the drill and the first player in line 2 picks up the ground ball, the second players in line 1 and line 2 will follow the same pattern as the players who went ahead of them. When the first player in line 8 picks up the ball, he will jog around the goal, run down the field, and go to the back of line 1.

This is a continuous drill. Once the first player in line 2 has touched the ball, the second player in line 1 will go; once the second player in line 2 has touched the ball, the third player in line 1 will go. This drill uses the full length of the field. For less-advanced players, however, it may be easier and more beneficial to shorten the length of the drill and move the lines a little closer together, in terms of both width and distance. This drill should last no longer than five minutes.

FULL-FIELD FOUR-ON-THREE FAST BREAK

Throughout this book we've discussed how important transition offense is in lacrosse. A great transition exercise to use, not only for more experienced players but also for youth-level players, is the full-field four-on-three fast-break drill (figure 17.11). This drill combines stickwork and offensive and defensive concepts, and probably most important—especially for youth players—it's fun. It is an enjoyable drill in which kids can run up and down the field and just play lacrosse.

Defensemen and attackmen take their respective positions at each goal area. Ten to twelve midfielders are divided into two lines near the sideline, with their lines beginning around the restraining box. One line wears the appropriate scrimmage vest to distinguish it from the other. Player O1 initiates the action by receiving a pass from the goalie to begin the fast break. When O1 catches the ball, he carries it down the side of the field, looking to begin the fast break with his offensive teammates. Player O2 chases him after having given him a head start of ten yards. As

pick it up with his strong hand. As he approaches the ball, he will shout "Ball!" to indicate that he's going to pick the ball up, and once he picks the ball up he yells "Release!" just as he would in a game. Once the first player in line 2 picks up the ball, the first player in line 3 will begin to move toward the first player in line 4. He will place his stick in his right hand with its head in the box area, providing the first player in line 2 with a target. When the player in line 2 passes the ball to the player in line 3 and he catches it, he will roll the ball on an angle toward line 4. The first player in line 4 will then run to pick up the ball with his strong hand, shouting the "Ball" and "Release" calls as he does.

This pattern of roll, pick up, pass, and roll will be repeated by the players in the remaining lines. Once a player rolls the ball or passes it, he will

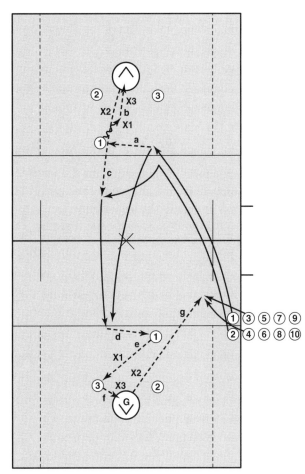

Figure 17.11 Full-field four-on-three fast-break drill.

passes the ball to O3, who is sprinting onto the field from the sideline and hopes to catch the ball somewhere near the face-off line. Once O3 catches the ball, he initiates the fast break with O4 chasing him. The same routine follows as described for O1 and O2. After five to eight minutes of action, the midfielders can switch to the other side of the field to practice the fast breaks from a different position. The normal length of time for this drill is ten to fifteen minutes.

If a team has a limited number of players, the drill just described is a great one. However, if a larger number is participating in the practice, this drill may leave some players standing around a little longer than a coach would like. To address that situation, the coach can simply split the midfielders into two lines, one on each sideline at the opposite ends of the field, diagonal to each other, and the fast breaks now can take place going both ways. For instance, O1 can receive the ball, and O2 can chase. Once they have executed the fast break down to the opposite end of the field and a shot is made, they will go to the end of a new line at the end of the field where the fast break occurred. O3 and O4, who are in a line at that end of the field, will then step onto the field and execute a fast break going the other way. Having defensemen and attackmen going each way, twice the number of players can be involved in initiating the fast break.

HALF-FIELD FAST BREAKS

All the various fast-break opportunities that we described in chapter 11 can be practiced on a half-field basis. The play should be started from about ten yards on the opposite side of the midfield line with an offensive player scooping a ground ball and driving to the goal. The normal length of time to practice any one of these various fast-break combinations is about ten minutes.

GOALIE REACTION

There are several reaction drills a goalie can use by himself. He can throw the ball against a wall and make the save. When he has control of the ball, he can simulate a clearing pass by throwing the ball

O1 carries the ball down, the attack will set up in their fast-break formation, which was described in the transition chapter, and the four offensive players will execute a four-on-three fast break. O2 will do his very best to catch O1, but chances are this won't happen. His role as a chaser in this drill is just to create a gamelike situation. After the four-on-three play is completed, the goalie initiates a fast break toward the other goal by passing the ball to O2, who makes a break as soon as the ball is shot. If the shot is missed or the goalie is unable to get control of it, he uses one of the many balls that he has in reserve in the goal. The action should be continuous.

After O2 carries the ball (with O1 chasing) to the other goal, the four-on-three is made at this goal. After the shot is taken, O1 and O2 are out of the play and go to the end of their respective lines. The goalie then at a particular spot on the wall, striving primarily for accuracy. When on the practice field, he can practice his positioning by moving on his arc and feeling for the pipes with his stick as he maintains position on an imaginary ball carrier moving in the midfield area. The goalie can also practice his turns on an imaginary feed from behind the goal to the crease. By reviewing his footwork and stick positioning by himself for several minutes each day, he can improve his techniques and quickness.

At the start of the season or when inclement weather forces practices indoors, the coach can give the goalie a concentrated workout in the gymnasium. The goalie assumes a position about six to eight yards from a wall and faces it. The coach stands several yards behind him and throws the ball against the wall (inside two lines, which are six feet apart). The goalie keeps his eyes on the wall, and when the ball hits it, he reacts quickly to play it. Once he has control of it, he flips it back to the coach, assumes a ready position, and waits for the next shot. The coach gives the goalie practice against both bounce shots and those thrown in the air. From his position behind the goalie, he is in an excellent spot to observe the goalie's movement into the ball.

FACE-OFF REACTION

There are several reaction drills that can help the face-off man. First, from his crouched position and without opposition, he responds to the whistle and plays a ball that is thrown by the coach to various positions within five yards of the center line. If the ball is too close to him, he pushes it with the head of his stick or kicks it with his foot. After scooping the ball, he listens for a call from his teammate in the wing area and makes a pass or flip to him.

The second drill requires just the face-off man and one other player. The ball is placed on the ground in front of the face-off man. The second player is positioned directly behind him as an opponent. When the whistle blows, the face-off man tries to screen off the opponent from the ball by using his body to protect it. The opponent moves in any way and from any position to try to get the ball. When the whistle blows again, the face-off man kicks the ball and then scoops it, with the opponent continuing to apply pressure.

DEFENSE VERSUS OFFENSE

Concentrated work can be given to both offensive and defensive players, plus the goalie, by using drills with one-on-one, two-on-two, the three-on-three as well as with two players on the crease, four-on-four. Close attention can be given to each player's reactions. Here at Hopkins, we are big proponents of the four-on-four. This drill combines not only individual skills but also team skills from both the offensive and defensive players.

III

Lacrosse at Johns Hopkins

The 1903 Hopkins lacrosse team in repose on the steps of Clifton, once the northeast Baltimore summer home of Johns Hopkins (1795–1873). *The Ferdinand Hamburger Archives of the Johns Hopkins University*

18

Building the Tradition 1883–1974

Almost from the beginning, Johns Hopkins has been recognized as a center of collegiate lacrosse in the United States. This is not a boastful statement. It is based on simple facts. Many exceptional lacrosse programs exist elsewhere. Some programs have storied histories as well, including Syracuse, Princeton, Maryland, Navy, Cornell, North Carolina, and others. Yet over the entire history of collegiate lacrosse, no institution has been more closely associated with the sport or done more to advance it nationally and internationally than Johns Hopkins.

Staying power has been the reason. From 1883 right up to the present, Hopkins lacrosse teams have been a force to be reckoned with. In other sports, Hopkins, with its small student body, has played opponents in its modest class. In lacrosse, it has always contended with the best and come out well: 43 national championships, either won outright or shared; 93 winning seasons and 10 all-even ones in 117 years of play; 62 out of 313 members of the Lacrosse Hall of Fame; and 174 first-team All-Americans since the selections first were made in 1922, by far the most of any school in the country. And Hopkins was the U.S. representative in the last two Olympic Games at which lacrosse was played, in 1928 and 1932. The Blue Jays have been invited to participate in the NCAA championship tournament for thirty-four years in a row. No other school has such a record— either in lacrosse or any other NCAA Division I sport.

Lacrosse always has been important in the life of Hopkins. Visitors at almost any game at Homewood Field will see top administrators, including the university president; deans, professors, and emeritus professors; old and young alumni; a cross-section of other Baltimore fans; and thousands of Hopkins students.

These are the reasons that the story of lacrosse at Johns Hopkins deserves attention.

The first game of lacrosse known to have been played in Baltimore was in 1878, only two years after the founding of the university. Four years later, on October 10, 1882, the Johns Hopkins Lacrosse Club was organized by Elgin R. L. Gould, a University of Toronto man who had earned a fellowship at Hopkins. The club's first game was played on May 11, 1883, when the Hopkins team lost a 4–0 decision to the Druid Lacrosse Club. After that game, Hopkins students did not field a team of their own again until 1888. Clinton L. Riggs, a former Princeton player who was doing postgraduate work at Hopkins, was captain and coach of that team. On April 19, 1888, Hopkins started its first official season, losing to the Druids 4–1. The only other game that season was against the Patterson Lacrosse Club of Baltimore, and Hopkins registered its first victory with a score of 6–2. Since that time, Hopkins has fielded a team every year but one—1944—when World War II curtailed intercollegiate athletics. (This is why the record of Hopkins lacrosse from 1888 to 2005 is only 117 years, not 118 years.)

In 1889, Hopkins had its first unbeaten team. The Jays were undefeated in collegiate play by virtue of a 6–0 win over then powerful Lehigh, their only collegiate opponent. Ties with two club teams, the Druids and Philadelphia, rounded out their abbreviated season.

Hopkins joined the Intercollegiate Lacrosse Association in 1890, and the Blue Jays won one game and lost two. After such a season, interest in the new sport wavered, but Brantz M. Roszel, who served as captain and coach for four years, persisted. In 1891, Hopkins's second season as a member of the Intercollegiate Lacrosse Association, the team won the championship, defeating the University of Pennsylvania twice as well as Lehigh and Stevens.

Up until the 1891 season, teams customarily made long passes to get the ball to attackmen before the opposition's defense could get set up. Hopkins's championship team resorted to a more deliberate type of play: passing to a man stationed near mid-field and then attempting to maneuver the ball into scoring position by running with the ball as well as passing it. This was the beginning of the modern carrying game.

After a lapse of six years, the intercollegiate championship returned to Hopkins in 1898. The championship banners of 1899 and 1900 soon hung in the gym as well, largely because of the efforts of William H. Maddren, who, though only a freshman, was elected captain and coach in 1897. Maddren had taken up the game in 1892 when he was a student at Brooklyn Polytechnic High School and had later played for the Crescent Club of New York. He instituted what later became known as the Hopkins System of play—taking the ball down the middle of the field with short diagonal passes and developing preset "crisscross" plays.

The 1902 team, which won the intercollegiate championship, was captained and coached by William C. Schmeisser, later affectionately known to generations of Hopkins players as "Father Bill." He coached the Blue Jays to further championships in 1903, 1906, 1907, 1908, and 1909. As noted in chapter 2, Father Bill was also instrumental in the early organization of the fabled Mount Washington Club team and wrote a textbook on the coaching of lacrosse in 1904 that became the standard instructional book for many years. His interest in coaching lasted until his death in the summer of 1941; throughout all this time he never asked for or received any pay for his coaching. He worked with the Hopkins varsity during his entire adult life and helped to introduce lacrosse to many other schools. He was with the Johns Hopkins team of 1928, which represented the United States in the Amsterdam Olympics, and accompanied an all-star team to England in 1937. He was long active in the affairs of the United States Intercollegiate Lacrosse Association (USILA), serving at various times on the rules committee and as chief referee and president. He was one of the first men elected to the Lacrosse Hall of Fame. In 1943, the national award for the finest defenseman in the game was named in his honor and is still known as the Schmeisser Award.

By the early twentieth century, Johns Hopkins had become so identified with championship lacrosse that the June 24, 1905, issue of *Tip Top Weekly*, "an ideal publication for the American youth," was devoted to "Frank Merriwell's Lacrosse Team, or, The Great Tussle with Johns Hopkins." Because Frank Merriwell was a popular, fictional scholar-athlete at Yale in a long-running series of stories by Gilbert Patten (1866–1945), the Hopkins players in this piece naturally were the villians!

Hopkins began playing football on Homewood Field in October 1907, and the championship lacrosse team of 1908 was the first to play there. Since then, Homewood has served as the site not only of all Hopkins home games but also of many North-South all-star games, national club lacrosse championship matches, numerous high school title games, and two International Lacrosse Federation World Championships (1982 and 1998) featuring teams from around the globe. Homewood Field's premiere position in the lacrosse world has led some to call it "The Yankee Stadium of Lacrosse," but in 1982, a player from Australia simply called it the world's lacrosse players' "Mecca."

Reaney Wolfe, one of the great players of the 1911 championship team, coached Hopkins to three championships in 1913, 1915, and 1919. In the crucial game of the 1913 season with Harvard, Johnny Knipp, all 115 pounds of him, made his presence felt, scoring three goals in a 6–3 victory. The 1915 team was unbeaten, but it did have one tie on its record, a 3–3 game with the Carlisle Indians. That game was played at Homewood Field during the period of the inaugural ceremonies of the third Johns Hopkins president, Frank J. Goodnow. Dr. Goodnow showed his interest in lacrosse by sitting on the Hopkins bench during the entire game with the Indians. After that game he frequently attended home games. Recent presidents Milton S. Eisenhower and Steven Muller as well as Hopkins's current president, William Brody, have been enthusiastic fans.

Hopkins won the Southern Division championship in 1918. In 1919, team captain C. Herbert Baxley led the Blue Jays to another USILA national championship. At the opening game of that season, Father Bill Schmeisser presented Baxley with a gold-star flag commemorating three former Hopkins lacrosse players who had lost their lives in World War I: Theodore Prince, Warren B. Hunting, and the captain's brother, W. Browne Baxley. The flag was fastened to the goal net before the game. To this day, flags commemorating Hopkins lacrosse players who died in both world wars and in Vietnam are hung on the Homewood Field nets at the beginning of each season and remain there for all home games.

In 1922 the first All-American lacrosse team was selected. Hopkins's representative on the first team was Douglas C. Turnbull Jr. His name became legendary at Hopkins, as he went on to make the first All-American team four straight years. This feat was unequaled for the next fifty-four years. In 1976, Maryland's Frank Urso became the second four-time, first-team All-American; in 1986, Hopkins's Del Dressel became the third four-time, first-team All-American. And in 2004, Syracuse's Mike Powell joined the exclusive club begun by Doug Turnbull. Doug led Hopkins to championships in 1923 and 1924, receiving strong support from two other All-American midfielders, John Murphy and Howard Benedict. Doug's younger brother, Jack, was a three-time All-American in 1930, 1931, and 1932 and is considered one of the game's greatest players. Jack was killed in combat during World War II, and in 1947, the national honor for the top attackman in lacrosse, the Turnbull Award, was created in his memory.

Ray Van Orman was head coach from 1926 through 1934, a period during which Hopkins won three championships and was the leading team in the country for three years when a champion was not named. The 1926 team went undefeated with a 9–0 record. Its defense, headed by Thomas N. Biddison and team captain Karl Levy, limited its opponents to just eleven goals for the season, while Norman Robinson and Walker Taylor led the offense, which tallied 103 goals. Norm Robinson captained the 1927 team to another unbeaten season (8–0). Tom Biddison and John Lang were first-team All-Americans, and Bill Logan scored 32 goals during the season, 9 against the University of Virginia.

To decide who would represent the United States in the 1928 Olympic Games at Amsterdam, a playoff of the country's top six teams was arranged. The

Figure 18.1 The 1928 national champion Hopkins lacrosse team, which represented the United States at the Olympics in Amsterdam. The team included future Hall of Famers Thomas N. Biddison Sr. (back row, far left), John D. Lang (back row, third from left), and C. Gardner Mallonee (back row, fifth from left), Robert Roy, future dean of engineering at Hopkins (back row, far right); and future Princeton head coach, Hopkins director of undergraduate admissions, and Hall of Famer William F. Logan (front row, second from left). *The Ferdinand Hamburger Archives of the Johns Hopkins University*

Mount Washington Club was the decided favorite, and Johns Hopkins was ranked sixth. The Hopkins team had lost to both Army and Navy during the regular season and would not have been in the play-offs at all had it not been for a startling win over previously undefeated Maryland. Hopkins's first-round game was with Mount Washington, the only unbeaten team to enter the Olympic play-off series. The club team had a 3–2 halftime lead, but Hopkins came on to win 6–4. In the semifinal round, Hopkins beat Army 4–2. The finals were played in Baltimore Stadium (then the city's equivalent of today's Oriole Park at Camden Yards), and Hopkins defeated Maryland 6–3. The leading Hopkins players that season were goalie Ray Finn, defensemen Gardner Mallonee and Carroll Leibensperger, midfielders Johnny Lang and Benny Boynton, and

attackmen Tom Biddison and Bill Logan. After making the first All-American team as a defenseman for two years, Biddison was a first-team All-American attackman in 1928.

At the Olympics, the Americans took the measure of Canada, 6–3, but the next day lost to Great Britain 7–6. When Canada beat Britain 9–5, it looked like a three-way tie. The United States offered to play another series; Canada agreed, but Britain declined.

Sandwiched between the 1928 Olympic squad and its 1932 successor were three Hopkins teams, two of which were very successful. In 1930, Purnell Hall and Jack Turnbull were first-team All-Americans at defense and attack, respectively, and the key figures in a 7–2 season. Turnbull and Lorne Guild led the 1931 team to an 8–1 record.

In 1932 Hopkins won all nine of its regular-season games. However, the play-off system was again used to determine the American representative at the Olympic Games. Eight teams were selected, and Hopkins won its first two games against St. John's (5–3) and the Crescents Club (10–2). In the final game with the University of Maryland, the Terps led 3–2 at halftime, and Hopkins did not take the lead until the last three minutes of play. The final score was 7–5. Jack Turnbull and Don Kelly were first-team All-American attackmen, and Lorne Guild, Millard Lang, and George Packard were first-team All-American midfielders.

The Olympic Games of 1932 were played at Los Angeles, and Canada was the only other nation entered. The teams met three times, on August 7, 9, and 12, and the total attendance was an unbelievable 145,000. The Americans won the opening game 5–3, Canada the second game 5–4, and the Americans the deciding match 7–4. The play of Jack Turnbull at attack and Fritz Stude in the goal earned special commendation. The internationally famous movie, stage, radio, and newspaper humorist Will Rogers, who was part Cherokee, provided lively commentary over the public address system.

Although a national collegiate champion was not selected in 1932, 1933, or 1934, Hopkins was considered by many the leading team each year. The 1933 team, captained by James "Moke" Merriken, was undefeated with a 7–0 record. Four Blue Jays made first-team All-American: Don Kelly and James "Boots" Ives (attack), Millard Lang (midfield), and Church Yearley (defense). The 1934 team compiled a 7–1 record, losing its last game of the season 10–9 to Mount Washington, a team it had already beaten 8–6. (The Mount Washington Club was a regular opponent on the Jays' schedule for decades.) Henry Beeler, a fine center, joined Kelly, Lang, and Yearley on the first All-American team.

Dr. W. Kelso Morrill, a brilliant former player at Hopkins who by then was a mathematics professor at the university, succeeded Ray Van Orman as the head coach in 1935. The Hopkins record was not impressive during his first four years, although several players were selected as first-team All-Americans: Lou Ruhling (goal) in 1935; Pete Swindell (defense)

in 1935, 1936, and 1937; and Don Naylor (defense) in 1936 and 1937.

In 1938, under the leadership of Dr. G. Wilson Shaffer, a psychology professor at Hopkins who also served as athletic director, the university took a dramatic step in intercollegiate athletics in an attempt to distinguish between recreation for college students and public amusement. The most important feature of Dr. Shaffer's new policy was the elimination of gate receipts. From 1938 to 1970, admission was free to all of Hopkins's athletic events, including lacrosse—and during this period, Hopkins won or shared the national lacrosse championship eleven times.

The 1939 team got Hopkins back in its winning ways with a 7–2 record, which included a 6–3 upset victory over the University of Maryland, the national champions. John Tolson was the defensive star of that team as well as of the 1940 team (8–2) and of the undefeated 1941 team (12–0). He was a first-team All-American each year.

The 1941 Hopkins team, under Kelso Morrill's direction, was one of Hopkins's greatest. Gardner Mallonee coached a superb close defense of Tolson, Nelson Shawn, and Benjamin "Bud" Kaestner Jr. LeRoy "Toy" Swerdloff was the goalie. This unit registered five shutouts and permitted the opposition only thirteen goals for the entire eleven-game regular season, which ended with a 10–3 victory over Maryland. Jack Williams scored three goals in that game, but the offensive leadership throughout the season was provided by George D. Penniman III. He was ably supported by Charlie Thomas, Dick Green, and Edgar Spilman. Mount Washington was also undefeated and had a string of twenty-four consecutive victories when it challenged Hopkins to play a postseason game for the benefit of the British War Relief Society. The Blue Jays were undecided until Father Bill Schmeisser spoke to the team. It would be the last time he would ever address a Johns Hopkins lacrosse squad. He assured them that this was the year they could beat the Wolfpack. The challenge was accepted, and the Blue Jays justified Father Bill's confidence in them. Dick Green scored the winning goal, with a little over one minute remaining in the game, to give Hopkins

Figure 18.2 The undefeated, and notable, 1941 Hopkins team. L–R: LeRoy "Toy" Swerdloff, Charles B. Thomas, E. H. Spilman, Nelson Shawn, John C. Tolson (later elected to the Hall of Fame), Benjamin H. "Bud" Kaestner Jr. (another Hall of Fame member and father of Benjamin "Hank" Kaestner III, also eventually in the Hall of Fame), George D. Penniman III (a World War II hero, killed in action), Dick Green, Frank D. Murnaghan (later a federal judge and university trustee), and Jack A. Williams. *The Ferdinand Hamburger Archives of the Johns Hopkins University*

a 7–6 victory. Two months later, Father Bill passed away.

Charlie Thomas and Bud Kaestner were the first-team All-Americans who led the 1942 team to a 9–2 record. Henley Guild (midfield) and George Riepe (defense) were also first-team All-Americans in the 6–2 season of 1943. With World War II at its height, Hopkins did not field an official team in 1944. G. Wilson Shaffer nevertheless kept the sport alive in the Baltimore area, arranging for players from Hopkins, Mount Washington, and other local affiliations to form the Johns Hopkins Lacrosse Club, with Kelso Morrill and Gardner Mallonee as coaches. The service academies were the only teams played. An informal Hopkins student team was organized in 1945, and it split a two-game schedule.

Shortly after World War II ended in 1945, a second commemorative service flag bearing seven gold stars was hung in one of the goals for all of Hopkins's home games. It represented the former Hopkins lacrosse players who had died in the war: Frank Cone, Walter J. Fahrenholz, David H. W. Houck, George D. Penniman III, Edward A. Marshall, Peter W. Reynolds, and John I. Turnbull.

The postwar era started slowly for Hopkins in 1946. The Blue Jays wound up with a 4–5 record, which, however, featured a 12–9 upset victory over Navy, with Gordon "Reds" Wolman scoring four goals. Jerry Courtney and Clarence Hewitt were first-team All-Americans at goal and defense, respectively.

In 1947, Howard "Howdy" Myers Jr. came to Hopkins as head coach. He combined veteran players with a wealth of new talent from the local high schools, in particular St. Paul's School in Baltimore, where he had just finished a brilliant career with seven consecutive championships. Howdy's Hopkins teams of 1947, 1948, and 1949 did not lose a single collegiate game, running up twenty-four consecutive victories. The closest game of the 1947 collegiate season was an uphill 8–7 overtime win over Princeton. Freshmen Lloyd Bunting (defense) and Wilson Fewster (midfield) were first-team All-Americans that year, along with attackman Brooke Tunstall.

The 1948 team again won all eight collegiate games but had several close calls. Army led the Blue Jays until the last forty-five seconds of play, when Hopkins scored the tying goal and went on to win in overtime, 11–9. Against Navy, Hopkins tallied three times in the final five minutes to win 9–8. It was Neil Pohlhaus who tied the score and Ray Greene whose goal won the game. The Maryland game was a hard-fought 10–8 victory for the Jays. Brooke Tunstall was a first-team All-American again and was joined in that select group by midfielder Ray Greene. Ironically, these two players had been first-team All-Americans at other schools during the war years, Greene at Drexel in 1943 and Tunstall at Cornell at 1944.

Howdy's last team at Hopkins swept through its college opponents without a close game. Navy and Hopkins did not play in 1949, and since Navy was also undefeated in the collegiate ranks, the two schools were declared cochampions. Lloyd Bunting, Jim Adams, and Corky Shepard were first-team All-Americans.

Before the 1950 season, Howdy left Hopkins to become the director of athletics, as well as football and lacrosse coach, at Hofstra University in Long Island, New York. There he became instrumental in popularizing lacrosse on Long Island. Dr. Shaffer called on his good friend Kelso Morrill to coach the Blue Jays one more time. With basically the same personnel as in the previous three years, the 1950 team defeated all its college opponents but lost a 6–5 heartbreaker to the powerful Mount Washington Club in the last game of the season. Joe Sollers gave a courageous performance in the Hopkins goal in that game, playing with a cast on his previously fractured right arm and with an ankle that was badly sprained in the first quarter.

The 1950 team, along with the 1947, 1948, and 1949 teams, belongs with the best in Hopkins's history. Eleven of its players made one of the All-American teams at least once during their playing careers. Four were already first-team All-Americans: Bunting, Fewster, Adams, and Shepard; in 1950 Bob Sandell joined that elite group. Fred Smith was among the greatest second-team All-Americans ever, having been so honored three times. Tommy Gough, Byron Forbush, and Joe Sollers were also second-team All-Americans. Mort Kalus was a third-team selection, and Ham Bishop was an honorable mention.

With the graduation of so many great players, Hopkins did not figure in the championship picture for the next six years. Fred Smith took over the head coaching reins in 1951 and began a career of dedicated service to Hopkins lacrosse. Princeton, led by Don Hahn and Reddy Finney, broke Hopkins's thirty-one-game collegiate winning streak with a 13–11 victory in a game during which the score was tied nine times. In Hopkins's 13–10 victory over Navy that year, Bill Carroll created a stunning Blue Jay benchmark, scoring three goals in twenty-seven seconds. At the conclusion of the season, Fred Smith left coaching to go into business but by no means separated himself from Hopkins lacrosse. He continued to have a profound effect on Hopkins players—and on the game of lacrosse itself—for more than thirty years.

Wilson Fewster succeeded Fred as head coach in 1952 and did an excellent job. The Blue Jays lost four games, but each was by only one goal, the most exciting being a 13–12 loss to the championship University of Virginia team at Homewood Field. In the homecoming game with the University of Maryland another fierce battle took place. Mike Dix, a fine goalie who had made twenty saves in our 8–7 upset victory over Army, was having difficulty with outside bounce shots by the Terps and was replaced by his substitute, Charles "Chubby" Wagner, at the end of regulation play, with the score tied 10–10. Maryland controlled the ball about 90 percent of the time in the two overtime periods, taking sixteen shots to only two for the Jays, but they just couldn't get the ball by Wagner, who had eight saves and was the hero of the game. Hopkins was also unable to score,

Figure 18.3 Bob Scott, who led Hopkins lacrosse to seven national championships from 1955 to 1974, stands ready for practice in the mid-1950s. At right, he shares strategic points with his players during the 1958 game at Princeton. The Jays won. *Sports Information, JHU: The Ferdinand Hamburger Archives of the Johns Hopkins University*

and the game ended in a 10–10 tie. Emil "Buzzy" Budnitz Jr., Bud McNicholas, and Don Tate were the offensive leaders of the team. Although the 1953 team had a mediocre record, it produced two first-team All-Americans in Budnitz (his second time) and Eddie Semler. Wilson Fewster left Hopkins after the 1953 season to become the coach at the University of Virginia. Fred Smith served as interim coach in 1954 while Bob Scott was finishing his tour of duty in the army. The 1954 team had a 4-4-1 record. An 8–8 tie with the University of Virginia, coached by Fewster, was the feature game.

Bob Scott's remarkable two decades as head coach at Hopkins began with the 1955 season and

ended in 1974. During that period, the Blue Jays won seven national championships and were almost always in the thick of the competition for the lacrosse crown.

Bob Scott—"Scotty" to almost everyone—became head coach at Hopkins at just twenty-four years of age. He considered himself only a slightly better-than-average player who hustled and knocked down more people than he scored goals—although he did bring the Homewood Field crowd to its feet in 1952, his senior year, when he scored two backhand goals within two minutes against the University of Virginia. He was captain of the team that year and an honorable-mention All-American midfielder—but clearly Dr. Shaffer and Marshall S. Turner Jr., then Hopkins's athletic director, saw more in Scotty's potential as a coach than his playing record indicated. When Wilson Fewster decided to leave Hopkins after the 1953 season, Mr. Turner called and offered Scotty the job after his military tour of duty was completed.

To help Scotty learn the game from a coach's perspective, Dr. Shaffer, by then dean of the Homewood schools, asked W. Kelso Morrill and William F. Logan, the former Hopkins player and Princeton coach who had returned to Hopkins as director of undergraduate admissions, to instruct him. Both of these men were great coaches. Dr. Morrill had coached championship teams at Hopkins, and Bill Logan, a former Olympic player for Hopkins, had done the same at Princeton. Dr. Morrill even had been Scotty's coach on the freshman lacrosse team in 1949 and the varsity team in 1950. As has been traditional throughout Hopkins lacrosse history, these former Blue Jay greats passed on a wealth of knowledge to the next generation. Scotty later observed that Dr. Morrill "worked me over with my lacrosse lessons as hard as he had done with many of his mathematics students over the years."[*] With Dr. Morrill and Bill Logan as his assistant coaches, Scotty began his career on the coaching sideline at Homewood.

The first year, 1955, was a difficult one for Scotty and his players—some of whom had been his teammates and friends only a few years earlier. It was awkward for him to act as a tough taskmaster and push them hard. The Jays won only four of ten games, but they did win the season opener with Harvard 14–1. Lou Ruland and Herbert "Buzzy" Williams captained the team. Overnight trips to Virginia and Rensselaer Polytechnic Institute turned out to be the highlights of the season. The Blue Jays came through with 23–9 and 10–6 victories, respectively.

Captains Dick Watts and Arlyn Marshall got the 1956 team on the winning track. After one-goal losses to Yale and Princeton, the Blue Jays won six

straight games. The pivotal point of the season was a second-half comeback victory over the undefeated Rensselaer. The Engineers held a 6–2 halftime lead, but George Breslau's four goals sparked a second-half rally and brought a 10–7 Hopkins victory. The following week Breslau scored the winning goal again in an 8–6 triumph over Navy. Arlyn Marshall, our leading scorer and one of the nation's best face-off men, was the first of Scotty's players to make the first All-American team, edging out a Syracuse junior by the name of Jim Brown, the future NFL legend and football Hall of Famer.

Dr. Morrill's son, Bill Morrill, and Mickey Webster were the leaders of a group of talented sophomores who were instrumental in guiding the Jays for the next three years. Morrill and Webster were first-team All-Americans for three years and teamed with John Jory in 1957 and 1958 to form one of Hopkins's most potent attack units. (In time, Mickey Webster and Bill Morrill would join Bill's father as members of the National Lacrosse Hall of Fame.) Walter Mitchell, a first-team All-American for two years, was the leader of the defense and was cocaptain with Jerry Bennett. Wilson Fewster, who had returned to Hopkins the previous year, played an important role in coaching the Morrill-Webster crowd on the freshman team, and he moved up with them to the varsity in 1957. The key game for the undefeated 1957 team was with the University of Maryland, the defending national champions for the preceding two years. The Terps were on a thirty-one-game winning streak. Although our sophomores were outstanding (in particular Morrill, Webster, Ed Bernstein, Bruce Duffany, Al Seivold, and John McNealey), it was two seniors who stole the show in the 15–10 Hopkins victory at College Park. Pete Banker was called upon to tend the goal early in the second quarter, substituting for Bob Powell (an excellent goalie who was an honorable-mention All-American for two years). He responded beautifully with twenty saves. Dick Steele was the other standout and scored five goals. The following week the Homewood Field spectators were treated to the battle of the unbeatens—Hopkins versus the Mount Washington Club. It was a classic, as both teams played even-up during regulation play

[*] Bob Scott, *Lacrosse: Technique and Tradition* (Baltimore: Johns Hopkins University Press, 1976), 208.

as well as in overtime, the score ending in an 11–11 tie. The 1957 season ended when the North-South all-star game was played on Homewood Field. Midfielders Carl Muly, Jerry Bennett, and Dick Steele represented the Jays on the South team and played well but were overwhelmed by Jim Brown, Syracuse's star midfielder, who put on a one-man show in the North's 14–10 victory.

The 1958 season was full of controversy in the collegiate lacrosse world, and Hopkins was in the thick of the action. After rolling through our first seven games of the season without a loss, we took on the undefeated Terps in our homecoming game. Hopkins dominated play in the first half with a 9–5 score but was unable to score in the third quarter, and Maryland tied it at 9–9. When we went on top, 11–9, with twelve minutes remaining in the game, we had two key players injured on the sidelines and chose to adopt a controversial slowdown tactic that we had learned from Princeton coach Ferris Thomsen. He had used this maneuver in our game with the Tigers earlier in the season. Many of the fans, even some of the old-guard Hopkins lacrossemen, were displeased with this tactic—but with two key players on the bench, we felt it was necessary, and it did give us an 11–10 victory. Maryland could have initiated action by coming out from their defensive perimeter to challenge Morrill and Webster, but they did not and lost.

The other key controversy of 1958 involved the selection of the national champion. A point system was used then as a guide by the executive committee of the USILA. Points were awarded based on the three levels of play: six points for defeating an A team, five for a B team, and four for a C team. Realizing that Hopkins had only scheduled six A teams, compared to Army's seven, Hopkins's athletic director, Marshall Turner, contacted the president of the association just before the season opened and asked if the Blue Jays should make a last-minute attempt to schedule another A team. The USILA president advised Hopkins not to do so because he didn't foresee a problem. But the problem did arise, as both Army and Hopkins went undefeated, and Army accumulated forty-two points to Hopkins's forty-one. Ironically, Army's seventh A-team win was over a Duke team that had won only one game

all season. Hopkins's B-team victory was over a team with a good won-loss record that had beaten Duke and given close games to both Maryland and Hopkins. Army did not play either Maryland or Hopkins in 1958, but the Cadets did beat Mount Washington in the opening game of the season, and Hopkins lost to the Mounties. The results of games with club teams were supposed to have no bearing on the determination of the champion, however, so it seemed logical to many observers that cochampions should have been declared. Instead, the USILA committee vote was 5–4 in favor of awarding Army the Wingate Trophy as sole champion.

Despite this severe postseason disappointment, the 1958 Hopkins team enjoyed a memorable six-week trip to England and Europe that summer. The Blue Jays won all eight of their lacrosse games, six played in Manchester and two in London.

The third season of the Morrill-Webster era got off to an excellent start in 1959. The Blue Jays averaged twenty goals a game in their first seven victories. The homecoming game with Navy figured to be an easy one. The Middies, under first-year coach Willis P. Bilderback, had close calls in several of their victories and had lost to Maryland 15–8 and to Princeton 9–8. Since Hopkins had beaten Princeton 24–3, almost everyone in lacrosse circles expected Hopkins to win with ease. Unfortunately, Hopkins was carried away with its role as favorite, and Navy pulled the upset of the decade by beating the Blue Jays 13–11. It was a bitter defeat for the seniors—their first collegiate loss in three years after twenty-three consecutive victories.

There was doubt in the minds of many as to whether Hopkins could win its last collegiate game of the season against the undefeated Terrapins, who had already trounced Navy. Nevertheless, the seniors went out in a blaze of glory with a resounding 20–8 victory over the Terps at College Park. Mickey Webster had seven assists, Billy Morrill six goals, and Al Seivold five goals. Hopkins goalie Emmett Collins had twenty-four saves. The Wingate Trophy was divided three ways, because Army, Maryland, and Hopkins each had one collegiate loss on its record. This was the only fair way to handle the championship—although given the controversy

Figure 18.4 All-American and future Hall of Famer William K. Morrill Jr. (JHU '59), son of Hall of Famer coach W. Kelso Morrill (JHU '27) and father of All-American Mike Morrill (JHU '88), scoring one of his then-record-high 107 career goals. *The Ferdinand Hamburger Archives of the Johns Hopkins University*

in 1958, it was ironic that the USILA executive committee somehow changed its thinking so radically in just one year.

The graduation of fourteen seniors, eight of whom had received All-American recognition during their careers, had its effect on the 1960 team. In addition, cocaptain Larry Becker, who was slated for a key role, broke his leg in a preseason game. Nonetheless, three sophomores—Henry Ciccarone, Jerry Schmidt, and Roy Mayne—teamed with junior Jimmy Ives to lead the team to a 7–1 collegiate record, including a 13–7 victory over Maryland. John McNealy and cocaptain Mike Byrne were outstanding on defense. In 1961, we repeated the seven victories but lost to Navy and Maryland. Captains Mike Byrne and goalie Jimmy Greenwood excelled at the defensive end of the field.

Ciccarone, Schmidt, and Mayne and defensemen Phil Sutley and Bill Flannery were the key players on the 1962 team, which compiled an 8–2 collegiate record. Jerry Schmidt led a high-powered offense, which averaged almost fourteen goals per game for the season. Three of our top opponents were undefeated when we met them. The first was Virginia, which had beaten Maryland the previous week. The game with the Cavaliers was a battle that featured outstanding play by Ciccarone and Virginia's goalie, Deeley Nice. Nice had thirty-four saves for the game, while Chic scored five goals for the Blue Jays and played about fifty-three minutes in the come-from-behind 12–8 Hopkins victory. The Army game featured a one-on-one confrontation between the nation's best attackman, Jerry Schmidt, and the nation's best defenseman, Army's

Bob Fuelhart. Jerry scored four goals to lead JHU to a 9–7 victory over the previously unbeaten Cadets. In the third major contest, then nearly unbeatable Navy kept its record unblemished by defeating us 16–11 at Annapolis. Prior to the Blue Jays' confrontation with Maryland in the last game of the 1962 season, Jerry Schmidt became the first and so far only lacrosse player featured exclusively on the cover of *Sports Illustrated.* Perhaps the celebrated "*SI* Cover Curse" played a part in Hopkins's subsequent heartbreaking 16–15 loss to Maryland.

E. Doyle Smith Jr. entered the Hopkins lacrosse picture in 1963. A native of Bend, Oregon, Doyle had never seen lacrosse before coming to Hopkins as a freshman, but it was at Homewood Field that he began a distinguished career as a team manager, statistician, and rule maker that made his name synonymous with collegiate lacrosse for more than a quarter century. Doyle was manager of the Blue Jay teams for six years—four as an undergraduate and two as a graduate student. Like so many of Hopkins's team managers, Doyle became an integral part of the Hopkins lacrosse tradition and made a valuable contribution to our teams, as have his successors. He was superefficient, and his statistical records were flawless. At times players might challenge him about the number of ground balls, saves, and assists for which he credited them, but they rarely, if ever, were able to catch him making a mistake. A true scholar, Doyle was elected to Phi Beta Kappa at Hopkins and then went to the University of Virginia to continue his studies. There he became the associate sports information director and for many years the executive secretary of the USILA, for which he served as information director for twenty-two years. In that capacity, he "wrote the book" on keeping statistics in men's lacrosse, and his standards remain part of the NCAA rule book. He was twice honored by Virginia for his devotion to Cavalier athletics, and he was named the USILA's Man of the Year in 1984 and 1993. He was inducted into the National Lacrosse Hall of Fame—representing both Hopkins and Virginia—in 2000. When he died in 2004, after a long battle against Parkinson's disease, the *Charlottesville Daily Progress* called him "Mr. Lacrosse."

In 1963, Henry Ciccarone began his coaching career at Hopkins as an assistant varsity coach. The 1963 team, captained by Dick Webster, posted a 6–3 collegiate record, with Virginia, Navy, and Maryland posting victories over the Jays. The big win of the season was again over Army, in a nip-and-tuck game. Skip Darrell, our sophomore attackman, was making his first trip back to West Point, where he had been a cadet for a brief period two years before. He was given a good bit of kidding by his old buddies but then proceeded to score four goals in a 10–9 victory. Jerry Pfeifer scored the winning goal with fifteen seconds to go in the game. It was Army's first collegiate loss of the season. Homer Schwartz and Jan Berzins were outstanding at midfield and defense, respectively.

The 1964 season started out well with five straight collegiate victories, including a 15–5 rout of Virginia, which turned around the following week to beat Maryland 13–3. Prospects were bright until the Army game, when the Cadets rallied from a 6–1 deficit to go ahead 7–6 by halftime. They won the game 13–10, and this loss had a demoralizing effect on our team. We lost the following week to Rutgers 10–9. Two days before the Navy game, our top defenseman, Dave MacCool, broke his leg, and we ended a 5–4 season by losing to Navy and Maryland. Lauren Scheffenacker, Homer Schwartz, and Joe Hahn represented Hopkins in the annual all-star game.

The 1965 team stands out as the one that reached its fullest potential throughout an entire season. Eleven seniors, headed by captains Frank Szoka and Chip Giardina, provided the leadership that guided the team to a 9–1 collegiate record. Stan Fine typified the excellent attitude and hustle of this team and did so as a member of our third midfield unit. This situation could have been difficult for him to handle, because he had been an honorable-mention All-American two years earlier. But Stan accepted his position, never stopped hustling, and was one of our top midfield scorers and ground ball men. Jerry Pfeifer was our leading scorer. Frank Szoka and Jerry Schnydman controlled the majority of face-offs. Hank Kaestner and Mike Oidick were outstanding on defense, and John Dashiells excelled in the goal. When Dennis

Figure 18.5 Joe Cowan (JHU '69), a future Hall of Famer, skirts a Navy defender, Carl Tamulevich, in the 1967 game that ended the Mids' eight-year dominance of the Jays, with Hopkins winning 9–6. Cowan became the only JHU lacrosse player drafted by the NFL. *Courtesy of Joseph W. Cowan*

Townsend was injured one week before the Army game, Joe Blattner took his place on the starting defense. Although his playing experience was limited to only one year on the freshman team, under Wilson Fewster, Joe did a superb job in helping to limit the Cadets to three goals, enabling us to win 6–3.

In the homecoming game with Navy, the team gave 100 percent effort but just could not contain Jimmy Lewis, and the Midshipmen handed us our only loss of the season, 15–6. In the last game of the 1965 season Hopkins met the 11–1 Terrapins at College Park. Although behind by two goals (8–6) with less than ten minutes in the game, the Blue Jays scored five unanswered goals for an 11–8 victory.

Jerry Schnydman scored the winning goal; Herb Better and Lucky Mallonee added two insurance goals.

Jerry Schnydman and Hank Kaestner (who would follow his father, Bud, Class of 1941, into the Lacrosse Hall of Fame) were the most outstanding players on the 1966 team, which compiled a 5–5 collegiate record. After the third game of the season, Mike Oidick, a third-team All-American defenseman in 1965, switched to the attack. Steve Levy started the season as a goalie but lost out in competition with Geoffrey Berlin. However, Steve had been a reserve defenseman the two preceding years and was moved into Oidick's position on the defense. He did an excellent job, and our defense held the opposition to an average of 5.7 goals per game. Steve was selected for the South all-star team and was one of the best defensive players in the game at Homewood Field.

Another championship era at Hopkins began in 1967. Joe Cowan was the superstar, but he had plenty of help. Joe teamed up with veterans Downie McCarty and Phil Kneip on the attack, Mike Clark joined Hank Kaestner on the defense, Charlie Goodell ran with Jerry Schnydman in the midfield, and Geoff Berlin was in the goal. The season opener was with Mount Washington, a team the Jays had not beaten since 1941. This year it was a different story: Hopkins 10–4. In a close game at West Point, Bobby Carter gave a courageous performance on a heavily taped knee and scored three goals in a 12–9 victory. The game of the season arrived two weeks later against Navy, a team we had not beaten since 1958. The Middies were riding a thirty-four-game winning streak. Our plans for the Navy game received a serious jolt when Joe Cowan severely bruised his leg the week before in a game with Syracuse. He spent most of the week before the Navy game in bed and was only able to jog at half speed at Friday's practice. He was ready to go on Saturday, however, even though only at 75 percent effectiveness. It was a psychological lift to our team to have Joe in the game, and he had four assists, three of which were to Phil Kneip, who led the scoring with four goals. The homecoming crowd went wild when we beat the Middies 9–6.

Unfortunately, this game was such a climax that our team was unable to get back to ground level to prepare properly for our last game of the season with Maryland. The Terps had already lost to Navy 10–8 but had an outstanding team. They upset us 9–5 and caused the championship to be shared by Maryland, Navy, and Hopkins.

In the spring of 1967, Charles E. Aronhalt, a member of the 1962–1964 teams, was killed in action in Vietnam. For heroism in combat, Chuck received the Distinguished Service Cross posthumously. Another gold star was added in his honor to one of the commemorative service flags that hang in the Homewood Field goals during every game.

The 1968 team became one of the most powerful

of the Bob Scott era, even though it lost its opening game against the Mount Washington Club in a free-scoring 16–14 contest. Led by captains Geoff Berlin and Wes Bachur, the 1968 team had a margin of victory that was seven goals or more in every game except the final one with the unbeaten Terrapins. Hopkins outshot the Terps by fifty-three to thirty attempts, but Maryland's goalie Norman Vander-Schuyte's twenty-four saves held the final score at 10–8 in Hopkins's favor. Hopkins's key personnel move of the season was the switching of Charlie Coker to the midfield after he saw only limited action as an attackman. Charlie became a great midfielder. After being shut out in the Princeton game, Downie McCarty came back with a four-goal effort against Virginia and then scored five goals each in the games against Army, Maryland, and the North-South all-star game, where he received the Most Valuable Player award. McCarty, Kneip, and Cowan formed an attack that was comparable to the Morrill-Webster-Jory combination of ten years earlier.

During the 1968 season, Dr. W. Kelso Morrill died suddenly of a heart attack. Dr. Morrill loved lacrosse as much as he did teaching mathematics. He was devoted to the game and continually strove to develop excellence in the Hopkins teams, both during his days of coaching and in his later years as an advisor to Bob Scott. As had Father Bill Schmeisser at the beginning of the twentieth century, Dr. Morrill wrote an influential book about lacrosse in 1952, entitled simply *Lacrosse*, providing guidance on the tactics and strategies of the game for coaches nationwide. When he died, Hopkins and the game of lacrosse lost a great man.

The 1969 season paralleled the 1959 season in several respects. Hopkins won all its collegiate games but one. And again the team that caught us napping was Willis Bilderback's Navy team. Before the Navy game we had beaten all collegiate opponents and defeated Mount Washington 10–4. The most exciting game was a 14–11 victory over previously unbeaten Army at Michie Stadium. However, our team was not mentally ready for Navy two weeks later. After all, Navy had lost to the Carling Club and Princeton, a team that we defeated handily. They barely edged Virginia 6–5, and we had beaten the Cavaliers 15–4. Sure enough, Navy upset us by a 9–6 score. But like the 1959 team, the Blue Jays bounced back and beat the Terps 14–8, with Joe Cowan and Charlie Goodell leading the scoring. Mike Clark, the best defenseman in the country, was given considerable help from his defensive teammates John Cardillo and Paul Weiss and goalie John Kelly. We shared the championship with Army.

The 1970 team, captained by Doug Honig and Russ Moore, holds a special place in Bob Scott's memories because it outperformed expectations considerably. Graduation had claimed four All-Americans, including three members of the Hopkins All-Time Team (Cowan, Clark, and Goodell), but Hopkins nevertheless put together a team that surprised many people. Charlie Coker was the star player, but he received excellent support from his teammates in the midfield—Honig, Bill Donovan, Gary Handleman, and Eric Bergofsky. The turning point of the season was our rebound from a 4–0 deficit near the middle of the second quarter to beat Mount Washington 10–9 at Norris Field. After the only loss of the season to Virginia, 15–8, the Blue Jays faced the previously unbeaten West Pointers. We moved out to a commanding 8–3 lead, with three minutes remaining in the third quarter. Army then scored five unanswered goals to tie the score 8–8 with six minutes to go in the game. Many felt that Army had the momentum to win, but with seven seconds showing on the scoreboard clock, Doug Honig fired the ball into the Army goal for a 9–8 victory. In the final two games, the defensive play of Rob MacCool, Paul Weiss, and Joe Cieslowski, along with goalie Ken Dauses, was outstanding, and we beat Navy 9–7 and Maryland 7–4. Paul Wallace was our leading scorer on the close attack.

Although the 1971 team was limited in talent and won only three games, it gave a good account of itself throughout the season. The Jays were inches away from pulling off the upset of the decade by battling Virginia to an 8–8 tie in regulation time before losing 9–8 in overtime. While the season's record prevented Hopkins from appearing in the first NCAA postseason play-offs (the only time that would happen in the next thirty-three years), the highlight of that year was a trip to the

Astrodome in Houston to play Navy and promote the game. Nearly 20,000 spectators witnessed an exciting game, which Navy won 9–6. Ralph S. O'Connor, Hopkins Class of 1951, was primarily responsible for this successful venture. Today, at least 3,480 young men and women play on Texas high school teams and another 670 are playing club lacrosse in the Lone Star State. We closed the season with an 8–5 loss to Maryland. Danny Hall, Bill Donovan, and Ken Dauses played in the North-South all-star game at Tufts University.

The backbone of Bob Scott's last three teams as Hopkins coach was the Class of 1974, headed by Jack Thomas and Rick Kowalchuk. We beat Princeton 16–8, and in the big game of the regular season we faced a previously unbeaten Virginia, riding a two-season winning spree. On a rainy day in Charlottesville, the Jays again used the slowdown offense and upset the Cavaliers 13–8. Two weeks later, Hopkins went to Annapolis to face Navy, which had just beaten Virginia 12–10. It was one of those days when the Jays could do nothing wrong and Navy could do nothing right. Billy Nolan had a four-goal performance in his hometown, and the defense—led by Jim Head, Jim Ferguson, and goalie Les Matthews—was superb. The final score was 17–3 in Hopkins's favor. The next week Maryland gave Hopkins its only loss of the regular season, 13–12. In our debut in the NCAA tournament, we beat Washington and Lee 11–5 and then surprised the Terps at College Park with a 9–6 victory in the semifinals. In the finals, Virginia had regained its stride and played like champions, edging the Blue Jays 13–12.

The script was almost identical in 1973. The Blue Jays had another 11–2 season and a one-goal loss in the NCAA finals. The first big game of the season was with Cornell, which had won the NCAA championship in 1971 and had been the Ivy League champion for five consecutive years. In our first meeting since 1940, Jack Thomas scored five goals and Les Matthews had twenty saves to lead us to a 17–8 victory at Ithaca. Virginia was unbeaten in seven games when they traveled to Homewood. Don Krohn scored four goals in our 14–9 win over the Cavaliers. In the final game of the regular season at College Park, the Terps humiliated us with a 17–4

Figure 18.6 On his way to the Hall of Fame, Jack Thomas (JHU '74) as a senior led the Blue Jays to a national championship (the first decided by an NCAA tournament) during Bob Scott's final year as head coach. By then, plastic and aluminum sticks had replaced the traditional wooden variety. *Johns Hopkins Sports Information*

score. Nonetheless, we recovered from that defeat and beat Army and Virginia, each for the second time of the season, in the NCAA quarterfinal and semifinal games. In the finals we did an excellent job in executing a slowdown offense against the high-powered Terrapins. We held a 5–2 halftime lead and a 9–7 lead with six minutes remaining in the game. But goals by Frank Urso and Doug Schreiber sent the game into overtime. A single goal by Frank Urso during the two overtime periods gave Maryland a

10–9 victory and the NCAA championship. As the team walked off the field at the end of the game, a standing ovation from the Hopkins fans helped to ease the sting of defeat. Matthews, Thomas, and Kowalchuk were first-team All-Americans for the second year in a row.

In 1974 the Jays, again led by Thomas and Kowalchuk, won twelve games and lost two, just as they had in the previous two years. But the two losses did not hurt as far as the NCAA championship was concerned. In fact, they helped. In the opener at Charlottesville, our players were somewhat overconfident because we had beaten Virginia twice the year before. The Cavaliers helped to straighten our thinking by trouncing us 15–10. We won the next eight games. Two freshmen were featured in the 20–10 victory over Washington College: Tommy Myrick scored six goals, and Richie Hirsch scored four. Hirsch also had four-goal performances against Cornell and Army. Jack Thomas put on a tremendous show at Annapolis, figuring in ten of our twelve goals, but it wasn't quite enough to beat Dick Szlasa's fired-up Navy team. The Middies upset us 13–12. Despite that disappointment, Scotty felt that the loss would actually help the Blue Jays gain an edge for the battle with the undefeated Terps the next week. Maryland had been averaging almost eighteen goals per game and had rolled over Virginia 25–13 and Navy 12–7. But our team was ready for the Terrapins, and it was a great thrill for Scotty and the Blue Jay fans to beat Maryland 17–13 in Bob Scott's last homecoming game as coach. There were many heroes in the game. Goalie Kevin Mahon had eighteen saves in his first varsity game. Rick Kowalchuk had four goals (two were our team's fifteenth and sixteenth goals, which stymied Maryland's rally), and Jimmy Cahill had two solo goals. Bob Maimone was very effective on faceoffs, as was Harry Stringer on ground balls.

The team was in high gear for the NCAA playoffs. Hofstra University, coached by Howdy Myers, was our first opponent. Howdy had recruited Bob Scott when he was a senior in high school. When Howdy removed several of his star players from Hofstra's squad on the day before the game for violating rules, the Hopkins players and coaches relaxed a bit, thinking they would have an easy time. Scotty joked before the game about Howdy giving him his start at Hopkins and how he had a chance to end his career in coaching on his first visit back to Homewood Field. Hofstra led at halftime 6–4, and when the score was tied 8–8 with one minute remaining in the third quarter, Scotty's joke about Howdy's return started to stick in his throat. However, Rick Kowalchuk's goal broke the tie, and we scored eight goals in the fourth quarter, the most important being

Bill McCutcheon's score, which gave us a two-goal lead. We won the game 18–10, and Franz Wittelsberger led the scoring with seven goals.

In the semifinal game at Homewood Field, Washington and Lee had Hopkins's back to the wall by virtue of a 10–7 lead with twelve minutes remaining in the game. Billy Nolan got us rolling by scoring our eighth goal. Richie Hirsch followed with a score, and then Dale Kohler tied the game with his second goal of the game. Kowalchuk scored the winning goal with less than two minutes showing on the clock to give us an 11–10 victory. Steven Muller, president of the university, was completely wrapped up in the game. When Wittelsberger scored a goal just before halftime, Dr. Muller jumped to his feet and threw his hands in the air triumphantly, accidentally striking the press-box window. A panel of glass fell out and cut the hand of one of his guests, the attorney general of Puerto Rico. Hopkins presidents had been known to sit on a team bench before, but Dr. Muller's name goes down in the record book as the only college president known to cheer with such fervor as to smash a press-box window.

The stage now was set for the NCAA championship against the University of Maryland at Rutgers Stadium. Although Hopkins had won the first meeting with the Terps, many felt that Maryland's offense was still too powerful for us. Nevertheless, our team was confident, and the seniors, in particular, were especially determined to win the gold.

Everyone on the squad gave his best; no one person could be singled out as the hero. With the Terps leading 2–0 early in the game, Rick Kowalchuk broke the ice and scored our first goal. We then jumped to a 10–4 halftime lead and then to 14–6 with five minutes to go in the third quarter. At this point, Maryland scored five goals in five minutes to bring the score to 14–11 early in the fourth quarter. Rick countered with his third goal of the game, and this allowed us to breathe easier. Wittelsberger scored our last two goals (he had five for the game), and we won 17–12. Thomas and Hirsch each had three goals, Nolan two, and Bob Barbera one. Kevin Mahon was outstanding in and out of the goal and was given strong support by Mike Siegert and Dennis Gagomiros, who had shut out Maryland's

All-American attackman, Pat O'Meally, for the second time that season.

The victory had special meaning for Scotty. It was a lot easier to bow out of the coaching ranks with a championship rather than a third second-place finish. And the eleven seniors on the team, who had never won a championship, finally made it. They were a fine group of lacrosse players, with two of Hopkins's best, Jack Thomas and Rick Kowalchuk, as their leaders.

After the 1974 championship game, the Blue Jays traveled to California for a three-week goodwill tour. Bob Scott officially turned the team over to Henry "Chic" Ciccarone when they arrived in California—and Chic then jovially gave Scotty one last time to shine as a player, putting him in the goal for the second half of a game with the University of California Lacrosse Club. (Chic felt that Hopkins had a safe enough lead of 18–1.) Scotty had eight saves and cleared the ball like the old pro he was—and remains to this day.

Hall of Fame goalie Larry Quinn (Hopkins '85) shows perfect
form in making a save against Maryland. *Photo by Sports
Unlimited, courtesy of Larry Quinn*

Henry Ciccarone, Hopkins's head coach from 1975 to 1983 and architect of three consecutive national championship teams (1978, 1979, 1980), explains a play with typical intensity. Future head coach Don Zimmerman, in jacket, looks on.
Courtesy of Steve Ciccarone

19

The Modern Era 1975–2000

Henry "Chic" Ciccarone was one of the finest coaches in the history of lacrosse. From 1975 to 1983, he led Hopkins through a phenomenal era of championship competitions and victories. Under Chic, the Blue Jays began the streak that led to their appearance in an unprecedented nine consecutive NCAA title games and were the first to win three championships in a row. Chic's won-loss statistics alone are stunning (105–16), but they only barely reflect his explosive, exuberant, enormously engaging personality—or the kind of coach he was. As a tribute to Chic in the National Lacrosse Hall of Fame observes, he "was demanding, hard-driven, fiercely determined to bring out the best in his athletes, and to make them better individuals by virtue of their experiences on the field. . . . He embodied the Hopkins lacrosse tradition. A players' coach, Chic was an incomparable motivator. . . . He made his players want to outperform their expectations, and he could convince them that whatever they lacked in firepower would be overcome by sheer force of will—and following his game plan."

In his first year as head coach, Chic's great leadership steered the 1975 team to an unexpectedly successful record. The Blue Jays were supposed to be in a rebuilding year after losing eleven seniors from the 1974 championship team (including five who were on one of the All-American teams). Freshman Mike O'Neill teamed with Franz Wittelsberger and Richie Hirsch to form a powerful close-attack unit. Midfielder Dale Kohler, defenseman Jim Moorhead, and goalie Kevin Mahon were also outstanding. The team registered ten straight victories—the most impressive being the opener with Virginia, 10–9, and the games with Cornell, 16–9; Long Island Club, 20–9; and Navy, 16–11. Mary-

Figure 19.1 All-American Mike O'Neill (JHU '78) won the Lt. Col. J. I. Turnbull Award (named for Hopkins great Jack Turnbull) as the nation's top attackman twice in a row on his way to a Hall of Fame career. *Johns Hopkins Sports Information*

land was primed for the Jays, remembering their two losses to Hopkins in 1974, and won decisively 19–11. In the first round of the NCAA tournament, Jack Emmer's Washington and Lee team surprised Hopkins with an 11–7 victory. Although the season ended on a disappointing note, overall it was very successful.

The 1976 Blue Jays also had a successful season, with Mike O'Neill and Dale Kohler again leading the offense and earning first-team All-America honors, while Kevin Mahon and Jim Moorhead continued performing impressively on their end of the field. In the NCAA play-offs, however, the Jays went up against a seemingly unstoppable Cornell in the semifinals. The Big Red's smothering defense held the powerful Jays scoreless for more than two quarters, and Cornell won 13–5. Cornell went on to win the championship by beating Maryland 16–13.

In 1977, the Jays continued their steady progression toward the top with an 11–2 season that included a thrilling come-from-behind 21–20 overtime win against Maryland during the regular season and a 22–12 trouncing of the Terps in the NCAA semifinal round. Mike O'Neill once more led the offense with sixty-five points and

was joined by young, rifle-armed midfielder Dave Huntley on the All-American first team. Freshman defenseman Mark Greenberg earned second-team All-America honors to launch a sparkling career that would—like O'Neill's—lead one day to the National Lacrosse Hall of Fame. Reaching the NCAA championship game for the first time under Chic, the Jays once again were bested by Richie Moran's overpowering Cornell team. Riding a twenty-nine-game winning streak, the Big Red became the first NCAA champion to successfully defend its title, walloping the Jays 16–8. "The only way to explain Hopkins's seeming collapse in the title game," Doyle Smith stated in the National Collegiate Athletic Association's official guide, "is that the semifinal rout of Maryland the week before left them mentally enervated for the title game." But, Doyle added, "Plenty of young talent returns to try to erase that memory."[*]

Indeed, the Ciccarone-led Hopkins teams of 1978, 1979, and 1980 would be the first to win three successive NCAA championships. Collaborating with Chic on the sidelines was a remarkable group of former Hopkins players—some destined, like Chic, to become members of the National Lacrosse Hall of Fame. These included Willie Scroggs, Class of 1969, who in a few years would single-handedly make North Carolina a major lacrosse power as its head coach; Joe Cowan, also Class of 1969; and Jerry Schnydman, Class of 1967, who is now the executive assistant to the president of Johns Hopkins. Former teammates Dennis Townsend, Class of 1966, and Jerry Pfeifer, Class of 1966, also made major contributions as assistant coaches, as did Jim Amen, now a highly respected high school coach on Long Island, who prepared incisive—and extremely funny—scouting reports on all the opposing teams.

By far the most important of Chic's assistant coaches was Fred Smith, who had been affiliated with Hopkins lacrosse since 1947. As described earlier, Freddie was an outstanding player on four great teams. He was head coach of the varsity team in 1951 and then again in 1954. During the remaining thirty-three years of his life, he volunteered his

* Doyle Smith, 1978 *NCAA Guide*, 30.

time and incomparable expertise as a varsity assistant coach, freshman coach, and chief scout. Not only was he knowledgeable in every technical aspect of the game, he also maintained a unique rapport with the players. In earlier years they referred to him as just plain "Fred," never "Coach Smith," and in later years as "Uncle Fred" or "Freddie." He was admired, respected, and liked by everyone, and the innovative defensive techniques he developed greatly influenced the way lacrosse is played to this day. Toward the end of his life, one of his protégés as an assistant coach at Hopkins was Bill Tierney—who readily acknowledges that what he learned from Fred Smith had a lot to do with his subsequent success as head coach at Princeton. Every time Bill comes to Baltimore, he tries to drive by Fred Smith's former home, just to pay his respects.

The 1978 team, captained by Mike O'Neill, had a 13–1 record, losing only to Cornell 16–11 during the regular season. During the NCAA play-offs, the Blue Jays handily beat Hofstra 20–8 and Maryland 17–11 and finally overcame Cornell 13–8 for Chic's first championship. A then record crowd of 13,527 at Rutgers Stadium saw Cornell's forty-two-game winning streak snapped decisively by a Hopkins squad whose young face-off expert, Ned Radebaugh, took twenty of the twenty-two matchups in which he took part. The Blue Jays scooped up seventy-five ground balls to Cornell's fifty-six and outshot the Big Red 48–41. Goalie Mike Federico made twelve saves as O'Neill, who was MVP of the game and later named Player of the Year, led an extremely efficient, well-rounded offensive onslaught. Also scoring goals were Bob DeSimone, Wayne Davis, Dave Huntley, Jim Bidne, Scott Baugher, and Joe Devlin. Half of the 1978 first-team All-American roster was made up of Hopkins players. In addition to O'Neill, other first-team All-American Blue Jays were Baugher, DeSimone, Federico, and Will Hazelhurst.

The 1979 Blue Jays are considered one of the greatest teams in Hopkins history, recording the program's first undefeated and untied collegiate season since 1941. On their way to a second consecutive NCAA championship, the 1979 Jays, captained by Dave Huntley and Steve Wey, demolished their opponents, scoring in the double digits against all

Figure 19.2 Mike Federico (JHU '80) won the Ensign C. Markland Kelly Award as the nation's top goalie and first-team All-America honors for three straight years. In 1999 he was inducted into the Lacrosse Hall of Fame. *Johns Hopkins Sports Information*

of them. A superb defense, anchored by Mike Federico and featuring Mark Greenberg, Dave Black, Curt Ahrendsen, LeRoy Katz, and Mike Sheedy, stifled the competition, which averaged only seven goals a game. (On only two occasions during the regular season did an opponent manage to score above nine goals. Maryland lost the regular-season game 13–12, and Navy lost 17–10.)

Figure 19.3 Members of the 1980 Hopkins team celebrate their double-overtime NCAA championship, Hopkins's fourth NCAA title — and third in a row. *Photo by Joachim Blunck, The Ferdinand Hamburger Archives of the Johns Hopkins University*

In the 1979 championship game, held at the University of Maryland's Byrd Stadium, a then-record crowd of 17,228 saw Hopkins defeat the Terrapins a second time, and far more decisively, 15–9. Although the first quarter had been tight, with Maryland tying the score at 3–3 with only twenty-eight seconds left on the clock, in the second quarter the Blue Jays exploded. They held the potent Terps scoreless for eleven minutes, thirty-three seconds and scored five unanswered goals to notch an 8–4 lead by halftime. The Jays outscored Maryland 4–3 in the third quarter and rolled on to victory by outscoring the Terps 3–2 in the fourth quarter. Dave Huntley and Jeff Cook each scored three goals; Scott Baugher, Wayne Davis, and Ned Radebaugh each scored twice; and Joe Garavente, Steve Wey, and Jim Bidne had one goal each. Cook had two assists, while Bidne, Huntley, Radebaugh, and Mike Donnelly each had one. Hopkins's first-team All-Americans in 1979 included Huntley, Baugher,

Federico, and Greenberg—who also became the first defenseman ever to win the Lt. Raymond Enners Memorial Award as the top Division I player. Mark—who, incredibly, played with a cracked vertebra all season—also won the Schmeisser Award as the top Division I defenseman.

In 1980, another first-team All-American, midfielder Brendan Schneck, a transfer from Navy, along with his brother, defenseman Lance Schneck, enhanced an already formidable Blue Jay team. The explosive offense continued to boast Jim Bidne, Jeff Cook, Howard Offit, Jeff Harris, Ned Radebaugh, Mike Donnelly, Jim Zaffuto, and Henry Ciccarone Jr. (Indeed, all four of Henry Ciccarone's sons—Henry Jr., Brent, Steve, and John—eventually would play for Hopkins.) Mike Federico remained incomparable in the goal, as did Mark Greenberg, Dave Black, LeRoy Katz, Howdy Nicklas, Kevin Keefer, Marty Bergin, and Haswell Franklin on defense. During the regular season, the Jays had a 13–1 record, losing only to Virginia 12–9. In the NCAA play-offs, Hopkins dispatched Harvard 16–12 and Syracuse 18–11 and then avenged their earlier loss to the Wahoos by edging them 9–8 in double overtime to win the championship on a humid afternoon at Cornell University's Schoellkopf Field.

Hopkins had entered its fourth straight championship game missing two of its top players: attackman Jeff Cook, out with a strained back, and face-off ace Ned Radebaugh, down with a virus. The Blue Jays nevertheless jumped out to a 4–0 lead in the first twelve minutes, but Virginia fought back fiercely and took an 8–6 lead early in the fourth quarter. The Wahoos actually dominated every phase of the game except the final tally, outshooting Hopkins thirty-five to twenty-seven, winning the battle for ground balls forty-seven to thirty-one, and scoring the only extraman goal. Without Radebaugh to fight, Virginia's face-off expert, Steve Kraus, dominated the midfield X, winning nineteen out of twenty matchups against Offit, Brendan Schneck, Henry Ciccarone Jr., and Kevin Keefer. Despite these heroics, quick goals by Henry Ciccarone Jr. and Jim Zaffuto knotted the game with four minutes to go, and tight defense on both sides pushed it into overtime. Mike Federico made eight of his twelve saves during the closing quarter and overtime periods—including two spectacular saves during the first four-minute sudden-death period. With forty-eight seconds remaining in the second sudden-death overtime period, Jim Bidne made a perfect feed to Harris on the crease, and Harris fired it into the net to win Hopkins's third straight title. Brendan Schneck, Mark Greenberg, and Mike Federico all received first-team All-American honors in 1980 and ultimately would be elected to the National Lacrosse Hall of Fame in 1997, 1998, and 1999, respectively.

The 1981 Hopkins team notched another 13–0 record during the regular season—continuing a twenty-two-game winning streak—but lost the championship in a nail-biting 14–13 game against North Carolina, coached by former Hopkins player and assistant coach Willie Scroggs. It was the Tar Heels' first appearance in the NCAA title game, held that year at Princeton's Palmer Stadium.

Willie's young, all-non-Carolinian team (including seventeen from Maryland, eleven from New York, two from Virginia, two from Connecticut, and one each from Massachusetts, New Jersey, and Ontario) staged a dramatic comeback, scoring six unanswered goals to overcome an 11–8 Hopkins lead. Carolina's offensive explosion was impressive, but three Hopkins shots on goal were disallowed. One by Jeff Cook hit the net as the whistle ended the first quarter, another by Joe Cantelli came at the last second of the third quarter, and a Jeff Cook rocket that apparently tore through a hole in the top of the Carolina net all were ruled not to be goals. Jeff nevertheless was the top scorer of the game, tallying six times and ending the season with fifty-two goals and twenty-eight assists for eighty points—surpassing the previous one-season Hopkins record of seventy-seven, held by Joe Cowan. Jeff Cook and Brendan Schneck were named to the All-American first team, and Jeff received the Turnbull Award as the top attackman in Division I.

The 1982 championship game was another Hopkins–North Carolina matchup decided by ferocious defense, with the Tar Heels completing a 14–0 season by successfully retaining the national title in a fierce 7–5 battle. The Blue Jays notched an 11–3 record, losing only to Army (11–10) and North Carolina (13–12) in overtime during the regular season. In the NCAA play-offs, we held both Maryland and Virginia to nine goals each while scoring fourteen and thirteen goals, respectively. In our sixth consecutive championship game, however, we ran up against an incredibly hot Carolina defense, anchored by MVP and Player of the Year goalie Tom Sears and featuring John Haus, who later would become an assistant coach and then head coach at Hopkins. On a sultry afternoon at the University of Virginia's Scott Stadium, Carolina's zone defense held Hopkins scoreless for the first twenty-four minutes of the game, despite tremendous offensive pressure from the Blue Jays. Hopkins outshot the Tar Heels 17–4 in the second period, but Sears recorded nine of his sixteen saves that quarter and only let in one goal. Hopkins had an intense defense as well, with goalie Brian Holman making twenty saves overall—but the halftime score was

Figure 19.4 Future Hall of Famer Del Dressel (JHU '86), twice the nation's outstanding midfielder, is one of only four players to be named a first-team All-American four years in succession. The others were Doug Turnbull (JHU '25), Frank Urso (University of Maryland, '76), and Mike Powell (Syracuse University, '04). *Johns Hopkins Sports Information*

4–1, with Carolina attackman Dave Wingate firing in all four Tar Heel tallies. He finished the game with five goals. As Henry Ciccarone told *Lacrosse* magazine afterward, "You win championships on defense, and their defense was better than ours today."[*] Nevertheless, Hopkins's defenseman Marty Bergin was named to the All-American first team and was joined there by Jeff Cook, who once again received the Turnbull Award as the nation's top attackman.

North Carolina was the only team to beat Hopkins during the regular 1983 season, winning 14–13 in overtime down in Chapel Hill, but the Blue Jays

beat the Tar Heels 12–9 in the NCAA semifinal game to send us to our seventh consecutive national championship game. This time our opponent was Syracuse, then making its first appearance in the NCAA final. It would turn out to be a contest that proved the truth of Yogi Berra's observation, "It ain't over 'til it's over." Hopkins dominated the first two quarters, outscoring Syracuse 8–4 on goals by John Krumenacker, Kirk Baugher, Brent Ciccarone, and Peter Scott. Goalie Brian Holman stifled a dozen Syracuse shots in the second period alone. And in the third quarter, Hopkins continued the onslaught with four straight goals, including a Del Dressel tally that left coach Roy Simmons Jr.'s Orangemen down 12–5 with six and a half minutes left in the period. Yet Syracuse proceeded to stage

[*] Gary Cramer, "UNC Report As NCAA Champs," *Lacrosse*, July/August 1982, p. 18.

an incredible comeback, scoring ten of the next eleven goals, including eight unanswered tallies, to give them a 15–13 lead with ten minutes left in the game. Hopkins goals by Henry Ciccarone Jr. and Bill Cantelli tied the score with two minutes, fifty-six seconds remaining. Then Syracuse's Brad Kotz and Randy Lundblad put the Orange ahead again. With fifty seconds left on the clock, Del Dressel scored an unassisted goal, but Syracuse still held on to win 17–16. This was Syracuse's first national lacrosse title since 1924—and the beginning of its exceptional record over the next twenty years. Del Dressel made his first appearance on the All-American first team for Division I and was joined there by Bill Cantelli, the Hopkins captain that year.

Henry Ciccarone decided to retire from coaching at the end of the 1983 season. His philosophy as a coach was simple and could be summed up in three words: "Discipline, sacrifice and respect." As he told veteran lacrosse writer James H. Jackson in 1981, "That's my idea of what you have to teach your players. . . . The competition and battle on the lacrosse field will go on in later life. . . . This is what collegiate sport is all about."[*] It is a philosophy with which I agree completely. Chic was inducted into the National Lacrosse Hall of Fame in 1987 but died just a year later at the age of fifty from a heart attack. Today, the Henry Ciccarone Center for the Prevention of Heart Disease at the Johns Hopkins Hospital, founded and directed by Dr. Roger Blumenthal, who was an assistant sports information director for Chic, is dedicated to the assessment of all the factors that contribute to heart disease. The name "Ciccarone" is not only legendary in lacrosse but is now also attached to heart research around the world.

Don Zimmerman, a former Hopkins player who had been an assistant to Willie Scroggs at North Carolina and to Chic at Hopkins, took over as the Blue Jays' head coach in 1984. He became the first rookie head coach to guide his team through an undefeated 14–0 season, capped with a 13–10 NCAA championship victory over Syracuse. In the title game at a muggy Delaware Stadium, Hopkins's ironclad defense, anchored by acrobatic goalie Larry Quinn and featuring John DeTommaso, Steve Dubin, Guy Matricciani, Brad McLam, and Steve Mitchell, held Syracuse—a team that had been averaging four goals a quarter—scoreless for the first fifteen minutes. The Jays controlled five of the first quarter's six face-offs, grabbed twenty-five ground balls to Syracuse's fourteen, and outshot the Orangemen fourteen to five for a 5–0 lead. Hopkins's well-balanced, powerful offense featured freshman phenom Brian Wood; veteran Willy Odenthal, the team captain; and Del Dressel, John Krumenacker, Peter Scott, John Tucker, Chris Schreiber, Brent Ciccarone, Steve Mutscheller, and Rich Glancy. Although Syracuse attempted one of its patented comebacks in the third quarter, managing to get within one goal of the Jays at 8–7 toward the end of the period, Mutscheller, Odenthal, and Dressel fired in three unanswered goals; Quinn continued making spectacular saves; and the Jays held off the Orange onslaught. Hopkins notched a 74–59 record on ground balls and 19–8 in face-offs, and Quinn, named the game's Most Valuable Player, finished with thirteen saves on Syracuse's surprisingly low thirty-three shots. Hopkins placed four players on the All-American first team: Del Dressel (for the second of his remarkable four-year first-team rankings), Peter Scott, John DeTommaso, and Larry Quinn.

In 1985, Hopkins, captained by seniors Larry Quinn, John Krumenacker, and Guy Matricciani, successfully defended its national title by dominating Syracuse even more in the championship game—the Jays' eighth in a row. Hopkins's stifling close defense of John DeTommaso, Dan Palace, and Chris Wickwire (coached by Fred Smith, Jerry Pfeifer, and a young Bill Tierney), with long-sticks Matricciani, Brad McLam, and Steve Mitchell, kept Syracuse scoreless for thirty-three minutes—more than half the game—and the Jays beat the Orangemen 11–4. Hopkins held Syracuse's tally that year to the lowest ever scored by a team in an NCAA lacrosse final. The Blue Jay's face-off ace Greg Matthews controlled twelve of the eighteen matchups at the X, while Del Dressel scored three goals; Craig Bubier, having a breakout season, scored twice, as

[*] James H. Jackson, "Super Coach but Not Coach of the Year," *Lacrosse*, June/July 1981, p. 13.

did Brian Wood and John Krumenacker; and Mike Morrill and Brad McLam scored once apiece. Larry Quinn made seventeen saves. Once again, Hopkins had four players on the All-American first team: Brian Wood, Larry Quinn, John DeTommaso, and Del Dressel (Quinn, DeTommaso, and Dressel are all now Hall of Famers).

As a high school senior who was going to be an incoming freshman at Johns Hopkins, I went to Brown University in Providence, Rhode Island, to watch that game. Hopkins and Syracuse had contrasting styles. Syracuse was well known for its offensive prowess; Hopkins was well known for its defensive prowess. In that game, hands down, the best player on the field was Larry Quinn. Larry absolutely shut the door on everybody. He stopped a long pole shot from Syracuse and make it look so easy. He dropped to his knees, made the save, controlled the ball, and from his knees cleared the ball forty yards up the field to a streaking Brad McLam, who went on in to score. It was unbelievable. Time and time again, Larry effortlessly swallowed up shots that I had never seen a goalie stop before. When he left the field toward the end of the game, the crowd gave him a standing ovation. He was named the outstanding player of the tournament—just as he had been in 1984—thus becoming one of only two players to win that honor twice and the only one to receive it in back-to-back seasons.

Later, as a U.S. Lacrosse Team member in 1990 and 1994, I had the distinct privilege of being a teammate of Larry Quinn. He had twice been Division I Goalie of the Year and twice Player of the Year, and he received tons of accolades, yet he was a low-key, witty guy who wasn't a great athlete. He was tall and thin, and he looked like a scarecrow. He was not a physically imposing player. But Larry Quinn, unlike a lot of better athletes, was a game-changing player. At any moment, Larry could take over a game. The confidence he instilled in his defense and the leadership he brought to the table were phenomenal. He was elected to the National Lacrosse Hall of Fame in 2000.

Although the 1986 team, captained by Del Dressel and John DeTommaso, recorded an impressive 10–2 record (losing only to Syracuse 11–10 in

the opening game of the regular season), Hopkins missed its first NCAA championship game in nine years. Thanks to a sudden-death overtime 10–9 loss to North Carolina in the semifinals, with Willie Scroggs's team besting the Blue Jays, coached by his former assistant (and fellow Hopkins alumnus) Don Zimmerman, the Jays were on the sidelines when the Tar Heels beat Virginia 10–9 in overtime. Despite missing the championship game, Hopkins still placed four players on the All-American first team: Del Dressel, John DeTommaso, Craig Bubier, and Brian Wood.

The 1986 season was my first as a Hopkins Blue Jay. We went into that semifinal game against a North Carolina team that we had beaten 16–4 in the regular season. We had great confidence—probably too much confidence. There was a feeling on the team that we couldn't lose, but we did. I learned two important lessons from that experience: first, that it is tough to beat a team twice, and second, that each game is its own game. What happened in the past is exactly that—it's the past, and you must prepare and be excited and motivated and have a good game plan for every game.

We played without leading defensemen Brad McLam and John DeTomasso, both of whom were injured. That thrust me into the lineup. It was perhaps the first or second game I ever started in my career at Hopkins, and it did not go well for me—it may have been the single worst game that I ever played at the collegiate level. I remember being taken to school by Brett Davy, a Carolina midfielder, who split dodged me for at least two goals; Pat Welsh, another talented Carolina player, beat me for another goal. It certainly was one of the most humbling experiences of my college lacrosse career to play on that national level and to perform so poorly. We had to take our hats off to Carolina. They played a tremendous game.

In 1987, when Hopkins wasn't given much chance to win the championship, we did so against great odds. We were a young team that had lost three All-Americans—Del Dressel, John DeTommaso, and Brad McLam—to graduation, and our top scorer, senior Brian Wood, was out with injuries for a month. We faced typically tough competition throughout the regular season, during which we lost to Syracuse (15–14), Virginia (9–7), and Maryland (11–7). Seeded fourth, we first had to face the defending champion, North Carolina, in the quarterfinals. Mike Morrill, a third-generation Blue Jay (grandson of Kelso, son of Bill), had perhaps his greatest day as a collegiate attackman, scoring six goals, and freshman goalie Quint Kessenich made an astounding twenty-two saves on our way to an 11–10 victory.

We then were faced with the challenge of beating two previously undefeated teams, Maryland and Cornell, in the semifinal and the championship games at Rutgers University. Maryland, ranked number one, was thought to have much more powerful midfielders and a superior defense. Instead, we surprised both the crowd and the Terps by holding Maryland to its lowest scoring total of the season, winning 13–8. Brian Wood, back from his injuries, scored five goals; Mike Morrill had a hat trick; Brendan Kelly scored twice; and John Wilkens, John Dressel, and Craig Bubier each scored once. Quint had another superb day in the nets, making nine saves. The all-sophomore starting close defense included James DeTommaso (the younger brother of John) and Greg Lilly. Along with sophomore Steve Ciccarone, senior Bruce Chanenchuck, and senior defensive midfielder Steve Mitchell—who would become the first long-stick middie to be named a first-team All-American—we managed to pull the plug on Maryland's high-powered offense. To keep our senior offense fresh, we used a "Jay Team" of attackmen, including Scott Marr (now head coach at the University of New York in Albany), Jeff Ihm, and Jay Clarke, along with midfielders Brendan Kelly, Patrick Russell, and John Wilkens, to keep the Terps moving—and tired.

Next up was Cornell, also undefeated and the reigning Ivy League champions. The Big Red had trounced Syracuse during the regular season 19–6, but in their semifinal matchup, the Orangemen—with freshmen Gary and Paul Gait making their first NCAA appearances—fought back furiously and tied the game at 15–15 with nearly six minutes remaining. Cornell dug deep and scored three unanswered goals to win 18–15. That set up a championship game between Cornell and Hopkins.

Once again, we were considered the underdogs—and once again, our veteran leaders on the offense stepped up to the challenge and inspired our young defense to match their effort. Our junior face-off specialist Greg Gunning won ten of thirteen draws, enabling our offense to control the pace in the first half. We were ahead 3–2 at the end of the first quarter and up 7–4 at the half. When senior Craig Bubier scored early in the third quarter, increasing our lead to 8–4, we may have relaxed a little too much. A goal by Cornell's Tim Goldstein narrowed the gap to 8–5, but Bubier quickly scored again to make it 9–5. Cornell came roaring back, scoring four goals in nine minutes to tie the game at 9–9. John Ciccarone scored an extraman goal early in the fourth quarter to put us back on top, but Cornell quickly rebounded with another goal to knot the score at 10–10. With just two minutes, twenty seconds left in regulation time, Cornell's goalie Paul Schimoler made a save on a shot by senior Larry LeDoyen and sought to clear by making a long pass down the field to a Big Red attackman. With lightning quickness, Quint saw that I was checking the stick of a Cornell attackman, sprinted from the goal, intercepted the pass, saw John Dressel free in the midfield, and passed it to him. John spotted Craig Bubier making a break toward the goal and passed the ball to him—and Bubier scored the winning goal with one minute, fifty-one seconds left in the game. We had to withstand a last-minute drive by Cornell, but they couldn't penetrate our defense. In all, Bubier—who was playing with an injured hamstring—scored four goals, Brian Wood hit the back of the net twice, and Mike Morrill, Larry LeDoyen, John Dressel, John Wilkens, and John Ciccarone each scored once. I was honored to be placed on the All-American first team along with Steve Mitchell and Brian Wood. Larry LeDoyen was placed on the second All-American team; Mike Morrill was placed on the third team; and Craig Bubier and Quint Kessenich, who had made twenty-one saves in the title game, received All-American honorable mention, the first of Quint's four-time All-American honors.

Cornell's frustrated attackman Tim Goldstein, who was named MVP of the tournament, told *Lacrosse* magazine that the one person most responsible for denying the Big Red the championship was Quint—proving, as I said in chapter 2, that the goalie can be the most important player on the field. "There's no question about it," Tim said. "If Hopkins had an ordinary goalie—even just a *good* goalie—we win the national championship."[*] Fortunately for us, in Quint we had an extraordinary goalie. Just as Larry Quinn often was a game-changing player, as in the 1984 and 1985 championships, Quint Kessenich was a season-changer in 1987. Quint took over the goaltending duties halfway through the season. His first game was down at North Carolina. Hopkins had not had great success at Fetzer Field up until that point, but Quint, a freshman guiding the efforts of the three sophomore defensemen starting in front of him, earned an important 11–10 win that turned the season around. He really led Johns Hopkins to the 1987 national championship, which is an unbelievable feat. Not many freshmen goalies have done that—and none in the spectacular fashion of Quint, whose work ethic is outstanding. Hopkins was indeed fortunate to have both him and Larry Quinn in the goal.

The 1987 championship also owed an incalculable debt to Fred Smith. Fred was dying of lung cancer that spring, but he gave every last ounce of his strength to guiding our defense. He was an immensely inspiring man and a wonderful coach. He rarely called us by name—usually by number—but everything he said and did made us better players and, I hope, better people. He managed to be on the sidelines during the semifinal game against Maryland, encouraging and counseling us as he always had, but you could see how weak he was. The terribly hot, humid weather drained him. He could not make the championship game two days later, but we knew he was listening to it on the radio. Many of us put pieces of tape on our gloves and wrote "FRED" or "FRED EE" on them. We dedicated the season to Fred, and it always will mean a lot to us that he knew we'd won that championship for him. He died three weeks later. As *Lacrosse* magazine observed after Fred's death, "Fittingly, it was *his* de-

fense, after all, which ultimately won the game; *his* defensemen who were good when they had to be."[*]

Many lacrosse writers—and the countless amateur commentators on the Internet today—made much of the fact that Hopkins took another eighteen years to win an NCAA championship after that 1987 victory. That eighteen-year lapse was the longest in the history of Hopkins lacrosse. Of course, we Blue Jays were not happy about that. We worked hard to end the drought.

If you really study lacrosse history, however, you'll find that eighteen years hardly sets a record for gaps between winning the gold. Syracuse went fifty-nine years between championships (1924 to 1983, including twelve years of the NCAA tournament). Princeton went almost forty years between titles (1953 to 1992, including twenty-one years of the NCAA play-offs). Maryland has not won a championship since 1975 (thirty years), Virginia was titleless for twenty-seven years (1972 to 1999), Cornell hasn't won a championship since 1977, and North Carolina hasn't won one since 1991. And Navy—like all these others, an exceptionally fine program—has never won an NCAA lacrosse championship. Put in that perspective, the recent Hopkins championship record is not that discouraging. The Blue Jays were in the running every one of those eighteen years, making every NCAA play-off series, appearing in the Final Four nine times and the championship game three times. Being the best is our goal every year, just as it should be the goal of every team in every sport. At Hopkins, we have every intention of continuing our quest to keep the championship trophy at Homewood Field.

The 1988 Blue Jays, captained by Jack Crawford and Mike Morrill, had a 9–2 record. This included a 9–0 victory over Princeton, then being coached for the first time by our former assistant defensive coach, Bill Tierney. It would take Bill a number of years to turn the Princeton program around—but as we all know, turn it around he did. Our only regular-season loss in 1988 was a 19–7 shellacking by Syracuse, where Gary and Paul Gait were beginning to make their mark on lacrosse. We beat Virginia 11–10 in the regular season, with our dy-

---

[*] Larry Needle, "Good When It Counted," *Lacrosse*, June/July 1987, p. 10.

namite face-off man, Joe Rzempoluch, setting us up to make seven third-quarter goals. In a tight game against North Carolina, our tough defense—which included Bill Dwan, now an assistant coach at Hopkins—held off a last-quarter rally by the Tar Heels, whom we beat 6–5. We entered the play-offs ranked second behind an undefeated Syracuse, but in the quarterfinals the Wahoos avenged their regular-season loss by reversing the score and beating us 11–10 in overtime. Syracuse swamped Navy 23–5 in another quarterfinal game, with Gary Gait scoring a then-record nine goals; Penn beat Loyola 10–9; and Cornell upset North Carolina 6–4. In the semifinals, Syracuse slipped past Penn 11–10, while Cornell surprised Virginia 17–6. In the championship game, the Orangemen completed their 15–0 season by defeating Cornell 12–5 in an all-Upstate New York final before a crowd of 20,220 in Syracuse's Carrier Dome. Gary Gait's fourteen goals in the play-offs passed the record of thirteen set by Hopkins's Franz Wittelsburger in 1974. In the All-American honors that year, Quint Kessenich, Mike Morrill, and I were placed on the first-team.

The 1989 Hopkins team, captained by Brendan Kelly, began the season with a 14–13 victory over Syracuse and registered impressive wins against Princeton (11–5), Virginia (12–3), Army (17–4), and North Carolina (16–10), plus tighter triumphs over Maryland (10–9) and Navy (7–5). Towson—a team to which we had never lost—put the only loss on our regular-season record, beating us 9–8 in overtime in the last game before the play-offs. Ranked number two, with Syracuse receiving the top seed, we beat Massachusetts (9–4) and Carolina (10–6) on the way to a championship game against Syracuse in the University of Maryland's Byrd Stadium. It was a remarkable matchup, almost destined to be another one-goal nail-biter—which it was.

We basically exchanged goals with the Orangemen in the first quarter, with Syracuse leading 5–4 at the end on the strength of three goals by Paul Gait. I was matched up against Gary Gait, succeeded in stripping him of the ball several times, and along with my defensive teammates managed to limit him to just two goals—an unusually low

output for him. Paul would take up the slack for Syracuse. Hopkins fought back in the second period, scoring four unanswered goals and holding Syracuse to just one (again by Paul Gait) with just twenty-four seconds remaining in the first half. The score at the break was 8–5 Hopkins. In the third quarter, we remained in control, finishing the period with an 11–9 lead. Syracuse midfielder Rodney Dumpson, who had played in the shadow of the Gait twins for most of the season, scored early in the fourth quarter, and Gary Gait then tied the game at 11–11 with eight and a half minutes left to play. Syracuse scored twice more in the next four minutes, and it looked like the Orange had iced the game. But we refused to surrender, and senior midfielder John Wilkens scored with two minutes, three seconds left in regulation time to get us to within a goal at 13–12. Our tough face-off man, Joe Rzempoluch, won the next face-off and passed the ball to Wilkens, who unfortunately had it forced from his stick with just forty-eight seconds left. Gary Gait brought the ball into play. I managed to check the ball loose from his stick with twelve seconds to go. Sophomore attackman Matt Panetta, who already had five goals and an assist, brought the ball into play and was forced to pass it to Jeff Ihm, who in turn passed it to John Dressel. He fired a point-blank shot at the goal, but Syracuse's goalie, Matt Palumb, made the save with two seconds left on the clock—and Syracuse won. The 23,893 fans at Byrd Stadium had seen one terrific game. Quint Kessenich, who had made seventeen saves in the championship game, was placed on the All-American first team, as were Matt Panetta and I. Five other Hopkins players received All-American honors that year: Greg Lilly, Joe Rzempoluch, Brian Voelker, Bill Dwan, and Brendan Kelly.

As detailed in chapter 2, the 1990s was an "Orange" decade, with the team color of Princeton and Syracuse dominating the championship game playing field, but the Blue Jays nevertheless fielded impressive teams featuring many outstanding All-American players during this period. The 1990 team, captained by James DeTommaso and Quint Kessenich, began its season with another rout of Prince-

Figure 19.5 Terry Riordan (JHU '95), a four-time All-American and winner of the Turnbull Award as the nation's top attackman, still holds the Hopkins record for career points (247) and goals scored (184). *Johns Hopkins Sports Information*

awhile. I had learned a lot about coaching from playing for and watching Zim. He is now head coach of the University of Maryland at Baltimore County. He was succeeded at Hopkins by Tony Seaman, the veteran coach at the University of Pennsylvania.

After serving a year as an assistant coach at Baltimore's Gilman School, I returned to Hopkins as an assistant coach in 1991. That year's Blue Jays, captained by Brian Voelker (who is now head coach at the University of Pennsylvania), Bill Dwan, and Seth Tierney (Dwan and Tierney now coach at Hopkins), had an 8–4 season. Although we sustained an opening-game loss of 15–10 to Princeton, coached by Seth's Uncle Bill, we recorded decisive wins against Syracuse (18–12), Virginia (16–6), Rutgers (13–5), and Washington College (22–5) before losing 11–6 to North Carolina. Our only other regular-season loss was against Maryland, 11–8. In the play-offs, however, Syracuse again avenged its regular-season loss by beating the Jays 11–8 in the quarterfinals. Brian Voelker and Adam Wright earned first-team All-America honors for their exceptional play. Bill Dwan, Scott Giardina, and Matt Panetta also received All-America honors.

In 1992, Blue Jay captains Brian Lukacz, Nick Shevillo, and Scott Giardina and their teammates recorded a similar 8–5 record. It included 15–14 victories over both Princeton (the eventual national champion) and Syracuse along with tough losses to Virginia, North Carolina, Maryland, and Towson. In the play-offs, we turned the tables on Towson, beating the Tigers 15–8 in the quarterfinals, but once more we found Syracuse ready to repay us for their earlier loss, defeating us in the semifinal 21–16. Attackman Adam Wright continued his fine efforts and was named to the first-team All-American roster for the second straight year. Also receiving All-America honors were Jeff Wills, Scott Giardina, Brian Lukacz, Brian Piccola, Terry Riordan, and Nick Shevillo.

Late in 1992, the Hopkins lacrosse family lost one of its greatest pillars when Dr. G. Wilson Shaffer, a renowned professor of psychology, director of sports, dean of the Homewood Schools from 1948 to 1967, and advisor to seven presidents of the university, died at the age of ninety-one. As Bob

ton, beating the Tigers 20–8, but then stumbled and lost to Rutgers, Syracuse, Virginia, and North Carolina. The Blue Jays' backs were against the wall: we had to win all four of our remaining games to make the play-offs. We did it, beating Army, Maryland, Navy, and Towson. In the first round of the play-offs, Princeton avenged its opening regular-season loss by beating us 9–8. Bill Tierney's Tigers had gotten their game legs. Despite our unaccustomed early departure from the play-off rounds, five Hopkins players— Bill Dwan, Quint Kessenich, Matt Panetta, Brian Voelker, and Adam Wright —received All-America honors.

Following the 1990 season, Don Zimmerman chose to leave the lacrosse coaching ranks for

Scott observed in the first edition of this book, Dr. Shaffer, a 1924 graduate of the university, was a genuine friend to generations of Hopkins lacrosse players. More than anyone else on the campus, Dr. Shaffer offered wise counsel that helped more students—athletes and nonathletes alike—deal with the problems that arise in any student's life. He and his wife of sixty years never had children, but as he told the *Sun* in 1973, "I always tell people I've had about 5,000 sons."* A classroom building on the campus is named in his honor.

The 1993 Blue Jays, captained by Tom Sullivan and Steve Vecchione, improved their record to 11–4, beating Georgetown, Rutgers, Virginia, Maryland, Loyola, and Navy, among others. In the play-offs, we beat Virginia again, 14–10, but were upended by North Carolina, 16–10, in the semifinals. Attackman Brian Piccola was the Blue Jays' representative that year on the All-American first team and was joined on the All-America roster by fellow Jays Terry Riordan, Steve Vecchione, Brian Kelly, Milford Marchant, and Tom Sullivan.

In 1994, under captains Brian Piccola and Todd Cavallaro, Hopkins beat Syracuse and Maryland during a regular season that included eight wins and four loses. In the play-offs, Princeton, which had beaten the Jays 20–11 in the opening game of the season, squeaked past us 12–11 in overtime during the quarterfinals and went on to win the championship by another one-goal margin, 9–8, again in overtime. Terry Riordan was named to the first All-American team, while Brian Piccola, Peter Jacobs, and Milford Marchant also received All-America honors.

The 1995 Blue Jays, captained by Peter Jacobs, Terry Riordan, and Chris Steer, had a spectacular, undefeated regular season, beating Princeton (15–14), Syracuse (14–13 in overtime), Virginia (22–13), North Carolina (13–9), Maryland (16–15), Navy (16–8), and Loyola (12–11), among others. We had a tremendous offensive team, featuring the players who turned out to be the top two goal-scorers in Johns Hopkins lacrosse history, Riordan and Piccola, and

the all-time leading assist-getter, David Marr. We had Casey Gordon, a transfer from Virginia, who had the best year in his Hopkins career. We had a great leader in Pete Jacobs, who was very workmanlike, playing good, solid defense and offense. We had Tom Rosko, a transfer from Navy who was a tremendous role player, and we had some gunslingers in Milford Marchant and Chris Macon, who could really let the ball go. It was a formidable offensive group that averaged sixteen goals a game. Brian Kuczma, Aaron Van Horn, and Jay Penn anchored the defense. In the goal we had Jonathan Marcus, who would go on to register the highest number of saves of any goalie in Hopkins lacrosse history.

Ranked number one at the end of the regular season, we once again beat Loyola in the quarterfinals, this time by a decisive 18–5, but in the semifinal, we ran up against Maryland goalie Brian Dougherty. He had a career day—particularly against our two best shooters. It seemed that wherever Terry Riordan and Brian Piccola shot, Dougherty knew ahead of time. He made twenty-three saves as the Terps upset us 16–8 before a then-record crowd of 30,327 at Byrd Stadium—the first sell-out in NCAA lacrosse championship weekend history. It was obvious that Maryland had prepared very well. Coach Dick Edell and his staff did a great job—and so did their players.

Eight Hopkins players nevertheless received All-America honors, with Terry Riordan, Brian Piccola, and Peter Jacobs all making the first team; Milford Marchant being placed on the second team; and Casey Gordon, Brian Kuczma, Jonathan Marcus, and David Marr receiving honorable mention. Terry Riordan also received both the Enners Award as the top player in Division I and the Turnbull Award as the nation's top attackman. Riordan and Piccola concluded their Hopkins careers with the first and second spots for most goals scored by a Blue Jay (Terry with 184 and Brian with 154) and the most points scored (247 and 245, respectively).

At halftime of the 1995 NCAA championship game, the twenty-fifth anniversary of the Division I lacrosse championships was marked by the naming of a twenty-five-member Silver Anniversary Team. Nearly half of the team—ten players—were from

---

* "Dr. G. Wilson Shaffer, Long-time Hopkins Dean," Obituary, *The Sun*, Baltimore, Md., September 22, 1992.

Hopkins, and they had won a combined seventeen NCAA championships (in a couple of cases, three apiece). I was honored to be among those named to this group, which included Mike O'Neill (1978), Jack Thomas (1974), Del Dressel (1986), Rick Kowalchuk (1974), Brendan Schneck (1981), John DeTommaso (1986), Mark Greenberg (1980), Mike Federico (1980), and Larry Quinn (1985). It was a privilege to stand on the field with these great Blue Jays and the outstanding players from other schools who were named to this team.

The 1996 Blue Jays weren't supposed to be very good. Gone were the All-Americans, the Riordans and the Piccolas and the Jacobses and the Macons and the Gordons. We lost a huge number of goal producers from the previous years. But then, in came freshman Dan Denihan, who joined David Marr and Adam Bond on our starting attack. It was a turbulent year. Led by captains Dave Marr, Jonathan Marcus, and Werner Krueger, we had an 8–6 record, beating, among others, Syracuse (14–10), North Carolina (9–8), Navy (18–11), and Army (13–12 in overtime). We lost to Princeton (12–9), Virginia (14–9), Maryland (12–9), Towson (13–12), and Hofstra (9–7). One of the great coaching moves by Tony Seaman late in the season that year was to back off in practice. We decided that everything was going to be positive: no negative feedback, no yelling. We cut back on practice time. We tried to make drills more enjoyable. We did that heading into our regular-season finale against Loyola. We felt that we had to win to make the play-offs, and we turned out to have one of our better games against Loyola, beating them 12–10.

In the first round of the play-offs, we beat Notre Dame 12–7. Then we had to face a Maryland team that the year before had beaten us in the play-offs and taken away our opportunity to play for the national championship. The Terps faced an extremely motivated Johns Hopkins team. In preparation, one of the adjustments that we made went against everything we had taught our players. We felt that Brian Dougherty was a goalie who baited people, trying to get them to shoot at an open area, then moving quickly to that area to block the shot. So in practices before that game, we worked on teaching

the guys to shoot where Dougherty was, instead of where he wasn't, so that we wouldn't fall for his bait and could catch him. We wound up shutting out the Terps in the first half. Our defense also put on a great effort, and we held on to win the game 9–7. We then faced Virginia in the semifinals and lost 16–10, but to get to that point with that team was a heck of an achievement. We'd had a lot of peaks and valleys and struggled to find our identity after the Riordan and Piccola era. Six Hopkins players received All-America honors. Brian Kuczma moved from 1995's honorable mention category up to first team, while Billy Evans, John Gagliardi, Milford Marchant, David Marr, and Jonathan Marcus were placed in the second team, third team, and honorable mention categories. Jon Marcus ended his career on Homewood Field with the most saves ever recorded by a Hopkins goalie, 877.

In 1997, Hopkins had a 10–4 record under captains Werner Krueger, Billy Evans, and Aaron Van Horn. We opened the season with a 7–6 loss to Princeton in overtime but went on to have lopsided victories over Maryland (13–9), Navy (24–5), Army (23–5), North Carolina (15–7), and Villanova (17–9), while registering tighter wins over Hofstra, Towson, and Loyola. We had regular-season losses to Syracuse (14–13) and Virginia (16–12). In the play-offs, we were surprised by Duke in the quarterfinals, losing a 12–11 heartbreaker in overtime. The disappointing conclusion to our season did not obscure the achievements of defenseman Brian Kuczma, who was awarded the Schmeisser Award as the top defenseman in the country and also was named to the All-American first-team along with his defensive teammate, John Gagliardi. Dudley Dixon, Billy Evans, and Andrew Godfrey also received All-America honors.

The 1998 team, captained by Dudley Dixon, Andrew Godfrey, and Rob Doerr, beat Virginia (13–10), North Carolina (16–9), Maryland (10–6)—before ten thousand fans packed into Homewood Field—and Navy (15–14) on its way to a 10–4 season that ended with a loss to Maryland (11–10) in overtime in the quarterfinals. The Blue Jays still placed three players on the All-American first team: goalie Brian Carcaterra, midfielder A. J. Haugen, and defenseman Rob Doerr. Andrew Godfrey, Dudley Dixon, Matt O'Kelly, and Dylan Schlott were also tendered All-America honors. In addition, Brian Carcaterra received the Ensign C. Markland Kelly Award as the nation's outstanding goalie in Division I.

Following the 1998 season, Tony Seaman left Hopkins (soon thereafter becoming the head coach at Towson University). He was succeeded by John Haus, the former All-American defenseman for North Carolina who had been an assistant coach at Hopkins from 1988 to 1994 and then head coach at the Division III perennial power, Washington College, where he had won a national championship.

Under Hausie, the 1999 Blue Jays, captained by Dylan Schlott, Rob Doerr, and Paul LeSueur, had an impressive 11–3 record. They beat Princeton (12–11), Syracuse (12–10), Virginia (16–15), North Carolina (21–12), Maryland (13–3), and Navy (11–1), among others. In the NCAA play-offs, the Jays beat Hofstra 11–7 in the quarterfinals (having just lost to the Dutchmen 9–8 in overtime in the last game of the regular season), then lost 16–11 to Virginia, which avenged its regular-season defeat. The All-

American roster that year again featured a hefty Blue Jay contingent of eight Hopkins players. A. J. Haugen and Rob Doerr once more were named to the All-American first team, while Dan Denihan, Matt O'Kelly, Brian Carcaterra, Dylan Schlott, Conor Denihan, and Brandon Testa received All-America honors, too.

The 2000 Blue Jays, led by Dan Denihan, A. J. Haugen, and Dave Rabuano, also made it to the NCAA semifinals after registering an 8–3 regular-season record that included victories over North Carolina (10–8), Maryland (20–11), Navy (7–6 in overtime), Towson (10–8), and Loyola (16–12). Losses included a season-opening defeat by Princeton (15–11); a 13–12 defeat by Syracuse in the Carrier Dome; and a 16–8 drubbing by Virginia in Charlottesville. In the NCAA semifinals, Syracuse once more had our number, defeating the Jays 14–12. Nevertheless, six Blue Jays made the All-American rosters. A. J. Haugen was named to the first team for the third straight year, and Dan Denihan joined him there. Brian Carcaterra, Brandon Testa, Conor Denihan, and Brendan Shook also received All-America honors.

Head Coach Dave Pietramala (JHU '90) is the only person to have won the NCAA Division I lacrosse championship as both a player (1987) and a coach (2005). Twice winner of the William C. Schmeisser Award (named for long-time Hopkins coach "Father Bill" Schmeisser) as the nation's top defenseman and a three-time first-team All-American, he was inducted into the Lacrosse Hall of Fame in 2004. Here he prepares for the 2005 game with Loyola. *Johns Hopkins Sports Information*

20

Into the 21st Century

The 2001 season presented a difficult situation for both the coaches and the players. We were a new staff coming in, and we planned to change everything—our offensive philosophy and our defensive philosophy. Some of the players were going to be playing for their third head coach, under their third offensive and defensive system. It was a tough transition.

On the bus coming home from our opening game against Princeton, which we had lost 8–4, Seth Tierney and I looked at each other and wondered how we were going to get through the season, having just scored only four goals. And it took some time. To the credit of the guys on the team, they stayed with us. Senior Eric Wedin, for example, turned out to have a banner year, his best and most productive. We took Wedin, who was predominantly a face-off specialist, and made him a prominent player in our midfield. He single-handedly helped us beat Syracuse 11–10 by scoring five goals in the Carrier Dome.

The 2001 Blue Jays were captained by Shawn Nadelen, Brendan Shook and Brandon Testa, who led the team to an 8–4 record. This included the victory over Syracuse (then ranked number one) as well as victories over North Carolina (12–4), Navy (13–11), Towson (14–13), and Loyola (13–10). We had that dispiriting, opening-game loss to Princeton; lost a heartbreaking 9–8 battle against Virginia in a record four overtimes; and lost to Maryland, 10–9, down at College Park. In the NCAA playoffs, a feisty Notre Dame surprised us in the quarterfinal, 13–9, to end our season. The Irish were a senior-laden team with great leadership, and on that day, they simply were better than we were. We committed several key offsides mistakes that gave

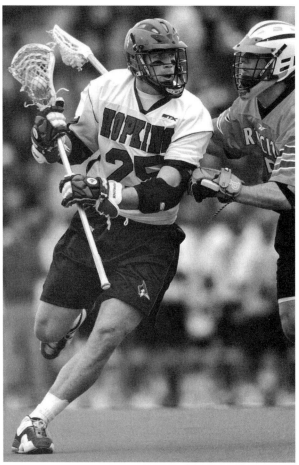

Figure 20.1 A few of the now-graduated players who made contenders of Pietramala-coached teams after the turn of the millenium: Adam Doneger (JHU '03), twice a first-team All-American midfielder. *Johns Hopkins Sports Information*

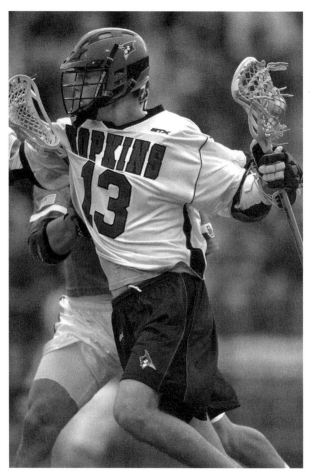

Figure 20.2 Bob Benson (JHU '03), a three-time All-American attackman, displayed an uncanny skill for positioning himself to score goals, hitting the back of the net 124 times in his career. *Johns Hopkins Sports Information*

the ball back to Notre Dame, missed some other opportunities, and were beaten fair and square. At the season's end, Bobby Benson, Shawn Nadelen, Brandon Testa, and Eric Wedin received All-America honors.

In the opening game of the 2002 season, we faced a defending national champion Princeton team. Nobody gave us a chance in that game—but we beat the Tigers 8–5, starting four freshmen and a brand new goalie: Kyle Harrison, Peter LeSueur, Kyle Barrie, Chris Watson, and Nick Murtha. Kyle Harrison took the opening face-off and scored the first goal, the first of his Hopkins career.

That Princeton game set the pace for the 2002 season. Under the leadership of captains Bobby Ben-

son, P. J. DiConza, Adam Doneger, Matt Hanna, and Nick Murtha, we had a 12–2 record. After Princeton, we proceeded to defeat Syracuse (9–8), by that time ranked number one; Albany (10–4); North Carolina (12–11); Villanova (10–7); Ohio State (12–9); Maryland (9–8 in overtime); Navy (9–8); Towson (14–11); and Loyola (8–4). Our only regular-season loss was to Virginia, down in Charlottesville, 12–6. Going into the play-offs ranked number one, we faced a tough University of Massachusetts in the quarter-finals, defeating them 13–12 in overtime. Then against Princeton, always ready in May, we suffered an 11–9 loss in the semifinals as Bill Tierney's Tigers reversed the outcome of our game in March. The outstanding performance of the Jays throughout the

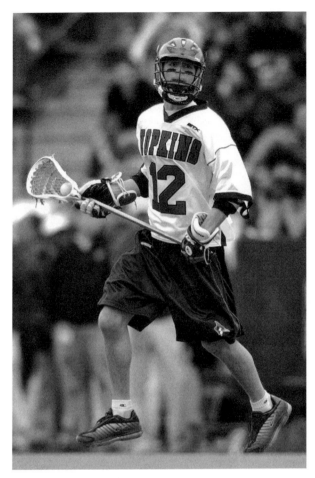

Figure 20.3 All-American Kevin Boland (JHU '04) stands as the all-time leader in assists among Hopkins midfielders. His 82 career assists surpassed the record of Hall of Famer Del Dressel. *Johns Hopkins Sports Information*

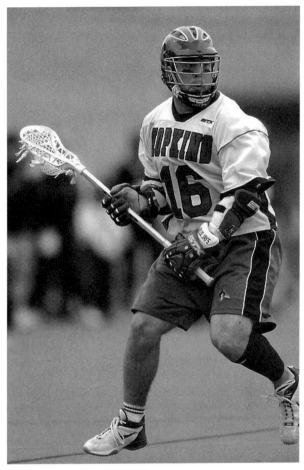

Figure 20.4 Conor Ford (JHU '04), an All-American selection who nonetheless made "quiet" contributions, recorded 101 career goals. *Johns Hopkins Sports Information*

2002 season was recognized, however, in postseason honors, which included the awarding of the Ensign C. Markland Kelly trophy for the nation's best goalie to Nick Murtha. Nick was also named to the All-American first team, along with midfielder Adam Doneger; third-team All-America honors went to midfielder Kevin Boland, defenseman P. J. DiConza (who also was elected to Phi Beta Kappa, the nation's top scholastic fraternity), and attackman Bobby Benson. Defenseman Michael Peyser received All-American honorable mention.

The 2002 team's efforts laid the foundation for our future success. We had outstanding leadership from Bob Benson and Adam Doneger. Along with Michael Peyser and some other veterans, they

really took a large group of freshmen under their wings and showed them the right way to do things: how to work and how to practice. They put demands on them to achieve academically, to do the right things socially.

Coming off the semifinal loss to Princeton in 2002, the 2003 Blue Jays were extremely motivated and did something no Hopkins team had accomplished since 1989—we advanced to the national championship game. Kyle Harrison, Chris Watson, Peter LeSueur, Kyle Barrie, and Tom Garvey all played significant roles in that achievement, as did Corey Harned, entering his second year as a long-stick midfielder. Conor Ford and Kevin Boland also emerged as major players. Bobby Benson, Adam

Figure 20.5 The 2005 national champion Johns Hopkins Blue Jays celebrate their 16–0 season. *Jay Van Rensselaer*

Doneger, Michael Peyser, Greg Raymond, and Rob Scherr were the captains of this outstanding group of young men, all of whom showed tremendous grit and class throughout a typically tough, demanding season. They really set the tone for that team, which completed the season 14–2, tying the school record for number of wins per season held by the NCAA champion 1980 and 1984 teams.

We began with a 10–8, on-the-road victory over Princeton, then ranked number two, and followed it with decisive victories at home against Albany (16–7) and Penn (14–5). Our only regular-season loss occurred against Syracuse, up in the Carrier

Dome, when we had an 8–2 lead with just one minute, fifty-six seconds left in the first half and then let Syracuse go on one of its legendary rallies. The Orange scored three unanswered goals in just nineteen seconds to gain momentum and leave for the halftime break trailing only 8–5. The Orangemen kept their rally going in the third quarter, scoring five straight goals to take a 10–8 lead with two minutes, fifty-four seconds left in the period. After another Syracuse goal in the fourth quarter, giving the Orange a 14–11 lead, Bobby Benson scored our last three goals, two of them assisted by Kevin Boland. It wasn't enough, as Syracuse scored once more in the fourth period as well, and when the clock ran out the score stood at 15–14.

The Blue Jays rebounded the following week, jumping out to a 5–0 halftime lead over the visiting Virginia Cavaliers on our way to an 8–7 victory at Homewood Field. Senior goalie Rob Scherr squelched a furious second-half rally by Virginia, then ranked number one, by making a career-high eighteen saves. We continued our winning ways down at Fetzer Field in North Carolina, rallying from a 10–8 deficit with only two minutes, twenty seconds left to play in the game and defeating the Tar Heels 11–10 in overtime. Adam Doneger and Peter LeSueur scored the goals to tie the game late in regulation, and Kyle Harrison fired in the game-winner just fifty-six seconds into overtime.

A 19–6 victory over Duke featured an outstanding performance by the Blue Devils' Matt Rewkowski, who scored four of the visitors' goals. (Matt later would transfer to Hopkins. It was a lot better having him on our side!) Hopkins's Kyle Barrie dented the net five times; Peter LeSueur had four goals; Bobby Benson, Conor Ford, and Adam Doneger each had three; and Joe McDermott had one. We then faced a typically tenacious Maryland Terrapin team at Byrd Stadium. We initially took control of the game and were winning 4–2 at the half when Maryland staged a comeback that knotted the score at 5–5. With two minutes, thirty-nine seconds remaining in sudden-death overtime, Joe McDermott scored to secure our second overtime victory over Maryland in as many years—and our second straight one-goal win against the Terps. Rob Scherr recorded fifteen saves; we won ten of fourteen face-offs and outhustled Maryland for ground balls thirty-two to twenty-five times.

After beating Navy 17–3, Towson 17–9, and Loyola 17–6, we were ranked number one going into the NCAA play-offs. We defeated Army 14–2 in the first round, then faced Towson in the quarterfinals. We were a little nervous going into that game. People thought we were supposed to win and head for the Final Four, but we knew that Towson was a talented team that was capable of beating anyone—and after losing to us 17–9 three weeks earlier, the Tigers were ready to take the game to

us. We handled the challenge. Our balanced offense—with Bobby Benson (three goals); Kyle Barrie, Adam Doneger, and Kyle Harrison (two goals and one assist each); and single goals by Kevin Boland, Greg Peyser, Peter LeSueur, Conor Ford, and Joe McDermott—more than countered the determined Towson team. Our tight defense, anchored by goalie Rob Scherr, who made fifteen saves, took care of the Tigers, 14–6.

In the Final Four, we first faced John Desko's Syracuse team, which had handed us our only regular-season defeat. Before 37,823 fans in the Baltimore Ravens' M&T Bank Stadium, Syracuse got off to a strong start. We found ourselves down 3–0 midway into the first period and down 7–6 at the half. During the halftime break, we assessed the situation. We knew that Rob Scherr was handling his goalie role as superbly as before, and defenseman Tom Garvey was holding Syracuse's All-American attackman Michael Powell at bay. And if we could control the face-offs, we could take away Syracuse's momentum. We did so in a manner that stunned the crowd—and Syracuse. Kyle Harrison tied the score just twenty-five seconds into the third quarter, fueling a terrific 14–0 scoring barrage that had begun with a Kevin Boland goal one minute before the first half ended and lasted until the last minute of the game. We defeated Syracuse 19–8, handing the Orangemen their worst NCAA tournament defeat since their 11–4 loss to Hopkins in the 1985 champion game. Once more, our offense was extremely balanced. Kyle Barrie and Bobby Benson each had four goals; Conor Ford had three; Peter LeSueur, Joe McDermott, and Kyle Harrison had two apiece; and Kevin Boland and Corey Harned each had one. Rob Scherr once more made fifteen saves.

Virginia was our championship game opponent, having beaten Maryland handily 14–4 in the semifinal. As so often is the case in lacrosse, it was the man in the goal who made the difference—and in this game, it was Virginia's Tillman Johnson. He had a fantastic day, making thirteen saves—several of them spectacular—to end our eleven-game winning streak and capture the championship 9–7.

Before a crowd of 37,944 in a soggy Ravens stadium, Dom Starsia's Cavaliers took control in the first quarter, scoring four unanswered goals and then a fifth early in the second quarter. We dug ourselves a hole, and you can't do that against a team as talented as Virginia was that year. We played a much better game in the final three quarters, but if you give your opponent a five-goal lead at the Division I level, your chances of emerging victorious are reduced considerably. We fought back in the second quarter and entered the half behind 6–4. Because we had been behind Syracuse at the half two days earlier, we thought we could make another comeback. We made some subtle adjustments during the break, and with five minutes, forty-one seconds remaining in the third quarter, scored and got within a goal of the Cavaliers at 6–5.

In the fourth quarter, we had several opportunities to tie the game and perhaps even go ahead, but Tillman Johnson doused our efforts with phenomenal play, at one point making three point-blank saves in less than seventeen seconds. We still felt we had a chance to come back, as Kyle Barrie beat Johnson with two minutes, fifty-two seconds left in the quarter to bring the score up to 8–6. With one minute, fifty-nine seconds remaining, Virginia's John Christmas scored to give the Cavaliers a 9–6 lead, but he then received a nonreleasable, unsportsmanlike penalty for taunting after he scored the goal. On the extraman opportunity, Adam Doneger quickly fired in our seventh goal. We might have been able to take advantage of the continuing man-up opportunity, but Virginia won the next face-off; we never again got possession of the ball within the Virginia zone, and time ran out on us. It was a tough defeat—but we had shown tremendous determination and drive during that game and the entire 2003 season. We placed four players on the NCAA All-Tournament Team: Bobby Benson, Kyle Barrie, Tom Garvey, and Corey Harned. Adam Doneger and Kyle Barrie received first-team All-America honors; Bobby Benson, Rob Scherr, Michael Peyser, and Kyle Harrison were placed on the second All-American team; and Kevin Boland received third-team honors.

The opening game of the 2004 season gave us a bit of a scare. We faced the University of Pennsylvania and jumped out to an early 2–0 lead in the first six minutes of the game, then held back Penn's scoring successes to enter the half ahead 7–4. Yet the Quakers—expertly guided by Brian Voelker, my former Hopkins teammate and assistant coach, and former Blue Jay face-off ace Peter Jacobs—outscored us 4–1 in the third quarter to knot the score at 8–8. Matt Rewkowski, playing in his first game as a Blue Jay, gave us the lead for good with a goal nine minutes, three seconds into the fourth quarter. Matt then assisted Conor Ford on his third goal of the game with two minutes, thirty-five seconds remaining to give us a two-goal cushion that held, despite a furious and near-successful attempt by Penn to tie the game with only seconds remaining in regulation time.

That wake-up call served us well in the next three games. We rolled past Princeton 14–5 with the aid of Kyle Harrison's then career-high four goals and an assist, along with Conor Ford's four goals, plus tight defense and excellent goaltending. Next came Albany, coached by another former teammate of mine, Scott Marr, to whom we were not particularly kind. We defeated the Great Danes 17–6, going on a 15–1 scoring streak that bridged the second and third quarters. Kyle Barrie scored four goals in our next victory, a 13–6 win over Hofstra up in Hempstead, Long Island—always a tough place to play. We outshot Hofstra fifty-two to twenty-four times, scooped up forty-three ground balls to the Pride's twenty-seven, and won nineteen of twenty-three face-offs—including all fifteen of the ones in which Greg Peyser was our man at the X.

In our next game, we handed Syracuse another stunning defeat, beating the Orangemen 17–5 at Homewood Field in a game during which our defensive ace, Tom Garvey, held Syracuse's potent Michael Powell pointless for only the second time in his career. We won twenty out of twenty-four face-offs, outhustled Syracuse forty-seven to twenty-eight on ground balls, and outshot them fifty to twenty-three times. Kyle Harrison won ten out of his eleven face-offs, grabbed fourteen ground balls, and ignited a 13–1 scoring run early in the second quarter. Conor Ford led the balanced attack with four goals and one assist; Kevin Boland had one goal and four assists, and Kyle Barrie had three goals. Our man-down defense held Syracuse scoreless on four extraman opportunities, while our man-up offense scored on three of our seven extra-man chances.

We seemed to be firing on all cylinders heading down to Charlottesville to meet the defending national champion Virginia Cavaliers, whose season had gotten off to a rocky start with three early losses. We exchanged leads with Virginia in the first half and went into the break tied 3–3. The nip-and-tuck battle continued through the third and fourth quarters, and when regulation time ran out, we were tied again, 8–8. Cavalier goalie Tillman Johnson once again frustrated us, making a crucial save forty-seven seconds into the sudden-death overtime on a shot by Conor Ford. Shortly thereafter, Virginia scored the winning goal. Ironically, this would prove to be the high point for Virginia in 2004. The Cavaliers did so poorly the rest of the season, winning fewer than half of their games, that they did not make the NCAA play-offs—becoming only the second such defending national championship team not to do so in thirty years.

The following week it was our turn to be on the positive side of a one-goal victory, with Peter LeSueur scoring the winning goal against a determined North Carolina team with less than a minute left in regulation time. It was our tenth straight victory over North Carolina—but the third straight one in the series that was decided by a single goal. The Tar Heels, especially when coached by John Haus, are always tough. We took an early 2–0 lead, but Carolina tied the game by the end of the first quarter, went on to lead 5–4 at the half, and then took a 6–4 lead early in the third period. We tied the game with two quick goals—only eighty-five seconds apart—but Carolina just as quickly scored twice again to lead 8–6 midway through that quarter. Kyle Harrison and Conor Ford then tied the game once more with a lightning-quick pair of goals just sixty-one seconds apart. With nine minutes, fifty-three seconds remaining in the game, Conor scored again on an assist from Matt Rewkowski to let us take the lead at 9–8, but with four minutes left to go, Carolina's Jeff Prossner fired in his third goal of the game to once again tie it. We successfully turned back a final offensive drive by

North Carolina, and Pete scored the winning goal off an assist from Kevin Boland. We won the next face-off and managed to run out the remaining fifty seconds on the clock to secure our twenty-fourth consecutive victory at Homewood Field.

On a trip to Durham a week later, we held off Mike Pressler's Duke team to win 6–5. The Blue Devils were the eighteenth consecutive opponent our defense had held to fewer than ten goals.

The following week was the one hundredth meeting between Hopkins and the University of Maryland—a game eagerly anticipated by both teams. The buildup to it was extraordinary. Maryland, coached by my old boss at Loyola, Dave Cottle, had been ranked number one following our lone loss to Virginia but was upset a week earlier by Navy. They were aiming to reclaim their top spot. The pregame press coverage was intense. *Sports Illustrated* planned a major story on the matchup; College Sports Television was there to cover the game live; and a standing-room-only crowd of 10,555 packed the stands at Homewood Field on a balmy night. We had prepared intensely and were ready for the Terps.

Kyle Barrie scored twice in the first two minutes to give us a lead we never relinquished. With a barrage of three subsequent goals in under ninety seconds, we were ahead 5–0 before the first television time-out—and were leading 8–1 at the end of the first quarter. After Matt Rewkowski made it 9–1 early in the second period, Maryland mounted a rally that inched them to within four goals, 9–5, but Kyle Harrison and Joe McDermott each scored to make the score 11–5 at the half. In the third quarter, we and the Terps matched each other goal-for-goal at three apiece. Maryland got two more goals in the fourth quarter, but it wasn't enough to overcome our earlier dominance of the game, which we won 14–10. We outshot the Terps fifty-three to thirty-two times, won the ground ball battle thirty-five to twenty, and took sixteen of the twenty-six face-offs. It was a very satisfying victory—our third straight over Maryland.

There was no letup in our schedule, however, as we next faced the Midshipmen of Navy, then ranked number two to our number one. The Naval Academy was considered the Cinderella team of the season, rebounding from a disappointing 2003 record of 6–7, which had prevented them from even getting into the NCAA play-offs. Under Coach Richie Meade, who would go on to be named Coach of the Year, they had ten wins, the most for Navy since 1978. Hopkins had beaten them for twenty-nine years in a row—a record that would have astonished the Blue Jays of the early to mid-1960s, who found it almost impossible to beat Navy. The Middies of 2004 gave us an amazing battle in their effort to end our three-decade streak. They nearly did it.

Navy took an early 2–1 lead in the first quarter, but we went on a run with goals by Conor Ford, Kyle Barrie, Kevin Boland, and Kyle Harrison in the second period to enter the halftime break leading 6–3. The Middies then showed that they were capable of lopsided scoring runs, making six goals to our one in the third and fourth quarters to take a 9–7 lead with a little more than five minutes left in the game. Following Navy's ninth goal, we won the face-off, and Kyle Harrison got his third goal of the game, inching the score up to 9–8 with four minutes, forty-two seconds remaining on the clock. When Navy was called for too many players on the field with less than a minute to go, giving us an ex-traman situation, Kevin Boland fed Conor Ford for the tying goal with just forty-eight seconds left in regulation time. In the sudden-death overtime, we outshot Navy 4–3, but their excellent goalie, Matt Russell, made two point-blank saves on Kyle Barrie shots before Conor Ford again succeeded in scoring on him to win the game for us 10–9.

We finished the regular season with a 13–8 victory over Tony Seaman's Towson Tigers and an 11–7 win against Bill Dirrigl's Loyola Greyhounds. In the Towson game, which ended a ten-game winning streak for the Tigers, Conor Ford tied his career-high five goals for the second consecutive game, and Matt Rewkowski scored three goals and had an assist. In the Loyola game, Conor became the nineteenth player in Hopkins lacrosse history to score more than 90 goals in his career, and he moved into seventeenth place on the list of Blue Jay scorers with 149 points, past Mike Morrill (1985–1988) and Mickey Webster (1957–1959). Kevin Boland's three assists in that game tied him with four-time, first-team All-American Del Dressel (1983–1986) for most assists by a midfielder (75) at Hopkins.

The Jays entered the play-offs ranked number one for the third consecutive year (the first time that had happened since Syracuse did it between 1988 and 1990). Our first opponents were the University of Providence Friars, whom we beat 15–3 in our twenty-seventh consecutive victory at Home-wood Field. Conor Ford and Kyle Barrie each had three goals and one assist, while Peter LeSueur had two goals and a career-high four assists to rack up six points. Kevin Boland had two goals and two assists—bringing his career assist total to 77 to become the all-time assist-leader among Hopkins midfielders. (Kevin would end his career with 82 assists.) Kyle Harrison also had two goals, while Matt Rewkowski and Frank Potucek each had one.

We felt we were playing good lacrosse. We drew a tough quarterfinal opponent in North Carolina and prepared intensely for them. The Tar Heels had given us a tenacious fight during the regular season. We knew the play-off game would be very difficult and thought that in order to win, we'd have to hold Carolina's scoring to single digits. Our defense did so, with Scott Smith having a very good day, keeping Carolina's goals to just nine as our offense notched 15 goals. We got off to a slow start, with Carolina taking an early 2–1 lead in the first quarter. Then Matt Rewkowski scored two quick goals back-to-back to put us ahead for good just a minute into the second quarter. Joe McDermott gave us another goal three minutes into the second period, and then Conor Ford took over, scoring five goals in just over eleven minutes to put us in the lead 8–4 at the half. The Tar Heels were not about to roll over, however, and fought back, scoring three quick goals in the third period. Kyle Harrison and Benson Erwin got us back on the scoreboard with a goal apiece in less than two minutes; in the fourth quarter, Kevin Boland scored twice, while Kyle Harrison and Matt Rewkowski each scored once. The five goals Conor Ford scored in that game put him in special company. He would end his career with 101 goals, tied with Richie Hirsch (1974–1977) for eleventh on the all-time Hopkins list, ahead of Dave Huntley (1976–1979), Brian

Wood (1984–1987), Del Dressel, and Peter Scott (1981–1984). In my opinion, Conor was the best All-American player no one ever wrote much about. He constantly amazed me by the way he put the ball in the net.

We felt that we were taking very positive momentum into the national semifinal against Syracuse. As we prepared for that game, however, our coaching staff was concerned with the fact that we had beaten Syracuse the last two games by a combined score of 36–13, and we worried that our guys might not be as prepared mentally as they should be. Although we had a good game plan and practiced hard, there was a feeling that we weren't going to lose, because we had beaten them so handily in the previous two games.

We took on the Orangemen before a crowd of 46,923 in Baltimore's M&T Bank Stadium. That day, Syracuse proved the better team, outshooting us forty-five to our thirty-seven, winning the ground ball battle thirty-four to our thirty-two times, and controlling the face-offs to beat us 15–9. In a game that was tied seven times, Syracuse took an early 4–2 lead in the first quarter and was up 6–5 at the half. In the 2003 semifinal, we also had been down by a goal going into the halftime break, so we figured we could recover the momentum as we often had done before. We appeared to do so early in the third quarter, forging ahead to an 8–7 lead with four minutes, thirty-six seconds remaining in the period. But then the come-from-behind Syracuse of old suddenly reappeared and scored three times in the final two minutes, seven seconds of the quarter to go ahead 11–8 and take a lead they would never relinquish. Our top scorer of the game was Matt Rewkowski, who had three goals, followed by Kyle Harrison and Conor Ford, who each had two.

The Syracuse coaching staff had done a great job. They changed the way they played and slowed the ball down. They took chunks of time off the clock. One of the biggest differences in that game, compared to the previous two, was our inability to be successful at the face-off X, where Syracuse proved very adept. We went into that game believing that we needed to prevent Syracuse's top scorers, such as Mike Powell, from excelling, but instead the Orange got great goal production from other players, such as Kevin Dougherty, who scored five times, and Brian Nee, who scored four times to set the Orange pace. They really stepped up and did extremely well.

It was a very disappointing end to a terrific season, in which we were ranked number one for nine out of eleven weeks under the leadership of captains Kevin Boland, Conor Ford, Corey Harned, Greg Raymond, and Chris Watson. Many of our players earned national recognition for their exceptional play—as well as their academic excellence. Kyle Harrison was named to the All-American first team and also received the Lt. Donald McLaughlin Jr. Award as the nation's outstanding midfielder, joining Dave Huntley (1979), Brendan Schneck (1981), and Del Dressel (1984 and 1985) as the Blue Jay recipients of that honor. Kyle Barrie, Kevin Boland, and Tom Garvey received All-American second-team honors; Matt Rewkowski was given third-team All-America honors; and Corey Harned received All-American honorable mention. Defenseman Chris Watson and attackman Peter LeSueur were named to the CoSIDA (College Sports Information Directors of America) Academic All-America At-Large Team with 3.69 and 3.65 cumulative grade point averages, respectively.

Despite the postseason accolades, we all spent the longest summer of our lives. Within three weeks of that loss, however, the tone for 2005 was set by Kyle Harrison in an e-mail he sent to all of the coaches and to each player. Kyle wrote that he had gone to the beach and was devastated. For three years in a row, we were the number one seed in the tournament, and for three years in a row, we hadn't come home with the prize. And we had been embarrassed on a national stage. He was extremely upset because he felt that he could and should have done more—he could have practiced harder; he could have pushed harder. He vowed that he would be the hardest-working guy on the team, and he demanded that everyone else follow him. The determination that characterized the 2005 season was created.

The 2005 season will rank as one of the most remarkable in the history of Hopkins lacrosse. The team was led by an exceptional group of seniors who had never lost a game on Homewood Field. Captains Kyle Harrison, Peter LeSueur, Greg Raymond, Matt Rewkowski, and Chris Watson, along with Kyle Barrie, Lou Braun, Benson Erwin, Tom Garvey, James Maimone-Medwick, and Joe "Kip" Malo, were inspirational exemplars of the Hopkins lacrosse tradition. With significant contributions by freshmen, sophomores, and juniors, it was a team that refused to lose. They completed a school-record 16–0 season, which included four overtime victories (the most ever in more than a century of Hopkins lacrosse), notched our first undefeated campaign since 1984, and won our first national championship since 1987.

We began the season at a snow-surrounded Princeton Class of 1952 Stadium, where the 2005 Jays defeated the then third-ranked Tigers 9–6 before a record 6,325 fans. Sophomore attackman Jake Byrne recorded his first career hat trick during a 6–0 first-half run that began when Kyle Harrison scored Hopkins's first goal just thirty-nine seconds into the game. Freshmen Paul Rabil and Stephen Peyser also scored their first goals as Blue Jays, while sophomore Jamison Koesterer and Kyle Barrie also hit the back of Princeton's net. Launching a standout season as starting goalie, sophomore Jesse Schwartzman had a then career-high ten saves—a mark he would surpass in a number of subsequent, crucial games. Hopkins's dominance of the face-off X also was key, with junior Greg Peyser joining Kyle Harrison and Lou Braun in winning twelve of the nineteen matchups.

Our second game may have been played under the coldest conditions ever faced by a Hopkins team, as the Jays faced the University of Maryland, Baltimore County, Retrievers under the guidance of my former Hopkins coach Don Zimmerman, on an Arctic-like night at Homewood Field. The wind chill was about ten degrees. Freshman Kevin Huntley, son of JHU's standout midfielder of the late 1970s, Dave Huntley, scored his first career goal on the game's first extra-man opportunity, and Greg Peyser scored a career-high four goals in the 9–6 victory. Two goals by Kyle Harrison and one each from Jake Byrne, Paul Rabil, and Peter LeSueur added to our total.

After defeating Hofstra 11–5 at Homewood during a game in which junior Joe Benson had a career-high three goals and one assist to lead the way, the Jays traveled up north to face the always-formidable Syracuse Orange in their fabled Carrier Dome. It was a game that would prove to be emblematic of the season, signaling that this group of Blue Jays would never quit. The Orange dominated the first half of the game. In their typical run-and-gun fashion, they outshot us twenty-nine out of forty-four times and sprinted to a 7–1 lead by late in the second quarter. Paul Rabil then initiated our comeback, scoring two of his career-high four goals in little more than a minute late in the second quarter to narrow the gap to 7–3. The third quarter began with another Rabil goal, followed quickly by one from Greg Peyser. Kyle Harrison and Jake Byrne added two more goals in between one from Greg Rommel of the Orange. We entered the fourth quarter trailing Syracuse 8–7. Orange freshman Mike Leveille sandwiched two of his game-high five goals around another Kyle Harrison tally, putting Syracuse ahead 10–8 before the fourth quarter was four minutes old. Then senior Kip Malo stepped up, scoring his first career goal with seven minutes, forty-four seconds left on the clock to narrow the score to 10–9. Syracuse's Jarett Park scored what proved to be the Orange's final goal with six minutes, thirty-seven seconds left on the clock. Greg Peyser scored again to make it 11–10, and then Paul Rabil forced the overtime by scoring his fourth goal of the game. Both Syracuse's goalie Jay Pfeifer and Hopkins's Jesse Schwartzman came up with impressive saves early in the overtime period, but Greg Peyser once more beat Pfeifer to secure the overtime victory. It was the first time Hopkins had erased a six-goal deficit since 1999—and demonstrated the determination of this Jays team to win.

Against Virginia the following week, Jesse Schwartzman posted a then career-high twenty saves and Kevin Huntley scored all three of his goals in a furious fourth-quarter explosion to propel the Jays to a 9–7 victory over then second-ranked Virginia at a packed Homewood Field. Despite being outshot ten of eighteen times in the first quarter, the Jays were able to build a 3–0 lead as Schwartzman stuffed the Virginia offense repeatedly. Paul Rabil scored the first two Hopkins goals with back-to-back, unassisted tallies just three minutes apart. Senior long-stick middie Greg Raymond netted the first goal of his career by running the length of the field and firing a high shot past Cavalier goalie Kip Turner with four minutes, forty seconds remaining in the quarter. In the second quarter, Virginia rallied to outscore the Jays 4–1 and tie the game at 4–4 by halftime. In the third quarter, Peter LeSueur and Kyle Harrison each scored for the Jays, while the Wahoos' Matt Ward tallied once for Virginia, ending the quarter with a score of 6–5. That set the stage for Huntley's heroics, which Schwartzman matched by posting six saves in the final period to preserve the win. Virginia had averaged 13.7 goals per game earlier in the season but were held to nearly half of that by the Hopkins defense.

We next went down to Chapel Hill for a defensive duel against North Carolina. The first quarter went by without either team scoring, but Paul Rabil once more began our run with back-to-back goals in less than two minutes. Carolina's Rob Driscoll scored once right before halftime, but Kyle Harrison gave the Jays a 3–1 lead with a goal just forty-six seconds into the third quarter. A thunderstorm interrupted play—and slightly cooled our momentum. When action resumed following a forty-five-minute delay, the Tar Heels were the first to score, narrowing our lead to one. Peter LeSueur quickly answered with back-to-back goals within only sixty-two seconds—the first of them a dramatic shot fired as he was falling to the turf. Tar Heel tallies by Andrew McElduff and Nick Tintle narrowed the score to 5–4 entering the fourth quarter, but Kevin Huntley and Paul Rabil quickly responded with a goal apiece to give the Jays some breathing room. Carolina's Mike McCall scored once more with one minute, twenty-four seconds left on the clock, but we came up with the final face-off and Carolina took only one more shot in the remaining minute and a half. Defensemen Chris Watson, Tom Garvey, and Matt Pinto had held North Carolina's starting attack unit to a single goal and two assists—and Schwartzman's twelve-save performance limited the Tar Heels to the lowest score against us so far that season, 7–5.

Three days later we broke the University of New York at Albany's three-game winning streak by defeating the Great Danes 19–6 at Homewood Field. Sophomore attackman Jake Byrne scored a career-high five goals and senior midfielder Joe Malo a career-high four goals to lead the Jays and tie a school record of thirty-one consecutive home victories. Ten different players scored for us in the course of the game, including Paul Rabil, Jamison Koesterer, Kevin Huntley, Greg Peyser, Michael Doneger, Joe Benson, Garrett Stanwick, and Kyle Harrison as well as Byrne and Malo. Jesse Schwartzman, freshman Graydon Locey, and senior James Maimone-Medwick all did duty in the goal, making a combined total of eleven saves. We won seventeen of twenty-six face-offs, including eleven of the first quarter's fifteen.

Our next opponent was second-ranked Duke, then 11–0 and off to its most successful season ever. The Blue Devils had made a dramatic turn-around from their dismal 5–8 season in 2004, becoming the best offensive team in the country. They had convincingly swept Maryland, North Carolina, and Georgetown on their home fields. We knew we had our hands full—and maintaining the Homewood Field winning streak was not our main concern.

It was an explosive seesaw battle before 7,136 fans, with Duke scoring first just two minutes, nineteen seconds into the game on a goal by Peter Lamade. That was followed by a 5–1 Hopkins run. Goals by Peter LeSueur, Greg Peyser, Kyle Harrison, and Kevin Huntley over a span of just ten minutes put us in the lead 5–2 at the end of the first period. The Blue Devils responded with their own surge of six goals to our one during the second and third quarters, which left the score tied at 6–6 by halftime and put Duke ahead 8–6 in the third. Early in the fourth quarter, Paul Rabil scored to inch us within a goal of the Devils; then Matt Rewkowski, who had transferred to Hopkins from Duke before the 2004 season, scored two goals within just forty-five seconds to give us a 9–8 lead. Kyle Dowd, a former Blue Jay who had gone down to Durham prior to the 2005 season, then tied the game again. With just two minutes, forty-one seconds remaining on the clock,

Duke's Matt Danowski quickly put the Devils ahead 10–9 with his third goal of the game. Moments later, Kyle Harrison knotted the score once more with an amazing jump shot that got past Duke's goalie Aaron Fenton. The first four-minute overtime period went by without either team scoring, as Fenton and Schwartzman each made a save. With just one minute, five seconds remaining in the second overtime period, Kevin Huntley made a spectacularly athletic and unassisted goal. He got the ball near the sideline, about seven yards above the goal line, and was driving toward the goal when he was checked high and began falling backward. He nevertheless managed to fire a low shot just inside the far post to beat Fenton and secure the record thirty-second consecutive victory for us on Homewood Field.

We headed down to College Park the following week for the 101st matchup in our historic rivalry with the University of Maryland, and a trio of freshmen—Kevin Huntley, Paul Rabil, and Stephen Peyser—led the way to an 11–6 victory before 10,117 fans at Byrd Stadium. Seniors Kyle Harrison and Kyle Barrie joined Peyser in powering us to a 3–0 lead in the first thirteen minutes of the game, but the Terps tied the score with a three-goal run in a span of just four minutes of the first and second quarters. We got back on top for good with a goal by Jake Byrne eleven minutes, twenty-six seconds into the second quarter. Jake took a feed from junior Greg Peyser, who had forced a turnover in our defensive end, scooped up the ball, and sprinted the length of the field before finding Byrne in position to fire a shot past Maryland goalie Harry Alford. Two minutes later, Paul Rabil fed the ball to Harrison, who found Kevin Huntley poised to beat Alford once again. Maryland's Dave Matz grabbed a rebound in midair and got a shot past Jesse Schwartzman just one minute, fifty-nine seconds into the third quarter, narrowing our lead to 5–4. Then Huntley, Rabil, and Stephen Peyser scored three goals to ignite a 6–1 Blue Jay run that put the game away. Peter LeSueur joined in the rally, which ended on Huntley's third goal of the game with five minutes, thirty seconds left on the clock. Maryland's Bill McGlone got a late goal after that to end the scoring. Huntley's hat trick was his third of the season, and Stephen Peyser's

two-goal effort was then a career high. Schwartzman made seven of his seventeen saves in the fourth quarter to stymie any Terp attempts to recover. Senior defensemen Chris Watson and Tom Garvey joined junior Matt Pinto in allowing Maryland only twenty-two shots through three quarters.

The next week, Navy came within fifty-eight seconds of ending a thirty-six-year drought at Homewood Field—and a thirty-one-year drought against Hopkins—but thanks to a career-high five goals by Kyle Harrison, including the game-winner one minute, thirty-seven seconds into overtime, we secured a come-from-behind 9–8 victory. In a game that was tied four times and saw four lead changes, we went ahead 2–0 in the first four minutes on goals by Matt Rewkowski and Peter LeSueur. Then a seven-minute three-goal run by Navy's Graham Gill, Bill Looney, and William Wallace gave the Midshipmen a 3–2 lead at the end of the first quarter. We regained the lead in under a minute with second-quarter goals by Harrison and Rewkowski and another tally from Jake Byrne on an assist from Greg Peyser, who won eight of thirteen face-offs in the course of the game. Following the halftime break, Joe Malo scored again for us, but Navy quickly rebounded with a five-goal run by five different Midshipmen that left the score at 8–7 with less than a minute to go in regulation time. We won the next face-off, took a time-out to set up a play, then worked the ball around before getting it to Harrison, slightly behind the goal. He beat his defender and got on top to put a leaping shot past Navy's All-American goalie, Matt Russell, that tied the game and sent it into overtime. Although Navy won the opening face-off in overtime, a shot by Navy's Steve Looney went wide, and we were awarded the ball. Once again, we called a time-out to arrange a play. We worked the ball around to Kyle, who was about ten yards to the right in front of Navy's goal. He sprinted past a Navy defenseman and took another leaping shot while being checked, firing a shot past Russell to secure the victory—our third one-goal win against the Middies in the past four years.

We completed our regular season undefeated, for the first time since 1995, by beating Towson University 8–4 and Loyola College 12–6. In the Towson game, Jesse Schwartzman again was superb in the net, recording a career-high twenty-one saves as we scored seven of the last eight goals in the victory over the Tigers at their Johnny Unitas Stadium. Towson led 3–2 at the half and retained that one-goal lead until just forty-three seconds into the fourth quarter, but then senior Matt Rewkowski put us ahead 4–3 on an assist from Paul Rabil. Shortly thereafter, Towson's Steve Mull intercepted a clearing pass and shot into an open net to tie the game at 4–4. From then on, however, all the scoring was by Hopkins as we went on an unanswered four-goal run. On a feed from Kevin Huntley, Peter LeSueur scored his second goal of the game with ten minutes, fifty-three seconds left on the clock; senior Benson Erwin followed up with his first goal of the season only eighty-one seconds later, giving us a two-goal lead. Jake Byrne and Kyle Harrison scored one goal apiece in the final eight minutes of the game to ice it.

Facing the Loyola Greyhounds, coached by Bill Dirrigl, for the Hopkins homecoming game, we scored the first eight goals of the second half to stretch a 4–3 halftime lead to 12–3 midway through the fourth quarter. Despite losing all five of the first-quarter face-offs, we jumped out to a 3–1 lead on goals by Kyle Barrie, Benson Erwin and Greg Peyser. A first-quarter goal by Loyola's Pat Shek and two goals by Greg Leonard kept the score close at the half, but only twenty-eight seconds into the third quarter, Paul Rabil sparked an eight-goal run that included three in less than three minutes of that quarter and another three in under three minutes in the fourth period. Jake Byrne and Greg Peyser both scored on assists from Joe Malo, who also scored a goal. Rabil scored again, and Stephen Peyser and Kevin Huntley also contributed tallies to the rally. Late Loyola goals by Andrew Spack, Craig Georgalas, and Paul Richards led to the final score.

In the first round of the NCAA play-offs we faced Metro Atlantic Athletic Conference champion Marist College and defeated the Red Foxes 22–6. Kevin Huntley had a career-high four goals; freshman Michael Doneger had his first Hopkins hat trick; junior Joe Benson also scored three times; Paul Rabil, Stephen Peyser, and Kyle Barrie each had two goals; and Kyle Harrison, Greg Peyser, Jake Byrne, Matt Rewkowski, Jamison Koesterer, and freshman Garrett Stanwick each tallied once. Our sixteen-goal margin of victory was our largest ever in NCAA tournament play, surpassing the 20–6 score the 1979 Blue Jays posted against North Carolina State. We had been preparing all season to play our best in May, and for the full sixty minutes we played really hard against Marist, never taking them—or any opponent—for granted. Two of the other 2005 first-round scores similarly were lopsided: Virginia hammered Albany 23–9, and Duke flattened Fairfield 23–4. The University of Massachusetts ended Syracuse's twenty-two-year record of advancing to the Final Four, beating the Orange 16–15. Maryland defeated Penn State 14–10, Navy beat Delaware 9–7, and Cornell got by Towson 12–11.

Giving the eighth-seeded University of Massachusetts all the respect its victory over Syracuse had earned, we also played intensely for the entire quarterfinal game against them, eventually winning 19–9. We knew it was important to get off to a quick start against UMass, and offensive coaches Seth Tierney and Dave Allan did a terrific job preparing our players to do so. Kyle Harrison got the first face-off and scored just forty-seven seconds into the game—the fifteenth time in his career that he began the scoring for us, and the fifteenth game in which his first goal signaled an eventual Hopkins victory. Matt Rewkowski scored a career-high four goals; Stephen Peyser had his first hat trick as a Blue Jay; Kyle Harrison scored a second goal later in the game; Peter LeSueur and Kyle Barrie also had two goals each; and Kevin Huntley, Michael Doneger, Jake Byrne, and Greg Peyser each scored once. Despite five extraman goals by Massachusetts, we logged our thirty-sixth consecutive victory at Homewood Field and headed up to Philadelphia's Lincoln Financial Field to face the Virginia Cavaliers, victors over Navy 10–8 in the second quarterfinal played at Homewood. Maryland advanced to the Final Four as Jesse Schwartzman's older brother Andrew scored the winning goal for the Terps in a 9–8 victory over Georgetown at Princeton. Maryland's semifinal opponent would be Duke, which had defeated Cornell 11–8, scoring seven unanswered goals in the third quarter of their quarterfinal game at Princeton.

Our semifinal 9–8 overtime victory against Virginia marked the eighty-first game Hopkins had played in NCAA tournaments—according to our sports information director, Ernie Larossa—and it surely was a classic unlike any of the preceding eighty. In terms of spectacular defense, explosive offense, surprising turnarounds, and sheer heart-pounding drama, the 45,275 fans in the Philadelphia Eagles' Lincoln Financial Field could not have asked for more.

The game began with a stunning display of defense by both the Blue Jays and Cavaliers that left the first-quarter scoreboard blank for the first time in Final Four history. Despite tremendous play by Virginia's sophomore goalie Kip Turner, who made sixteen of his eighteen saves in the first three quarters, Hopkins senior Joe Malo finally got the scoring under way twenty-five minutes, eleven seconds into the game with an unassisted goal. His tally was followed less than three minutes later by a Peter LeSueur goal to give us a 2–0 lead. Virginia's Matt Ward got the first of his game-high four goals with just one minute, six seconds left in the first half, but Kyle Barrie needed only ten seconds of the third quarter to take a feed from Kevin Huntley and push our lead to 3–1. Less than a minute later, Jake Byrne gave us our fourth goal, and Joe Malo fired in our fifth just under four minutes later. Then in a span of forty-seven seconds, Virginia's John Christmas and J. J. Morrissey each scored to narrow the margin to 5–3. Matt Rewkowski scored an extraman goal off a feed from Paul Rabil with three minutes, forty-one seconds left in the third period, sending us into the fourth quarter holding what looked like a still-comfortable 6–3 lead.

With thunderstorm clouds rushing in, what had been a bright, sunny sky suddenly turned ominously dark as the fourth quarter began. High winds started whipping the stadium, blowing wrappers from pretzels, Philly cheesesteaks, and hot dogs all over the field. Virginia just as suddenly rediscovered its offensive power and launched a four-goal rally. Matt Ward initiated the spree with his second goal of the game two minutes into the quarter; Morrissey then got the next face-off and fed freshman Ben Rubeor for a goal. Five minutes

later, Ward scored his third goal, tying the game for the first time. Junior Matt Poskay then took a pass from senior Brendan Gill behind the Hopkins cage to fire in the Cavalier's first go-ahead goal. Moments later, a flash of lightning forced suspension of play. Torrential rains descended on the stadium, fans ducked for cover, and the teams went to the locker rooms to cool their heels.

During the ensuing forty-six-minute delay, our team showed great maturity—never panicking, never doubting its preparation or ability. Just before we left the locker room to resume play, captain Greg Raymond told his teammates that we would get the first face-off and tie the score—which is exactly what Kyle Harrison proceeded to do in the first twenty seconds. Virginia wasn't through, however. Their face-off ace Jack deVilliers won the next battle at the X, and the Cavs held the ball tightly for four minutes before calling a time-out with only thirty-seven seconds left to set up a play. When Ward got his fourth goal of the day, giving the Cavaliers an 8–7 lead with twelve seconds left on the clock, many spectators probably thought that the Blue Jays were done for. Not our players. "This team has the ability to really believe we aren't going to lose," Kyle Harrison later told the *Philadelphia Inquirer*. "We came in the huddle, calm as always."[*] Greg Peyser beat deVilliers on the next face-off, dashed toward the goal, spotted Jake Byrne about ten yards from the crease, and passed the ball to him. Byrne dodged past Morrissey and slipped a left-handed shot through Kip Turner's legs to tie the game once more with a scant 1.4 seconds remaining in regulation time.

Defense again ruled the action during overtime, as both Turner and Jesse Schwartzman made several spectacular saves. After his second save on a shot by Virginia's Kyle Dixon, Jesse made a perfect clearing pass to Tom Garvey, who moved the ball forward to Paul Rabil as he sprinted toward the Virginia zone. Paul found Benson Erwin unguarded some twelve yards from the goal and passed the ball to him; Benson, a superb defensive middie with

[*] Marc Narducci, "Johns Hopkins Clocks In, Overtime Win Earns Spot in Final vs. Duke," *Philadelphia Inquirer*, May 29, 2005.

just seven career goals, took only a few steps before closing his eyes (he claims) and firing a low shot past Turner to win the game. Benson later called it "a lucky shot," but I believe you make your own breaks as a player and as a team. Along with the other seniors—who together scored seven of our nine goals in that game—he had experienced plenty of play-off disappointment in the previous three years; past heartbreak helped us rebound to beat Virginia. In any case, we did not have much time to relish our Virginia victory. We had one day to prepare for Mike Pressler's great Duke Blue Devil team, which had demolished Maryland 18–9 in the other semifinal.

Although our seniors had been the motivational backbone of the 2005 Blue Jays, a pair of sophomores—goalie Jesse Schwartzman and attackman Jake Byrne—were the keys to our come-from-behind 9–8 championship victory over Duke. Jesse, with the tight defense of seniors Chris Watson and Tom Garvey and junior Matt Pinto in front of him, was named MVP of the tournament, making seven of his twelve saves in the second half and stifling the potent Duke for nearly twenty-eight minutes. And Jake scored the unassisted, game-winning goal with thirteen minutes, thirty-five seconds remaining in the fourth quarter, putting us ahead for good.

Duke's defense was also remarkable during the course of the game, proving that defense is what wins championships. It was the Blue Jays' Watson, Garvey, and Pinto, however, who were extraordinary in forcing Duke's shooters away from prime areas and, as Jesse later acknowledged, making his job—tough as it was—a little easier.

Before a record championship game crowd of 44,920, Paul Rabil got on the scoreboard first with a goal just thirty-three seconds into the game, but Duke—beginning with Hopkins transfer Kyle Dowd, followed by Matt Danowski and Dan Flannery—responded with three straight goals to take a 3–1 lead at the end of the first quarter. The defenders on both teams saw to it that eighteen minutes would elapse between Flannery's first-quarter goal and the next scoring flurry, which featured two Hopkins goals within just forty-eight seconds. One of these was scored by Greg Peyser and the other

by Kevin Huntley, on an assist by Benson Erwin. In a rapid reply, Duke's Flannery scored his second goal of the game off an assist from Danowski, but his tally was answered almost immediately by Kyle Harrison, who tied the game again at 4–4. Duke's Matt Zash scored on an extraman opportunity to give the Blue Devils another lead, and Bret Thompson added another even-strength goal to give Duke a 6–4 lead. Kyle Harrison responded with a running jump shot past Fenton, and just seven seconds later Kevin Huntley tied the score again with a goal off an assist from Jake Byrne. On another extraman opportunity, Duke's Zash scored with one minute, thirty-three seconds remaining in the second quarter, putting the Devils ahead 7–6 going into the half.

Duke increased its lead to 8–6 only two minutes, seventeen seconds into the third quarter. Nick O'Hara stripped Harrison of the ball in the Devils' defensive zone, passed it on a fast break to Zack Greer, who passed to Danowski, who fired it past Schwartzman. Given the Devils' impressive offensive record all season—averaging thirteen goals a game—that tally, astonishingly, would be the last Duke goal. Hopkins's defense smothered the Blue Devils for twenty-seven minutes, forty-three seconds. Chris Watson continued to hold Duke freshman Greer, who had recorded fifty-seven goals during the season, scoreless for the second time, and Tom Garvey limited Danowski (who had a Duke record ninety-two points in 2005) to just two goals and four assists. Our offense, in turn, took only high-percentage shots.

With five minutes, fifty-six seconds remaining in the third quarter, Rabil began our rally by beating Fenton with a left-handed shot between his legs. Then with less than a minute remaining in the quarter, Greg Peyser sent a right-handed, twelve-yard rocket past Fenton to tie the score. In the fourth quarter, with thirteen minutes, thirty-five seconds left on the clock, Jake Byrne fired a perfect bounce shot past Fenton to give Hopkins the lead that would last. Duke would continue trying. Danowski fired five unsuccessful shots, including a point-blank bullet that Jesse blocked with eight minutes, twenty-two seconds left in the quarter, and then another with three minutes, forty-eight seconds left that Jesse also stopped. That was Duke's last volley. Kyle Harrison and Kevin Huntley—a senior and a freshman—controlled the ball for the rest of the game, with Kevin even drawing two Duke fouls in the last minute to put a comeback out of reach.

When we won, the feeling that came over me was almost indescribable. I simply felt tremendous appreciation for what those kids had done. I was so happy for them. The jubilation on their faces and their excitement were incredible. Now that some time has gone by, the feeling that stays with me is one of gratitude. My coaches and I are grateful for everything our team did for Hopkins, and I'm thankful that they are the national champions. I also can't begin to say how important the wonderful relationships are that my staff and I developed with those players, in particular the senior class. They call us, and they e-mail us regularly. We have lifelong bonds with these guys. That is truly remarkable.

We are immensely proud of the 2005 team. Some people said that we were the team of destiny, but I am not someone who believes in destiny. I believe in hard work. Luck is when opportunity meets preparation. The sophomores, juniors, and seniors had handled both winning and losing with dignity. Along with the freshmen, they made a commitment at the beginning of the 2005 season to focus on just one game at a time, constantly improve, and do all they could to return the championship trophy to Homewood. Just prior to the championship game, seven Blue Jays received All-America honors—Kyle Harrison and Tom Garvey on the first team, Paul Rabil on the third team, and Jake Byrne, Matt Pinto, Chris Watson, and Jesse Schwartzman on the honorable mention roster. Kyle later received the Tewaaraton Foundation Award as the top lacrosse player in the nation, as well as the United States Intercollegiate Lacrosse Association's Enners Award as the year's outstanding player and its McLaughlin Award as the country's best midfielder. Chris Watson and Peter LeSueur were also honored for their academic achievements—something we especially value at Hopkins—receiving first-team *ESPN the Magazine*

District II Academic All-America At-Large awards, both for the second time.

As hard as we work to be the best team in Division I lacrosse, we also know that the success of lacrosse at Johns Hopkins isn't measured only in championships. The impact that former Hopkins players and coaches continue to have on the sport is not calculated by the number of athletic awards in our trophy cases—numerous though they are.

Hopkins's influence on the spread of lacrosse, both nationwide and overseas, has been profound. As mentioned earlier, Blue Jay coaches William Schmeisser (1905–1909 and 1923–1925), W. Kelso Morrill (1935–1946 and 1950), and Bob Scott (1955–1974) each wrote books about lacrosse that influenced generations of coaches and players. Howdy Myers, the Blue Jays' head coach from 1947 to 1949, perhaps did more than anyone else to introduce lacrosse on Long Island in the 1950s, helping to make it the important center of the sport that it is today. When Willie Scroggs, who had played on three national championship teams at Hopkins in the 1960s and then had been an assistant Blue Jay coach on two more title teams, went down to North Carolina in 1979, few in the Tar Heel state had heard of lacrosse. He single-handedly made North Carolina a power in the sport. During his twelve years as Carolina's coach, Willie compiled a 120–37 record and won three NCAA championships and six Atlantic Coast conference titles. As his former Hopkins teammate, Charlie Coker, observed in 2004 when presenting Willie for induction in the Lacrosse Hall of Fame, he not only made the University of North Carolina a lacrosse power but also moved the sport into the state's elementary, middle, and high school athletic programs. Similarly, Bill Tierney, an assistant coach at Hopkins from 1984 to 1987, went on to bring Princeton back to prominence in lacrosse after nearly forty years in the shadows—and helped spark the still-growing popularity of lacrosse in New Jersey.

Hopkins's influence on lacrosse has not been limited to the United States. In addition to writing the first edition of this book, Bob Scott joined Ross Jones, vice president of the Johns Hopkins University, to personally introduce lacrosse into Japan, paying a goodwill visit to Keio University in 1986 at the request of a Hopkins alumnus who lived there. They donated ten lacrosse sticks to the athletic department—and soon those sticks multiplied significantly. In 1987, Don Zimmerman and Quint Kessenich held a lacrosse clinic in Japan, and five months after that, the first competitive lacrosse game was held there. Since then, Zim has made six more trips to teach and promote lacrosse in Japan, and enthusiasm for the sport has grown tremendously there. The first edition of this book has even been translated into Japanese. It is estimated that thirteen thousand Japanese college and high school students now play lacrosse, mostly on club teams. The Japanese competed in both the 1998 World Games held in Baltimore and the 2002 World Games held in Perth, Australia, where on the final day they defeated 13–12 one of international lacrosse's oldest participants, Great Britain, for fifth place in the tournament. Larry Quinn was instrumental in introducing lacrosse into China in 1992, joining a delegation from US Lacrosse on a trip to Beijing University to demonstrate the basics of the game to Chinese youngsters. And as a lacrosse analyst on television for the past twelve years, including for ESPN and College Sports Television, Quint Kessenich has become one of the most recognized lacrosse broadcasters and an important national popularizer. Potential fans and players all over the country (and even overseas) get their first taste of lacrosse's excitement from seeing Quint's coverage.

Lacrosse has meant so much to the entire Johns Hopkins University community—students, faculty, alumni, and friends. Sharing in the thrill of the Hopkins lacrosse tradition has been a tremendously satisfying experience for many people, and their enthusiasm means a great deal to the Hopkins lacrosse family.

In many ways, John N. Richardson (1876–1971) symbolizes the remarkably strong bond that Hopkins lacrosse continues to forge between players and fans. "Uncle John," as he came to be known to generations of Hopkins players, never attended Hopkins or even played lacrosse. He went to Baltimore City College (a public high school) before the

turn of the twentieth century, became interested in lacrosse, and followed the sport closely throughout his long life. When he retired from his insurance company job in 1944 at age sixty-eight, he adopted Hopkins as his team. He hardly missed a practice or home game from the postwar era until his death at age ninety-four. He knew every player by name and even knew the names of their girlfriends. The 1950 Hopkins team made him an honorary member, and he became an integral part of the Hopkins lacrosse tradition. When he could no longer drive, he would have his daughter deliver him to away games; when he could no longer climb the stairs in the Homewood Field stands, a folding chair was placed on the track surrounding the field for him. There he would puff a cigar (or a hand-rolled cigarette), regardless of the weather, while watching the games. The 1970 championship team created the John N. Richardson Award in his honor. It is given annually to the person who has made significant contributions to Hopkins lacrosse over the years, whether they were on the field or the sidelines. The winners of this award indicate the broad base of interest and support that make lacrosse a vital part of Hopkins, and the award shows how deeply Hopkins lacrosse appreciates their devotion.

In 1971, on his fiftieth anniversary as director of the Hopkins band, Conrad Gebelein received the first Richardson Award. "Gebby" had been a spirited booster of our teams and devised the program of traditional songs with which the Blue Jay band enlivens every game. He always stood beside the team, whether in the pouring rain at West Point, the comfort of the Astrodome, or the whipping winds at Pebble Beach, California, creating the tradition of playing "To Win" after every Hopkins goal, of counting out the number of JHU goals after each tally, and then shouting, "We want more!" The original stands at Homewood Field are now named in his honor and feature a bronze plaque with Gebby's portrait.

Other early recipients of the Richardson Award include three more people who had no official connection with the university but were just Hopkins fans who got wrapped up in the sport and gave tremendous support and friendship to both players and coaches. Mr. and Mrs. Talbott Anderson began following Hopkins lacrosse in 1933 and did not miss a game at home or away for more than fifty years. At the team's traditional postseason barbecue, the elderly Andersons never tired of standing over blazing hot grills to fix hamburgers and hot dogs for the players and their families and friends. George Pohler was another early winner of the Richardson Award. When his daughter became the athletic department's secretary, George started to attend practices, helped to arrange the layout of our fields with his surveying equipment, and even backed up the goal—becoming the oldest ball boy in the NCAA. When Bob Scott discovered that George left home at 5:00 A.M. on a Saturday to make commercial bus connections to Charlottesville for Hopkins's game against Virginia, he arranged to make George an official member of the Blue Jays' travel party. He remained the team's favorite ball boy until his death in 1992 at age eighty-six.

When Bill Tierney left Hopkins to go to Princeton in 1987, he received the Richardson Award. And in more recent years, its honorees have included Rich Moscarello, the long-time equipment manager for the team; Kathleen Wisner, secretary to the lacrosse team; team manager Carlo Vigorito; sports information director Ernie Larossa; and William Brody, president of Johns Hopkins. Dr. Brody was instrumental in Hopkins's successful effort in 2003 to retain its NCAA Division I status for lacrosse while maintaining its Division III status for other sports.

On-the-field championships, scores, goals, assists, and saves don't begin to tell the whole Hopkins lacrosse story. Some of my clearest and most prized memories are of the courage and self-sacrifice that spectators never saw. Here are a few examples from recent seasons.

In recent years we have faced some difficult situations—twice deciding which of two quality goalies should start. In 2001, we had to decide between Nick Murtha, a junior, and Rob Scherr, a sophomore. Nick had received more playing time the previous year as a backup to Brian Carcaterra. I think it was just assumed that Nick was going to be the starting goalie. We went through fall ball, but the staff felt

that neither Nick nor Rob really separated himself from the other. We went through the winter, planning to have these guys competing against each other during the early scrimmages in the spring, believing one of them would clearly take the lead. After watching these goalies during the spring scrimmages, we felt that Rob Scherr deserved the starting job, but we still weren't certain. We even evaluated the warm-up before our opening game against Princeton, and Rob had the better warm-up. He was named the starter about thirty minutes before the Princeton game. At that time, it might not have been the most popular decision. Even though we lost that game, Rob Scherr did a terrific job—and went on to have an outstanding season.

The thing that was most notable, however, was how Nick Murtha handled the situation. Nick dealt with it like a true winner and a true gentleman. He continued to work hard and was still a positive contributor to our practices. He was the first one to greet Rob when he came off the field and was extremely supportive, which reflected the spirit of our team. The following year, Nick took back the starting goalie job—and Rob Scherr repaid the favor. He was extremely supportive of Nick and was always the first to greet Nick on the sideline and cheer for him. It was unbelievable. When the roles were reversed, they were great. And Nick went on to be named to the first All-American team that season. In 2003, Rob's senior year, he was back as our starting goalie and received second-team All-America honors.

A short time later, in 2005, we had a similar situation. We had Jesse Schwartzman, a talented young sophomore, and Scott Smith, our returning starter from 2004, who had led us to the national semifinals and had a good, solid year. We went through the fall, and neither goalie separated himself from the other. By the spring, we just felt that Jesse had begun to emerge. Our decision didn't hinge on stopping the balls; it was based more on intangible factors, such as leading the defense, understanding the defense, and communicating the changes from one defense to the other. Jesse was very competitive, and in our scrimmages we felt that Jesse played better. It was a very difficult decision. As a staff, we sat down several times for hours to discuss it, going back and forth and back and forth. It became a decision we probably wrestled over more than we had with Nick and Rob. Yet we've always said that we were going to put in the player who would give us the best chance to be successful, and we felt at the time that it was Jesse. We hadn't lost faith in Scott at all. It wasn't anything that Scott did. He performed well. We just felt that Jesse, for a lot of intangible reasons, was the better fit, and we named him the starter. To Scott Smith's credit, he handled it wonderfully. I'll never forget leaving a high school game at Homewood Field about ten o'clock one night, and who did I see walking out together but Jesse Schwartzman and Scott Smith. They have remained very close and are very supportive of one another. I think those two are indicative of the camaraderie and chemistry we want to have on our teams.

Corey Harned had been a high school All-American attackman when John Haus recruited him, but when my staff and I took over the Hopkins program, we first moved him to the midfield, then made him a long-stick defensive middie. As he always did, Corey handled these changes extremely well. He was selfless and said, "Coach, whatever you guys need." Then in his junior year, 2003, he began to have some arthritic problems in his knee. By his senior year, the pain that Corey went through was staggering. It got to the point that by the end of a game, he could no longer run. By late in the season, he was practicing one day a week, just to get out there. The situation was even worse on grass. When you knew the kind of treatments he was getting, how much time he was spending in the training room, and how he could barely walk after games, it was just unbelievable to see how he would run up and down the field each week, doing a terrific job on the wings in face-offs and playing good, solid defense. When we went to the Final Four, he gave everything he had. People never knew the pain with which that young man played. You could see it on the sidelines. He'd come off the field in pain. Yet he never missed a shift because of it. He never missed games. He was playing at a high level without practicing. Corey's dedication embodied the sacrifices that players were willing to make for their team and for Hopkins.

Matt Rewkowski faced a similar situation in 2005. In the fall of 2004, he tore his anterior cruciate ligament, the knee's major stabilizing ligament, but insisted, "I will be back." And he came back. Although he wasn't anywhere near full strength, he was back for the Syracuse game in mid-March, which was very early to return from that kind of significant injury. Throughout the season, he continued to work hard, to rehab, to sprint, to participate in practices—and it was tough. Nevertheless, Matt was intent on finishing his career with his senior class. There were days when he could just do stickwork; there were days when he just couldn't do anything. Matt got better when the weather warmed, but as we played him more, the recovery time between games grew longer. Our regular-season game against Duke really stands out in my mind. Matt put us on his back a bit and gave us a lift with two huge goals. The fact that he scored those goals against Duke, where he once had played, lifted us even more—and we wound up winning that game by one goal. As we headed into the latter part of the season and the play-offs, Matt could not practice except on Fridays. That was all his knee could handle. What people don't realize was how difficult it was for him to play in the semifinal against Virginia on Saturday with that knee injury, then turn around and play again in the championship game on Monday against Duke. If you ask Matt, he'll say he played one of his worst games in the national championship, but that's not important, because the grit he demonstrated throughout the season inspired everyone on the team. Indeed, as Matt got better, we moved him to the first midfield, and asking more of him was a big part of our success. The fact that Greg Peyser was willing to move to the second midfield to make way for Matt really helped us as well. Their selflessness again is indicative of the sacrifice these guys were willing to make for each other.

Far more than individual courage was demonstrated in the week prior to the 2005 Final Four, which in many respects makes our championship win even more remarkable. We arranged to practice down at the Baltimore Ravens' stadium, which has a field like the one at the Philadelphia Eagles' stadium. We were a banged-up team. Paul Rabil had a groin injury, Greg Peyser had a groin injury, and Kevin Huntley was coming off an injury to his ribs. Peter LeSueur had a fractured ankle. Joe Malo was coming off of a hamstring injury. Kyle Barrie had just returned from an ankle injury. As we were practicing on Tuesday afternoon, Kyle Harrison made a move to go one-on-one, screamed, and fell to the ground like he had been shot. None of us knew it at the time, but Kyle had a back problem. TV cameras were there, and we were all looking on in disbelief, thinking we had just lost our best player. Kyle tried to get up and fell down again. He couldn't walk. We helped him off the field, and our trainer got him a doctor right away.

At that point, we pulled everyone with any kind of injury out of practice. We later caught Paul Rabil and Kevin Huntley trying to sneak into drills because they wanted to practice—they wanted to play—but we were fighting just to get them to rest and be healthy. We went until Friday without Rabil, Peyser, Malo, Huntley, LeSueur, Rewkowski, and Harrison practicing. That's seven guys. It was a tough week of practice. We did everything we could. We backed off to just make sure everybody was healthy enough to play. We didn't know until about a day before Virginia that Kyle was going to play. He was still very banged up, but he played and we got the job done. It was an interesting week, as you can imagine.

These behind-the-scenes stories, as much as any heroics on Homewood Field, demonstrate the qualities of discipline, sacrifice, and respect that form the core of the Hopkins lacrosse family's philosophy.

The lacrosse tradition will live on at Hopkins. The names and faces will change, but the same spirit and enthusiasm will continue for players, coaches, students, alumni, and friends of lacrosse at the Johns Hopkins University.

Index

Page numbers in italic represent captions.